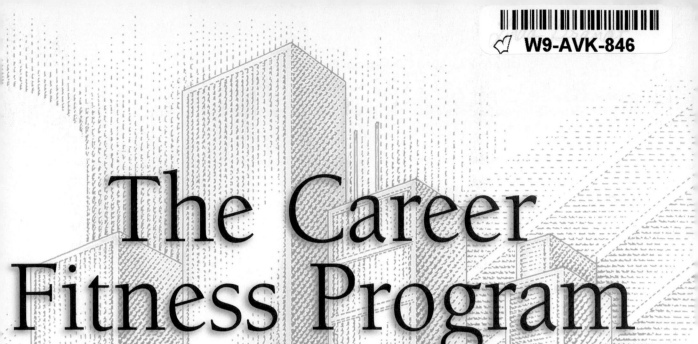

The Career Fitness Program

EXERCISING YOUR OPTIONS

SEVENTH EDITION

Diane Sukiennik

William Bendat

Lisa Raufman

PEARSON

Prentice Hall

Upper Saddle River, New Jersey
Columbus, Ohio

Library of Congress Cataloging-in-Publication Data

Sukiennik, Diane.
    The career fitness program : exercising your options / Diane Sukiennik, William Bendat,
Lisa Raufman.—7th ed.
        p. cm.
    Includes bibliographical references and index.
    ISBN 0-13-049615-4
    1. Vocational guidance.   2. Job hunting.   3. Personality assessment.   I. Bendat, William.
II. Raufman, Lisa.   III. Title.

HF5381.S914 2004
650.14—dc21   2003049822

Vice President and Executive Publisher: Jeffery W. Johnston
Senior Acquisitions Editor: Sande Johnson
Development Executive Editor: Heather Doyle Fraser
Assistant Editor: Cecilia Johnson
Editorial Assistant: Erin Anderson
Production Editor: Holcomb Hathaway
Design Coordinator: Diane C. Lorenzo
Cover Designer: Thomas Borah
Cover Art: Peter Siu
Production Manager: Pamela D. Bennett
Director of Marketing: Ann Castel Davis
Marketing Manager: Christina Quadhamer
Compositor: Aerocraft Charter Art Service
Printer/Binder: Courier Kendallville, Inc.
Cover Printer: Phoenix Color Corp.

Photographs from Corbis Images, Digital Graphics, Digital
Vision, EyeWire, and PhotoDisc royalty-free resources.

Pearson Education Ltd.
Pearson Education Australia Pty. Limited
Pearson Education Singapore Pte. Ltd.
Pearson Education North Asia Ltd.
Pearson Education Canada, Ltd.
Pearson Educación de Mexico, S.A. de C.V.
Pearson Education–Japan
Pearson Education Malaysia Pte. Ltd.

10 9 8 7 6 5 4 3 2

ISBN 0-13-049615-4

THE CAREER FITNESS PROGRAM

Contents

Preface xiii

About the Authors xvi

INTRODUCTION: ON YOUR MARK . . . GET SET . . . xvii

Part One   Personal Assessment   1

CHAPTER 1   TAKING STOCK   2

Personal Assessment   3

   Super's Self-Concept Theory   4

Overview of Life Stages   6

Understanding the Differences Between a Job and a Career   8

   BOX: *Greatest contributors to quality of life*   9

   Striving for Career Satisfaction   9

Real Stories: *Meet Sandra*   10

   BOX: *Sample career changers*   12

Choosing and Changing Careers   12

   BOX: *More career changers*   13

Summary   14

EXERCISES

   1.1   First Impressions   15

   1.2   Your Lifeline   16

   1.3   Identify Your Interests   18

   1.4   Describe Yourself   18

   1.5   Consider Occupational Status   19

   1.6   WWWebwise   20

   1.7   Exercise Summary   20

CHAPTER 2   PROGRAMMING YOURSELF FOR SUCCESS   22

I Am Building Self-Esteem   24

I Maintain a Positive Outlook   24

I Am Assertive   26

I Have a Sense of Humor   26

I Am Self-Confident   27

I Am Enthusiastic   27

I Use Positive Self-Talk (Affirmations)   28

I Visualize Success   29

I Have a Positive Self-Image   30

I Have Multiple Intelligences   30

I Learn from Role Models   32

I Initiate Action   32

I Am Persistent   33

I Am Disciplined   33

Real Stories: *Meet Alan*   *34*

I Demonstrate Emotional Intelligence   34

   BOX: *What makes workers succeed . . .*   *36*

I Identify My Goals   36

I Am Self-Reliant and Career Resilient   36

I Am Flexible   37

Summary   37

EXERCISES

2.1   Past Actions and Influences   38

2.2   Two Perfect Days   39

2.3   Emotional Intelligence Checklist   40

2.4   Positive Self-talk (Affirmations)   40

2.5   Your Fantasy Careers   41

2.6   Making a Fantasy Real   43

2.7   Building Your Success Profile   43

2.8   Think About Enthusiasm   44

2.9   WWWebwise   44

2.10 Exercise Summary   45

CHAPTER 3   VALUES CLARIFICATION   46

Defining Values   48

Clarifying Your Values   48

Real Stories: *Meet Maria*   *50*

Needs and Motivators   50

   BOX: *Life balance*   *52*

Finding Balance   52

Role of Leisure   53

   BOX: *True values*   *54*

Summary   54

EXERCISES

3.1   Values Grid   55

3.2   Explore Your Values   57

3.3   Your Values—Some Hard Choices   59

3.4   Reflective Questions   60

3.5   Top Five   60

3.6   Values Related to Careers   61

3.7   Values Related to Ethics   61

3.8   WWWebwise   62

3.9   Exercise Summary   62

CHAPTER 4   FOCUSING ON YOU: PERSONALITY AND INTERESTS   64

Exploring Personality   66

  ACTIVITY: *Identifying Your Personal Preferences*   67

  BOX: *Exploring majors*   72

Identifying Fields of Interest   73

Real Stories: *Meet Holly*   74

RIASEC (Holland Interest Environments)   74

  ACTIVITY: *Sample Majors Related to Holland Types*   7 7

  BOX: *Holland Interest Environments and hobbies, abilities, and careers*   78

  ACTIVITY: *Interest Checklist for Worker Trait Groups*   80

  BOX: *Worker Trait Groups*   84

  ACTIVITY: *Identifying occupational interest areas*   85

Career Clusters   86

Summary   86

EXERCISES

  4.1   Your Personality Type   89

  4.2   Your Holland Interest Environment   89

  4.3   Your Occupational Interests   90

  4.4   Job Clusters   90

  4.5   Interest Inventories   90

  4.6   Classified Careers   90

  4.7   College Catalogs   91

  4.8   WWWebwise   91

  4.9   Exercise Summary   91

CHAPTER 5   SKILLS ASSESSMENT   92

Defining Skills   94

Identifying Your Skills   94

Real Stories: *Meet John*   96

  Analyze Your Accomplishments   96

  BOX: *Sample job descriptions from the DOT*   98

  Use the DOT to Identify Skills   98

  ACTIVITY: *Assessing your skills*   100

  The Portfolio Employee   102

Identifying Transferable Skills   102

Transferable Skills of a Liberal Arts Major   *102*

   BOX: *People skills*   *103*

Your Most Valuable Assets: Your Personality Traits   103

   BOX: *Identifying the transferable skills of a teacher*   *104*

   BOX: *The SCANS report*   *105*

   BOX: *Using SCANS skills*   *108*

   BOX: *Describing skills*   *109*

Summary   109

EXERCISES

  5.1   Experiography   110

  5.2   Accomplishments   110

  5.3   Description of Accomplishments   111

  5.4   The Skills   111

  5.5   Your Favorite Skills   111

  5.6   Ideal Jobs   112

  5.7   SCANS   112

  5.8   Skills Review   114

  5.9   WWWebwise   114

  5.10   Exercise Summary   115

Part Two   The World of Work   117

CHAPTER 6   THE WORLD AND YOU   118

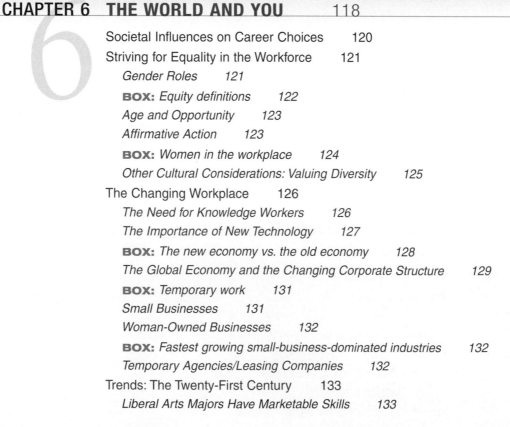

Societal Influences on Career Choices   120

Striving for Equality in the Workforce   121

  Gender Roles   *121*

   BOX: *Equity definitions*   *122*

  Age and Opportunity   *123*

  Affirmative Action   *123*

   BOX: *Women in the workplace*   *124*

  Other Cultural Considerations: Valuing Diversity   *125*

The Changing Workplace   126

  The Need for Knowledge Workers   *126*

  The Importance of New Technology   *127*

   BOX: *The new economy vs. the old economy*   *128*

  The Global Economy and the Changing Corporate Structure   *129*

   BOX: *Temporary work*   *131*

  Small Businesses   *131*

  Woman-Owned Businesses   *132*

   BOX: *Fastest growing small-business-dominated industries*   *132*

  Temporary Agencies/Leasing Companies   *132*

Trends: The Twenty-First Century   133

  Liberal Arts Majors Have Marketable Skills   *133*

Real Stories: Meet Jessica   *134*

   Lifelong Learning   135

     BOX: *Multimedia revolution ignites creative industries   137*

   Job Growth Trends   137

     BOX: *Internet-related growth areas   138*

Finding Your Place in a Changing World   138

     BOX: *Job growth throughout the next decade   139*

Facts and Figures   141

EXERCISES

  6.1 First Impressions   149

  6.2 Gender Roles Questionnaire   150

  6.3 Pros and Cons   150

  6.4 Famous People   151

  6.5 Small Businesses   152

  6.6 Globalization of the Work World   152

  6.7 Changing Nature of Work   152

  6.8 WWWebwise   152

  6.9 Exercise Summary   153

CHAPTER 7   INFORMATION INTEGRATION   154

Brainstorming Career Options   156

Understanding Career Paths and Common Organizational Divisions   157

Strategies for Researching Career Options   160

     BOX: *Questions to ask when researching a job   160*

     BOX: *Local government   161*

Government Employment Opportunities   161

     BOX: *DOT entry for copywriter   162*

U.S. Department of Labor Publications   162

Employer Directories   164

     BOX: *Research   164*

Other Written Sources of Information   166

   Newspapers   166

   Trade Journals   166

   Magazines   166

   In-House Bulletins and Announcements   167

Computerized Information Sources   167

   Selected Computerized Sources   167

Real Stories: Meet Jackie   *168*

   The Internet   170

     BOX: *Job market research sites   171*

EXERCISES

  7.1 A Tempting 10   173

  7.2 I'd Do This Even If I Didn't Get Paid   173

  7.3 The Grass Is Always Greener   174

7.4 Job Research   174

7.5 Local and Internet Resources   175

7.6 Gathering the Facts   175

7.7 WWWebwise   176

7.8 Exercise Summary   177

CHAPTER 8 MAKING DECISIONS   178

Overcoming Barriers to Decision Making   180

Decision-Making Strategies (Good and Bad)   180

   BOX: *Ways to make decisions (strategies)*   *181*

Real Stories: *Meet Art*   *182*

Conditions for Change   184

A Decision-Making Model   185

Rational/Linear Decision Making   185

   BOX: *Decision styles*   *185*

Intuitive Decision Making   185

Goal Setting   187

   BOX: *Sample goal and objectives*   *187*

   BOX: *Time management strategies*   *188*

Stress Management   189

   BOX: *Stress management techniques*   *189*

   BOX: *Tomorrow*   *190*

Deciding on a Major   190

Deciding on Training   191

Deciding on Change   191

Summary   192

EXERCISES

8.1 Ranking Yourself   193

8.2 Reviewing Goal Setting   193

8.3 Write a Goal Statement   194

8.4 Task Identification   195

8.5 One Year to Live   195

8.6 Meeting Your Needs   195

8.7 Your Energizers   195

8.8 Recent Decisions   196

8.9 Priorities   196

8.10 Irrevocable Decisions   196

8.11 Harmful Decisions   196

8.12 Limiting Decisions   197

8.13 Contingent Decisions   197

8.14 Values   197

8.15 Factors Adversely Affecting Decisions   197

8.16 What If . . .   199

8.17 Specific/Nonspecific Objectives   199

8.18 Test Your Assumptions   200

8.19 Time-Savers   200

8.20 Short- and Long-Term Goals   200

8.21 WWWebwise   201

8.22 Exercise Summary   201

Parts One & Two Chapter Summaries   203

PUTTING IT ALL TOGETHER TO REACH A TENTATIVE CAREER GOAL

Chapter 1   Exercise Summary   203

Chapter 2   Exercise Summary   204

Chapter 3   Exercise Summary   205

Chapter 4   Exercise Summary   206

Chapter 5   Exercise Summary   207

Chapter 6   Exercise Summary   207

Chapter 7   Exercise Summary   208

Chapter 8   Exercise Summary   208

Quick Impressions   209

Information Integration and Goal Setting   210

Part Three Job Search Strategy   213

CHAPTER 9   TARGETING YOUR JOB SEARCH   214

BOX: *Your comprehensive job search strategy*   216

Designing a Comprehensive Job Search Strategy   217

Your Job Search: Getting Started   218

Understanding and Using Classified Ads   218

Promoting Yourself Through Mail and E-Mail   218

Understanding and Using Employment Agencies   219

Volunteering   219

Real Stories: *Meet Xiao-Ying*   220

BOX: *Internships*   220

Interning   220

BOX: *The* Princeton Review Online: *America's top internships*   221

Real Stories: *Meet Felipe*   222

BOX: *Employers rate experience*   222

Starting Your Own Business   223

Home Businesses   223

BOX: *Women-owned firms*   223

Getting Help to Start Your Own Business   223

BOX: *Franchise information*   224

Franchising   224

Using Career Planning Services   224

    BOX: *Job hot lines   225*

Interviewing for Information   225

    Information Interviewing—The Purpose   226

    Information Interviewing—The Process   226

    Information Interviewing Outline   227

    Practicing Information Interviews   230

Networking   230

    ACTIVITY: *Information interviewing outline   231*

    Moving Beyond the Fear of Networking   233

Job Search While Unemployed   233

Real Stories: *Meet Susan   234*

Planning for Action   235

Implementing Your Job Search: A Lifelong Venture   237

Summary   237

    BOX: *Selected online employment databases   238*

EXERCISES

    9.1   Support Network Checklist   240

    9.2   Information Interviews   241

    9.3   Personal Contact Log   241

    9.4   WWWebwise   242

    9.5   Exercise Summary   243

CHAPTER 10   PREPARING A WINNING RESUME   244

The Resume   246

    Portfolios   246

    Preparation for Composing Your Resume   247

    Using Action Words   248

    BOX: *Resume/portfolio review   249*

    Using the Right Key Phrases   249

Real Stories: *Meet Eduardo   250*

    BOX: *Action words   250*

    References   251

The Appearance of Your Resume   251

    BOX: *Resume problems   252*

Electronic Resumes   252

    BOX: *Guidelines for preparing and submitting electronic resumes   253*

Types of Resumes   253

    BOX: *Resume template   254*

    BOX: *Sample functional entry under professional experience;*

        Sample chronological entry under professional experience   255

    The Functional Resume   255

    The Chronological Resume   257

The Combination Resume   *258*

Cover Letter Guidelines   258

BOX: *Resume cover letter template*   *259*

Application Forms   260

BOX: *Filling out application forms*   *261*

Neatness Counts   *261*

Summary   261

EXERCISES

10.1 Resume Review Sheet   263

10.2 Create a Card File   263

10.3 Write Your Resume   263

10.4 Save Sample Work for a Portfolio   263

10.5 Critique Your Resume   265

10.6 Ask Others to Critique Your Resume   266

10.7 Write a Cover Letter   266

10.8 WWWebwise   267

10.9 Exercise Summary   267

Sample Resumes   268

Sample Cover Letters   280

Sample Letter of Introduction   285

CHAPTER 11   INTERVIEWING SUCCESSFULLY   286

Before the Interview   287

BOX: *Job search tips*   *288*

BOX: *Company knowledge*   *290*

Interview Guidelines   290

Dressing for Success   *290*

Practical Preparation   *291*

Segments of an Interview   292

Practice Questions   293

BOX: *Sample thank-you letters*   *294*

How to Handle Illegal Questions   295

The Behavioral/Situational Interview   297

Real Stories: *Meet Jose*   *298*

Body Language   298

Video Interviewing   299

Learning from the Interview   301

BOX: *Sample questions to ask at the interview*   *302*

Factors Influencing Hiring   302

BOX: *Factors that influence your success*   *303*

If You Are Offered the Job   304

Negotiating for Salary and Benefits   *304*

BOX: *Summary: Reviewing the interview process*   *305*

If You Do Not Get the Job   306

EXERCISES

11.1 Question Review   307

11.2 Practice Interview   307

11.3 WWWebwise   307

11.4 Exercise Summary   307

CHAPTER 12   **FUTURE FOCUS**   308

Managing Your Career   310

Developing Your Relationship Savvy   311

Developing Career Stamina   311

Embracing Career Fitness as a Way of Life   312

BOX: *Risking*   *313*

References   *315*

Index   *321*

Preface

Welcome to the Seventh Edition of *The Career Fitness Program: Exercising Your Options.* As authors, we are immensely gratified by the positive feedback from the field, which tells us that we continue to make a contribution to the quality of life for the thousands of students who use our book. We say "use our book" rather than "read our book" because the process of career planning is action oriented at its base. We have attempted to balance the text with a variety of exercises to encourage our users to "get into the process" and allow the process to unfold in the many unexpected ways that careers do take shape. We are committed to the process of career planning, which is part science and part art, part logic and part intuition, part inspiration and part perspiration. We recognize the critical role of the teacher/counselor/coach in this process as the voice of experience, reassurance, validation, and wisdom. Just as a personal trainer keeps a well-intentioned exerciser on track, so too, does the teacher keep students on track and moving forward in a process that all too often seems circuitous and convoluted rather than linear and straightforward.

Our book attempts to be a comprehensive and current compendium of the best art and science in the field of career planning. As such, the Seventh Edition has more fully incorporated the electronic medium into the text and exercises without implying that the Internet is the only or even preeminent tool in the process. In this edition, as in previous ones, we have updated the facts and figures and have added topics that have become relevant to the subject, such as a discussion of multiple intelligences and the role of benefits in a salary negotiation. We have also expanded real-life stories in each chapter and added critical-thinking questions to each chapter.

Of particular note is this book's usefulness to the undecided and the liberal arts-oriented students. These students have heard all too often that technology is the promise of the future, and while that may be true, they need the latitude to explore other career avenues that may be more compatible with who they are. We encourage and support them in this exploration.

Companion Website:
A Virtual Learning Environment

Companion
Website

echnology is a constantly growing and changing aspect of our field that is creating a need for content and resources. To address this need, we have significantly revised the Companion Website for the Seventh Edition. Moreover, to better facilitate student learning and comprehension of chapter content, we have integrated the Companion Website into the text. In creating a Companion Website, our goal is to build on and enhance what the textbook already offers.

The Companion Website, located at **www.prenhall.com/sukiennik,** is a valuable resource for both the professor and the student.

- **For the Professor**—Every Companion Website integrates Syllabus Manager™, an online syllabus creation and management utility that allows instructors to create and customize syllabi online. Your completed syllabus is hosted on our servers, allowing convenient updates from any computer on the Internet. Changes you make to your syllabus are immediately available to your students at their next logon.

- **For the Student**—The Companion Website helps students gauge their understanding of chapter content through the use of chapter objectives, reflection questions that connect chapter content to the "Real Stories" and "Facts and Figures" features in the text, and interactive self-assessments. It also provides web links mentioned in the text and a variety of other online resources (such as articles that relate to chapter content), as well as WWWebwise Activities at the end of chapters and chapter summary exercises.

Acknowledgments

e would like to thank the following individuals, who reviewed this project in various stages of completion and offered suggestions as to how it might be improved. The book is better as a result of their efforts.

For the Seventh Edition: Howard J. Bachman, Creighton University; Dora Clarke, Whittier College; Angela Dillavou, Westwood College of Technology; Sue Eckberg, Career Focus; Theresa Green Ervin, The University of Mississippi; Sue Gannon, Vista Community College; Laura Goppold, Central Piedmont Community College; Jacqueline Hing, Rice University; Marilyn Joseph, Florida Metropolitan University; Gina Larson, Doane College; Christine Laursen, Westwood College of Technology; Jackie Lewis, Minnesota State University–Mankato; Lea Beth Lewis, California State University, Fullerton; Carole Mackewich, Clark College; Kathleen McGough, Broward Community College; Carmen McNeil, Solano College; Cynthia Moore, The University of Alabama; Victoria Sitter, Milligan College; Belen Torres-Gil, Rio Hondo College; and Laurie Williamson, Appalachian State University.

For previous editions: Cheryl Matherly, Rice University; David White, College of San Mateo; Carla Mortensen, Simmons Graduate School of Management; Susan Ekberg, Webster University; Bruce Bloom, DeVry Institute of Technology, Chicago; Bob Stanelle, Tulane University; Patrick Schutz, Mesa State College; Joe Ritchie, Indiana University of Pennsylvania; Rita Delude, New Hampshire Community Technical College; Barbara Allen-Burke, Clackamas Community College; Michael Brooks, Texas Christian University; Beverly Brown, Southern Illinois University; Pam Conyngham, Kent State University; Mariah Daniel-Platt, Rancho Santiago College; David Davis, Delta College; Ricardo Diaz, Chaffey Community College; Robert Ehrmann, Santa Barbara City College; John Evans, Hillsboro Community College; Christina Friedman, Triton College; Sheila Goethe, Hillsborough Community College; Kathy Hanahan, Harper College; Tim Haney; Karen Hardin, Mesa Community College; Mary Harreld, McHenry County College; Kenneth Harris, College of DuPage; Sandi Krantz, Moorhead State University; Ruth McCormick, Edmonds Community College; Paul Neal, Sierra College; Judy Patrick, Community College of Aurora; Sonjia Peacock, Lewis and Clark Community College; Bob Peters, College of DuPage; Hue Pham, Orange Coast College; Susan Rhee, College of DuPage; Dennis Sadler, Rancho Santiago College; Geri Shapiro, Los Angeles Mission College; Joseph Spadafino, Arizona Department of Transportation; Peggy Sullivan, Purdue University; Tanya Wahl, Inver Hills Community College; and David Young, Cerritos College.

We would like to thank Janis Pizer of Cerritos College for her help in developing new case stories and other content. We also appreciate the input of many other professional contacts and colleagues throughout the country and are grateful for the stimulating opportunities to share ideas. In particular, we want to mention Cheryl Matherly of Rice University and the entire academic team who steered the development of the "Career Advantage" telecourse available through PBS. These contacts have served to influence and enhance this Seventh Edition. Additionally, we extend our sincere thanks to all those instructors who have used the book throughout the past six editions. We hope you find this Seventh Edition even more comprehensive and helpful to your students in their career search. We are, as always, interested in hearing your feedback.

Finally, we are indebted to our friend and previous publisher, John Gorsuch, for his encouragement throughout our many years of association. We are also grateful for the professional production assistance we receive from Gay Pauley. Special acknowledgment is given to our editor, Sande Johnson, and our publisher, Jeffery Johnston, for their enthusiasm and great ideas for the future of *The Career Fitness Program*.

Last but not least, on a personal note, special thanks to each of our significant supporters and partners: Jean Bendat, Bernard Natelson, and Michael Reiss.

About the Authors

Dr. Diane Sukiennik is a career counselor; a licensed marriage, family, and child therapist; and a nationally recognized lecturer and workshop facilitator. She holds an advanced degree from Columbia University and has extensive postgraduate training in industrial psychology, management, and organizational development. Currently Dr. Sukiennik is on the faculty of Moorpark College in California, where her areas of expertise are career development, personal and professional presentational skills, and managerial effectiveness. She is a consultant, has a private practice, and has contributed to the development of a nationally distributed telecourse on career and life development called "Career Advantage" distributed by PBS.

Dr. William Bendat is a recognized leader and innovator in career development theory. While serving as Dean of Student Services at Moorpark College, he managed the award-winning counseling and career programs that gained both California and national eminence. His advanced degrees in counseling psychology, with emphasis in decision making and self-concept, have enriched the material within the text of *The Career Fitness Program*. Dr. Bendat is the Director of Careerscope, offering specialized career workshops to public and private agencies. He is also a licensed therapist, past President of the California Managers of Counseling, and a contributor to numerous workshops and professional journals.

Dr. Lisa Raufman has been Dean of Counseling and Career Center Coordinator at El Camino College in Torrance, California. She is a career counselor and consultant, as well as a licensed marriage, family, and child therapist. Her master's degree is in counseling with a specialization in the community college and vocational rehabilitation. Her doctoral degree from University of California at Los Angeles focused on higher education, work, and adult development. Previously Dr. Raufman coordinated the Career Transfer Center at Moorpark College. She is past president of the Los Padres chapter of the American Society for Training and Development (ASTD) and the California Community College Counselors Association. For the past decade, Dr. Raufman has been a member of the California Community College Chancellors Office State Advisory on Career Development.

Introduction

On Your Mark . . . Get Set . . .

The world of work is spinning at a dizzying pace. We have entered the new millennium, and the job market is more unpredictable than ever. Companies are downsizing, rightsizing, restructuring, outsourcing, and undergoing radical technological change. Bigger mega-mergers are occurring and more small businesses are being created. The globalization of industries and organizations presents us with competitive challenges and unprecedented opportunities. You can benefit from becoming aware of the changing job market, by keeping up with trends, and identifying how they fit your personal preferences. Seven major trends are shaping the workplace:

1. The majority of jobs are created by small businesses employing fewer than 50 employees.

2. The traditional hierarchical organization is changing into a variety of forms, with a flat (reduced middle management) organizational chart becoming more common. Flexible networking of specialists who come together for a short-term project, then reform into a new group for the next project will be commonplace.

3. Smaller companies are able to expand and contract with the changing economy by employing temporary and contract employees.

4. Just as manufacturing used to be our mainstay, the United States is now considered a service economy that depends on knowledge workers. (See the section in Chapter 6 titled "The Need for Knowledge Workers.")

5. Lifelong learning is the rule; getting a degree to get a job may allow you entry into a company, but if you don't continually upgrade your knowledge, you will lose your competitive edge. The winners are rethinking, reinventing, and reengineering products, ideas, and services to meet continually changing needs.

6. Global competition and multinational corporations will influence more and more companies. The most valuable employee will be the one most familiar with several languages and cultural customs. The number of women and immigrants will continue to increase in the workforce.

7. The Internet will continue to influence the way we think, act, learn, do business, and manage our careers.

A broad rainbow of possibilities makes this an exciting time in history. Yet many of us are overwhelmed by lack of knowledge about our choices and our place and purpose in the world. One thing that is certain is change. It is essential to prepare ourselves to expect change, accept it, and plan for it. We can best prepare for it by learning "who we are" in terms of lifetime goals and by taking responsibility for shaping our lives. As we gain information about ourselves and begin to make our own decisions, we acquire self-confidence. In a deep, personal way, we begin to realize that no matter how drastically the world changes, we can deal with it.

The expectations and demands of today's job market require us to be physically agile, mentally alert, and psychologically able. *The Career Fitness Program* will prepare you to exercise your options whether you are planning for your first job, reentering the workforce, or rethinking your career. This program will help you build the mental stamina and psychological strength you need to be successful and satisfied today. You will also develop the mind-set and acquire the tools for continuing success despite the inevitable surprises and challenges that you will face. *The Career Fitness Program* is designed to assist you in the process of self-discovery and realization. The main goal of this book is to lead you through the process of career planning, which includes self-assessment, decision making, and job search strategy; our primary objective is to assist you in making satisfying career choices. By following our chapter-by-chapter program, you will learn more about yourself and how self-knowledge relates to your emerging career plan.

Let's preview the content of this book to see how it will help you achieve your career goals. The career-planning process is divided into three main parts: personal assessment (Chapters 1 to 5); the world of work (Chapters 6 to 8); and job search strategy (Chapters 9 to 12).

- In Chapter 1, you will come to understand how the process of self-assessment *begins* the process of career planning. You will explore the concept of *life stages* and examine your current life stage. Chapter 1 also discusses the difference between a job and a career.

- In Chapter 2, you will learn how building self-esteem greatly affects your actions. This chapter's goal is to help you develop a positive approach to life and career planning.

- In Chapter 3, you will identify your needs, wants, and values and explore how they influence your career choice.

- In Chapter 4, you will develop an understanding of and appreciation for your unique personality and interests—factors that will influence your career choice.

- In Chapter 5, you will learn about different types of skills; you will learn to identify and describe your own skills with job requirements in mind.

- In Chapter 6, you will explore societal and cultural norms and biases that may affect your career choices. In this chapter, you will also read about workplace trends, promising occupations, and salary predictions.

- In Chapter 7, you will investigate published and computerized sources of information about careers and specific jobs, including government publications and Internet resources.

- In Chapter 8, you will identify how people make decisions and learn how to improve your own decision-making skills. This process includes learning to set and pursue short- and long-term goals.

- In Chapter 9, you will learn about job search strategies, including informational interviewing, networking, and electronic job search techniques.

- In Chapter 10, you will learn how to write an effective resume and cover letter.

- In Chapter 11, you will prepare for job interviews. This chapter discusses all aspects of the interview process, includes sample questions that you may encounter, and advises you about handling illegal employer queries.

- In Chapter 12, you will learn what it takes to manage your career and embrace the philosophy of career fitness as a way of life.

Even if you are not yet in the full-time job market, the job search strategy chapters (9–12) will be a valuable resource for you now. If you are in school, planning to work part-time, already employed, or seeking an internship, you can begin to prepare your resume and practice interviewing skills.

The Process

In many ways, the process of preparing to meet job and career challenges is much like the process athletes use to prepare to meet the challenges of competition in their particular sport. It involves establishing a fitness program in which the competitor sharpens existing skills, adds needed skills, and, most important, develops a mental attitude of success.

Any good fitness program is a combination of theory and exercise, and our career fitness program maintains this balance. For each step of the planning process, we will explain the theory behind that step, how it relates to the previous and next steps, and how it moves us closer to our final goal of identifying career options.

The chapters conclude with a series of exercises designed to bring each step of the process to life. These exercises will help make you more aware of your strengths, weaknesses, and attitudes, and they will also help you summarize what you think is important to remember after each chapter. You will notice that each chapter also contains a section called WWWebwise. These exercises are intended to build your skill in utilizing the Internet and to broaden your exposure to material that is related to the information presented in the chapter. Remember that reading a chapter or a book is a passive activity. However, responding to questions makes you an active participant in the career exploration process. You may find that it helps to share your answers with at least one other person; a classroom setting in which group discussion is encouraged is even better because it adds to your own awareness and perspective.

It is easy for someone to sit back and read about career planning and simply agree with the text, theories, and exercises. *But until you make the commitment to actually get involved in the process, to actively participate, and to experience both progress and occasional discomfort along the way, you will not be able to reap the benefits of the process.*

The Challenge

Yes, we did mention the word *discomfort* just now. What do we mean by that? Anytime you begin a new physical exercise program, even if you start cautiously and sensibly in relation to your current level of activity, new muscles are stretched, and they let you know about it. They feel awkward. They ache. You become aware of parts of your body that you may never have noticed before. You can also expect this to happen in the process of career planning. Along the way, confusion and some discomfort may occur. We will ask questions to help you dig deep into yourself for answers. In this process of enhancing self-awareness, you will discover much about yourself that you like, as well as some things that you would like to change.

Because of this self-discovery process, at certain points along the way in our fitness plan you may feel a bit confused, a bit anxious, a bit impatient. All of these feelings are normal. When you start out on a physical fitness program, you idealistically hope that in a week or two you will have the body that you visualize in your mind, even though you know realistically that developing a good physique is going to take a lot longer. Similarly, with your career plan you may begin to feel impatient and want things to move along more quickly or more clearly. It is important to remember that any change or growth typically includes some discomfort, uneasiness, or anxiety. Frankly, if you begin to experience some of those feelings, it is a good sign! It indicates that you are stretching, that you are growing, and that you are moving toward a newly developed awareness of who you are and how you relate to the world of work.

Committing to the Process

Whether you are taking the time at the beginning of your adult career to examine your options carefully and thoroughly or are finding at midlife it is time to explore new directions, you will reap tremendous benefits in the future. The satisfaction you experience at "the finish line" will be directly proportional to your willingness and ability to deal with the anxiety and uncertainty you will experience at some points in the career-planning process. In essence, the more you put into any activity, the more you are likely to get out of it. Stories that we have heard and read about our cultural heroes and heroines, whether athletes, performers, scientists, or political figures, tell us that the results they achieve, which look so easy and so glamorous, are always and only the consequence of tremendous sustained effort, commitment, and perseverance. A statement attributed to famed artist Michelangelo seems to say it all: "If people knew how hard I had to work to gain my mastery, it wouldn't seem so wonderful after all."

Your career search requires a similar commitment. It requires your willingness to go with the process; to seek out specialized assistance; and to move through points of frustration, uncertainty, and confusion in the belief that you will come out with more awareness and a good sense of the next steps to take along your career path. We invite you to participate in an adventure and endeavor that are every bit as exciting and rewarding as preparing for the Olympics. You are identifying your own mountain peaks and are setting out to climb them. Among your resources is this career-planning textbook, which incorporates the insights and experience of the authors and other successful career planners over several decades. Most of all, the important attributes of your own spirit, vitality, and intuition, together with the desire to improve yourself, will serve you well throughout your search. This career fitness program will help you master the inevitable changes that occur within yourself and are associated with your evolving career choices and the work world around you. It will help you identify options that are consistent with who you are. It will enable you to be the champion of your own career.

Personal Assessment

PART ONE

CHAPTER 1
Taking Stock

CHAPTER 2
Programming Yourself for Success

CHAPTER 3
Values Clarification

CHAPTER 4
Focusing on You:
Personality and Interests

CHAPTER 5
Skills Assessment

1

Taking Stock

2

Do you want to have a career that meets your needs, complements your personality, and inspires you to develop your potential? Are you someone who deliberately chooses the type of life you live rather than settling for what's convenient and available? If so, you need to set goals that will lead you from where you are now to where you want to be. However, to be realistic, goals must reflect your experiences, desires, needs, interests, values, and vision of the future.

LEARNING OBJECTIVES

At the end
of the chapter
you will be able to . . .

- Differentiate between a job and a career

- Identify life stages as they relate to career planning

- Discuss why personal assessment is the key factor leading to career satisfaction

Personal Assessment

As the first step in self-assessment, this chapter helps you examine your personal experiences, who you are right now, your current stage of career and life development, and your ability to deal with new information. Once you begin to identify what energizes you about life, you can begin to incorporate those insights into a career. Self-awareness is the first stage of both the career choice and career change process. As we look for insights that will help us chart our careers well into the 21st century, it is useful to take a look at career development models. Renowned psychologist Donald Super (1957) is credited with developing the theory that a career makes it possible for you to actualize or express your self-concept. Your **self-concept** is essentially *how you see yourself*. Consider the following principles of Super's theory on career development and how they relate to you.

3

SUPER'S SELF-CONCEPT THEORY

1. We differ in abilities, interests, and personalities.
2. Every occupation requires a characteristic pattern of abilities, interests, and personality traits. Within each occupation are workers with varying degrees of these characteristics.
3. Each of us is qualified for a number of occupations.
4. Vocational preferences and skills, the situations in which we live and work, and our self-concepts change with time and experience. These factors make choice and adjustment a continual process based on our maturity and lifestyle.
5. Selecting a career involves the following stages. As we will discuss later in this chapter, many people experience these stages more than once in life. Thus, although Super discusses the stages in a more traditional sense, remember that you may return to the stages discussed below at various times in your life.

   a. **Growth.** This includes both physical and emotional growth as you form attitudes and behaviors that relate to your self-concept. What did you learn about yourself from childhood games or family roles? For example, "I am a team player," "I am an individualist," "I am a mediator," or "I would rather read than play games." A child begins having fantasies during this period, e.g., a dream of becoming a doctor.

   b. **Exploration.** This is divided into *fantasy* (e.g., a child's dream of becoming a doctor), *tentative* (e.g., high school and post–high school periods of exploration in which ideas are narrowed down), and *reality testing* (e.g., in high school or early college, working part-time or volunteering in a hospital, taking math and science classes, or raising a family). You start learning about the kind of work you enjoy and the kind of worker you are, for example, "I am good with detail," "I enjoy working with people," "I enjoy working alone," "I take criticism well."

   c. **Establishment.** This includes initial work experience that may have started only as a job to earn a living but that offers experiences for growth so that it becomes part of the self-concept. For example, "I am an assistant manager, I am responsible for the bookkeeping, and I look forward to becoming the manager," rather than, "This is just a job, and I will be doing bookkeeping until I can finish my bachelor's degree and get into law school." Very often several changes in jobs will occur over a few years.

d. **Maintenance.** This is a time when we maintain or improve in our career area. Advancement can be to higher levels or laterally across fields. For example, you may start thinking: "I am extremely competent," "I can compete with others," "I can cooperate and share my knowledge," or "I can train others."

e. **Disengagement.** Super defines this as the stage just before retirement or one when we see no new challenges or chances for mobility. Traditionally, it is a period during which there is a shift in the amount of emphasis you place on your career; you may even seek a reduction of the hours you work. Disengagement may also occur some time prior to retirement. You may think: "I have many things other than this job I want to do," "I want to spend more time at home," "I want to work on my hobbies," "I want to travel more," or "I want to make a living from my leisure pursuits." Job or career changes are a form of disengagement, whether prompted by personal choice or circumstances beyond your control (a layoff, for instance).

6. The nature of any career pattern is influenced by parental socioeconomic level, mental ability, personality characteristics, and opportunities to which the individual is exposed. Both limitations and opportunities may be apparent as a result of these factors. People are affected by the realities of everyday life. A teenager living in an affluent suburb may have unlimited opportunity to focus on high school classwork because of ample financial support. On the other hand, a teenager living in the inner city with several siblings may work 20 hours or more each week to help out with the family finances. Such limitations can be overcome with effort and perseverance.

7. The process of career development is essentially that of self-concept development and implementation. All of us try to maintain a favorable picture of ourselves.

8. Work satisfaction and life satisfaction depend on the extent to which our work and our life provide adequate outlets for our abilities, interests, personality traits, and values.

What has influenced your self-concept? Do you have an accurate view of your likes and dislikes, desires, attributes, limitations, needs, wants, and values? An accurate self-assessment will enable you to make better career decisions by increasing your personal awareness and understanding. Self-awareness improves your ability to seek and select jobs that fit your unique self-concept. Super's theory applies each time you make a career change: you will reexperience the stages of growth, exploration, establishment, maintenance, and disengagement.

Self-awareness = first step

Our discussion of Super's theory briefly mentioned the general career stages that many people have experienced: growth, exploration, establishment, maintenance, and disengagement. Because you are probably somewhere between the stages of exploration and maintenance right now, it is useful to understand that you are also experiencing the transitional stages that relate to your age and affect your career planning.

Overview of Life Stages

he following life stage descriptions, derived from a variety of research on adult life stages, suggest that we emphasize different needs at different times of our lives. Planning a career involves thinking about the past, present, and future. Reviewing life stage information allows a career searcher or changer to gain and accept insight regarding certain personal and emotional issues that tend to influence values, planning, and goal setting.

Ages 16–22—late adolescence

Leaving parents' world; independence being established but not stable; uncertainty about ability to make it in the adult world; openness to new ideas.

Ages 22–28—provisional adulthood

Gaining independence in work, finances, marriage, or intimate relationships; gathering relevant work skills and setting goals; testing and choosing which to retain in adulthood. Still proving competence to peers and parents; becoming more self-reliant, building for the future; adjusting to personal or alternative lifestyle preferences.

Ages 28–32—the thirties transition

Questioning the commitments to traditional marriage and relationships, family and career; reassessments and changes may take place. A particularly vulnerable stage for continuity, although many choose to continue their earlier choices.

Ages 32–39—the time of rooting

Being involved in career and personal life decisions; helping children grow, giving priority consideration to childbearing; recognizing parental messages; modifying personality; accepting choices; giving more attention to business matters; establishing reputation—until about age 35 when the question "Will I have time to do it all?" begins to arise; more awareness of time and renewing the important matter of "What do I really want to be?" This may be the first time a woman experiences freedom from child rearing and begins to consider career options.

Ages 39–43—the turning-point years

Experiencing a period of great upheaval and midlife crisis; may appear that earlier dreams are not attainable; wondering "Why am I here, where am I going?"; additional lifestyle changes, often not planned; feeling there is something missing in life; possible further thoughts about raising a family; starting or changing a career.

Ages 43–50—restabilization/bearing fruit

Being more at peace with questions of mortality, career and lifestyle transitions; children testing their independence; personal review of child-raising patterns; career blossoming; attention to personal growth; activity in community; reevaluating relationships as one's children become adults.

Ages 50–65—renewal

Either enjoying a time of relative calm, boredom, or acceptance and enjoyment of life or facing new challenges due to an abrupt career change; planning for retirement; physical energy and strength may decline; spouses and/or friends die; new life structure emerges; risk taking seems less likely to occur; acceptance of parents' role in one's life; spiritual questioning; potential for creative growth; disengaging from concept of "work," though some people will start a new career at this time; dealing with caretaking responsibilities for aging parents; possible tension between a wife in the prime of her career after completing child rearing and a husband eager to retire and start a new phase of life.

Ages 65 and up—transition toward retirement

As life is extended and retirement is not mandatory, this period may become the true "golden years" of continued usefulness to society and growth for oneself.

Retirement

Ending traditional work patterns for extended time; involvement with hobbies and other interests; opportunities to increase social and civic activities; enjoying travel, family, and leisure.

Remember that these life stages are based on social norms of the past and present. People are changing careers and employment at a rapid rate as we experience the new millennium. The world is changing at such a pace that social norms will surely be different in the future. For example, two-car families, single-parent households, later marriages and/or alternative lifestyles, longer life spans, fewer good entry-level jobs, and the need for lifelong learning will all influence the direction of people's lives and will lead to more fluidity and ambiguity between life stages. Decisions will vary greatly, with some people still choosing early marriages or delaying career and professional plans for more education or training. A future scenario may incorporate a flexible and adaptive work schedule both permitting and addressing leisure and longevity.

Author Gail Sheehy (1996) has explored how people change as they age and found that as longevity has increased, so have concepts and definitions of career and retirement. There is no longer a clear-cut point when we end our training or move into retirement. Finding challenging or rewarding employment may ultimately mean retraining and an early exit from a stale or boring job in order to find one's passion and pursue it. The idea is to think long-range and anticipate an active lifestyle into later years—perhaps into one's 80s or 90s. Being personally productive may now mean anticipating retiring in stages. This may mean going to an alternate plan should a primary career end by either choice or economic factors.

Because it will take longer to grow up and grow old, we need to seek meaning to our existence and be open to new experiences. These can include nonprofit ventures, volunteering, hobbies turned into businesses, or part-time hours to help others and increase earnings. Taking risks to supplement and expand our personal horizons can help us at any age to avoid becoming vulnerable, being stuck, or even being directed by unforeseen events. In essence, our later adulthood can be a time of renewal, leisure, service to society, activity, and productivity.

Understanding the Differences Between a Job and a Career

We will be using the words *job* and *career* throughout this book, so let's define them. There is an important difference between them. Basically, a job is a series of tasks or activities that are performed within the scope of what we call work. These tasks relate to a career in that a career is a series of jobs. But more than jobs, a career is a sequence of attitudes and behaviors that are associated with work and that relate to our total life experience. *A career is the integration of our personality with our job activities.* Therefore, our career becomes a primary part of our identity or our self-concept.

A career is the integration of personality with work activities

In the past, people chose a career early in life, and they tended to stay in it most of their lives. Farmers worked on their farms, secretaries stayed in the office, and teachers taught until retirement. More recently the trend in America has shifted toward multiple careers. We can now expect to have four or more careers in our lives. Furthermore, with the rapid changes in society as well as in economic conditions, jobs, and technologies, many traditional jobs are becoming obsolete. In fact, William Bridges in his book *Jobshift* (1995) suggests that jobs as we know them will be different in the future. He means that a person hired to take a particular job can be certain the job tasks will change rapidly. Even if the job title remains the same, new and different skill sets will continually be required—the original position may become dramatically different or even disappear altogether.

Follow intuitions and not trends

This is markedly different from the world in which your family worked. Thus, the expectation that once you find a job, you are home free, secure, or set for life is no longer realistic. The traditional employee contract, although unwritten, implied an honest day's work for an honest day's wage, employee loyalty in exchange for job security, and raises and promotions in return for seniority. Today's new employee contract simply implies continued employment for individuals who possess skills that continue to meet a business need.

Be prepared to manage your career

More than ever it is important to give considerable thought to what you want to do and structure your training and education to be relevant both to your interests and to trends in the job market. You will find it beneficial to assess your skills and identify those that are transferable from a previous career to a newly emerging field with a minimum amount of retraining. Knowing yourself and developing a plan of action based on both your needs and the needs of the job market will help you embark on the career most satisfying for you rather than just following the latest trends in one field or another.

Demands in the job market rapidly come and go. Some time ago, teachers were in great demand. Then, for about a decade, there was a glut of teachers on the market. Now there seems to be a renewed need for teachers in the workforce. If you base your career decision primarily on current trends, by the time you obtain the training necessary to get into the hot field, it may well have cooled down. This strategy leaves you with slim prospects for a job that can lead to a career, and quite possibly with skills and training in a field that you weren't terribly excited about in the first place (except as a quick opportunity).

Each of us has the potential to be satisfied in any number of occupations. Getting to know yourself better through self-assessment will help you identify careers that are best suited to your personality. People who are not prepared for change allow that change to make decisions for them. They are often frustrated and unhappy because they are forced to work at jobs they don't enjoy. They may never have realized that they have choices, or perhaps they never took the time or energy to become aware of their preferences. They settle for less than what might be best for them. Dad says "get a job in business" even though his child has a special talent in art. The high school adviser recommends engineering because scholarships are available. The employment department directs a job applicant into an electronics training program because there's an opening. By knowing your own preferences, you will be ready to manage your career path instead of merely following others' suggestions.

STRIVING FOR CAREER SATISFACTION

Survey after survey on job satisfaction among American workers indicates that well over 50 percent are dissatisfied with their jobs. In a study for *U.S. News & World Report,* people were asked to name the three things that contribute most to their quality of life. The top categories for men and women

Greatest contributors to quality of life

MEN

Job/career satisfaction (32%)

Relationship with family (28%)

Money (18%)

WOMEN

Job/career satisfaction (28%)

Relationship with family (33%)

Money (17%)

THINK ABOUT IT

1. Give an example of job satisfaction. Describe the type of work, a routine day, the location and commute time, and the workplace (including your work space). List pros and cons of this job.

2. Describe your idea of a satisfying family relationship. Include the role of each participant.

3. Support or refute the statement: "Money is the root of all evil."

4. Which of the three factors would you rate most highly as contributing to your quality of life?

5. How does your current situation support the factor that you selected?

6. Have you made career decisions based on the factor that you selected?

7. Are there any other factors that you consider most important to your quality of life?

To answer these questions online, go to the *Facts and Figures* module in Chapter 1 of the Companion Website.

Meet Sandra

After graduating from high school, Sandra didn't know what she wanted to do. Many of her friends were enrolling in college, but Sandra wasn't interested in continuing with her education; she was tired of going to school and wanted to experience the "real world." Since she did well in her high school business classes, she thought that clerical work might be interesting. With the help of a friend, Sandra put together a resume and went on the Internet to search for jobs. There were hundreds of clerical positions, and Sandra didn't know the type of business she might find interesting, so she decided to go back to her high school counselor for some help. The counselor said that in order to make a career or job decision, it was important for Sandra to determine her interests, values, and goals. Once she had an idea of "who" she was, she could then investigate businesses that would be right for her. The counselor suggested that

she make an appointment with the career counselor at the local community college.

The counselor gave Sandra several assessments, and they revealed an interest in the legal field. Sandra went back to the Internet, but she soon discovered that the jobs that interested her required special skills. Sandra had a decision to make: return to school or look for work in a different field. Since Sandra thought she would really like the legal field, she decided to do both. She began looking for general office positions and enrolled in community college to begin a legal secretary certificate program. Sandra found a job as a receptionist with Transamerica Corporation. She learned the work quickly and found the hours allowed her to attend school and study. Although the pay did not allow her to live on her own, she took advantage of the opportunity to live at home and save money for her own apartment.

were "job/career satisfaction," "relationship with family," and "money." Because people may be changing jobs and careers several times in their lives, it is more important than ever before to have accurate knowledge about yourself and the world of work.

In March 2001 the Gallup Poll organization analyzed its massive database and determined that 55 percent of employees have no enthusiasm for their work! In another Gallup survey, two-thirds of a group of adults said if they were starting all over, they would try to get more information about their career options. The Conference Board, a business research organization, recently released a survey of 5,000 people in the United States indicating that, across different ages and income levels, workers were less satisfied with their jobs in 2002 than in 1995, despite good economic times during a majority of those years. Only about half of those surveyed said they are happy in their jobs, down from 59 percent. The largest decline in overall satisfaction was from 60.9 percent in 1995 to 47.4 percent by 2002 among 35- to 44-year-olds. People in this age group were once the happiest group in the American workforce. Trust between employers and employees is at an all-time low. Similarly, Watson Wyatt Worldwide in Bethesda, Maryland, found in a study of 7,500 employees that only half trusted their senior managers (*Wall Street Journal,* "Work and Family" column, June 21, 2000).

After two years, Sandra was close to receiving her certificate.

One day at work she was reading her Legal Terminology text when one of the executives walked by. Sandra liked Mr. Owens; he was always interested in her opinions and she enjoyed talking to him about her studies. When she told him her career plans, he indicated that he knew several attorneys and perhaps he could be of help when she was ready. Over the next few months, Sandra worked hard, and in early April she felt ready to make a move. She called Mr. Owens and said, "I wanted you to know that I will be completing my legal secretary certificate in May, and I remember you mentioned to me that if I needed any assistance in finding employment you might be able to help. I was wondering if I could meet with you to discuss my qualifications." Mr. Owens told Sandra how proud he was of her and that he would be happy to meet with her.

1. Do you think Sandra made a wise choice by not attending a four-year college? List the pros and cons of her decision.

2. If Mr. Owens had not offered to help Sandra, what other resources could she have investigated?

3. While Sandra was attending college, what organizations could she have joined that would have given her networking connections?

4. What other types of jobs or careers could Sandra have selected based on her high school diploma?

5. What type of career ladder can you build for Sandra based on her legal secretary certificate?

 To answer these questions online, go to the *Real Stories* module in Chapter 1 of the Companion Website.

You will face the need to reevaluate yourself and your career path continually. It is useful to know about the changing world of work and which occupations allow you to best express yourself and best use your strengths and talents. When analyzing your personal assets, it is to your advantage to think ultimately about the total job market. Search for jobs that will lead you into a career. You will benefit greatly from identifying a variety of alternatives that allow you to express your personality. Once you have looked within yourself and identified what you want and need in a job, changes will be easier to make because you'll know when you have outgrown one job and need a new one.

Be prepared to revise your career plan continually

For most of us, career planning is not a simple, straightforward, linear process in which we follow certain prescribed steps, end up at a specific destination, and live happily ever after. It is instead a feedback loop that continues to self-correct as we add information about our changing self and the world around us. We are constantly revising our career plan as we grow and change. This means that there isn't any one "right" career. Instead, there are many careers in which we could be equally happy, equally successful, equally satisfied.

There is no single "right" career

We are looking, then, not for the *one* right career but for the series of alternatives and career options that seem to make sense for each of us given our background, our personality, our career and life stages, and the changing world.

Sample Career Changers

Here are some examples of the kinds of career selections we've been discussing:

Professor Nguyen had reached his life goal, or so he thought. He was one of the few chosen to be a professor of religion at a small college in the San Francisco area. One day he woke up with stomach pains and body aches and had little energy. He dragged himself out of bed. When the pains lasted longer than three days, he visited his family physician only to find there was no medical reason for his discomfort. He then began some soul searching. His pains and nightmares continued over a period of months and seemed to occur only during the work-week. On weekends, when he was with his family or volunteering at a hospital, he felt energetic and healthy. Soon he took a leave of absence from his job and devoted more time to his hospital avocation. The physical ailments mysteriously disappeared. He spent one year examining his needs, consulting with a career counselor, and talking things over with friends. He found that his real satisfaction came from helping people in the hospital rather than from teach-

ing religion. Shortly thereafter, a friend told him about a job opening as an ombudsman in a hospital. He got the job and now lectures to local classes in career development on the hazards of keeping a job that is making you ill! Professor Nguyen needed to reexamine his original goals to discover why his career as a professor wasn't meeting his needs.

David Chan spent two years at a state college with a major in pre-law but a love for art. He wished to choose a career with strong financial potential that would be acceptable to his parents. During his junior year David realized he constantly daydreamed about a career in art. So he enrolled in an evening community college class and then transferred full-time to a technical art school where he specialized in drawing and sketching. David completed his degree, sought career counseling, and decided to try for his dream job. Within two years, he had a part-time job with an animation studio. He is now a full-time animator, creating characters for feature films. David was able to find a career that used his artistic talents and surpassed his financial goals.

Choosing and Changing Careers

Each one of us, regardless of our stage in life, is in some phase of career development. You may be starting your first job or looking for a job. You may be planning for your first career, reentering the job market after some time at home, considering your next career, planning for part-time employment, or looking for meaningful volunteer experience.

As there is no crystal ball that will predict the one right career for you, you will want to consider several options as you explore career development. The previous examples described people who reassessed their needs and made satisfying changes. It is also possible to survey your needs, values, interests, skills, aptitudes, and sources of information about the world of work in order to create a broader career *objective*. Some careers do have established or common career paths. In teaching, one often starts out as a tutor, works up to student teacher, and then becomes an assistant teacher before becoming a full-time teacher. In the marketing profession, people

More Career Changers

Taylor Jordan is a sophomore at a community college. For the past two years, largely on the advice of her parents, she has been preparing to transfer to the local university to complete a degree in business. Taylor now realizes that she wants to follow her true talents and interests, and pursue a career in interior design. Although she has spent much time and effort accumulating credits toward a bachelor's degree in business, she knows that many of her core courses will apply toward her associate's degree in interior design. She is determined to do what is necessary to achieve her new goal. To prepare for her discussion with her parents, Taylor has researched local job opportunities with furniture and home improvement stores, home builders, and interior design firms. She has talked to a college adviser about possible internships and volunteer work. Most important, she believes that her decision is the right one and is determined to follow through with it.

Jose Marcado emigrated to the United States in the 1980s. In 1990, after improving his language skills by attending adult school, he enrolled in a restaurant and hotel management program at a community college and began working as a parking attendant. Jose was very sociable and positive, often making friendly conversation with his customers. By the time he finished his schooling, he was the supervisor of parking facilities. One of his customers told him about a job possibility with a large hotel chain and recommended he apply. Jose not only got the job but within three years was managing the hotel's restaurant at an annual salary of $60,000. His ability to network, be friendly, learn on the job, and combine studies and work experience led him to a great job.

Rhonda Speer spent five years in college completing a bachelor's degree program in teaching with an emphasis in special education. After two and a half years working in the field, she decided that she needed a change. Working with children all day was making it difficult for Rhonda to concentrate at the end of the day on her own young daughter. She found a job as a stockbroker trainee. Within six months she was a full-fledged stockbroker. Now she's a corporate financial adviser.

---

often start in sales. Therefore we need to think about career goals in the sense of their being both short term and long term. A short-term career goal is one that can be rather quickly attained. For instance, in the process of career planning, you may discover you want to be a lawyer. We would normally consider law a long-term career option because it generally takes many years of study and preparation. However, a short-term career goal related to law might be obtaining a job as a legal secretary or a paralegal. Either of these would give you the opportunity to work in an environment that excites and energizes you long before you actually achieve your final and ultimate career goal. In addition, relevant experience enhances your appeal to future employers.

Preparation = short-term and long-term goals

If you examine enough options during the career-planning process, you may be able to use career experiences to move into related areas just as Sandra did. Subsequent chapters in this book will help you identify your related options.

There is a final, very important reason that this effort at personal assessment is crucial as the first step in your career-planning process. Once you know who you are and what your preferences and talents are, you can better make sense of the information that continually bombards you regarding the world of work. It's almost impossible to read a newspaper, listen to a news broadcast, visit a website, or watch a television show that does not have some implication for you and your career. In fact, you may feel you suffer from information overload. Surfing the Web, looking at the classified ads, and reading about employment projections and trends can cause confusion, frustration, and often discouragement about what place you might have in this elusive job market.

One of the best ways to achieve a sense of control and perspective on this constant stream of information is to know who you are, so that when you are surfing, listening, reading, watching, and experiencing, you will have a means of processing information through your consciousness, through your personality and preferences, and through your values and skills. Eventually, you will be able to recognize and reject information that does not apply to you, and to internalize and add to your career plan information that does. If a group setting such as a career class is available to you, all the better! The opportunity to discover yourself and expand your horizons is multiplied by the added benefit of group interaction.

Self-knowledge helps decision making

Summary

The best approach to the process of career planning is first to examine who you are, what you know about yourself, and what you need and want, and next to mesh that information with the world of work. You then have the distinct advantage of being able to choose training for a career about which you are truly excited and enthusiastic. These two qualities are among the most important to potential employers. Even if the job market for the field you have chosen is extremely competitive, you will have an edge because of your sense of commitment, your passion, and your joy in what you are doing. We will elaborate further on these attitudes for success in Chapter 2 and will identify and discuss the attitudinal components that will make you a success in whatever career you choose.

Attitude influences action: knowing yourself is critical in an unpredictable job market

Taking Stock

The first set of exercises will help you explore your current feelings and attitudes and thus better understand yourself. Begin with Exercise 1.1, First Impressions. This will help you take stock of where you are currently. Exercise 1.2 is a review of where your life focus has been. You will learn more about how personality and interests relate to career planning in Chapter Four. For now, Exercise 1.3 asks you to begin thinking about your interests, and Exercise 1.4 asks you to identify your personal strengths. (Later when you are reading about the personality requirements of different careers, you can use this list as another piece to complete the "personality puzzle.") Exercise 1.5 encourages you to identify job preferences by ranking occupations according to how you perceive their status.

> To answer these questions online, go to the *Exercise* module in Chapter 1 of the Companion Website.

First Impressions

Here is your first chance to think about yourself and record your responses. Fill in each blank carefully and honestly. Be true to yourself; don't try to please anyone else with your answers. Try to be spontaneous; the longer you think before answering, the more likely you are to censor your answers.

1. I am _____

2. I need _____

3. I want _____

4. My current life stage in selecting a career is _____

5. I would like to change _____ about myself.

6. If all goes well in the next five years, I will be doing the following things:

   _____

   _____

7. If things go poorly in the next five years, I will be doing

   _____

   _____

8. Reviewing past jobs or volunteer experiences I have had, what did I like best/least about each one? Is there a pattern?

   _____

   _____

Your Lifeline

Review the information on life stages. As we noted, these life stage descriptions suggest that we emphasize different needs at different times of our lives. Can you remember the highs and lows in your personal and career life and then place them on a line? It is helpful to place symbols on a line graph of your life indicating times of major decisions such as moves or new jobs; periods when mentors or other influential people entered or affected your life; and times when you had particular problems or acquired important new skills. To assist your memory, divide your life into four time periods and write four important memories (activities, people, events) in each period.

Ages 0–12 (Try remembering friends, birthday parties, holidays, or school events to recall your earliest memories. What did you excel at?)

1. _____
2. _____
3. _____
4. _____

Ages 13–19

1. _____
2. _____
3. _____
4. _____

Ages 20–29

1. _____
2. _____
3. _____
4. _____

Ages 30–39

1. _____
2. _____
3. _____
4. _____

Ages 40 Plus

1. _____
2. _____
3. _____
4. _____

Now you can transfer these memories onto the lifeline. It may help to use symbols to save space (e.g., A = people, B = events, C = jobs).

A sample lifeline and the space to draw your own lifeline at bottom. EXHIBIT 1.1

1. Leadership award in sixth grade (age 12).
2. Chosen student ambassador to France—sophomore in college (age 19).
3. Spent senior year in France (age 21).
4. Met significant person in my life (age 21).
5. Graduate school in New York (age 22).
6. Move from New York to Missouri (lost friends and career contacts) (age 23).
7. First professional job (but not my ideal job) (age 24).
8. Fired! (A bona fide case of sexual harassment!) (age 25).
9. After being unemployed for nine months, volunteered at career planning center and learned new skills (age 26).
10. Began my own serious job search, identified my ideal job (career counselor) in ideal setting for me (community college) (age 27).
11. Success! Landed perfect job for me! (age 30).
12. Was still learning on my job and began to explore further options and career enrichment opportunities (age 44).
13. Began to deal with my parents' mortality and my own aging (ages 50–54).
14. Seeking balance, giving back to the community, planning for increased leisure and continuous lifelong learning (age 55).
15. Exploring the possibilities and challenges of retirement (55+).

Now draw your own lifeline below:

HIGHS

Age   0   10   20   30   40   50   60   70

LOWS

Identify Your Interests

1. What subjects in school do I like?

_____

_____

2. What books or magazines do I read? What kinds of music, art, theater, and cinema do I like? What are my favorite websites?

_____

_____

_____

3. What do I like to do for fun? How do I spend my spare time?

_____

_____

_____

4. What jobs have I had (including volunteer work) and what did I like about them?

_____

_____

Describe Yourself

Circle those adjectives that best describe you. Place an "X" in front of those adjectives that are least like you.

R REALISTIC		I INVESTIGATIVE		A ARTISTIC	
practical	persistent	careful	introverted	emotional	impulsive
athletic	conforming	achieving	confident	expressive	flexible
rugged	down-to-earth	curious	analytical	imaginative	idealistic
stable	self-reliant	precise	intellectual	unordered	original
frank		independent		creative	

S SOCIAL		E ENTERPRISING		C CONVENTIONAL	
helpful	understanding	energetic	adventurous	conscientious	moderate
insightful	popular	driving	powerful	persistent	orderly
kind	cooperative	ambitious	persuasive	organized	efficient
friendly	responsible	assertive	competitive	obedient	detailed
tactful	flirtatious	enthusiastic		dependable	thorough

Next, review the adjectives you circled. Note the list is divided into six clusters: Realistic, Investigative, Artistic, Social, Enterprising, and Conventional (RIASEC). Which groups of adjectives best describe you? Also note that most of the words are positive personality traits. This exercise gives you a chance to acknowledge your positive attributes.

From which three of the six groups do most of your adjectives come? Rank the groups from which most of them come as 1, second most as 2, and third most as 3.

1 _____   2 _____   3 _____

Each group of adjectives describes a certain kind of person. What kinds of people do you like to be around? Rank the top three types of people you like to be around.

1 _____   2 _____   3 _____

Consider Occupational Status

EXERCISE 1.5

Rank the following occupations in numerical order according to the *status* you attribute to them. Number 1 should be the occupation that in your mind is most significant—how you define *significant* is, of course, up to you. For example, a police officer could appear as number 1 on your list if you place most value on societal order and safety. Number 20 should reflect the occupation you regard as least significant.

_____ administrative assistant		_____ lawyer
_____ agriculture supervisor		_____ movie director
_____ auto technician		_____ musician
_____ computer operator		_____ plumber
_____ construction worker		_____ police officer
_____ dental hygienist		_____ psychiatric nurse
_____ doctor		_____ public school teacher
_____ engineer		_____ restaurant manager
_____ hairdresser		_____ robotics technician
_____ landscape designer		_____ salesperson

Think about the aspects of these positions that impress you or seem of value to you. Next, think about how you define *status*. Is it based on probable income, amount of education required, societal standards? How individualistic do you think your rankings are? For example, was *musician* ranked in your top five because you appreciate music? There are, in actuality, no correct or incorrect answers in this exercise. However, your rankings may reflect some of your basic preferences. If most of your top-ranked occupations were higher-salaried or if your rankings were based on potential for high pay, you may be motivated by a need for security; if your highest rankings were for service-related occupations (e.g., doctor, public school teacher), your motivation might be different.

WWWebwise

For additional activities, go to the WWWebwise module in Chapter 1 of the Companion Website.

Exercise Summary

Write a brief paragraph answering these questions.

What have I learned about myself? My current life stage? How does this knowledge relate to my career/life planning? How do I feel?

_____

_____

_____

_____

_____

_____

_____

_____

_____

_____

_____

_____

_____

_____

_____

_____

_____

_____

_____

_____

_____

_____

_____

_____

_____

Go to page 203 of the chapter summaries, and complete the Chapter 1 exercise summary now.

Programming Yourself
for Success

CHAPTER 2

Through the process of career planning, you learn how to take what you've got (values, skills, interests, aptitudes, qualities, limitations) and do what it takes (job search strategy) to reach your career goal. A satisfying career *is* attainable *if* you decide you want it. We begin the process of career planning with an assessment of your self-esteem and your attitudes because your mental outlook is the crucial variable that will move you toward (or keep you from) identifying and achieving your career goals. No book, set of exercises, system, or counselor will affect your future as much as your own belief system and your own commitment to achieving success. Your beliefs are reflected by your actions.

How many times have you told yourself, "I'm going to start on a new exercise program today" and then found a "legitimate" excuse to postpone your efforts? Are you really ready to work on your career fitness? If so, let's examine some of the beliefs and attitudes that can assist you with your plan.

Because we believe in positive attitude and imagery (both of which we'll discuss shortly), we have used positive statements to begin each section in this chapter. This is done to provide you with models of statements that reflect attitudes that lead to successful behavior.

At the end of the chapter you will be able to . . .

- Discuss why building self-esteem is important in developing a successful career plan

- Identify specific components of the success profile

- Recognize approaches and techniques for creating opportunities for success in your career planning

Act as if it were impossible to fail.

I Am Building Self-Esteem

Our sources of self-esteem are deeply rooted; at a very young age, we begin to formulate a concept of ourselves based on our upbringing, our schooling, our culture, and a multitude of other factors. It is an unfortunate truth that many of us reach adulthood with low self-esteem, which manifests itself in many ways. For example, we may be afraid to try new things for fear of being embarrassed. We may let others make decisions for us, or we may stay in a job that we dislike rather than risking loss in order to find one we do like.

Obviously, one book or course cannot miraculously repair low self-esteem, and we do not mean to imply that such a quick fix is possible. *However,* this book can help you identify possible problem areas, give you the incentive to make changes, and start you in the right direction. Today, many colleges offer courses on building self-esteem, learning to be assertive, and related issues. Thus, you have resources available if you discover you need help; making that discovery is an important step in the right direction.

The ultimate goal is to like yourself. The higher your appreciation of yourself, or your self-esteem, the greater are your chances of feeling and being successful in your personal and career goals. This chapter identifies several building blocks of self-esteem, listed at left and discussed below.

As you read each section, take a quick pulse. How would you rate yourself on each of these essential components? Which ones do you need to work on first? As you identify the areas in your life that need work, pay attention to the suggestions for improvement. Later, Exercises 2.1 and 2.4 will help you further your goal of building self-esteem. This should be a lifelong goal. Establish small goals that you can meet along the way, and give yourself credit for small successes.

Although the word *success* means many things to many people, success in general usually means the progressive external demonstration of internalized life goals. In other words, success refers to the step-by-step movement toward the attainment of an object, quality, or state of mind that we value and wish to possess.

- I maintain a positive outlook.
- I am assertive.
- I have a sense of humor.
- I am self-confident.
- I am enthusiastic.
- I use positive self-talk (affirmations).
- I visualize success.
- I have a positive self-image.
- I have multiple intelligences.
- I learn from role models.
- I initiate action.
- I am persistent.
- I am disciplined.
- I demonstrate emotional intelligence.
- I identify my goals.
- I am self-reliant and career resilient.
- I am flexible.

I Maintain a Positive Outlook

Do you have your own personal definition of success? Regardless of the particular goals you have in mind, you need to think positively to attain them. Have you ever heard the saying, "It's all in your head"? People who say this believe that our mental attitudes have control over our body and our life and can, therefore, program our success or failure. Although many of our attitudes and beliefs come from early messages we received from our parents and teachers, as adults we can choose to keep or change these messages, depending on how helpful they are to us in achieving success and satisfaction in life.

Examine your philosophy of life. How you see life in general is how you lead your life. A quick way to identify your philosophy is to examine how you visualize the future.

Read the following scenarios and select the one that best relates to your point of view (Kauffman, 1976).

The future is a great roller coaster on a moonless night. It exists, twisting ahead of us in the dark, although we can see each part only as we come to it. We can make estimates about where we are headed and sometimes see around a bend to another section of track, but it doesn't do us any real good because the future is fixed and determined. We are locked in our seats, and nothing we may know or do will change the course that is laid out for us.

The future is a mighty river. The great force of history flows inexorably along, carrying us with it. Most of our attempts to change its course are mere pebbles thrown into the river: they cause a momentary splash and a few ripples, but they make no difference. The river's course can be changed, but only by natural disasters like earthquakes and landslides or by massive, concerted human efforts on a similar scale. On the other hand, we are free as individuals to adapt to the course of history either well or poorly. By looking ahead, we can avoid sandbars and whirlpools and pick the best path through any rapids.

The future is a great ocean. There are many possible destinations, and many different paths to each destination. A good navigator takes advantage of the main currents of change, adapts the course to the capricious winds of chance, keeps a sharp lookout posted, and moves carefully in fog or uncharted waters. Doing these things will get the navigator safely to a destination (barring a typhoon or other disaster that one can neither predict nor avoid).

The future is entirely random, a colossal dice game. Every second, millions of things happen that could have happened another way and produced a different future. A bullet is deflected by a twig and kills one person instead of another. A scientist checks a spoiled culture and throws it away or looks more closely at it and discovers penicillin. A newly renovated home is destroyed by an earthquake. Since everything is chance, all we can do is play the game, pray to the gods of fortune, and enjoy what good luck comes our way.

One of these scenarios may reflect your perception of life. Is your life a roller coaster, beyond your control; a mighty river to which you must adapt; a great ocean with many directions and options; or just a game of chance? Are you a positive thinker or a negative thinker? The second and third scenarios are the more positive reflections. Your belief system will affect how you see life. Have you ever noticed how your most dominant thoughts reinforce what happens to you? This phenomenon is called the self-fulfilling prophecy.

Your mind tends to believe what you tell it. And, yes, you can if you *think* you can. Cultivating a positive, assertive outlook on life is the most crucial

Remember the times you've thought the following:

"That's just the way I am."

"I can't control what I do."

"I just can't seem to finish anything I start."

"I would like to do that differently, but it's just too hard to change."

"Yes, it happened again."

"I've never been good at that."

factor in the difference between those people who have successful, satisfying lives/careers and those who don't. Let's examine some of the aspects of this positive, assertive outlook so that we can get into a mind-set for success.

I Am Assertive

One of the basic choices we make moment to moment is whether to be assertive, aggressive, or passive in response to life situations. Being assertive means being the ultimate judge of our own behavior, feelings, and actions and being responsible for the initiation and consequence of those actions. In essence, assertive people choose for themselves and build themselves up *without* putting others down. Aggressive people choose for themselves and others; they build themselves up *by* putting others down. Passive people allow *others* to choose *for* them; they put themselves down or allow others to do so.

An assertive attitude helps to maintain control

An assertive attitude will help you maintain some control over today's competitive job market. An assertive outlook enables you to be persistent, seek more information when you run out of leads, weigh all alternatives evenly (incorporating both your logic and your intuition), revise your goals when necessary, and pursue your goals with commitment and purpose. Assertiveness specifically enables you to say what you feel, think, and want. It allows you to be expressive, open, and clear in communication. You are able to say no under pressure, recognize and deal with manipulation, and stand up for your rights in negative, confrontational situations. You gain the ability to be a better listener. Others appreciate your directness and ability to hear them. You enjoy more positive interactions with people and feel more positive about being able to handle life situations.

Assertive personal traits include body language as well as words. Studies indicate that 93 percent of the meaning of any message is communicated nonverbally. Look at your appearance, facial expressions, and typical physical movements and stance when you are feeling assertive compared to when you are feeling passive. What does your style of dress say about you? Can changing the color or style of your outfit change the mood you project to others? Have you ever noticed your gesturing? Assertiveness is often associated with expansive gestures rather than limited ones. Finally, how do you deal with touch or physical closeness? Being assertive means feeling comfortable within your own body space.

Positive, assertive behavior shows self-confidence

Positive, assertive behavior suggests that you truly have confidence in yourself. This behavior conveys verbally and nonverbally that you believe in your abilities and in your own worth. That positive, confident, and enthusiastic self will set you apart, make people take notice of you, and ultimately enable you to exercise control over your career and your life.

I Have a Sense of Humor

According to journalist Norman Cousins, laughing is internal jogging, and when you laugh, you are exercising all your internal organs. Not only does laughter feel good, it is essential to good health and a sense of well-being. Cousins has good reason to believe this. Some years ago he was diagnosed with a terminal illness and given just two months to live. Instead of spending his precious time remaining in the hospital, he checked into a hotel and watched, read, or listened to every humorous movie, book, and audiotape he could get his hands on. He virtually laughed himself well. Many years later, still in excellent health, Cousins was convinced, as were his doctors, that laughter accounted for his recovery! In fact, the medical school at U.C.L.A. invited him to join its faculty to teach interns how to lighten up.

Cousins' amazing story holds a lesson for all of us. We can all stand to lighten up a little—to find the genuine humor in an embarrassing moment, in a mistake, in a situation that is so serious that we need to laugh to keep from crying. Humor at its best means being able to laugh at yourself. Look for opportunities to see the lighter side of life and to share the experience of being human with others who can laugh with you, not at you. Cultivate the habit of walking on the "light" side of life.

I Am Self-Confident

Self-confidence, perhaps more than any other factor, is the secret to success and happiness. It is the ability to recognize that even though you are imperfect, you are a unique, worthwhile, and lovable person who deserves and can attain the best in life. You project a sense of self-confidence in your body language, your dress, your pace, your ability to take pride in your accomplishments, your ability to learn from your mistakes, and your ability to accept suggestions and praise from others. Because you believe you deserve the career of your choice, you can attain it.

Discover your own self-worth

You can begin to develop more self-confidence by recognizing and rewarding yourself for something you do *well* each day. It may feel more natural for you to review, in great detail, each and every negative event that has occurred. This is a common and understandable human reaction that can be neutralized by deliberate positive thinking. At times you may have to force yourself to think of something positive and give yourself a pat on the back. Better yet, make it a point to share the good news with a friend, a support person, someone who you know will delight in your small personal achievement. Consider starting a support group consisting of individuals who want to share their personal victories with each other. The reinforcement and support of others are powerful tools in our personal quest for success. Start small, remembering that an Olympic gold medal, just like self-confidence, is built on hours, days, weeks, months, and years of small personal victories.

I Am Enthusiastic

You can identify achievers by their consistently optimistic and enthusiastic demeanor. They know that life is a self-fulfilling prophecy, that people usually get what they actively imagine and expect. They choose to start the day on a positive note by listening to music, singing in the shower, or telling themselves this will be a good day. They view problems as opportunities to be creative. They learn to stay relaxed and calm under stress. They associate with people who share their optimism about life and who support each other through praise, encouragement, and networking. When asked about their career goals, instead of saying, "I don't know," they say, "I'm in the process of discovering my career goals."

Employers rate enthusiasm highly

When employers are asked what traits they look for in prospective employees, enthusiasm is always among those at the top of the list. What kind of people do you want as friends, associates, and colleagues? Chances are you want people who are optimistic and have a zest for life. You can become more enthusiastic about life by getting involved in something that has meaning for you. A hobby, volunteer work, mastery of a skill, a new relationship all provide opportunities to generate and express enthusiasm. On the job, displaying a professional attitude includes acting as if things are fine even when you feel upset or depressed. Although it may seem phony, you will find that acting positively pays off. Not only do you come across as mature and professional, but as you begin to act enthusiastically, you receive positive feedback from others. The smiles, nods, and positive words of others begin to make you feel enthusiastic, and you soon discover you are no longer acting: you genuinely feel better!

I Use Positive Self-Talk (Affirmations)

One of the most effective ways to improve your self-image is the deliberate use of positive self-talk. You already talk to yourself; we all do, constantly! But we usually do not consciously listen to our internal dialogue; consequently, we often hear only negative, self-defeating messages that create and reinforce a poor self-image. Once you decide to take charge of your self-talk, you can begin to repeat positive messages that will reinforce a positive self-image. These messages are commonly called affirmations.

Positive self-talk improves self-image

An *affirmation* is a statement or assertion that something is *already* so (Gawain, 2000). It is an existing seed or thought in the here and now that will grow as life unfolds. It is not intended to change what already exists but to create new, desired outcomes. Remember, all events begin with a thought. If you think you can, you can! Anything a person can conceive can be achieved. Good gardeners cultivate not only flowers but also the soil in which they grow. The thoughts you are thinking and sending out are the "soil" of your life: If you constantly project thoughts of lack of ability, you will have barren soil; if you project thoughts of ability and strength, your soil will be rich. Therefore, any career in which you can imagine yourself being happy and successful can be achieved.

However, when developing your affirmations, remember that you are planting a seed and that the seed must carry information on the exact thing you want to grow into, or produce—the result you desire. When you become specific about what you want, you are focusing the power of your mind's energy (your thoughts) on your desires. The more specific you are about your goals, the more focused you become about what must be done to reach them. You know you are being specific enough when you can visualize details about what you want. For example, if you want to become a college professor, you must be able to see yourself on a college campus in a specific classroom, standing before a room of students, lecturing, interacting with other professors, and correcting papers!

Let's put this technique into action. Think of a quality that you want to develop in yourself; we'll use enthusiasm as an example. Your first instinct might be to say or think, "I'm not very enthusiastic." As soon as this thought comes to mind, replace it with the opposite thought, "I am enthusiastic." Repeat the phrase over and over, day and night, until you feel you own it; soon it will feel comfortable. At the same time, picture yourself doing something enthusiastically, such as explaining to your boss why you deserve a day off, starting a conversation with a stranger, or confidently disagreeing with an instructor during class. Picture yourself making your statement and being positively reinforced: Your boss says yes, you deserve it; the stranger becomes a friend; the instructor praises you for your insight.

Thus, even before you implement your affirmation by enthusiastically taking some action, you have prepared yourself mentally for a positive outcome of your action. Your chances of experiencing the positive outcome improve because you are projecting a positive self-image. Try it!

SUCCESS STRATEGIES

Here are some hints to follow when stating or writing down your own affirmations:

1. Always phrase the affirmation in the present, never in the future; otherwise it may remain in the future. For example, if your goal is to be less tense or nervous in challenging and stressful situations, use an affirmation such as "I am calm; I am in control of my feelings and this situation," rather than "I will be calm."

2. Phrase your affirmation in the positive rather than the negative. In other words, avoid affirming what you don't want. Instead of writing "My present job doesn't bother me anymore," it would be much more effective to write, "My work is wonderful" or "I enjoy my job."

3. Maintain the attitude that you are creating something new and fresh. You are not trying to manipulate, redo, or change an existing condition.

I Visualize Success

Visualization, much like affirmations, is mental practice. It is the conscious implanting of specific images in your mind. Through repetition, these images will become part of your unconscious and then conscious mind, evoking and enhancing abilities, habits, and attitudes. Visualization differs slightly from affirmations because it involves specific mental imagery as opposed to verbal expression of positive thoughts. Visualization is also referred to as *mental imagery* and *mental rehearsal*.

Use mental rehearsal for success

When we marvel at the mastery of an expert, we often assume that the person was born with superhuman talents or skills. We forget that every champion athlete, every great performer, every skilled surgeon, and every professional developed expertise through endless hours of physical and mental practice. They visualize their performance, they engage in positive self-talk ("I can," "I'll do better each time"), and through repetition they become more and more of what they desire to be.

Until you begin to understand yourself, it is difficult to contemplate success fully, in both personal matters and a career. Choose your own vision in which specific results, qualities, and abilities are evident and consistent with winning.

Visualization is one of the most powerful tools promoting personal change. It is the process of maintaining a thought long enough for the mental picture we create to evoke an emotional response. This emotion causes conviction, and conviction influences reality. Thus, a change in reality begins with visualization, which turns to emotion, and results in conviction.

Visualization can have a profound impact on your mind. Your subconscious does not distinguish between imagining something and actually experiencing it. (Try imagining you are biting into a lemon; can you taste it?) You can change your opinions, beliefs, aspirations, and levels of expectation by vividly imagining the circumstances and experiences you select. Of all the species on earth, only human beings can visualize the future and believe it can happen (Dyer, 1992).

A pessimist says, "I will believe it when I see it," whereas an optimist says, "I always see it when I believe it." What you see is what you get. The critical first step is a mental one. You must believe in and be able to see the possibilities and outcomes in your mind before you can hope to realize them in your life.

A high-jumper visualizes a successful route to clear the bar; a golfer sees in his mind the putt dropping into the cup and follows that vision. Strong visual messages are often reinforced with appropriate positive affirmations. This process will assist you in achieving what you want to accomplish. Conscious visualization of yourself as a winner is a key step toward a self-fulfilling prophecy.

Those who use visualization successfully do so regularly over a period of time. This is the key to the success of mental rehearsal. Research indicates that a goal must be visualized a minimum of 30 minutes a day for at least a month to obtain results. This discipline distinguishes visualization from random daydreaming, an effortless activity in which we all engage from time to time!

I Have a Positive Self-Image

Successful people *like* themselves, visualize themselves at their best, and monitor their self-talk to reinforce their images of success in word and action. They know that self-image acts as a regulator, an unconscious thermostat. If you cannot picture yourself doing, being, or achieving something, you probably will not be able to do, be, or achieve it. Your self-image absorbs information, memorizes it, and guides your actions accordingly. Every time you say, "I can't," you are adding to a negative self-image. Every time you say, "I can and will," you are giving yourself permission to be your best. Successful people recognize how potent their beliefs about self are, and they take responsibility for shaping their own self-images, rather than allowing others' opinions to shape or limit them.

I Have Multiple Intelligences

Scientists used to believe that there were only two ways to demonstrate intelligence, either verbally or mathematically. The research of Dr. Howard Gardner (1993) now indicates that there are at least seven distinct areas of intelligence. Gardner proposes that each person possesses all seven intelligences to a greater or lesser degree and that we can all work on developing even more of each intelligence. As you read about each one below, ask yourself which ones you have already developed highly and which ones you would like to develop further:

1. *Verbal/linguistic intelligence* focuses on the use of language and words. Individuals with this intelligence tend to enjoy school subjects such as English, foreign languages, history, and social sciences. They participate in debate, drama, TV and radio work, newspaper and yearbook editing, and writing of newsletters and magazines. Common career choices include author, attorney, teacher, salesperson, and religious leader.

2. *Musical/rhythmic intelligence* focuses on the ability to be aware of patterns in pitch, sound, rhythm, and timbre. These individuals enjoy such school subjects as music and dance. They are involved in band, orchestra, choir, and dance productions. Some common career choices include singer, composer, dancer, conductor, disc jockey, and sound engineer.

3. *Logical/mathematical intelligence* includes the ability to think abstractly, to problem-solve, and to think critically. Favorite school subjects for these individuals include math, science, economics, and computer programming. They tend to be involved in science projects and enjoy reading maps, spreadsheets, budgets, and blueprints. Common career choices include engineer, scientist, mathematician, banker, economist, and computer programmer.

4. *Visual/spatial intelligence* includes the ability to create mental images and transform them into an art form. Individuals with this intelligence enjoy art, shop, drafting, and photography. They enjoy projects such as designing brochures, ceramics, costumes, structures, and websites. Popular careers include visual artist, designer, architect, and Webmaster.

5. *Bodily/kinesthetic intelligence* involves the ability to connect mind and body and often relates to excelling at sports. Popular subjects include dance, drama, sports, and culinary arts. Common career choices include athlete, coach, physical therapist, dancer, trainer, and chef.

6. *Intrapersonal intelligence* involves the ability to comprehend one's feelings. Popular school subjects related to this intelligence include psychology and creative writing. These individuals enjoy reading and journal writing. Common careers include psychologist, author, and religious leader.

7. *Interpersonal intelligence* involves the ability to comprehend others' feelings. Individuals who possess this intelligence enjoy such school subjects as literature, psychology, and sociology. Typical career choices include counselor, psychologist, nurse, social worker, teacher, and politician.

Because each person possesses some of all seven intelligences, it's useful to recognize which are most highly developed, which come naturally, and which should be consciously targeted for improvement. Most research on career satisfaction suggests that in order to be satisfied, you need to identify and capitalize on areas that seem natural and take advantage of your multiple intelligences.

I Learn from Role Models

So far we have explored the components for developing a positive self-image, that is, personal behaviors and attitudes that help us identify and best use our values, skills, and interests. Now it's time to look outside ourselves at people who display the qualities of success we want to cultivate. Think about the people you admire and begin to make a list. First, think globally about prominent individuals on the national and international scene. Then, think locally about people with whom you work; individuals who are part of your community, your neighborhood, or your religious affiliation; those who attend your school; or those who share your hobbies. Finally, think of the people who are most dear to you—your family and friends. Which of their qualities do you admire? In what ways do you want to be more like them?

Spend time observing them in action. You may want to consider telling them what you admire about them and asking them to tell you how they developed those qualities. Ask them for insights and suggestions that you might use in developing your own success profile. Make these people part of your network of contacts. You will probably find that even the most successful people have struggled with moments of self-doubt or crises of self-confidence. Ask them what they do when the going gets rough.

No doubt you choose your friends and associates deliberately and carefully, knowing that you are influenced by the attitudes of the company you keep. Similarly, when you seek out individuals and acknowledge the qualities you admire in them, you are giving them the gift of recognition and appreciation, a valuable commodity in today's fast-paced, all-too-impersonal world. Also, in speaking with your role models you are practicing information interviewing (to be discussed in Chapter 9) and taking the first steps in developing networking skills.

In fact, this is a good time for doing some volunteer work, exploring internships, and getting involved in the community. It is not too soon to use the newspaper or local magazines to find leads and meet people who can give you ideas. Look for articles describing successful people or interesting jobs. Then call these people and interview them about how they chose and trained for their careers. Their strategies may also work for you. (See Exercise 2.6.) You are making connections that can later assist you in the job search process. Of course, you are also projecting the positive self-image you are cultivating.

I Initiate Action

Successful people realize that goals activate people and fears stop people. If you dwell on your fears, whether real or imagined, you will be immobilized in the pursuit of your goals. If you concentrate on your goals, you will move toward them. People who are afraid to tell the world what they want don't get it. The difference between those who are successful and those who are not is attitude. Which side of the coin do you choose to look at—fears or goals? In what direction are you going—away from or toward your goals?

Imagine yourself in your dream job, your fantasy career, the kind of job you would pay to do. Take the job of cruise ship director, for example. Now identify someone who has that occupation. If you don't know of anyone, ask your friends, relatives, neighbors, and classmates, all of whom are part of your extended network (see Exercise 9.1, page 240, for a list of people who make up your network). Ask if they know someone who actually has your dream job. Next, contact that individual in person, if possible, and arrange a brief information interview. Read the section in Chapter 9 on information interviewing, and plan to ask the sample questions.

After you have gathered some facts about your fantasy career, ask yourself if it still holds its appeal for you. If so, you may wish to talk to others in the field to further develop an accurate and detailed assessment. If not, you may want to choose another fantasy career to investigate.

I Am Persistent

ersistent people take responsibility for initiating desired action. They know that life is full of choices, not chances. They realize they have the personal power, both physical and psychological, to take control of their own lives. They know that blaming Mother Nature for a less-than-perfect body or calling it fate when they don't get a job is simply copping out. Successful people make things happen for themselves. What appears to be luck is usually opportunity met by preparation.

Luck = opportunity, preparation, and persistence

Perhaps nowhere is this more evident than in the Olympics. Only the most persistent and committed athletes will be chosen to participate, and all know full well the slim chance of coming home with a medal. Nevertheless, many return time after time, and some eventually triumph. Those fortunate enough to compete gain public acclaim, knowing their participation places them in elite company. The successful person is the one who keeps trying after *not* reaching a goal or after experiencing rejection, the one who keeps trying until the dream is attained.

In today's unpredictable economy, many of us feel as if we, too, are preparing for the Olympics; this especially holds true for students and job seekers, who must face such hurdles as degree and training decisions, financial hardships, interviews, and rejections. Never has persistence in the face of limited opportunity been more necessary.

Through tenacity, determination, and consistent effort, you can achieve much. Talent and education are not automatic keys to success: nothing can take the place of persistence and enthusiasm.

I Am Disciplined

elf-discipline can also be called *self-control*. It is the ability to control or manage some aspect of your life, to have power over it. A simple example is that most of us have the self-discipline to get out of bed every morning at a particular time even though we'd probably prefer to sleep later.

Discipline yourself for success

Meet Alan

Alan began working for Sony's Music Division in Hollywood, California, after he received his associate's degree. He started out as an assistant to the sound cutter and then was promoted to lead sound cutter. After 12 years, his division was reorganized and Alan was laid off. Not knowing exactly what he wanted to do, Alan went to see the outplacement counselor offered to him through Sony. The counselor used a variety of career resources to uncover Alan's interests, skills, and values.

After several meetings and some serious soul-searching, Alan realized that surfing the Web and spending time in the library were two of his strongest interests. The counselor suggested that he check out his local library for volunteer opportunities while he was trying to decide what career direction he would take. With his current skills, Alan was less than confident about his ability to volunteer in the library, and he was sure that he didn't want to return to school to become a librarian.

After several months, Alan was getting discouraged and needed a place to go every day, so he decided to talk to the volunteer coordinator at the library. The coordinator was happy to have him; however, the work he was assigned was not very challenging or interesting. He was stocking shelves and erasing pencil marks from the children's books. He expressed his frustration to one of the other volunteers, who asked him what he really wanted to do in the library. Alan thought that working with the library's media collection might be interesting. Alan's volunteer friend suggested that he call the media specialist and meet with him.

After thinking about it, Alan decided he had nothing to lose so he made an appointment. The two men established an instant rapport and after checking with the volunteer coordinator, it was decided that Alan could work in the media department. After several months, Alan was making a significant contribution to the department. One day

---

Self-discipline is a vital component of success. If you lack the discipline to complete a task or spend the hours needed to accomplish your immediate goal (e.g., to contact four potential employers, study for an important test), your long-term goals will not be accomplished. Each time we allow a task to go undone or a goal to go unaccomplished, we train ourselves to believe that it is okay, that there's always tomorrow. In the meantime, someone else is out there doing it. As is true of persistence and attitude, self-discipline is part of the foundation for success; it must be the basis of other strategies for success we have discussed.

I Demonstrate Emotional Intelligence

Our competitive and achievement-oriented society places great value on intellectual ability. Early in your life your parents and teachers probably tried to determine your IQ (intelligence quotient). The results of such tests are highly regarded, even though these tests are often judged to be inaccurate and incomplete. The results are often unreliable predictors of future success in life. Were you the media specialist and Alan started to brainstorm ideas to create a permanent job for Alan. They decided to explore writing a grant. They spoke with the grant writer associated with the library and discovered there were several grants they could apply for. After six months, the grant was submitted and the library received $250,000 to automate the media center. The library management was so impressed with Alan's initiative and abilities that they offered him a position.

1. What strategies did Alan use to realize his goal of working in the library? What strategies could you use to realize your goals?

2. What skills, if any, did Alan have that made him a good candidate to volunteer in the library? (To help you answer this question, use the skills section in O*Net (http://online.onetcenter.org) resource to look up Alan's job title from his job

at Sony.) Remember to look at soft skills as well as specific job skills.

3. How did networking help Alan pursue his goal? What networking opportunities do you have?

4. If Alan had not met the media specialist, what else could he have done to make his volunteer experience at the library more satisfying?

5. What strategies are effective in dealing with difficult work situations?

6. What affirmation could Alan have used when he first began working in the library?

7. Do you think Alan used visualization when he was looking for work after he left Sony?

8. Do you think Alan used visualization when he started working with the media specialist?

To answer these questions online, go to the *Real Stories* module in Chapter 2 of the Companion Website.

---

labeled an overachiever or underachiever? Average or below average? Were you inspired by these labels—or did they cause you to lose motivation? We have all heard stories of high-IQ individuals who were not successful at chosen paths or who were unhappy in life. Conversely, many people with low to average "intelligence" have defied all predictions and become successful by any definition of the term. In fact, research on college grade point average as a predictor of success indicates the B to C student often enjoys more success in later life than the solid A performer! What explains this apparent paradox?

Research by Daniel Goleman, discussed in his books on emotional intelligence (1995, 2002), offers some answers. The common sense, wisdom, maturity, humor, and street smarts that distinguish successful individuals are the manifestation of emotional intelligence (EQ). The awareness of and ability to monitor and control our emotions, thoughts, and feelings and the ability to be aware of and sensitive to others define emotional intelligence. Complete Exercise 2.3 to test your own EQ. The better developed your EQ, the more successful you are likely to be. Although you are born with IQ, you can learn and cultivate EQ. It may be IQ that gets you the job, but it's EQ that keeps you employed and gets you promoted!

FACTS AND FIGURES

What makes workers succeed . . .

Executives say these personality traits are most important in successful workers:

Enthusiasm 80.6%

"Can Do" Attitude 65.1%

High Energy 40.3%

Assertiveness 30.5%

Source: Management Dimensions, Inc.; survey of 241 executives from all types of companies. Elys McLean-Ibrahim, *USA Today.*

THINK ABOUT IT

1. Why do you think more people ranked enthusiasm as the most important personality trait?

2. Of the four traits listed, which do you feel you express the most of and least of in a work-related environment? Are these the same traits you express most and least in your home life (not work-related)? If not, why do you think there is a difference?

3. Ask three people who have worked with you the same question. What did they say?

4. Do you see yourself as others see you? Why or why not?

5. Given this information, which of these traits should you try to express more often? How will you do this on a daily basis? (Hint: Write an affirmation.)

6. What is the difference between enthusiasm and high energy? Give examples.

7. What is the difference between a "can do" attitude and being assertive? Give examples.

 To answer these questions online, go to the *Facts and Figures* module in Chapter 2 of the Companion Website.

I Identify My Goals

People who succeed have clearly defined plans and objectives that they refer to regularly to keep in mind their lifetime goals, as well as to order their daily priorities. Clearly defined, written goals help move us to completion. The reason most people don't reach their goals is that they don't identify them. They don't know what they want. (See Chapter 8 for information on setting goals.)

If you don't know where you are going, you probably won't get there. Even though you're just embarking on your career fitness plan and you probably don't have a specific career in mind as yet, you can still begin the process of goal setting. Your *first goal* might be to read this book (one chapter a week) and complete all the exercises after each chapter with the intent of learning more about yourself so you can make appropriate career choices when the time comes. Ideally, you should set aside a specific time and place each week so that you will get into the habit of working on your career fitness plan in the same way that you would work on a physical fitness plan—with consistency and commitment.

I Am Self-Reliant and Career Resilient

In the face of events such as downsizing and rightsizing, successful employees must demonstrate self-reliance and resilience. These involve the ability to continually learn and develop new skills, initiate activities, demonstrate flexibility, and continuously align work with the business need. It is essential to ask constantly—and be able to answer—the question, "How does my work add value to the organization?" The question conveys a sense of commitment and a sense of loyalty to your current project. As the job tasks and business needs change, those who want to remain employed must be in a *continuous learning* mode. Simply doing a good job is no longer enough!

I Am Flexible

The world of work has never offered a greater array of choices and possibilities. A common response to this seemingly endless horn of plenty is to look desperately for the one right choice that will offer certainty and stability. Although it is an understandable response, it is unrealistic in our work life in the 21st century. Instead, we must cultivate a sense of comfort regarding the ambiguity, uncertainty, and change that challenge our every plan. We must learn to recognize and accept the fact that life happens as we're making plans.

The ability to appreciate and incorporate the unexpected twists and turns along the path is the secret to success in the new millennium. Rather than resisting change and the unexpected, learn to delight in the unpredictable. Cultivate the ability to incorporate new information quickly and adeptly into your current or emerging career plan. Challenge yourself not only to experience the unsettled feeling that comes with surprise but to think positively about the unanticipated possibilities that present themselves. Recognize that for every door that closes, a new door opens.

Knowing what you want is step number one.

Summary

Career success is based on a knowledge of self. The more you understand and accept your uniqueness, the better able you will be to make appropriate life and career choices.

Programming yourself for success is the first step of your personal assessment program. As you cultivate and engage in each of the practices addressed in this chapter, you will raise and reinforce your self-esteem, the root of all success. *Your opinion of yourself will grow in proportion to the time and energy you give to developing your most valuable asset—yourself.*

Programming Yourself for Success

These exercises are designed to review your attitude and assertiveness skills. Try to answer the first set of questions as quickly and spontaneously as possible. Do not censor your answers. These are called *open-ended questions.* Open-ended questions sometimes make people think about different responses each time they see them, so it's all right to have more than one answer, as well as to change an answer whenever you review the questions. These questions will also cause you to review past actions so that you can better identify how they affected who you are today. Answer the questions in the rest of the exercises to reflect your ideal environment and how you see yourself.

To answer these questions online, go to the *Exercise* module in Chapter 2 of the Companion Website.

Past Actions and Influences

Fill in each blank carefully and honestly. Be true to yourself; don't try to please anyone else with your answers.

1. I am proud that _____

   _____

   _____

2. One thing I can do now that I couldn't do a few years ago is _____

   _____

   _____

3. Name the person you most admire. This person can be living, historical, or fictional. Write down the specific characteristics that you admire in this person (e.g., smart, famous, rich, loving, generous).

   _____

   _____

4. Name a person who is like you, and describe this person. _____

   _____

   _____

5. In the last two weeks, which activities or people gave you a feeling of being energized?

   _____

   _____

f. What have you always wanted to do in your life? What's keeping you from doing it? What action could you take in the next year to get closer to this goal?

_____

_____

_____

g. What negative habit have you successfully changed? _____

_____

_____

h. What three words would you like others to use in describing you? _____

_____

_____

Two Perfect Days

1. Written description

    In order to be clear about what you want in life, write a one-page description of two ideal days in your future. One day should be related to leisure, and one day should be related to work. Think about where you would be; what you'd be doing; who, if anyone, would be with you, and so on. Try to be as detailed as possible. Use Chapter 7, Exercise 7.8 as your outline for the workday.

    Use this space for notes: _____

    _____

    _____

    _____

    _____

    _____

2. Summary in two or three words

    Write down three or more words or phrases that capture the *essence and quality* of each of these two days (e.g., peaceful, challenging, fun, harmonious, exciting, restful, productive).

    Leisure day: _____

    _____

    _____

    Workday: _____

    _____

    _____

Emotional Intelligence Checklist

Answer the following questions for a better idea of how your attitude is reflected in your actions. Consider asking several important people in your life to respond to these questions about you as well. Compare their answers with yours. Choose two or three areas that you think are important to work on to improve your attitude and emotional intelligence.

	I Am Satisfied	I Need to Improve
a. Do I always do my best?	○	○
b. Do I tend to look on the bright side of things?	○	○
c. Am I friendly and cooperative?	○	○
d. Am I prompt and dependable?	○	○
e. Do I do my share (or more than my share)?	○	○
f. Do I appear confident, poised?	○	○
g. Am I believable?	○	○
h. Do people ask my opinions?	○	○
i. Do I appear to be trustworthy?	○	○
j. Am I well-mannered, tactful, considerate of others?	○	○
k. Do I dress appropriately?	○	○
l. Do I put others before myself? To what extent?	○	○
m. Can I accept compliments?	○	○
n. Do I give compliments?	○	○
o. Do I make suggestions?	○	○
p. Can I say no?	○	○
q. Do I wait for others to decide for me?	○	○
r. Do I try to understand how others are feeling?	○	○

For an additional survey of your emotional intelligences, go to the Companion Website for Chapter 2 and click on Weblinks.

Positive Self-Talk (Affirmations)

1. Write six affirmations related to being successful in your career and life planning. Put them on 3 × 5 cards (one per card). Some examples:

   I am a confident and competent person.

   I have many transferable skills.

   I am a valuable employee.

   I am a risk taker.

I am a skilled networker.

I enjoy talking to people about their careers.

a. _____

b. _____

c. _____

d. _____

e. _____

f. _____

2. Read your affirmations to yourself two times during the day, once in the morning as you awake and once just before you go to sleep. Consider sharing your affirmations with a close friend or a classmate.

3. To accelerate their effectiveness, try the following suggestions:

   a. Write your affirmations in longhand while speaking them aloud to yourself 10, 20, or more times.

   b. Try writing in different persons, such as "I, Marilyn, am highly employable"; "You, Marilyn, are highly employable"; "She, Marilyn, is highly employable."

   c. Record your affirmations on a cassette tape recorder, and listen to them as you drive or while you do chores around the house.

   d. Before going to sleep at night or on arising in the morning, visualize yourself as you are becoming. For example, see yourself as more assertive, loving, social, enthusiastic.

   e. Chant or sing your affirmations aloud while driving or during any appropriate activity.

   f. Meditate on your affirmations.

   g. Tape them up around the house, on the telephone, on mirrors, on the refrigerator, on the ceiling above your bed, on the dashboard of your car, in your dresser drawers.

   h. Use affirmations as bookmarks.

4. Finally, ask yourself, "Is it what I really want?" George Bernard Shaw once commented, "The only thing worse than not getting what you want is getting what you want!" In other words, many go fishing all their lives, only to realize it wasn't the fish they wanted.

Your Fantasy Careers

EXERCISE 2.5

"WOULDN'T IT BE GREAT TO BE . . ."

List your current fantasy careers below. Then think back chronologically to earlier age levels and try to recall some of your past fantasy careers; list them as well. We develop fantasy careers at a very young age. Most children see cartoons, television dramas, and movies about doctors, lawyers, police officers, firefighters, astronauts, teachers, and scientists, to name a few popular careers. Books about solving mysteries create an image of excitement about being a detective. Current movies influence many to dream of being a jet pilot or gifted performer. What have you read about, seen in the movies, or dreamed about doing?

1. For each career on your list, ask yourself this question: "What about this career is or was appealing to me?" Many of us might have the same fantasy career but for different reasons.

CURRENT FANTASY CAREER	WHAT ABOUT THIS CAREER APPEALS TO ME?
a.	
b.	
c.	
d.	

PAST FANTASY CAREERS, BY AGE	WHAT APPEALED MOST TO ME ABOUT THIS FANTASY CAREER?
1–10	
11–15	
16–20	
21–30	
31–40	
41–50	
51 plus	

2. Now choose the one fantasy career that is most appealing. Try to locate someone who earns a living in this career. If you are part of a class, ask your instructor and classmates if they can refer you to someone. Otherwise, try to make a connection by asking people you know at school, work, and social gatherings. Read the section on information interviewing in Chapter 9. Arrange an interview, preferably in person, and ask the questions in the sample list of typical questions under Information Interviewing Outline.

Making a Fantasy Real

1. Find a newspaper or magazine article describing a job that seems like a fantasy job to you. Or find a story about a person you consider to be truly successful. (Remember, you have a right to your own definition of success.)

2. Summarize the features that make the job or the successful person interesting. What are the personality traits of the person holding the job? What adjectives best describe this person? (See Exercise 1.4.) How do these traits compare to your own personality traits?

_____

_____

_____

_____

_____

_____

_____

_____

Building Your Success Profile

1. Review all of the affirmations in this chapter. Together, they comprise the formula for the success profile of the 21st century. Identify the six affirmations that are most true of you today (e.g., I have a sense of humor, I am persistent). Write them on the lines below. They are already part of your success profile.

MY TOP SIX SUCCESS FACTORS

(1) _____   (4) _____

(2) _____   (5) _____

(3) _____   (6) _____

2. Now, identify the three affirmations that are currently least like you. List them below. These are the three that are most likely to keep you from experiencing optimal success. Think about one action step you could take this week to further develop these three areas.

THREE AREAS TO DEVELOP   **THREE ACTION STEPS TO TAKE**

(1) _____   (1) _____

(2) _____   (2) _____

(3) _____   (3) _____

Think About Enthusiasm

1. Give three examples of enthusiastic behavior in the workplace. _____

_____

_____

_____

2. How can enthusiasm help a new employee? Is a "can do" attitude learned? If yes, how?

_____

_____

_____

_____

3. Give an example of an assertive behavior that can be misinterpreted. _____

_____

_____

_____

_____

4. Explain the difference between affirmation and visualization. _____

_____

_____

_____

_____

_____

_____

_____

WWWebwise

 For additional activities, go to the WWWebwise module in Chapter 2 of the Companion Website.

Exercise Summary

1. What have I learned about myself? _____
   _____
   _____

2. I want to improve the following: _____
   _____
   _____

3. I admire the following qualities in people: _____
   _____
   _____

4. My affirmations are as follows: _____
   _____
   _____
   _____
   _____
   _____

5. In the next two weeks, I can do the following to improve my self-confidence and build
   my success profile:

   _____
   _____
   _____
   _____
   _____
   _____
   _____
   _____
   _____
   _____
   _____
   _____

Go to page 204 of the chapter summaries and fill out the Chapter 2 exercise summary now.

Values Clarification

What is it that causes someone to study for years to enter a career such as medicine or law while others are looking for the quickest, easiest way to make money? What causes someone to switch careers midstream after spending years developing mastery and a reputation in a field? The answer to these questions is *values*. Your values are the often unidentified forces that guide and influence your decisions throughout your life. Values are *the deeply held convictions that influence your thinking when you are faced with choices.* They provide you with a frame of reference for evaluating information and options. If you value fitness and good health, you make time for daily exercise, positive self-talk, and proper nutrition. If you value career satisfaction, you take time to examine your values and make choices consistent with them.

At the end of the chapter you will be able to . . .

- **Define and clarify your values**

- **Discuss how your values motivate you**

- **Describe how your values affect your career decisions**

Destiny is not a matter of chance.
It is a matter of choice.

Defining Values

Values are the self-motivators that indicate what you consider most important in your life. Values are reflected in what you actually do with your time and your life. This chapter will help you identify what is needed in your work environment to make you feel satisfied with your job. You may discover that the reason you are dissatisfied with your present job is that it incorporates few of your values and interests.

From time to time it may be necessary to settle for a job just to pay the bills; in such circumstances you may feel empty, frustrated, and unfulfilled by the job. Once you learn how to identify your values, it will be natural for you to take them into account and make meaningful and satisfying decisions about jobs. In other words, your decisions can be based on what's really important to you. If you are determined to follow your chosen career path and stay committed to your values, you will find that even when times are tough, you will make every effort to stick to your long-range goal.

Clarifying Your Values

Now that you have begun to take charge of your mental attitude, identifying your values becomes the next step in your personal assessment program. By the age of 10, most of us have unconsciously adopted the values of our parents, teachers, and friends. By adolescence, we have begun to sort out which of these adopted values we want to freely choose as our own. This process of rejecting some of our family's values and developing our own is often called teenage rebellion. Parents, in particular, often take offense when we question or reject a value they believe important. In fact, however, this process of values clarification is an essential part of growing up. Mature, independent, successful individuals act on their own values rather than those of others. This frees them from unnecessary guilt ("What would my mother say if . . . ?") and indecision ("What would my boss do in this situation?"). It fosters satisfaction and self-confidence ("Regardless of the outcome, I'm in control of my life").

Adults often fail to reassess their values as life goes on. Research about life stages indicates that adults can and do make dramatic changes in their personal and career lives based on changes in values. This process of change can be less traumatic for all individuals involved if, as adults, we periodically review and reassess what is important to us.

How can you identify your values? The more intense your favorable feelings are about some activity or social condition, the more you value it. Is there an issue currently in the news that excites you or makes you angry? Are there certain activities that energize you? Are there circumstances in your life that lead you to certain activities? All of these are indicators of your values.

More specifically, the following criteria will help you determine your values. Values that are alive and an active part of you have the following qualities:

Prized and cherished. When you cherish something, you exude enthusiasm and enjoyment about it. You are proud to display it and use it.

Publicly affirmed. You are willing and perhaps even eager to state your values in public.

Chosen freely. No one else is pressuring you to act in a certain way. You own these values. They feel like a part of you.

Chosen from alternatives. If given a choice to play a leading role in a Hollywood film or be provided with a full scholarship to study at Harvard Business School, which would you choose? Choosing to act in Hollywood highlights such values as creativity, prestige, glamour, monetary returns, and risk taking, whereas choosing to acquire a Harvard MBA suggests prestige, monetary returns, education, intellectual stimulation, and security.

Chosen after consideration of consequences. We usually consider the consequences before we make an important decision. What impressions come to mind when you consider the following scenarios?

- You have been offered a job at a firm across the country far from the place you've lived all your life.
- You are offered a well-paying job as a defense contractor in your town.
- You are presented with a dinner check that doesn't charge you for all the food ordered.

What values come into play as you think about the decisions involved and their possible consequences?

Acted on. Again, values are reflected in what you do with your time and your life; they are more than wishful thinking or romantic ideals about how you *should* lead your life.

Acted on repeatedly and consistently, forming a definite pattern. The premise here is that you repeatedly engage in activities that relate to your highest values. To identify specific examples for yourself, complete the Values Grid in Exercise 3.1 at the end of this chapter. List five aspirations or goals you have achieved in your lifetime (e.g., finished high school, was member of debate team, planned a surprise party, found a job), and then check the values that were involved in each goal. When you're done, the values with the most checks are those most important to you.

As you begin to think about it, you will come to realize how much you rely on your values to make decisions. People facing career planning often wonder how they will ever choose a career when they have so many possibilities in mind. This is precisely the time when knowing your values is most important. Let's say you've discovered that economic return, helping others,

Meet Maria

Maria was the oldest of four siblings. Her parents owned a small mortgage brokerage company. Maria was an excellent student in high school, but her parents never encouraged her to or discouraged her from attending college. They felt that Maria would always be able to make a living no matter what. Before Maria graduated from high school, her counselor told her that she had a very good chance of getting a scholarship to attend college, but Maria never took advantage of the opportunity.

After graduation, she went to work in her parents' business and her life changed very little. Being a shy, quiet young woman, Maria usually let decisions happen to her, or she let others make them for her. One morning Maria awoke and she couldn't get out of bed. She felt very tired and had a bad headache. Her mother told her to see the doctor, who told her that she was probably starting to get the flu, but weeks went by and she was still feeling poorly.

One night Maria was having dinner with a friend and she started to cry. With some encouragement, Maria started to talk about how unhappy she was with her work and her life in general. Her friend suggested that she talk with a career counselor who might be able to help her look at career options. Not knowing how to find a career counselor, Maria decided to call her local community college. She discovered that she could meet with the counselor in the career center.

The counselor spent some time talking with Maria and together they felt it would be beneficial for Maria to take some assessments to examine her interests, personality preferences, values, and skills. The tests revealed a pattern of interests that were very different from the type of work Maria was doing and a value system that supported a strong moral code, creativity, and self-expression. After several appointments with the counselor,

and security are your top three values. You are thinking about becoming an artist, an actor, or a speech teacher. You might well be able to do all three, even simultaneously! However, in order to choose one direction, try deciding which career would best satisfy your top three values. You are likely to experience the most success and happiness from this kind of choice. In this case, speech teacher most closely incorporates the values mentioned.

Needs and Motivators

So far we have discussed motivation based on successful personal attitudes and values. In addition, inner drives or needs also influence how you choose a career. People experience psychological discomfort when their needs are unmet. We best satisfy our needs by identifying them and then engaging in behaviors that meet them. Once our needs are met, tension and discomfort are reduced. You may have read about five primary types of needs as identified by Abraham Maslow (1970), a famous psychologist.

As you can see, these needs progress from the most basic and biologically oriented (survival needs) to more complex and socially oriented levels of needs. When people are preoccupied with finding ways to put food on the

Maria began to understand why she was so unhappy.

The counselor suggested that Maria develop some goals and objectives to help her move from her current situation. She also suggested that Maria speak with her parents to help them understand her feelings. A year later, Maria had made some specific changes in her life. She enrolled in college and discovered that she was really interested in psychology. Because she was still very close to her parents, she kept her job, but with school and more social activities, she felt that she had some balance in her life.

1. Do you think Maria was unhappy with her job because it didn't satisfy her values or her interests or both? Why?

2. Do you think values are more important than interests when it comes to making career decisions? Why or why not?

3. Do you think Maria had problems with decision making? Why?

4. What are some of the signs that indicate you have made a poor decision?

5. What values are most critical to your career satisfaction right now?

6. To what extent does your current job or lifestyle support your most critical values?

7. Can you recall a recent decision that you've made that supported these values?

8. How easy was it to make that decision? Were you aware of the role that your values played?

 To answer these questions online, go to the *Real Stories* module in Chapter 3 of the Companion Website.

---

table (physiological needs), they have little time or desire to work on developing relationships or to search for a job that can utilize their talents. Rather, they tend to work at any job that will immediately bring in money. A person becomes aware of a higher-order need only when a lower-order need has been met. These basic needs are such primary and intense self-motivators that our *values* may be eclipsed when we are struggling to meet primary *needs*.

One example of changing needs often occurs among divorcing couples with children. Most newly single parents have to readjust from the shared responsibilities of a two-parent family and the greater financial security of a two-person income. For some, the reduction in income and addition of responsibilities may be so great that the individual returns to a focus on meeting survival needs such as securing food and shelter. If parents in this situation are out of work, they will likely be far less concerned about having the perfect job than with simply finding a job. As we discussed earlier, however, people should certainly take their values into account in career decisions whenever possible.

It is also important to assess needs from a cultural perspective and to realize that individuals may function and see things differently, depending on the cultural context. For example, recent immigrants need time to adapt or adjust to a new environment. Even if their survival needs for food, clothing, and shelter are met in the new culture, their lack of familiarity with local customs and

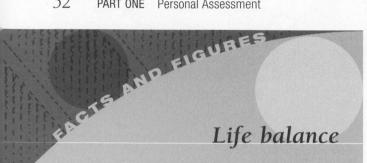

Life balance

In a survey of graduating business students from eleven countries, 57 percent said that balancing work and personal life is their top career goal.

Source: PricewaterhouseCoopers, 2000.

"In survey after survey, Gen X men, those born between 1965 and 1980, say they intend to put family ahead of work. Companies are starting to pay attention. The most progressive corporations, including many on this year's 100 Best list, are striving to let young men, as well as women, know that they can work a flexible schedule, take time off after the birth of a child, and go home at a normal hour, without fearing that their job is at risk."

"Nearly 80 percent of men and women ages 24 to 34—the core of the Gen X cohort—said that time with family was more important than earning a higher salary."

Source: Working Mother. Annual 100 Best Companies, 2002.

WHAT DO YOU THINK?

1. How would you rate work versus leisure?

2. If you were continually asked to sacrifice your leisure time to ensure job promotion in the future, would you find this an acceptable arrangement? Why or why not?

3. Do you think this survey would hold up in a difficult economic period when it is hard to find a good job? What makes the concept of balance in one's life so compelling?

4. Would you be willing to earn less income and work fewer hours for the opportunity to pursue balance in your life?

 To answer these questions online, go to the *Facts and Figures* module in Chapter 3 of the Companion Website.

Job satisfaction: internal vs. external motivators

their homesickness for familiar people and customs may diminish their sense of security, psychological well-being, and competence, as outlined by Maslow.

When your ability to meet your physiological and safety needs is stable, you may find that you demand more feedback (satisfaction of social needs) in your work environment. Renowned industrial psychologist Frederick Herzberg (1966) examined the factors that produce or contribute to job satisfaction for most workers. We have already discussed how a job that reflects your top values contributes to job satisfaction. Herzberg found that we have both external motivators and internal motivators. External motivators include salary, working conditions, company policies, and possibility for advancement, elements that fulfill physiological and safety needs. However, internal motivators involving amount of responsibility, type of work accomplished, recognition, and achievement also all contribute to job satisfaction. These motivators appear to be most important for people with values and needs related to status and self-actualization. People do not necessarily respond to each need with identical intensities of desire. For your own benefit, it would be useful to examine what brings you satisfaction on the job. Look at Exhibit 3.1 to see how Herzberg's research on job satisfaction overlaps with Maslow's identification of needs.

Finding Balance

Balance is the ability to include all your top priorities and values in your career and life plan. Some people who live to work (*workaholics*) and claim to be happy may not experience balance.

In today's challenging economic environment, it may seem more difficult than ever to consider your values, interests, and overall happiness when making career decisions. Nevertheless, as you learn more about what makes you happy and successful, you are indeed more likely to take all factors into account when choosing schooling or training and when making job and career decisions, even in tough economic times. Ideally, this process of identifying interests, talents, and values will begin much earlier in life for the generations to come. More and more high schools, for example, are offering career courses and

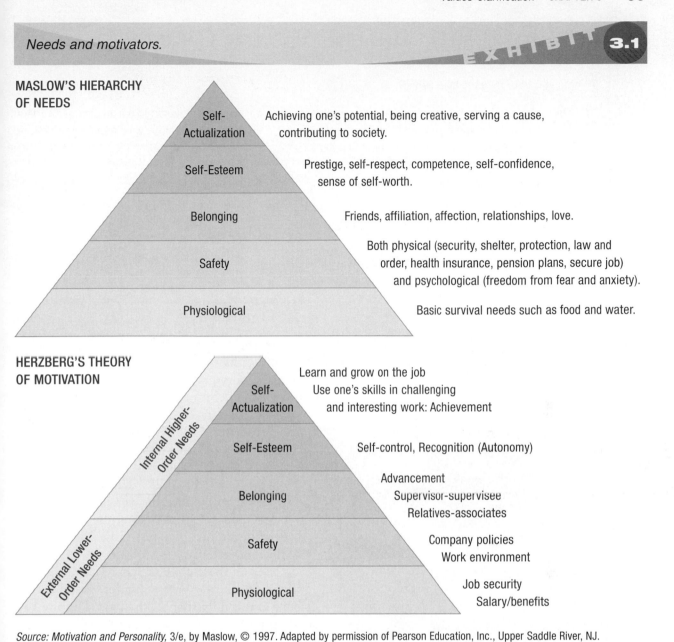

Needs and motivators.

EXHIBIT 3.1

MASLOW'S HIERARCHY OF NEEDS

- Self-Actualization — Achieving one's potential, being creative, serving a cause, contributing to society.
- Self-Esteem — Prestige, self-respect, competence, self-confidence, sense of self-worth.
- Belonging — Friends, affiliation, affection, relationships, love.
- Safety — Both physical (security, shelter, protection, law and order, health insurance, pension plans, secure job) and psychological (freedom from fear and anxiety).
- Physiological — Basic survival needs such as food and water.

HERZBERG'S THEORY OF MOTIVATION

Internal Higher-Order Needs

- Self-Actualization — Learn and grow on the job / Use one's skills in challenging and interesting work: Achievement
- Self-Esteem — Self-control, Recognition (Autonomy)
- Belonging — Advancement / Supervisor-supervisee / Relatives-associates

External Lower-Order Needs

- Safety — Company policies / Work environment
- Physiological — Job security / Salary/benefits

Source: Motivation and Personality, 3/e, by Maslow, © 1997. Adapted by permission of Pearson Education, Inc., Upper Saddle River, NJ.

encouraging students to find volunteer jobs and internships and take courses in those subjects and areas that interest them. When these students reach college or some other form of post–high school training, they are likely to have a much better idea of what they want to do and to have more experience to offer.

Role of Leisure

t one time, an employee who diligently honored family obligations and pursued leisure and other nonwork activities may have been considered uncommitted. The workplace now, however, acknowledges and even often encourages these pursuits. A satis-

True Values

To help you identify your true values:

1. Think about 10 decisions you've made this week. Consider how you spent your money and your time; what you watched on TV; what you surfed on the Web; what you read; and with whom you spent time.

2. As you review your choices, observe the patterns that emerge.

3. Begin to compare what you say your values are with what you actually choose.

4. Reflect on any differences that may surface as you do your comparison.

5. Consider adjusting your decisions to reflect y values more closely, or reevaluate what you thought were your values and identify those do reflect your decisions.

6. This process of values clarification will help identify your true values so that you can mak wise career choices that are consistent with values. This will confirm who you are and gi a deeper sense of satisfaction when you act your true values.

fied, balanced individual is likely in the long run to be a more productive employee. Leisure activities allow individuals to let go, be spontaneous, and nurture their creativity, self-expression, and personal growth. All these qualities enhance performance on the job and counteract the negative effects of stress in many work situations. (In addition, many people have turned leisure pursuits into careers. Consider Mrs. Fields and her cookies or Tiger Woods and his golf.) The more an individual can balance the demands of family, work, and personal leisure, the better he or she can embrace the inevitable changes that challenge us daily.

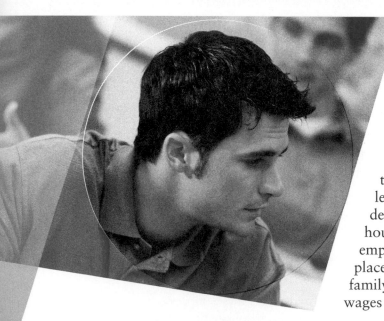

Even in these challenging economic times, today's workers place a higher premium on leisure and family than in the past. Despite evidence that some employees are working longer hours to make up for corporate downsizing, employees today, when given the choice, typically place greater emphasis on finding quality time for family and outside interests than on increasing their wages by working extended hours.

Summary

In Chapters 2 and 3, we discussed several types of forces that propel you to act on your goals: attitudes, values, and needs. In Chapter 4 you will learn more about your specific interests and personality type and how these can and should affect your career decisions.

If you wish, describe your accomplishments 1 through 5 in more detail here:

1. _____

2. _____

3. _____

4. _____

5. _____

Explore Your Values

1. List five things you love to do. What values are reflected in these activities? (See Exercise 3.1, Values Grid, for ideas.)

_____

_____

2. What is one thing you would change in the world? In your town? About yourself?

_____

_____

3. What is something you really want to learn before you die? _____

_____

4. List several values that are most important to you in your job (e.g., independence, creativity, working outdoors):

_____

_____

5. Work environments are people environments. Some people add to your energy, productivity, and self-esteem; others drain you. Think of three people and describe their influence on you:

_____

_____

6. If you had unlimited funds so that you would not have to work:

   a. How would you spend your time? (Try to think beyond a summer vacation; envision a daily lifestyle.)

_____

_____

   b. To what charities or causes would you contribute?

_____

_____

Job descriptions

From the list of 15 job descriptions that follow, choose the three you find most interesting as career possibilities. Then list the values each of those job descriptions implies. Some possible answers appear on page 63.

1. _____

   _____

2. _____

   _____

3. _____

   _____

1. An opportunity to help people in a personal way. Meet and deal with the public in a meaningful relationship. Help to make the world a better place to live. Pay and benefits in accordance with experience.

2. Do your own thing! Work with abstract ideas. Develop new ideas and things. Nonroutine. A chance to work on your own or as a member of a creative team. Flexible working conditions.

3. A professional position. Position of responsibility. Secretarial assistance provided. Pay dependent on experience and initiative. Position requires a high level of education and training. Job benefits are high pay and public recognition.

4. A job with a guaranteed annual salary in a permanent position with a secure, stable company. Supervisory assistance is available. Minimum educational requirement is high school. Slightly better pay with one or two years of college or vocational training. Position guarantees cost-of-living pay increases annually. Retirement benefits.

5. Looking for an interesting job? One that requires research, thinking, and problem solving? Do you like to deal with theoretical concepts? This job demands constant updating of information and ability to deal with new ideas. An opportunity to work with creative and intellectually stimulating people.

6. This job requires an extraordinary person. The job demands risk and daring. Ability to deal with exciting tasks. Excellent physical health a necessity. You must be willing to travel.

7. An ideal place to work. An opportunity to work with people you really like and—just as important—who really like you. A friendly, congenial atmosphere. Get to know your coworkers as friends. Pay and benefits dependent on training and experience.

8. Work in a young, fast-growing company. Great opportunities for advancement. Starting pay is low, but rapid promotion to midmanagement. From this position, there are many opportunities and directions for further advancement. Your only limitations are your own energy and initiative. Pay and benefits related to level of responsibility.

9. Set your own pace! Set your own working conditions. Flexible hours. Choose your own team or work alone. Salary based on your own initiative and time on the job.

10. Start at the bottom and work your way up. You can become president of the firm. You should have the ability to learn while you work. Quality and produc-

tivity will be rewarded by rapid advancement and recognition for a job well done. Salary contingent on rate of advancement.

11. Ability to direct work tasks of others in a variety of activities. Leadership qualities in controlling workforce and maintaining production schedules. Ability to maintain a stable workforce. Coordinate work of large management team. Instruct workforce. Evaluate work completed. Hiring and firing responsibilities.

12. Great opportunity for money! High salary, elaborate expense accounts, stock options, extra pay for extra work. Christmas bonus. All fringe benefits paid by company. High pay for the work you do.

13. Are you tired of a dull, routine job? Try your hand at many tasks, meet new people, work in different situations and settings. Be a jack-of-all-trades.

14. Does the thought of a desk job turn you off? This job requires brisk and lively movement and is for the active person who enjoys using energy and physical abilities.

15. Opportunity to express your personal convictions in all phases of your job. Devote your lifestyle to your work.

Your Values—Some Hard Choices

EXERCISE 3.3

In this exercise you are asked to choose the best and worst among sets of options, all of which are more or less undesirable. Rank the situations and individuals, however unpleasant, that you could best and most easily accept as number 1, and the worst bad case, the situations you would find hardest to accept, as number 5, with the intervening cases ranked accordingly.

JOB SITUATIONS

_____ To work for a boss who knows less than you do about your work and over whom you have no influence.

_____ To be the key person in a job while someone else gets better pay and all the credit for what you do.

_____ To work with a group in which trust is very low.

_____ To work in an organization whose job is to serve the poor but which wastes huge amounts of its resources on red tape.

_____ To work day to day with someone who is always putting in second-rate work.

ENVIRONMENT

_____ The desert (120 degrees F) with a well-paying job.

_____ A small subsistence-level farm in Appalachia.

_____ An efficiency apartment in New York on a tight budget.

_____ A congested, smoggy urban area that is a short walk to work from your comfortable low-rent apartment.

_____ A middle-income suburban housing development, with an hour commute (one way) that is totally dependent on a freeway route.

RISKS

_____ Bet $10,000 on a gambling wager.

_____ Put $10,000 into a new and uncertain business venture.

_____ Go into business for yourself, with minimum resources.

_____ Without an assured job, move to a place where you always wanted to live.

_____ Risk arrest in a public demonstration for something about which you feel strongly.

Reflective Questions

EXERCISE
3.4

1. Which of the needs outlined by Maslow are currently being met by your job? By your lifestyle?

_____

_____

2. Think of several family members. Which of Maslow's needs do you think are being met by their jobs?

_____

_____

3. When someone is suddenly laid off or fired from a job, what happens to their needs? What becomes foremost in their minds?

_____

_____

4. How do world events such as the terrorist attacks on September 11, 2001, affect your values? Those of your family and friends?

_____

_____

Top Five

EXERCISE
3.5

List five things you want in life. Examine each of these to see what is most important to you. What have you done to support or express these values? What actions have you taken or do you need to take to move toward what you most want in life? The difference between what you say is important and what you are actually willing to do deserves close examination.

1. _____

2. _____

3. _____

4. _____

5. _____

EXERCISE
3.6

Values Related to Careers

List below your top five values and three job descriptions (from Exercise 3.2) that you believe would allow you to fulfill many of those values. For example, creativity, variety, money, and independence might all be associated with a career as a lawyer, writer, or sales representative. Which job description best describes your values? What job title would you give to this job description?

VALUES

1. _____
2. _____
3. _____
4. _____
5. _____

JOB DESCRIPTIONS

1. _____
2. _____
3. _____
4. _____
5. _____

EXERCISE
3.7

Values Related to Ethics

1. In a class or group setting, discuss how values affect ethical behavior. Consider current events and prominent figures in the worlds of

athletics	entertainment	military
business	government	science
education	law enforcement	

2. Choose one example from a newspaper or magazine article, and explain how you would act if you were in the same situation—for example, an athlete takes steroids to be competitive. What values are reflected in your actions?

   _____
   _____
   _____
   _____
   _____
   _____
   _____

WWWebwise

 For additional activities online, go to the WWWebwise module in Chapter 3 of the **Companion Website.**

Exercise Summary

1. List the values that are most frequently reflected in your answers to this chapter's exercises:

   a. _____

   b. _____

   c. _____

   d. _____

   e. _____

2. Rank the values listed above, from most important to least important:

   a. _____

   b. _____

   c. _____

   d. _____

   e. _____

3. List the top values that could most likely be satisfied by a future career:

   _____

   _____

   _____

4. What I have learned from reading and answering the exercises:

   _____

   _____

   _____

5. I feel _____ after completing this chapter (e.g., more aware, confused, satisfied).

6. I am energized by the following types of activities (use Values Grid, past jobs, or hobbies):

   a. _____

   b. _____

   c. _____

   d. _____

   e. _____

JOB DESCRIPTION ANSWERS (FOR EXERCISE 3.2)

Job Number	Value	Job Title (examples)
1	Helping others	Social worker, teacher, counselor
2	Creativity	Writer, artist, graphic designer
3	Prestige	Executive, politician, doctor, police officer
4	Security	Education administrator, administrative assistant
5	Intellect	Researcher, mathematician, scientist
6	Adventure	Archaeologist, CIA investigator, firefighter
7	Association	Educator, restaurant worker, tour guide
8	Advancement	Assistant sales manager, engineer
9	Independence	Landscape artist, contract worker, marketing representative
10	Productivity	Sales representative, clerk, bookkeeper
11	Power	Manager, team leader, company president, coach
12	Money	Stockbroker, accountant, real estate developer
13	Variety	Electrician, plumber, lawyer, freelance editor
14	Physical activity	Game warden, physical trainer, physical education teacher
15	Lifestyle	Minister, guidance counselor, consultant

Go to page 205 of the chapter summaries and fill out the Chapter 3 exercise summary now.

Focusing on You: Personality and Interests

The more you know about your natural tendencies and preferences, the easier it will be for you to identify a career path that enables you to maximize what comes naturally. If you take your personality and interests into account when starting down your career path, you are much more likely to enjoy your work and be fulfilled by it.

Many of us dismiss the notion that we can have careers based on who we are and what we like to do. Somewhere along the line, we lose track of early dreams inspired by our true selves and begin focusing on more practical matters: What degrees are offered and what classes are needed? What occupation offers security and good pay? In many cases, we might have been able to explore careers much more closely aligned with our interests than we thought possible. For example, a young man who loves baseball might not enjoy the many hours of practice needed to become a professional ballplayer and might abandon the field altogether. Yet he might be able to pursue a career related to his interests, perhaps as an athletic trainer for a team, a facility manager at a ballpark, or a park recreation leader. These careers might be more congruous with his personality and interests than that of ballplayer or a completely unrelated position.

LEARNING OBJECTIVES

At the end of the chapter you will be able to . . .

- List differences in personality types

- Explain your own personality type

- Recognize how personality type relates to career planning

- Identify college majors that interest you

- Match your interests to occupations, using the Worker Trait Groups and other inventories

*I am a great believer in luck, and I find
that the harder I work, the more I have of it.*

This chapter will help you explore some aspects of your own personality and interests. You will learn how to interpret this knowledge and apply it to your career decisions. Perhaps you will identify a career path you hadn't considered before, based on who you are and what you really like to do.

Exploring Personality

Have you ever said to a friend, "That's not like you"? Has anyone ever said to you, "You're not acting like yourself today"? These are common ways for us to talk about the complex set of tendencies, behaviors, attitudes, and characteristics that makes each of us unique. The sum total of these qualities is called your *personality.*

The more you know about yourself and your personal preferences, the better able you will be to identify work and outside activities that complement your personality type. Several different assessment instruments are available to help you learn about yourself. Like the following activity, some of these instruments are based on the work of noted Swiss psychologist Carl Jung (1923), who developed a way to help us understand and categorize our inborn tendencies. Katherine Briggs and Isabel Briggs Myers (1962) later expanded on Jung's theory to develop an assessment tool that helps identify personality preferences. This widely used survey is called the Myers–Briggs Type Indicator® instrument (MBTI).* It might be possible for you to arrange through your instructor or career center to take this or some other survey to learn more about your personality type than is possible here.

The following activity is not intended to give you an exact description of your personality, nor to indicate that a certain personality fits exactly within a certain career. In fact, there is debate about the extent to which personality relates to career choice or satisfaction. Instead, this discussion and the accompanying exercise are intended to make you aware of some characteristics of your personality and give you some insight into what types of interactions and activities might be more comfortable and satisfying for you than others.

The information you gain about your personality can help you make practical decisions about the types of classes to take and the career you pursue. Career success is based on a knowledge of self. The more you know, understand, and accept your unique self, the better able you will be to make appropriate life and career choices. Learning about personality will also make you better able to understand and accept differences in others.

Next, identify your personal preferences from the four parts in the following activity.

---

*MBTI, Myers-Briggs, and Myers-Briggs Type Indicator are trademarks or registered trademarks of the Myers-Briggs Type Indicator Trust in the United States and other countries.

Identifying Your Personal Preferences   **ACTIVITY**

The work of Jung, Myers, and Briggs provides us with a four-part framework in which to examine our inborn tendencies; thus, the following exercise consists of four parts. In each part, you will determine which of two characteristics or preferences better describes you. Briefly, in Parts 1 through 4 you will select items that indicate personality tendencies toward (1) extraversion or introversion; (2) sensing or intuition; (3) thinking or feeling; and (4) judging or perceiving. Each of these characteristics will be explained below.

Instructions: Read the following pairs of descriptions and check the item in each pair that is like you *most of the time.* (All of us have aspects of all of these qualities to some degree.)* To help you decide, think of your most natural self, your behavior if no one were looking.

PART 1. In describing your *flow of energy,* which pattern more closely resembles you, E or I?

E	I
○ Likes action and variety	○ Likes quiet and time to consider things
○ Likes to do mental work by talking to people	○ Likes to do mental work privately before talking
○ Acts quickly, sometimes without much reflection	○ May be slow to try something without understanding it first
○ Likes to see how other people do a job, and to see results	○ Likes to understand the idea of a job and to work alone or with just a few people
○ Wants to know what other people expect of him or her	○ Wants to set his or her own standards

E's interest turns mostly outward to the world of action, people, and things. I's interest turns more often to the inner world of ideas and personal concerns. Of course, everyone turns outward to act and inward to reflect. You too must do both, but you are more comfortable doing one or the other and rely on one more often than the other, just as right-handers are more comfortable using their right hands.

Go to next page

---

*The checklists in this exercise are adapted from *People Types and Tiger Stripes: A Practical Guide to Learning Styles,* 3rd edition, by Dr. Gordon Lawrence, Center for Applications of Psychological Type, Gainesville, FL, 1993. This exercise is NOT a type indicator, nor does it replicate the Myers–Briggs Type Indicator® instrument, which is a validated instrument. MBTI, Myers-Briggs, and Myers-Briggs Type Indicator are trademarks or registered trademarks of the Myers-Briggs Type Indicator Trust in the United States and other countries. Parts of this exercise are also based on an exercise in *Building Self-Esteem: Strategies for Success in School and Beyond,* 2nd edition, 1997, by Bonnie Golden and Kay Lesh (Upper Saddle River, NJ: Prentice Hall).

E stands for Extraversion, which means outward turning.

I stands for Introversion, which means inward turning.

SAMPLE EXTRAVERSION TYPE

Jesse is a computer consultant. He thrives on attending meetings at which several people at a company explain their computer needs, and he loves providing training for clients on their upgraded systems. His hobbies include attending conferences and serving as a Boy Scout leader for his son's troop, which he has also taken on weekend outings. Jesse gets energy from being around groups of people.

SAMPLE INTROVERSION TYPE

Jennifer is a computer consultant. She works in computer systems design. She meets individually with a company's computer networking specialist who provides her with a list of company needs; then she manipulates the company's system until it is operating as requested. She lets others train the staff. Jennifer gets her energy from working intensively with a technical system. She also gets recharged by spending time alone. Her hobbies include reading and exploring new ways of learning through the Internet and other distance-learning programs.

PART 2. In describing the ways in which you *take in information*, which pattern resembles you more closely, S or N?

S	N
○ Pays most attention to experience as it is	○ Pays most attention to the meanings of facts and how they fit together
○ Likes to use eyes, ears, and other senses to find out things	○ Likes to use imagination to come up with new ways to do things, new possibilities
○ Dislikes new problems unless there are standard ways to solve them	○ Likes solving new problems, and dislikes doing the same thing over and over
○ Enjoys using skills already learned more than learning new ones	○ Likes using new skills more than practicing old ones
○ Is patient with details but impatient when the situation gets complicated	○ Is impatient with details but doesn't mind complicated situations

S and N represent two kinds of perception, that is, two ways of finding out or giving attention to experiences. Everyone uses both sensing and intuition, but we are likely to use one more than the other. S pays most attention to the facts that come from personal experience. S can more easily see the details, while N can more easily see the big picture. N pays most attention to meanings behind the facts.

S stands for Sensing.

N stands for iNtuition.

Go to next page

SAMPLE SENSING TYPE

Georgette has a good memory for numbers and has been a bookkeeper at a car dealership for several years. One day, she commented to her boss that spoilers and dash covers were selling well. Upon reviewing the sales figures, the boss confirmed Georgette's observations and promoted her to work with inventory management. The boss found it helpful that Georgette enjoyed keeping track of materials.

SAMPLE INTUITIVE TYPE

Santos is a freelance writer and teaches scriptwriting at a community college. He uses his creative and real-life experiences to assist others in creating scripts for independent producers. He often gets ideas while daydreaming or exercising at the gym. Santos keeps a journal in his car to jot down his thoughts, and he teaches others how to keep track of their ideas for writing assignments.

PART 3. In describing your ways of *making decisions*, which pattern resembles you more closely, T or F?

T	F
○ Likes to decide things logically	○ Likes to decide things with personal feelings and human values, even if they aren't logical
○ Wants to be treated with justice and fair play	○ Likes praise, and likes to please people, even in unimportant things
○ May neglect and hurt other people's feelings without knowing it	○ Is aware of other people's feelings
○ Gives more attention to ideas or things than to human relationships	○ Can predict how others will feel
○ Doesn't need harmony	○ Gets upset by arguments and conflicts; values harmony

T makes decisions by examining data, staying less personally involved with the decision. F makes decisions by paying attention to personal values and feelings. Each of us uses both T and F judgments every day, but we tend to use one kind of judgment more than the other.

T stands for Thinking judgment.

F stands for Feeling judgment.

Go to next page

SAMPLE THINKING TYPE

Malcolm is a student trying to decide if he wants to major in business. He is basing his decision on the facts that he has collected: he has talked to a college counselor, researched his interests in the career center, taken classes related to business, and visited workplaces that hire people with such majors. He has even investigated graduate degrees related to the types of business specialties that employers have suggested they need.

SAMPLE FEELING TYPE

Shareen has always wanted to be a model but was influenced by her husband and adult children to get a college degree. She stays in shape and is taking modeling classes in the community while also attending college full-time. After meeting with a college counselor, she's decided that majoring in fashion merchandising will allow her to study something related to her ideal job as well as please her family.

PART 4. In describing your day-to-day lifestyle, which pattern resembles you more closely, J or P?

J	P
○ Likes to have a plan, to have things settled and decided in advance	○ Likes to stay flexible and avoid fixed plans
○ Tries to make things come out the way they "ought to be"	○ Deals easily with unplanned and unexpected happenings
○ Likes to finish one project before starting another	○ Likes to start many projects but may have trouble finishing them
○ Usually has mind made up about situations, people	○ Usually looks for additional information about situations, people
○ May decide things too quickly	○ May decide things too slowly
○ Wants to be right in forming opinions, making decisions	○ Wants to miss nothing before forming opinions, making decisions
○ Lives by standards and schedules that are not easily changed	○ Lives by making changes to deal with problems as they come along

J people show to others their thinking or feeling judgment more easily than they show their sensing and intuitive perception. The opposite is true of P people; they show their sensing or intuition rather than judgment in dealing with the world outside themselves.

J stands for Judgment.

P stands for Perception.

Go to next page

SAMPLE JUDGING TYPE

Marion is a film editor. He has a computerized appointment calendar programmed with alarm beeps to remind him about important dates. All of his clients know that when he makes a deadline to finish a project, the project will be delivered on time. He lets nothing interrupt his plans. Rush jobs, given to his department by higher-level management, drive him crazy; he doesn't want to start a new project before he finishes his current obligations.

SAMPLE PERCEIVING TYPE

Cathy is also a film editor. Some colleagues think that Cathy is scattered. She works on several projects at the same time. Even though her office is a mess, she seems to be able to find the tapes, telephone numbers, and accessories she needs. She often takes on new assignments before she is finished with old ones because she doesn't want to miss out. She gets irritated when her supervisor reminds her that a project should have been completed yesterday and tends to get projects done just in time.

Reviewing each of the four areas, which do you resemble most closely in each pair? (Circle the appropriate letters.)

E   or   **I**

S   or   **N**

T   or   **F**

J   or   **P**   Your 4-letter preferences are: _____ _____ _____ _____

You now have a four-letter personality preference based primarily on the work of Jung and of Myers and Briggs. This preliminary self-assessment offers one way to appreciate and value your natural individuality. Although we all represent combinations of each characteristic described, we have natural preferences, revealed in our type, that have implications for our career choices. To understand your preferences further, arrange to take the Myers–Briggs Type Indicator® instrument (MBTI) at your college counseling or career center.

Your career choices may be based in part on your temperament or personality preferences. If you enjoy detail and structure, fields such as accounting, engineering, math, sciences, law, and health sciences might interest you. If you prefer unstructured, global thinking, then majors and fields such as the creative arts and social sciences may better suit your temperament. It is essential to note, however, that all types are found in all fields. In order to truly do well, you must stretch yourself in areas that do not come as naturally for you. This stretching takes extra effort above and beyond the demands of the occupation. Keep this in mind as you experience yourself responding to various work settings and demands.

Be aware that a major or career choice that does not mesh with your personality preferences typically takes more energy and concentration than one

Exploring Majors

The first and last letters of your personality type often indicate your preferred style of exploring majors. The descriptions below may help you become more aware of your preferred style, or suggest alternative strategies.

EJ TYPES (ESTJ, ESFJ, ENFJ, ENTJ)
"I want to decide and get on with my life."

EJ students often put choosing a major on their "to do" list soon after reaching college. It is not uncommon for them to seek career counseling early, hoping to declare a major before the first semester ends. Early decision making can have its drawbacks. For example, an EJ student may decide at an early age to be a doctor, lawyer, or engineer but then discover that he or she lacks the necessary ability or the continuing interest. The student may then become disappointed and want to hurry up and choose another major because "I don't want to waste any more time." Ironically, what such students often need to do is slow down and collect more information. Managers, school administrators, and organizers are found in this category.

EP TYPES (ESTP, ESFP, ENFP, ENTP)
"I want to experience it before deciding."

For **EP** types, deciding tends to be an ongoing process. They often decide by trial and error. They typically want, and try, to do it all—every course, major, or extracurricular activity that appeals to them. Changing their mind helps to reassure them that they still have options open, but they often don't know how to choose among the options. Their style, however, can be very difficult for their parents to understand, especially parents who have a Judging style. EP types can become better decision makers by accepting that the decision is part of a journey, not the final destination. Psychologists, counselors, authors, and helping types are often found in this category.

IJ TYPES (ISTJ, INFJ, ISFJ, INTJ)
"I want to be sure about my selection."

The **IJ** types will probably spend a lot of time researching and reflecting before reaching a final decision. They often consult books and other resources on majors and careers. Because they tend to stick with a decision once it's made, the information they collect must be carefully considered. Because their thinking is done alone, however, they may surprise people when they announce their plans. Accountants, computer programmers, and engineers are often found in this category.

IP TYPES (ISTP, ISFP, INFP, INTP)
"I wonder what I'll be when I grow up."

IP students often want to delay a decision about a major until they can consider all options, which they do at their own pace. Although they may resist deadlines imposed by others, they sometimes need the outside influences to help them make a decision. When they can tell themselves that no decision is ever final, they can move ahead. Even in mid-life, they often say they don't know for sure what they want to be when they grow up. Their style of decision making often reflects a struggle between the vast amount of information they are exploring from the outer world (which can be overwhelming) and their need to be true to their inner world. The world's artists and creative types are often found in this category. A career path for them is a never-ending quest for more knowledge, facts, or inspiration.

that more closely matches your preferences. The purpose of understanding personality type in relation to your classes and major is not to discourage you from pursuing a specific career, but to help you become more aware of why you might master certain subjects more easily than others and be attracted to certain careers over others.

Identifying Fields of Interest

The rest of this chapter explores the ways that interests can be grouped into job categories or clusters so that you can begin to select specific fields of interest to investigate.

We will be highlighting three different approaches to identify interests. The first refers to the *Holland Interest Environments* (or categories) (Holland, 1985), which are Realistic, Investigative, Artistic, Social, Enterprising, and Conventional. The second system is an *interest inventory* from the Department of Labor organized around *Worker Trait Groups,* which are described in the *Guide for Occupational Exploration* (GOE). Interest inventories ask if you like or dislike a variety of subjects or activities and offer you a profile of the results. The results from the GOE are clustered into interest categories such as Artistic, Scientific, Nature, Mechanical, Industrial, Business Detail, Persuasive, Accommodating, Humanitarian, Social–Business, and Physical Performing. This inventory is provided especially for readers who do not have access to other interest assessments. The third system is provided by the *American College Testing (ACT) Program.* ACT clusters, as well as the tech-prep and school to career clusters listed later in this chapter, have been used in secondary-school career centers.

Although many readers have access to career inventories, it is important to remember that the information gathered by printed or electronic assessments is not magic. Assessments simply provide a quick, efficient way of gathering and organizing the information that you know about yourself. Remember that the answers come from you. In the absence of an inventory, you are still able to collect the same information by completing the exercises and activities provided throughout this book.

Interest clusters, known as *personality types* or *environments,* are based on the following assumptions: (1) People express their personalities through their vocational choices; (2) people are attracted to occupations

FACTS AND FIGURES

A study of college students has shown that developing a sense of purpose is associated with EJ preferences. Also, when career counselors ranked students on how well they made appropriate educational plans, the following order of preferences emerged: EJ, EP, IJ, and IP.

This study showed that EJ types are the most decisive about their majors and careers while IPs are the least decisive. In two other studies, the ISTPs were the most likely types to have undecided majors, and the IPs were the most likely to be attracted to special advising programs.

Source: Allen L. Hammer (Ed.), *MBTI Applications: A Decade of Research on the Myers–Briggs Type Indicator,* 1996. Consulting Psychologists Press.

WHAT DO YOU THINK?

1. Did you find yourself in the descriptions listed here?

2. Does the type that you have selected fit the way you act?

3. If you could change your type, which type listed above would you choose and why?

 To answer these questions online, go to the *Facts and Figures* module in Chapter 4 of the Companion Website.

Meet Holly

"I've taken several inventories now and have gotten the results! My results for the Myers Briggs were ENFP, which means that I am extraverted, intuitive, feeling, and perceptive. On the Strong Inventory, my results were mainly high in Social and Enterprising areas, with a medium interest in Investigative and Conventional-type activities.

"The MBTI results suggest that I like to use my creativity to help others reach goals and realize their dreams. I like to solve problems using a person-oriented approach and I make decisions by relying on my values and the values of others. I prefer to solve problems as part of a team rather than deciding alone. Because I am social, I will benefit from working with people, especially people who are friendly and who like to socialize outside of work too. Because I am intuitive and perceptive, I like to be able to connect my daily routine to a bigger picture. I need to know why I am doing my work and I am able to help others to see the bigger picture too. Because I am social, enterprising, and global, I enjoy leading others while helping them to see the bigger picture.

"The inventories indicate that I would enjoy teaching, counseling, social work, managing community organizations, and human resource management. I also was reminded that dietitian and athletic trainer fit my personality. It is important to me that my career will allow me to work with a cooperative, supportive group of people who are committed to helping, nurturing, and caring for others.

that they feel will provide experiences suitable to their personalities; (3) people who choose the same vocation have similar personalities and react to many situations in similar ways. Using the descriptions below, select the category that best describes you.

If you review Chapter 1, Exercise 1.4, you will notice the adjectives are grouped by the six types described below. Most interest inventories relate your interests to these six types and provide a list of jobs related to these interests. If you are in a class that uses the Self-Directed Search® or the Strong Interest Inventory®, your instructor will explain which jobs are related to these six environments. If you don't have access to separate inventories, the interest inventory developed by the U.S. Department of Labor (see pages 80–83) should give you a general idea of how your interests relate to potential jobs.

RIASEC (Holland Interest Environments)*

Doers

(Realistic—R) These types like jobs such as automobile mechanic, air traffic controller, surveyor, farmer, electrician. They like to work outdoors and to work with tools. They prefer to deal with things rather than with people. They are described as:

---

*To explore Holland's ideas more fully, ask your instructor or counselor for the Self-Directed Search, available from Psychological Assessment Resources, Inc., P. O. Box 990, Odessa, Florida 33556.

"The results of these inventories really fit me because I have always been a helper-type person and an organizer. In high school, I was the junior class secretary and the senior class vice president in charge of special events. I was a tutor, and I helped organize the tutorial program. I also planned recognition activities for clubs at my high school. The reminder about dietitian and athletic trainer relates to my early life as a gymnast, which I gave up when I sprained my back at age 12. I have read about and used almost every diet there is! But I also know that I do not want to take the science and math classes necessary to be a nutritionist or athletic trainer major. At this point, with the help of these assessments, I am leaning towards being a teacher or a counselor."

1. What are your Myers Briggs and Strong Assessment results? Are your results as true about you as Holly's were for her?

2. Which descriptors from these results are true for you?

3. Which descriptors are not true for you?

4. Which of the occupations suggested by your results might you consider?

5. What other information do you need to consider before making an informed decision about your career?

To answer these questions online, go to the *Real Stories* module in Chapter 4 of the Companion Website.

conforming	humble	natural	shy
frank	materialistic	persistent	stable
honest	modest	practical	thrifty

Thinkers

(Investigative—I) These types like jobs such as biologist, chemist, physicist, anthropologist, geologist, medical technologist. They are task-oriented and prefer to work alone. They enjoy solving abstract problems and understanding the physical world. They are described as:

analytical	curious	introverted	precise
cautious	independent	methodical	rational
critical	intellectual	modest	reserved

Creators

(Artistic—A) These types like jobs such as composer, musician, stage director, writer, interior designer, actor/actress. They like to work in artistic settings that offer opportunities for self-expression. They are described as:

complicated	idealistic	impulsive	nonconforming
emotional	imaginative	independent	original
expressive	impractical	intuitive	unordered

75

Helpers

(Social—S) These types like jobs such as teacher, clergy, counselor, nurse, personnel director, speech therapist. They are sociable, responsible, and concerned with the welfare of others. They have little interest in machinery or physical skills. They are described as:

convincing	generous	insightful	sociable
cooperative	helpful	kind	tactful
friendly	idealistic	responsible	understanding

Persuaders

(Enterprising—E) These types like jobs such as salesperson, manager, business executive, television producer, sports promoter, buyer. They enjoy leading, speaking, and selling. They are impatient with precise work. They are described as:

adventurous	domineering	optimistic	risk-taking
ambitious	energetic	pleasure-seeking	self-confident
attention-getting	impulsive	popular	sociable

Organizers

(Conventional—C) These types like jobs such as bookkeeper, word processing technician, banker, cost estimator, tax expert. They prefer highly ordered activities, both verbal and numerical, that characterize office work. They have little interest in artistic or physical skills. They are described as:

careful	conservative	orderly	reserved
conforming	efficient	persistent	self-controlled
conscientious	obedient	practical	structured

Sample Majors Related to Holland Types | ACTIVITY

Now that you are familiar with Holland Interest Environments, the following chart will help you review some sample majors that may be of interest to you. Underline or circle those areas that seem to fit you. Note that this is a list of just some available majors.

REALISTIC
architectural/mechanical drafting technology
architectural construction technology
civil engineering
civil engineering technology
forestry
criminal justice technology
dietitian
medical technology
industrial engineering
mechanical engineering

INVESTIGATIVE
biological science
biology
chemical engineering
chemistry
computer sciences
dental hygiene
earth sciences
economics
electrical engineering
electrical engineering technology
electronics
environmental sciences
geography
geology
law
materials science
mathematics
paralegal
physics
psychology

ARTISTIC
advertising art
art
art history
commercial art
computer animation
computer graphics
design drafting
design technology
English
graphic technology
instructional media
multimedia technology
music
studio art
theater

SOCIAL
American studies
anthropology
child care
classical studies
communications
dental hygiene
elementary and secondary education
English
foreign languages
health
history
home economics
medical assistant
nursing
nutrition
physical education
political science
pre-law
religious studies
sociology
special education
speech

ENTERPRISING
advertising technology
business administration
business education
business management
finance
industrial and transportation management
industrial management and retail marketing
law enforcement administration
management engineering
marketing technology
public administration
real estate

CONVENTIONAL
accounting
administrative assistant
computer information systems
computer technology
court reporting
executive technology
legal/medical office management
library science
transportation management technology
word processing

Holland Interest Environments and Hobbies, Abilities, and Careers*

	Realistic "Doers"	Investigative "Thinkers"	Artistic "Creators"
Hobbies	Refinishing Growing Tinkering Using hands Building things	Book clubs Computers Doing puzzles Visiting museums Collecting rocks, stamps, etc.	Photography Performing Writing stories, poems Sewing Playing music
Abilities or Interests	Repair Plant Operate tools Play a sport	Think abstractly Solve math problems Do complex calculations Use a microscope Interpret formulas	Sketch, draw, paint, etc. Sing, dance, act Design fashions or 　interiors Play a musical instrument Write stories, poems, music
Sample Careers	Air conditioning mechanic (RIE) Archaeologist (IRE) Architectural drafter (RCI) Athletic trainer (SRE) Automotive engineer (RIE) Automotive mechanic (RIE) Baker/chef (RSE) Carpenter (RCI) Commercial airline pilot (RIE) Construction worker (REC) Dental assistant (RES) Electrical engineer (RIE) Fiber optics technician (RSE) Floral designer (RAE) Forester (RIS) Industrial arts teacher (IER) Optician (REI) Petroleum engineer (RIE) Police officer (SER) Radio/T.V. repair (REI) Software technician (RCI) Truck driver (RSE) Ultrasound technologist (RSI)	Actuary (ISE) Anesthesiologist (IRS) Anthropologist (IRE) Archaeologist (IRE) Biochemist (IRS) Biologist (ISR) Chemical engineer (IRE) Chemical technician (IRE) Computer analyst (IER) Computer programmer Dentist (ISR) Ecologist (IRE) Economist (IAS) Geologist (IRE) Hazardous waste technician Medical technologist (ISA) Nurse practitioner (ISA) Physician (ISE) Psychologist (IES) Statistician (IRE) Technical writer (IRS) Veterinarian (IRS) Webmaster	Actor (AES) Advertising (AES) Artist Broadcasting executive (EAS) Camera operator Clothing designer (ASR) Copywriter (ASI) Dancer (AES) Drama/music/art 　teacher (ASE) English teacher (ASE) Fashion designer (ASR) Fashion illustrator (ASR) Furniture designer (AES) Graphic designer (AES) Interior designer (AES) Journalist (ASE) Landscape architect (AIR) Librarian (SAI) Medical illustrator (AIE) Museum curator (AES) Musician Photographer (AES) Writer (ASI)

*Compiled from online career search sources.

Holland Interest Environments, continued

	Social "Helpers"	Enterprising "Persuaders"	Conventional "Organizers"
Hobbies	Volunteering Caring for children Religious activities Playing team sports	Starting own service or business Campaigning Leading organizations Promoting ideas	Collecting memorabilia Arranging and organizing household Playing computer or card games Studying tax laws Writing family history
Abilities or Interests	Teach/train others Express yourself Lead a group discussion Mediate disputes Cooperate well	Initiate projects Persuade people Sell things or promote ideas Organize activities Lead a group	Work within a system Be organized Keep accurate records Use a computer Write effective business letters
Sample Careers	Air traffic controller (SER) Athletic coach (SRE) Chaplain (SAI) College faculty (SEI) Consumer affairs director (SER) Cosmetologist (SAE) Counselor (SAE) Dental hygienist (SAI) Historian (SEI) Homemaker (S) Hospital administrator (SER) Mail carrier (SRC) Medical records administrator (SIE) Nurse (SIR) Occupational therapist (SRE) Paralegal (SCE) Police officer (SER) Radiological technologist (SRI) Real estate appraiser (SCE) Schoolteacher (SEC) Social worker (SEA) Speech pathologist (SAI) Youth services worker (SEC)	Advertising executive (ESA) Automobile sales worker (ESR) Banker/financial planner (ESR) Buyer (ESA) Claims adjuster (ESR) Computer operator (ESI) Credit manager (ERS) Dental assistant (E) Financial planner (ESR) Flight attendant (ESA) Food service manager (ESI) Funeral director (ESR) Hotel manager (ESR) Industrial engineer (EIR) Insurance agent (ECS) Journalist (EAS) Lawyer (ESA) Office manager (ESR) Politician (ESA) Public relations representative (EAS) Real estate agent (ESR) Stockbroker (ESI) Urban planner (ESI)	Accountant (CSE) Administrative assistant (ESC) Bank teller (CSE) Budget analyst (CER) Building inspector (CSE) Business teacher (CSE) Catalog librarian (CSE) Claims adjuster (SEC) Clerk (CSE) Computer operator (CSR) Congressional-district aide (CES) Cost accountant (CES) Court reporter (CSE) Customer inspector (CEI) Elementary school teacher (SEC) Financial analyst (CSI) Insurance underwriter (CSE) Internal auditor (ICR) Legal secretary (CSA) Medical records technician (CSE) Paralegal (SCE) Tax consultant (CSE) Travel agent (ECS)

ACTIVITY   *Interest Checklist for Worker Trait Groups**

It is important to each of us that we like our job; doing so will increase our chances of success.

This Interest Checklist may help you decide what kinds of work you would like to do. It lists activities that are found in a broad range of industries and occupations in the United States today.

Read each of the statements carefully. If you think you would *like* to do this kind of activity, make a check (✓) under the *L*; if you *wouldn't like* the activity, make a check under the *D*; if you are not certain whether you would like the activity, make a check under the *?*. After you have checked each activity, go back and circle at least five activities that you think you would enjoy most.

You may check an activity even if you do not have training or experience in it, if you think you would enjoy the work. Check the ? only when you cannot decide whether you would like or dislike the activity, or when you do not know what the activity is. There are no right or wrong answers. Check each activity according to how you feel about it.

Like/Uncertain/Dislike	L	?	D	Like/Uncertain/Dislike	L	?	D
01.01 Write short stories or articles				**01.08** Model clothing for customers			
Edit work of writers				Pose for a fashion photographer			
Write review of books or plays				Be a stand-in for a television star			
01.02 Teach classes in oil painting				**02.01** Develop chemical processes to solve technical problems			
Carve figures of people or animals				Analyze data on weather conditions			
Design artwork for magazines				Develop methods to control air or water pollution			
01.03 Direct plays				**02.02** Study causes of animal diseases			
Perform magic tricks in a theater				Develop methods for growing better crops			
Announce radio or television programs				Develop new techniques to process foods			
01.04 Conduct a symphony orchestra				**02.03** Examine teeth and treat dental problems			
Compose or arrange music				Diagnose and treat sick animals			
Play a musical instrument				Give medical treatment to people			
01.05 Create routines for professional dancers				**02.04** Prepare medicines according to prescription			
Dance in a variety show				Study blood samples using a microscope			
Teach modern dance				Test ore samples for gold or silver content			
01.06 Restore damaged works of art				**03.01** Manage a beef or dairy ranch			
Carve designs in wooden blocks for printing greeting cards				Operate a commercial fish farm			
Design, cartooning, or animation				Manage the use and development of forest lands			
01.07 Analyze handwriting and appraise personality							
Introduce acts in a circus							
Guess weight of people at a carnival							

Go to next page

*Source: U.S. Dept. of Labor, Employment and Training Administration, U.S. Employment Service.

Like/Uncertain/Dislike	L	?	D
03.02			
Supervise farm workers	___	___	___
Supervise a logging crew	___	___	___
Supervise a park maintenance crew	___	___	___
03.03			
Train horses for racing	___	___	___
Feed and care for animals in a zoo	___	___	___
Bathe and groom dogs	___	___	___
03.04			
Pick vegetables on a farm	___	___	___
Catch fish as a member of a fishing crew	___	___	___
Trim branches and limbs from trees	___		
04.01			
Direct police activities	___	___	___
Issue tickets to speeding motorists	___	___	___
Enforce fish and game laws	___	___	___
04.02			
Guard inmates in a prison	___		
Guard money in an armored car	___	___	___
Fight fires to protect life and property	___	___	___
05.01			
Plan and design roads and bridges	___	___	___
Design electrical equipment	___		
Plan construction of a water treatment plant	___	___	___
05.02			
Direct operations of a power plant	___		
Direct construction of buildings	___		
Supervise operations of a coal mine	___	___	___
05.03			
Survey land to determine boundaries	___	___	___
Make drawings of equipment for technical manuals	___	___	___
Operate a radio transmitter	___	___	
Design and draft master drawings of automobiles	___	___	___
Direct air traffic from an airport control tower	___	___	___
Conduct water pollution tests	___	___	___
05.04			
Pilot a commercial aircraft	___	___	___
Operate a ferry boat	___	___	___
Captain an oil tanker	___	___	___
05.05			
Build frame houses	___	___	___
Make and repair dentures	___	___	___
Prepare and cook food in a restaurant	___	___	___
Plan, install, and repair electrical wiring	___	___	___
Repair and overhaul automobiles	___	___	___
Set up and operate printing equipment	___	___	___
05.06			
Operate generators at an electric plant	___	___	___
Operate boilers to heat a building	___	___	___
Operate water purification equipment	___	___	___

Like/Uncertain/Dislike	L	?	D
05.07			
Inspect fire-fighting equipment	___	___	___
Inspect aircraft for mechanical safety	___	___	___
Inspect cruise control in automobiles	___	___	___
Grade logs for size and quality	___	___	___
05.08			
Drive a tractor-trailer truck	___	___	___
Operate a train	___	___	___
Operate a motorboat to carry passengers	___	___	___
05.09			
Prepare items for shipment and keep records	___	___	___
Receive, store, and issue merchandise	___	___	___
Record amount and kind of cargo on ships	___	___	___
05.10			
Develop film to produce negatives or prints	___	___	___
Repair small electrical appliances	___	___	___
Paint houses	___	___	___
05.11			
Operate a bulldozer	___	___	___
Operate a crane	___	___	___
Operate an oil drilling rig	___	___	___
05.12			
Recap automobile tires	___		
Operate a duplicating or copying machine	___	___	___
Clean and maintain office buildings	___	___	___
06.01			
Set up and operate a lathe to cut and form metal	___	___	___
Drill tiny holes in industrial diamonds	___	___	___
Hand polish optical lenses	___	___	___
06.02			
Operate a drill press	___	___	___
Operate a power saw in a woodworking factory	___	___	___
Assemble refrigerators and stoves in a factory	___	___	___
Operate a power sewing machine to make clothing	___	___	___
Operate a dough-mixing machine for making bread	___	___	___
Assemble electronic components	___	___	___
06.03			
Inspect bottles for defects	___	___	___
Sort fruit according to size	___	___	___
Test electronic parts before shipment	___	___	___

Go to next page

Like/Uncertain/Dislike	L	?	D
06.04 Work on a factory assembly line	___	___	___
Operate a machine that fills containers	___	___	___
Hand package materials and products	___	___	___
Assemble parts to make computer components	___	___	___
Drive a forklift truck to move materials in a factory	___	___	___
07.01 Take dictation, type, and handle business details	___	___	___
Search records to verify land ownership	___	___	___
Maintain records on real estate sales	___	___	___
07.02 Maintain spread sheets	___	___	___
Keep time card records	___	___	___
Compute average weekly production from daily records	___	___	___
07.03 Receive and pay out money in a bank	___	___	___
Sell tickets at places of entertainment	___	___	___
Operate a cash register in a grocery store	___	___	___
07.04 Answer questions at an information counter	___	___	___
Interview persons opening checking accounts	___	___	___
07.05 Check printed material for errors	___	___	___
Compile and maintain employee records	___	___	___
Deliver mail to homes and businesses	___	___	___
07.06 Input letters and reports	___	___	___
Operate a computer keyboard to send or receive information	___	___	___
Operate a billing system to prepare customer bills	___	___	___
07.07 File office correspondence	___	___	___
Locate and replace library books on shelves	___	___	___
Hand stamp return addresses on envelopes	___	___	___
08.01 Sell telephone and other communications equipment	___	___	___
Sell newspaper ad space	___	___	___
Select and buy fruits and vegetables for resale	___	___	___
08.02 Sell automobiles	___	___	___
Demonstrate products at a trade exhibit	___	___	___
Sell articles at auction to highest bidder	___	___	___
08.03 Sell merchandise door-to-door	___	___	___
Sell candy and popcorn at sports events	___	___	___
Persuade nightclub customers to pose for pictures	___	___	___

Like/Uncertain/Dislike	L	?	D
09.01 Supervise activities of children at vacation camp	___	___	___
Greet and seat customers in a restaurant	___	___	___
Serve meals and beverages to airline passengers	___	___	___
09.02 Give haircuts	___	___	___
Style, color, and treat hair	___	___	___
Give scalp-conditioning treatments	___	___	___
09.03 Drive a bus	___	___	___
Drive a taxicab	___	___	___
Teach automobile driving skills	___	___	___
09.04 Wait on tables in a restaurant	___	___	___
Park automobiles	___	___	___
Cash checks and give information to customers	___	___	___
09.05 Check passenger baggage	___	___	___
Help hotel guests get taxicabs	___	___	___
Operate a carnival ride	___	___	___
10.01 Plan and carry out religious activities	___	___	___
Work with juveniles on probation	___	___	___
Help people with personal or emotional problems	___	___	___
10.02 Provide nursing care to hospital patients	___	___	___
Plan and give physical therapy treatment to patients	___	___	___
Teach the blind to read Braille	___	___	___
10.03 Give hearing tests	___	___	___
Care for children in an institution	___	___	___
Prepare patients for examination by a physician	___	___	___
11.01 Plan and write computer programs to help solve scientific problems	___	___	___
Plan collection and analysis of statistical data	___	___	___
Apply knowledge of statistics to set insurance rates	___	___	___
11.02 Teach courses in high school	___	___	___
Teach vocational education courses	___	___	___
Manage the library program for a community	___	___	___
11.03 Conduct research to develop new teaching methods	___	___	___
Conduct research to understand social problems	___	___	___
Review and analyze economic data	___	___	___

Go to next page

Like/Uncertain/Dislike	L	?	D
11.04 Serve as a court judge			
Advise clients on legal matters			
Settle wage disputes between labor and management			
11.05 Manage a department of a large company			
Plan and direct work of a government office			
Purchase supplies and equipment for a large firm			
11.06 Examine financial records to determine tax owed			
Approve or disapprove requests for bank loans			
Buy and sell stocks and bonds for clients			
11.07 Direct administration of a large hospital			
Serve as principal of a school			
Direct operations of a museum			
11.08 Write news stories for publication or broadcast			
Broadcast news over radio or television			
Direct operations of a newspaper			
11.09 Plan advertising programs for an organization			
Direct fund-raising for a nonprofit organization			
Lobby for or against proposed legislation			

Like/Uncertain/Dislike	L	?	D
11.10 Direct investigations to enforce banking laws			
Inspect work areas to detect unsafe working conditions			
Inspect cargo to enforce customs laws			
11.11 Manage a hotel or motel			
Direct activities of a branch office of an insurance company			
Manage a grocery, clothing, or other retail store			
11.12 Investigate and settle insurance claims			
Obtain leases for outdoor advertising sites			
Sign entertainers to theater or concert contracts			
12.01 Manage a professional baseball team			
Referee sporting events			
Drive in automobile races			
12.02 Perform as a trapeze artist in a circus			
Perform stunts for movie or television scenes			
Perform juggling feats			

Now go back and circle at least five activities that you would like most.

Worker Trait Groups

The number beside each group of activities in the Interest Checklist refers to a *Worker Trait Group.* The trait groups are broad, general categories of interest that describe many of the occupational functions and factors related to these areas of interest, such as physical requirements, necessary academic skills, and specific vocational preparation time. These descriptions then lead to a listing of some possible occupations that fall within the interest categories and trait groups. Look at each of the five activities that you would enjoy most (the ones you circled), note the number beside its group, and find the corresponding number in the following list. This gives you some idea of the kinds of occupations that are of greatest interest to you. The boldface letter(s) to the left of each trait group title indicates the related Holland Interest Environment.

   More complete and detailed descriptions may be found in the *Guide for Occupational Exploration* (GOE) and McKnight's *Worker Trait Group Guide* (1997), which can be found in college career centers, in libraries, and on the Internet.

A   01. ARTISTIC

01.01   Literary Arts
01.02   Visual Arts
01.03   Performing Arts: Drama
01.04   Performing Arts: Music
01.05   Performing Arts: Dance
01.06   Technical Arts
01.07   Amusement
01.08   Modeling

I   02. SCIENTIFIC

02.01   Physical Science
02.02   Life Science
02.03   Medical Science
02.04   Laboratory Technology

R   03. NATURE

03.01   Managerial Work: Nature
03.02   General Supervision: Nature
03.03   Animal Training and Care
03.04   Elemental Work: Nature

R   04. AUTHORITY

04.01   Safety and Law Enforcement
04.02   Security Services

R   05. MECHANICAL

05.01   Engineering
05.02   Managerial Work: Mechanical
05.03   Engineering Technology

05.04   Air- and Water-Vehicle Operation
05.05   Craft Technology
05.06   Systems Operation
05.07   Quality Control
05.08   Land-Vehicle Operation
05.09   Materials Control
05.10   Skilled Hand and Machine Work
05.11   Equipment Operation
05.12   Elemental Work: Mechanical

R   06. INDUSTRIAL

06.01   Production Technology
06.02   Production Work
06.03   Production Control
06.04   Elemental Work: Industrial

C   07. BUSINESS DETAIL

07.01   Administrative Detail
07.02   Mathematical Detail
07.03   Financial Detail
07.04   Information Processing: Speaking
07.05   Information Processing: Records
07.06   Clerical Machine Operation
07.07   Clerical Handling

E   08. PERSUASIVE

08.01   Sales Technology
08.02   General Sales
08.03   Vending

R   09. ACCOMMODATING

09.01   Hospitality Services
09.02   Barbering and Beauty Services
09.03   Passenger Services
09.04   Customer Services
09.05   Attendant Services

S   10. HUMANITARIAN

10.01   Social Services
10.02   Nursing and Therapy Services
10.03   Child and Adult Care

S/E   11. SOCIAL–BUSINESS

11.01   Mathematics and Statistics
11.02   Educational and Library Services
11.03   Social Research
11.04   Law
11.05   Business Administration
11.06   Finance
11.07   Services Administration
11.08   Communications
11.09   Promotion
11.10   Regulations Enforcement
11.11   Business Management
11.12   Contracts and Claims

R   12. PHYSICAL PERFORMING

12.01   Sports
12.02   Physical Feats

Identifying Occupational Interest Areas | ACTIVITY

Check off (✓) the areas or words in 1, 2, and 3 that you find most interesting. If you had two hours to research careers, which area(s) would you select?

1. WHAT FIELDS INTEREST YOU?

○ Social

Do you like to work with people? Do you help others organize activities? Are you active in social events?

○ Sales–verbal

Do you like to sell, convince, persuade, influence, lead? Do you like to talk, write, read?

○ Mechanical

Do you like to fix things? Do you use and repair machines, appliances, equipment? Do you like to make or build things?

○ Scientific

Are you curious about ideas and abstract processes? Do you like to experiment and solve problems?

○ Clerical–computational

Do you like to keep things orderly? Do you like to keep records, use a keyboard, be accurate?

○ Artistic

Do you like music, dance, art, literature, photography, decorating? Do you like to express yourself creatively?

2. OCCUPATIONAL CATEGORIES ACCORDING TO THE SIX HOLLAND TYPES

○ Realistic (R)   Occupations include jobs in industry, trade, and service.

○ Investigative (I)   Occupations include jobs in the fields of science and technology.

○ Artistic (A)   Occupations include jobs in the fields of art, music, and literature.

○ Social (S)   Occupations include jobs in the fields of education and welfare.

○ Enterprising (E)   Occupations include jobs in sales and management.

○ Conventional (C)   Occupations include office and clerical jobs.

3. OCCUPATIONAL FIELDS—JOB FAMILIES OR JOB CLUSTERS (letters relate to Holland types described above)

○ Agriculture and Home Economics—R & I

○ Arts and Letters—A

○ Business—C

○ Education and Welfare—S

○ Engineering and Architecture—R & I

○ Government and Law—E & S

○ Health—I & S

○ Industry, Trade, and Service—R & C

○ Science—I & R

Career Clusters

areer centers often organize their materials by the following career clusters (created by the U.S. Office of Career Education and used in tech-prep or school to career programs):

Agriculture

Arts/Communications/Human Services

Business

Consumer and Family Services

Engineering Technology

Health Services

Industry and Technology

The American College Testing Program (ACT) has also devised a useful system of organizing jobs into career clusters (Exhibit 4.1). If you are attending school and have chosen a major, you might research the cluster in which your major falls. Otherwise, select the area that seems to relate to your interests, values, and skills, and explore it.

Understanding your interests will be a great aid to you in making satisfying educational and career choices. Exhibit 4.2 arranges career clusters into 12 "regions" based on primary work tasks that are found in jobs: dealing with data, people, ideas, and things. Please note that this figure also uses the letters RIASEC (Realistic, Investigative, Artistic, Social, Enterprising, and Conventional) to show the relationship of each region to Holland's Interest Environments, discussed earlier in this chapter.

The more you are able to incorporate your interests into your work, the more you will enjoy your work. Once you have completed an interest inventory, plan to explore those occupations associated with your interests. Find out what people actually do, and compare these jobs to your interests.

Summary

ow that you have completed this chapter, you are aware that your satisfaction in a career is related to how much you can incorporate your unique personality and interests into your work.

In the next chapter, we will focus on skills: you will learn how to identify the skills you possess, and you will get ideas about the types of skills you may need in the future. With this information, you will be well into your career fitness program!

ACT Career Clusters and Career Areas (A–Z), illustrating how jobs can be clustered into related categories.

ADMINISTRATION AND SALES CAREER CLUSTER

A. Employment-Related Services   Managers (human resources, training/education, employee benefits, etc.); recruiter; interviewer; job analyst.

B. Marketing & Sales   Agents (insurance, real estate, travel, etc.); buyer; sales/manufacturers' representatives; retail sales-worker; telemarketer.

C. Management   Executive; executive secretary; purchaser; general managers (financial, office, property, etc.); specialty managers (retail store, hotel/motel, food service, etc.). For other managers, see specialty—e.g., Social service (Career Area Y).

D. Regulation & Protection   Inspectors (customs, food/drug, etc.); police officer; detective; park ranger; security manager; guard.

BUSINESS OPERATIONS CAREER CLUSTER

E. Communications & Records   Receptionist; secretary (including legal and medical); court reporter; clerks (order, billing, hotel, etc.).

F. Financial Transactions   Accountant/auditor; cashier; bank teller; budget/credit analyst; tax preparer; ticket agent.

G. Distribution & Dispatching   Shipping/receiving clerk; warehouse supervisor; mail carrier; dispatchers (flight, cab, etc.); air traffic controller.

TECHNICAL CAREER CLUSTER

H. Transport Operation & Related   Truck/bus/cab drivers; locomotive engineer; ship captain; aircraft pilot; sailor; chauffeur.

I. Agriculture, Forestry, & Related   Farmer; nursery manager; pest controller; forester; logger; groundskeeper; animal caretaker.

J. Computer & Information Specialties   Programmer; systems analyst; information systems manager; computer repairer; desktop publisher; actuary.

K. Construction & Maintenance   Carpenter; electrician; bricklayer; tile setter; painter; plumber; roofer; firefighter; custodian.

L. Crafts & Related   Cabinetmaker; tailor; chef/cook; baker; butcher; jeweler; silversmith; hand crafter.

M. Manufacturing & Processing   Tool & die maker; machinist; welder; bookbinder; printing press operator; photo process worker; dry cleaner.

N. Mechanical & Electrical Specialties   Mechanics/technicians (auto, aircraft, heating & air conditioning, electronics, dental lab, etc.); repairers (office machine, appliance, electronics).

SCIENCE AND TECHNOLOGY CAREER CLUSTER

O. Engineering & Technologies   Engineers (aerospace, agricultural, nuclear, civil, computer, etc.); technicians (electronics, mechanical, laser, etc.); surveyor; drafter; architect; technical illustrator.

P. Natural Science & Technologies   Physicist; astronomer; biologist; statistician; soil conservationist; food technologist; crime lab analyst.

Q. Medical Technologies   Pharmacist; optician; prosthetist; technologists (surgical, medical lab, EEG, etc.); dietitian.

R. Medical Diagnosis & Treatment   Physician; psychiatrist; pathologist; dentist; optometrist; veterinarian; physical therapist; audiologist; physician's assistant.

S. Social Science   Sociologist; experimental psychologist; political scientist; economist; criminologist; urban planner.

ARTS CAREER CLUSTER

T. Applied Arts (Visual)   Artist; graphic artist; photographer; illustrator; floral/fashion/interior designers; merchandise displayer.

U. Creative & Performing Arts   Writer/author; musician; singer; dancer; music composer; movie/TV director; fashion model.

V. Applied Arts (Written & Spoken)   Reporter; columnist; editor; ad copywriter; P. R. specialist; TV announcer; librarian; interpreter.

SOCIAL SERVICE CAREER CLUSTER

W. Health Care   Administrator; nurse; occupational therapist; psychiatric technician; dental hygienist/assistant; geriatric aide.

X. Education   Administrator; teachers & aides (preschool, elementary, & secondary, special education, PE, etc.). For others, see specialty—e.g., Physics teacher (Career Area P).

Y. Community Services   Social service director; social worker; lawyer; paralegal; home economist; career counselor; clergy.

Z. Personal Services   Waiter/waitress; barber; cosmetologist; flight attendant; household worker; home health aide; travel guide.

EXHIBIT **4.2**   *The World-of-Work map.*

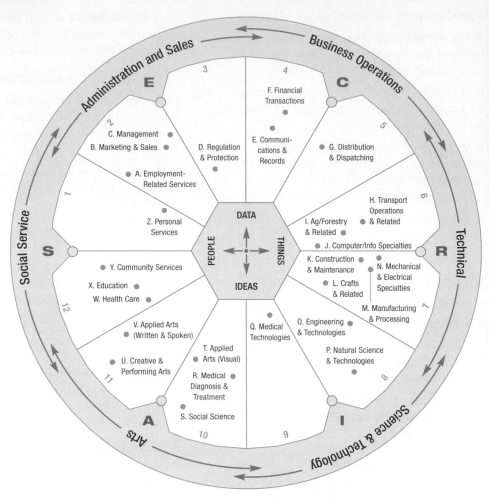

ABOUT THE MAP

- The World-of-Work Map arranges 26 career areas (groups of similar jobs) into 12 regions. Together, the career areas cover all U.S. jobs. Most jobs in a career area are located near the point shown. However, some may be in adjacent map regions.

- A career area's location is based on its primary work tasks. The four primary work tasks are working with

    Data: Facts, numbers, files, accounts, business procedures.

    Ideas: Insights, theories, new ways of saying or doing something, for example, with words, equations, or music.

    People: People you help, serve, inform, care for, or sell things to.

    Things: Machines, tools, living things, and materials such as food, wood, or metal.

- Six general types of work (Holland Interest Environments) are shown around the edge of the map. The overlapping career cluster arrows indicate overlap in the occupational content of adjacent career clusters.

- Because of their People rather than Things orientation, the following two career areas in the Science & Technology cluster are located toward the left side of the map (Region 10): Medical Diagnosis & Treatment and Social Science.

Focusing on You

The following exercises serve to help you summarize information. Exercise 4.1 asks you to record your personality type as determined earlier. Exercise 4.2 is a review of the Holland Interest Environments as they describe you. Exercises 4.3 and 4.4 ask you to list information about your interests, and Exercise 4.5 asks you to record the results of any additional assessments you have taken. Exercise 4.6 asks you to list interesting jobs found in the classifieds; Exercise 4.7 asks for your list of interesting courses taken from a college catalog. The exercise summary encourages you to put this information together and describe an ideal job or set of activities that best reflects who you are.

To answer these questions online, go to the *Exercise* module in Chapter 4 of the Companion Website.

Your Personality Type

EXERCISE 4.1

Check your four-letter personality preference (page 71):

- ○ Extraversion   ○ Introversion
- ○ Sensing   ○ Intuition
- ○ Thinking   ○ Feeling
- ○ Judging   ○ Perception

Your Holland Interest Environment

EXERCISE 4.2

1. Check your top three Holland Environments (pages 74–76):
- ○ Realistic   ○ Investigative
- ○ Artistic   ○ Social
- ○ Enterprising   ○ Conventional

2. What adjectives from these environments best describe you (pages 74–76)?

_____

_____

_____

3. List three interesting majors from your top categories (page 77):

_____

_____

_____

4. List three interesting jobs/careers from your top categories (pages 78–79):

_____

_____

_____

Your Occupational Interests

List the occupational interest areas you have checked off in this chapter (page 85):

_____

_____

_____

Job Clusters

List three ACT job clusters that are most interesting to you (page 87):

1. _____

2. _____

3. _____

Interest Inventories

Record below the results of any other interest or personality inventories you have taken (e.g., top three career choices):

_____

_____

_____

Classified Careers

Locate the Sunday classifieds section from two or three weeks of newspapers in hard copy or on the Internet. These do not need to be recent or local papers. Scan the entire section of the Sunday job classifieds and identify those jobs that look interesting, *regardless of whether you consider yourself qualified*. Review the jobs that you identified and look for patterns in the announcements that caught your eye. Write the job titles and industries that interested you in the space that follows.

_____

_____

_____

College Catalogs

ocate the general catalog for the college or university you are currently attending or
for a local college. The general catalog is the publication that contains the entire listings and descriptions of courses offered at that college. Read the catalog and course
descriptions, marking those classes on topics about which you would like to learn more.
Review the classes you have marked and notice which subjects seemed most interesting.
Write the subject areas in the space below:

_____

_____

_____

WWWebwise

 For additional activities online, go to the WWWebwise module in Chapter 4 of the
Companion Website.

Exercise Summary

hat kinds of activities or job descriptions would your ideal job reflect, based on
what you have learned about your personality and interests?

_____

_____

_____

_____

_____

_____

_____

_____

_____

_____

Go to page 206 of the chapter summaries and fill out the Chapter 4 exercise summary now.

Skills Assessment

CHAPTER 5

The next step in the career-planning process is to identify your skills. Skills are the building blocks of your future career just as muscles are the building blocks of your future body shape. A career fitness program helps you to identify your current skills and the skills you want to develop. A thorough skills analysis is a critical component of the career-planning process.

Skills are the currency used by job seekers. In the job market you receive pay in exchange for skills. Individuals who can describe themselves to a potential employer in terms of their skills are the people most likely to enjoy their careers because they are the most likely to obtain jobs that use their particular skills. People who enjoy their work tend to be more productive and healthy. After completing this chapter, you will be able to analyze a potential job on the basis of how the skills required by the job compare with both the skills you possess and enjoy using and the skills you want to develop. Furthermore, you will have a broader vocabulary to use in describing your strengths when you prepare your resume and when you are interviewed for jobs.

LEARNING OBJECTIVES

At the end of the chapter you will be able to . . .

- Discuss the importance of skills in your career search

- Define and identify your skills

- Recognize the power of the transferability of your skills

- Use the language of skills in writing your resume and preparing for an interview

*Ability is what you are capable
of doing. Motivation determines what
you do. Attitude determines how well you do it.*

Defining Skills

Skills include the specific attributes, talents, and personal qualities that we bring to a job as well as the tasks we learn on the job. Every job requires skills. We also develop skills simply through the process of living, by interacting with others and going through our daily routines. Our personal preferences often affect our skills and abilities. We tend to be motivated to repeatedly use skills that are part of enjoyable activities. Our repeated use of and success with certain preferred skills identifies them as our *self-motivators*. Self-motivators are skills we enjoy and do well.

Skills are the currency of the job market

By learning the vocabulary of skills, you can recognize the hundreds of skills that may be within your grasp. Skills are generally divided into three types: functional, work-content, and adaptive. All of these can be considered transferable. *Functional skills* are those that may or may not be associated with a specific job, such as maintaining schedules, collecting data, and diagnosing and responding to problems. They are called functional skills because they are used to accomplish general tasks or functions of a job. *Work-content skills* are specific and specialized to one job (e.g., bookkeeping is done by bookkeepers, assigning grades is done by teachers, interpreting an electrocardiogram is done by specific medical practitioners). *Adaptive* or *self-management skills* are personal attributes; they might also be described as personality traits. The ability to learn quickly, the ability to pay close attention to detail, task orientation, self-direction, congeniality, and cooperativeness are some examples of adaptive skills.

Identifying Your Skills

If you were asked right now to list your skills, what would your list look like? It might be a short list, not because you do not have skills but simply because you have never been asked to identify them and are not accustomed to thinking and talking about them. Reflecting on your skills may also be difficult because most of us have been taught to be modest and not to brag. We often feel that something we do well doesn't take any special skills, that is, we discount our own special talents. We may also feel that if we are not currently using a skill, we can no longer claim it—that somehow it has escaped us. Or, if we haven't been paid to use the skill, we may not recognize its value.

All of these false assumptions make it difficult to list our skills honestly and accurately. Your goal now will be to recognize the many skills you possess that make you valuable in the job market. You have acquired hundreds of skills just by virtue of your life experiences, and, paid or not, they are part of your portfolio!

Once you begin to recognize your skills, you will become more aware of your identity as extending beyond the narrow limits you tend to apply to yourself. We all unconsciously tend to categorize ourselves too narrowly. For instance, you might typically answer the question "Who are you?" with statements such as "I am a student," "I am a history major," "I am a graphic artist," "I am a conservative," or "I am a homemaker." The problem with these labels is that they tend to stereotype you. This is especially true when you are interviewing for a job. If you say you are a student, the interviewer might stereotype you as not having enough experience. If you say you are a secretary, the interviewer may consider you only for a secretarial job or may insist that you start as a secretary. But suppose you say your experience has involved public speaking, doing organizational work, coordinating schedules, managing budgets, researching needs, problem solving, following through with details, motivating others, resolving problems caused by low morale and lack of cooperation, and establishing priorities for allocation of available time, resources, and funds. Not only does this sound impressive, but you appear eligible for many positions that require these skills.

A particular challenge may be faced by homemakers who feel that because they have been out of the job market, they have no transferable or marketable skills. To the contrary, homemaking is a full-time job requiring a wide range of skills that can translate into paid employment. (Review the creative functional resume in Chapter 10 for ideas on skills in the areas of management, office procedures, personnel, finances, and purchasing that might be included in a homemaker's list of transferable skills.)

Employers look for employees who are task-oriented and who think and talk in terms of what they as employees can do to make the employer's operation easier, better, and more efficient. The best way to describe what you can do for an employer is to talk about your skills and how they apply to the job. Unfortunately, we tend to discount our accomplishments and the related skill development. Although climbing a mountain and running a four-minute mile are noteworthy accomplishments, so are the following:

Can you talk about your skills?

raising a child	raising funds
getting into college	giving a speech
delivering papers on a route	writing a term paper
using a software program	getting a job
repairing a car	consoling a child
designing a costume	graduating from high school
completing a computer course	planning a trip and traveling
planning a surprise party	working as a food server
surfing the Internet	mastering a sport
completing a degree	overcoming a bad habit

Sample accomplishments

In reviewing this list, you may be thinking that some of these activities are simple, no big deal. Some are activities that you can do without much thought or preparation. However, just because they don't take much preparation does not mean they aren't accomplishments. Start thinking of goals that you have set and then later met as accomplishments!

Meet John

John, a 16-year-old high school junior, was always someone friends went to when they needed a plan. When he was younger, John was known as a schemer, and most of the time he was in trouble for his schemes—but as he got older he learned to turn his schemes into plans. Well liked, John never thought of himself as anything special, but his friends thought he had a real talent for making things happen.

John's girlfriend, Alicia, was turning 18 and he wanted to throw a really great surprise party for her. He called all his friends and Alicia's and told them his ideas. He divided everyone into groups to cover the food, entertainment, transportation, and decorations. The party was a huge success (even though Alicia says she knew about it all along).

The following week when John had to write a paper for his career class describing an accomplishment, he used the party. He described his initial plan, how he organized and divided up the work, how he made a checklist and communicated with everyone. From a list of skills given to each student by the teacher, John identified leadership, creativity, communication, determination, organization, dependability, and attention to detail as the skills in putting together the party.

In his senior year, a friend told John of an internship opportunity with a congressman in his district. The friend felt that John's organizational skills would make him a perfect candidate. Since John did not have any real work experience, he used the party-planning activity on his resume to demonstrate his skills. His resume got him an interview and his outgoing personality and strong organizational skills got him the internship.

One of John's assignments was to organize meetings and special events. He loved the work and he was able to use the full resources of the congressman's office to put together impressive events.

ANALYZE YOUR ACCOMPLISHMENTS

You can begin to recognize your skills by identifying and examining your most satisfying accomplishments, because your skills led you to these accomplishments. By analyzing these accomplishments, you are likely to discover a pattern of skills (your self-motivators) that you repeatedly use and enjoy using. Again, accomplishments are simply completed activities, goals, projects, or jobs held.

There are several ways to analyze accomplishments. One way is to describe something that you are proud of having completed, and then list the skills that were required to complete it. Let's look at John, whose accomplishments are described in the Real Stories box. Read it now. Then reread the list of skills that John identified in the third paragraph.

Can you think of any that he missed? We all have many more skills than we credit ourselves with having.

Another method to identify skills is to write a story about one of your accomplishments and then list the skills used. Richard Bolles has popularized this approach in his *Quick Job Hunting Map* (1996), a booklet that lists hundreds of skills. Following is an example of one student's story and the skills involved. The student's classmates listened to her story and helped her identify 18 skills.

After graduation, John felt more confident than he ever felt before. With an excellent reference letter from the congressman, John decided to enroll in community college. He took some marketing classes and looked for another internship. He was lucky to land a position with an ad agency that promoted Britney Spears. He learned a great deal working with the ad agency and the people associated with Ms. Spears.

When the internship ended, John began researching careers to see what education and training he needed to continue with this type of work. He discovered that event planning fit with his interests and his skills; however, the salary was not as much as he had hoped for. John met with a counselor and they agreed that in order to do the type of work he loved and make a decent salary, he would need a four-year degree. The counselor helped John create an educational plan to prepare him to transfer to the university.

1. What other types of jobs require the skills that John possesses?

2. Are some people born with organizational skills? If not, how can people develop these skills?

3. What gave John the confidence to attend college?

4. Which is more difficult—learning to like doing something you dislike but do well, or learning to be competent at something that you do not feel competent doing?

5. List an activity or project you have accomplished and indicate the skills that you used to complete it.

6. Write yourself a letter of reference.

 To answer these questions online, go to the *Real Stories* module in Chapter 5 of the Companion Website.

Writing My Term Paper on the Computer

It was necessary for me to learn how to use the computer at a simple level to complete my term paper. I knew the traditional keyboard and could type. I went to our campus computer center for instruction on how to use all the additional keys. I wrote down on paper all the key functions I had to use in order to give the correct commands to the computer. I got a mini-operations course. I learned to do the following:

1. find any page
2. enter the file
3. transfer material to different pages
4. create simple graphs
5. print out on printer
6. make corrections
7. delete and insert characters

I proofread, corrected, and typed 60 pages in three weeks; then I edited it down to 35 pages. The paper received an A. I'm now taking a class in Word and computer graphics!

Skills used in writing a term paper on the computer:
1. learns quickly
2. displays flexibility
3. meets challenges
4. directs self
5. follows through
6. faces new situations
7. proofs and edits
8. translates concepts
9. word processes
10. organizes
11. gets the job done
12. displays patience
13. attends to detail
14. overcomes obstacles
15. communicates clearly
16. works under stress
17. displays persistence
18. asks questions

131.067.014 COPYWRITER (PROFESS. & KIN.)

Writes advertising copy for use by publication or broadcast media to promote sale of goods and services: consults with sales media and marketing representatives to obtain information on product or service and discuss style and length of advertising copy. Obtains additional background and current development information through research and interview. Reviews advertising trends, consumer surveys, and other data regarding marketing of specific and related goods and services to formulate presentation approach. Writes preliminary draft of copy and sends to supervisor for approval. Corrects and revises copy as necessary. May write articles, bulletins, sales letters, speeches, and other related informative and promotional material. Prepares advertising copy, using computer.

O*Net Code: 27-3034.04

241.267.030 INVESTIGATOR (CLERICAL)

Investigates persons or business establis applying for credit, employment, insurance, lo settlement of claims. Contacts former em neighbors, trade associations, and others phone to verify employment record and to health history and history of moral and socia ior. Examines city directories and public rec verify residence history, convictions and property ownership, bankruptcies, liens, and taxes of applicant. Obtains credit rating from and credit concerns. Analyzes information g by investigation and prepares reports of findir recommendations. May interview applicant phone or in person to obtain other financ personal data for completeness of report. Wh cializing in certain types of investigations, designated CREDIT REPORTER (bus. ser.); ANCE–APPLICATION INVESTIGATOR (insu

No description listed in O*Net

USE THE DOT TO IDENTIFY SKILLS

You can research the skills associated with jobs by reading the job descriptions, often located in the employer's personnel office, or by researching the jobs in the *Dictionary of Occupational Titles* (referred to as the DOT). The DOT is an excellent reference source for identifying tasks required in more than 21,000 different occupations.

In addition to identifying specific tasks in each job, the DOT identifies the primary skills required for each job according to the three broad categories of *data* (instructions and information), *people* (supervisors, coworkers, or the public), and *things* (materials, equipment, or products). The nine-digit number that precedes each job title (refer to the two sample job descriptions) includes an indication of how the job is related to data (the fourth digit), people (the fifth digit), and things (the sixth digit). For example, by finding the middle three digits for *Investigator*—2, 6, 7—in their appropriate columns in Exhibit 5.1, we know that the position involves *analyzing* data, *speaking to and signaling* people, and *handling* things. For a teacher, the fifth digit would likely be 2, signifying *instruction*. For a crane operator, the sixth digit would probably be 3, representing *driving and operating*.

The DOT can be of great use to you in identifying types of skills involved in jobs. Perhaps more important, it can alert you to the existence of thou-

Skills relationships of jobs to data, people, and things, as identified in the Dictionary of Occupational Titles (DOT).

EXHIBIT 5.1

DATA (4TH DIGIT)		PEOPLE (5TH DIGIT)		THINGS (6TH DIGIT)	
0	Synthesizing	0	Mentoring	0	Setting up
1	Coordinating	1	Negotiating	1	Precision working
2	Analyzing	2	Instructing	2	Operating–controlling
3	Compiling	3	Supervising	3	Driving–operating
4	Computing	4	Diverting	4	Manipulating
5	Copying	5	Persuading	5	Tending
6	Comparing	6	Speaking–signaling	6	Feeding–offbearing
7	No significant relationship	7	Serving	7	Handling
		8	No significant relationship	8	No significant relationship

sands of jobs and careers you never knew existed. In Chapter 7, the DOT will be discussed as one of many sources of career information.

If your local career center or One Stop Career Center has access to O*NET (http://online.onetcenter.org/), you may find it easier to discover the relationship between occupations and skills. O*NET is the acronym for the Occupational Information Network developed by the U.S. Department of Labor. The program is an easy to use, interactive computer database that collects, analyzes, and disseminates skill and occupational information in more than 1,100 occupational areas. Simply type three skills and the computer will bring out various occupations that use them. O*NET has crosswalks with the DOT. Therefore, knowing your DOT code allows you to find several related occupations using O*NET. For example, if you searched for "counselor," you would find these related jobs: Supervisor; Special Services; Veterans Contact Representative; Counselor; Director of Counseling; Residence Counselor; Foreign-Student Advisor; and several others. When you click on any of these job titles, then you find the skills and job tasks describing these jobs.

Move now to the next page and complete the Activity Checklist. This list includes more than 200 skills in 13 different categories. These categories are useful because they're familiar to employers and often show up in job announcements. As you complete the checklist, carefully consider how each skill applies specifically to you.

Identify your skills

If you are currently working, think of ways to use those skills you identify in the activity checklist as your self-motivated skills as often as possible to give you job satisfaction. Talk to your supervisor and identify additional ways to use these skills now or in the future; for example, if you were hired because of your word processing skills, you might suggest that you become the company expert on formatting documents and reports to give them a consistent look! If your people skills are one of your strengths, make sure your boss keeps you in mind for office supervisor, or as a member of a committee, or as the company liaison with an important client. Don't take your skills for granted and don't let others do so!

ACTIVITY *Assessing Your Skills*

For each item in this table, mark an *X* next to each skill you enjoy using (even if you aren't expert at it!). Then go back over the list and place a check (✓) next to each skill that you perform particularly well. Underline any skills that you have never used. Finally, place an *O* next to any skills that you would like to develop or acquire. Under personal qualities, check all that apply to you.

Once you have completed these steps, review those skills that are marked with both an *X and* a check. These are your *self-motivated* or preferred skills. These skills represent your areas of mastery and probably your areas of greatest satisfaction as well. If you use these skills on the job whenever possible, and look for additional ways to use them, you will increase the enjoyment and satisfaction you derive from your job.

Review your list and identify five skills that interest you and that you would like to develop. Think of ways you can develop these skills, such as taking a course or class, getting on-the-job training, joining a club, volunteering, or asking a friend, associate, colleague, or mentor for help. To further clarify your responses, complete Exercise 5.7 at the end of the chapter.

X = skills you enjoy using   O = skills you would like to develop or acquire
✓ = skills you perform especially well   underlining = skills you have never used

---

CLERICAL SKILLS
- Examining
- Evaluating
- Filing
- Developing
- Improving
- Recording
- Collating
- Computing
- Recommending
- Following
- Bookkeeping
- Keyboarding
- Transcribing
- Indexing
- Arranging
- Systematizing
- Tabulating
- Photocopying
- Collaborating
- Sorting
- Retrieving
- Organizing
- Purchasing
- Handling people
- Problem solving

TECHNICAL SKILLS
- Financing
- Evaluating
- Calculating
- Adjusting
- Aligning
- Observing
- Verifying
- Drafting
- Designing
- Cataloging
- Examining
- Adjusting
- Problem solving
- Creating
- Detailing
- Restructuring
- Reviewing
- Revising
- Synthesizing
- Structuring
- Solving
- Refining
- Reviewing
- Following specifications

PUBLIC RELATIONS SKILLS
- Planning
- Conducting
- Informing
- Consulting
- Writing
- Researching
- Representing
- Negotiating
- Collaborating
- Communicating
- Promoting
- Convincing
- Hosting
- Entertaining
- Mediating
- Performing
- Endorsing
- Recruiting
- Demonstrating
- Creating
- Problem solving

AGRICULTURAL SKILLS
- Inspecting
- Costing

- Lifting
- Cultivating
- Assembling
- Problem solving
- Devising
- Scheduling
- Demonstrating
- Inspecting
- Evaluating
- Estimating
- Diagnosing
- Repairing
- Maintaining
- Replacing
- Constructing
- Operating

SELLING SKILLS
- Contacting
- Persuading
- Reviewing
- Inspecting
- Informing
- Promoting

Go to the next page

_____ Positioning
_____ Influencing
_____ Convincing
_____ Comparing
_____ Differentiating
_____ Representing
_____ Asking
_____ Closing
_____ Costing
_____ Negotiating
_____ Communicating
_____ Calculating
_____ Advising
_____ Contracting
_____ Recommending
_____ Problem solving

MAINTENANCE SKILLS
_____ Operating
_____ Repairing
_____ Maintaining
_____ Dismantling
_____ Adjusting
_____ Cleaning
_____ Purchasing
_____ Climbing
_____ Lifting
_____ Assembling
_____ Problem solving
_____ Devising
_____ Scheduling
_____ Demonstrating
_____ Inspecting
_____ Evaluating
_____ Estimating

MANAGEMENT SKILLS
_____ Planning
_____ Organizing
_____ Scheduling
_____ Assigning
_____ Delegating
_____ Directing
_____ Hiring
_____ Measuring
_____ Administering
_____ Conducting
_____ Controlling
_____ Coordinating
_____ Enabling
_____ Empowering
_____ Initiating
_____ Formulating
_____ Supervising
_____ Sponsoring
_____ Modeling

_____ Supporting
_____ Negotiating
_____ Decision making
_____ Team building
_____ Conceptualizing
_____ Problem solving

COMMUNICATION SKILLS
_____ Reasoning
_____ Organizing
_____ Defining
_____ Writing
_____ Listening
_____ Explaining
_____ Interpreting
_____ Reading
_____ Speaking
_____ Editing
_____ Instructing
_____ Interviewing
_____ Collaborating
_____ Presenting
_____ Formulating
_____ Proposing
_____ Synthesizing
_____ Integrating
_____ Connecting
_____ Summarizing
_____ Articulating
_____ Interpreting
_____ Translating
_____ Problem solving

RESEARCH SKILLS
_____ Recognizing
_____ Interviewing
_____ Questioning
_____ Synthesizing
_____ Writing
_____ Diagnosing
_____ Compiling
_____ Reviewing
_____ Designing
_____ Theorizing
_____ Testing
_____ Equating
_____ Evaluating
_____ Investigating
_____ Summarizing
_____ Communicating
_____ Collaborating
_____ Demonstrating
_____ Analyzing
_____ Refining
_____ Problem solving

FINANCIAL SKILLS
_____ Calculating
_____ Projecting
_____ Budgeting
_____ Recognizing
_____ Accounting
_____ Processing
_____ Computing
_____ Correlating
_____ Costing
_____ Forecasting
_____ Comparing
_____ Compiling
_____ Examining
_____ Leveraging
_____ Verifying
_____ Problem-solving

MANUAL SKILLS
_____ Operating
_____ Monitoring
_____ Controlling
_____ Setting up
_____ Driving
_____ Cutting
_____ Assembling
_____ Drafting
_____ Drawing
_____ Inspecting
_____ Programming
_____ Tabulating
_____ Constructing
_____ Creating
_____ Repairing
_____ Problem solving

SERVICE SKILLS
_____ Counseling
_____ Guiding
_____ Leading
_____ Listening
_____ Coordinating
_____ Teaching
_____ Responding
_____ Collaborating
_____ Facilitating
_____ Monitoring
_____ Integrating
_____ Motivating
_____ Persuading
_____ Evaluating
_____ Summarizing
_____ Planning
_____ Correcting
_____ Mediating
_____ Encouraging

_____ Contracting
_____ Demonstrating
_____ Problem solving

PERSONAL QUALITIES
_____ Adaptable
_____ Adventuresome
_____ Aggressive
_____ Alert
_____ Ambitious
_____ Assertive
_____ Calm
_____ Capable
_____ Confident
_____ Conscientious
_____ Creative
_____ Cooperative
_____ Candid
_____ Dependable
_____ Determined
_____ Diplomatic
_____ Discreet
_____ Dominant
_____ Efficient
_____ Energetic
_____ Enterprising
_____ Enthusiastic
_____ Flexible
_____ Forceful
_____ Frank
_____ Idealistic
_____ Initiating
_____ Innovative
_____ Logical
_____ Loyal
_____ Methodical
_____ Objective
_____ Optimistic
_____ Organized
_____ Patient
_____ Persistent
_____ Practical
_____ Precise
_____ Quiet
_____ Realistic
_____ Reliable
_____ Resourceful
_____ Risk taking
_____ Self-starting
_____ Sensitive
_____ Serious
_____ Sincere
_____ Tactful
_____ Tenacious
_____ Versatile

THE PORTFOLIO EMPLOYEE

As we have discussed, your skills are your most valuable asset in the job market because they are transferable. For example, the word processing and data management skills you use in your current job as administrative assistant or insurance claims processor will be equally valuable in other jobs that you seek in the future, such as journalist or lawyer. The more skills you develop, the more valuable and versatile you are in the job market. In his book *The Age of Paradox* (1995), Charles Handy proposed that in this decade the number of portfolio workers will grow dramatically. Such workers would not be a full-time part of one organization but instead will sell their portfolio of skills to several employers on a freelance basis. Thus, the person who has word processing and data management skills may work for more than one firm in various capacities. A greater number of workers in the future will be self-employed, and their job security will come not from the traditional employer–employee relationship, but from their ability to offer needed skills to many employers. This increased trend toward self-employed portfolio employees means that each of us will benefit from being able to identify our skills and from determining which skills we want to use, improve, and develop to stay competitive in the job market.

Identifying Transferable Skills

s we've discussed throughout this chapter, transferable skills are those skills that you carry from one job to another and can utilize in performing many jobs. Perhaps you are concerned about a lack of paid job experience, or you may have chosen a liberal arts major and are concerned that you will not learn specific job skills or be trained for a job when you graduate.

Note how many SCANS skills you are using by reading Exhibit 5.2 and by completing exercises in this book related to resume writing, career information searching, information interviewing, and making a budget (see Using SCANS Skills, p. 108).

Let's examine the transferable skills that a liberal arts major can and should develop while in school. We will also explore the notion that your *personal, natural abilities* and *attitude* are perhaps the most important set of skills you have for selling yourself and your talents to a potential employer.

TRANSFERABLE SKILLS OF A LIBERAL ARTS MAJOR

A liberal arts degree is preparation for a variety of careers. In fact, the majority of those who graduate with a liberal arts degree do not find employment in fields related to their major (e.g., history majors do not necessarily become historians).

Whether you are an anthropology, English, or history major, you have (or will develop) transferable skills that are useful in the workplace as a result of being a successful college student. As you read the following clusters of skills, think about which skills you have gained as a student. The *cluster* approach to skills will be further explained in Chapter 10 when we discuss the functional resume. Do you have research skills? Do you have organizational skills? Chances are, you do!

Examples of the skills learned in a typical college liberal arts degree program include the following (note how these mirror the skills identified by the SCANS report):

Communication skills. Listening effectively, writing essays and reports, convincing individuals and groups of the importance of your ideas, negotiating disputes and differences.

Problem-solving or critical-thinking skills. Analytical thinking, thinking abstractly, determining broader issues, defining an issue, identifying several solutions to the same problem, creating new ways to handle an issue, persuading others to act in the best interests of the group.

Human relations skills. Speaking with colleagues, advising people, helping people resolve problems, communicating ideas effectively, cooperating with others to solve problems and to complete projects, working well with diverse groups of people, teaching or coaching others.

Organizational skills. Assessing needs, planning or arranging presentations or social events, designing programs, coordinating events, delegating responsibility, evaluating programs, managing the implementation of projects.

Research skills. Searching computerized databases and published reference materials, identifying themes, analyzing data, classifying data, handling detail work, investigating problems, recording data, writing reports and term papers.

By now, it should be apparent that you carry many skills from one job to another. Once you are able to describe a job by its skills, you can use these skills in your own letters of application, in your resumes, and during job interviews to reinforce the fact that you have what it takes to do the job, even if you have never had the exact job title.

FACTS AND FIGURES

People skills

From the manager of the accounting department at Sony Technology Center:

> "The number one thing that I look for when I am hiring someone is their people skills because it is very important that you have the skills to talk to people and find out what you need to know. I believe that everyone has the ability to learn anything in this world, but if you have the ability to find the answers to things you want, then you will succeed. . . . I spend 80 percent of my time or so dealing with other divisions within Sony . . . and my staff also deals with these people."

Source: http://cord.org/workplacelibrary/sony/katie5.html

WHAT DO YOU THINK?

1. Why is it important to have people skills if you plan to be an accountant?

2. From this description, what do you think an accountant does besides accounting?

3. What did you learn from reading this information?

To answer these questions online, go to the *Facts and Figures* module in Chapter 5 of the Companion Website.

Your Most Valuable Assets: Your Personality Traits

e've talked about transferable skills that were learned or acquired at school, work or home, or through leisure and volunteer activities. Many of your skills may have come to you naturally, without training or education. We call these skills *nat-*

Identifying the Transferable Skills of a Teacher

Do you think a teacher would have the skills necessary to find employment in the business world? If you know or have read about anyone working in sales, marketing, or management, you may notice that similar skills are involved in all these jobs.

ASSESSMENT OF TEACHER SKILLS

Teaching. Training, coordinating, communicating, arbitrating, coaching, group facilitating, accessing the Internet, using computers.

Making lesson plans. Designing curricula, incorporating learning strategies, problem solving, creating visual aids.

Assigning grades. Evaluating, examining, assessing performance, interpreting test results, determining potential of individuals, monitoring progress.

Writing proposals. Assessing needs, identifying targets, setting priorities, designing evaluation models, identifying relevant information, making hypotheses about unknown phenomena, designing a process, estimating costs of a project, researching funding sources.

Advising the yearbook staff. Planning, promoting, fund-raising, group facilitating, handling detail work, meeting deadlines, assembling items of information into a coherent whole, classifying information, coordinating, creating, dealing with pressure, delegating tasks, displaying ideas in artistic form, editing, making layouts.

Supervising interns. Training, evaluating, mentoring, monitoring progress, diagnosing problem areas, inspiring, counseling, guiding.

Interpreting diagnostic tests. Screening, placing, identifying needs, diagnosing.

Interacting with students, parents, and administration. Confronting, resolving conflicts, establishing rapport, conveying warmth and caring, drawing people out, offering support, motivating, negotiating, persuading, handling complaints, mediating, organizing, questioning, troubleshooting.

Chairing a committee or department. Administering, anticipating needs or issues, arranging meetings, creating and implementing committee structures, coordinating, delegating tasks, guiding activities of a team, having responsibility for meeting objectives of a department, negotiating, organizing, promoting.

ural abilities—we're referring here to aspects of your personality such as the ability to stay calm in a crisis, the ability to manage many things at once, a natural ability with math and numbers, a natural ability with words, and so forth. More important, we're referring to personal characteristics such as enthusiasm, a good attitude, persistence, confidence, a sense of humor, and many other qualities of success that we discussed in Chapter 2.

These abilities will help you *sell yourself and your talents*. It is often these personal characteristics, called *adaptive skills*, that in the end separate you from many other qualified applicants and enable you to get the job, top evaluations, raises, and promotions. They may even help you keep your job in tough times.

We don't mean to imply that an employer will look at your enthusiastic, smiling face and say, "It doesn't matter that you have no experience—we want

The SCANS Report

IDENTIFYING THE BASIC SKILLS REQUIRED BY EMPLOYERS

In 1991, the U.S. Department of Labor issued the SCANS *(Secretary's Commission on Achieving Necessary Skills)* report. The goal of this report was to sum up the competencies and skills that form the basis of solid job performance. The results are based on extensive questioning of employers and educators.

Review the core competencies, qualities, and skills identified by the SCANS report below. These are considered essential skills that workers must possess to be competitive in the 21st-century job market. In how many of these areas do you currently feel you have adequate skill levels? If an employer asked you to prove your competencies, could you identify an area of accomplishment in which you demonstrated your use of these skills?

WORKPLACE KNOW-HOW

The know-how identified by the SCANS report is made up of a three-part foundation of skills and personal qualities along with five competencies; both the foundation and the competencies are needed for solid job performance.

THE FOUNDATION

Basic skills: Reading, writing, arithmetic and mathematics, speaking, and listening. These are the *minimum* skills needed by today's workers. If you are unsure about your skills in these basic areas, now is the time to take steps to improve them. Don't shy away from basic testing and coursework or assume that, as an adult, you naturally have these abilities. Begin thinking in terms of doing all of these things *well* and taking steps to achieve this level of proficiency.

Thinking skills: Thinking creatively, making decisions, solving problems, seeing things in the mind's eye, knowing how to learn, and reasoning. Thinking skills allow you to identify your strengths and weaknesses and take steps to remedy the latter. They allow you to acquire new skills, think creatively, and identify problems and solutions. Once again, if you are unsure of your abilities in these areas, talk to your career counselor or instructor about testing and coursework that can help.

Personal qualities: Individual responsibility, self-esteem, sociability, self-management, and integrity. Included are the personality characteristics described in Chapter 2 and the adaptive skills described in this chapter.

THE COMPETENCIES

Effective workers can productively use:

Resources: Allocating time, money, materials, space, and personnel.

Interpersonal skills: Working on teams, teaching others, serving customers, leading, negotiating, and working well with people from culturally diverse backgrounds.

Information: Acquiring and evaluating data, organizing and maintaining files, interpreting and communicating, and using computers to process information.

Systems: Understanding social, organizational, and technological systems; monitoring and correcting performance; and designing or improving systems.

Technology: Selecting equipment and tools, applying technology to specific tasks, and maintaining and troubleshooting technologies.

EXHIBIT 5.2 Tasks from diverse occupations representative of level of performance in SCANS know-how required for entry into jobs with career ladder.

POSITION AND TASK

RESOURCES	Travel Agent: Sets priorities for work tasks on a daily basis so that travel arrangements are completed in a timely manner.	Restaurant Manager: Prepares weekly sales projections; conducts inventory of food supplies; calculates the costs of purchased and on-hand food; determines sales.	Medical Assistant: Acquires, maintains, and tracks supplies on hand—inventories supplies and equipment, fills out reorder forms, and obtains extra supplies when merchandise is on sale.	Quality Control Inspector: Establishes a system for inspecting items within a given area and time frame while allowing for other contingencies.	Chef: Performs a cost analysis on menu items in order to turn a profit.
INTERPERSONAL SKILLS	Childcare Aide: Works as a member of a team in the classroom.	Outside Equipment Technician: Coordinates with a peer technician to install a point-to-point data circuit in two different cities.	Carpenter: Shares experiences and knowledge with other workers, and cooperates with others on a variety of tasks to accomplish project goals.	Accounting/Financial Analyst: Teaches a coworker the procedure for sending bimonthly memos.	Customer Service Representative: Assists customers in selecting merchandise or resolving complaints.
INFORMATION	Travel Agent: Uses online computer terminal to retrieve information relating to customer requests, plans itinerary, and books airline tickets.	Blue-Collar Worker Supervisor: Records and maintains purchase requests, purchase invoices, and cost information on raw material.	Childcare Aide: Compiles accurate written records including all facets of the child's play for the office and the parents.	Order Filler: Communicates a downtime situation to coworkers, and explains the situation so that everyone can visualize and understand it.	Cosmetologist: Keeps abreast of new and emerging styles and techniques through magazines and attendance at fashion shows.
SYSTEMS	Medical Assistant: Understands the systems of the organization and the organization's ultimate goal (i.e., excellent patient care).	Accounting/Financial Analyst: Performs analysis comparing current expenditures with projected needs and revenues.	Shipping and Receiving Clerk: Unloads and directs material throughout the plant to storage and the assembly line in accordance with company policy.	Food Service Worker: Evaluates the performance of workers and adjusts work assignments to increase staff efficiency.	Plastic Molding Machine Operator: Monitors gauges and dials to ensure that the machine operates at the proper rate of speed.

(continued)

Continued.

EXHIBIT 5.2

POSITION AND TASK

TECHNOLOGY	Travel Agent: Uses the online computer terminal to retrieve information relating to the customer's request, plan the itinerary, and book the airline ticket.	Accounting/ Financial Analyst: Prepares the monthly debt schedule, including reviews of financial statements.	Expeditor/ Purchasing Agent: Accesses the computer to retrieve required forms used to request bids and to place purchase orders.	Industry Training Specialist: Uses available computer and video technology to enhance the realism of training and to conserve time.	Order Filler: Operates a forklift and ensures that it is in proper operating condition.
BASIC SKILLS	Dental Hygienist: Reads professional manuals to understand issues related to new techniques and equipment.	Sales Representative, Hotel Services: Assesses client accounts to determine adherence to company standards.	Optician: Measures a customer's facial features to calculate bifocal segment height.	Law Enforcement Officer: Prepares written reports of incidents and crimes.	Contractor: Prepares a letter to a subcontractor delineating responsibilities for completion of an earth-grading contract.
THINKING SKILLS	Expeditor/ Purchasing Agent: Decides what supplier to use during a bid evaluation based on supplier information stored in the computer.	Blue-Collar Worker Supervisor: Sets priorities for processing orders to resolve a conflict in scheduling.	Truck Delivery Salesperson/ Outside Sales: Collects money from delinquent customers and uses judgment on extending credit.	Contractor: Analyzes and corrects the problem when timber piles break before reaching specified bearing loads.	Travel Agent: Compensates a customer who is dissatisfied with his or her travel experience.
PERSONAL QUALITIES	Optician: Responds appropriately to customer requests, demonstrates understanding of customer needs, and exhibits friendliness and politeness to customers.	Quality Control Inspector: Performs independent research to assess compliance.	Computer Operator: Assumes responsibility for the arrangement and completion of jobs run on the mainframe.	Telemarketing Representative: Displays a sense of concern and interest in customers' business and company.	Sales Representative, Hotel Services: Asserts self and networks with people at conventions in order to obtain hotel business.

Source: School to Career Handbook (California Community Colleges, Chancellor's office, 1995).

Using SCANS Skills

Sample skills used to complete assignments in a career planning class.

Resume Writing	Career Info Search	Informational Interview	Making a Budget	SCANS FOUNDATION
				Basic Skills
X	X		X	Reading
X				Writing
			X	Arithmetic
		X	X	Listening
	X	X		Speaking
				Thinking Skills
X	X	X	X	Creative thinking
			X	Decision making
		X	X	Problem solving
	X	X		Seeing things in the mind's eye
X	X	X	X	Knowing how to learn
	X		X	Reasoning
				Personal Qualities
X			X	Responsibility
X	X	X		Self-esteem
X		X		Sociability
X	X		X	Self-management
X	X	X	X	Integrity/honesty

Resume Writing	Career Info Search	Informational Interview	Making a Budget	SCANS COMPETENCIES
				Resources
X	X	X		Time
	X		X	Money
	X	X		Material and facilities
X	X	X		Human resources
				Interpersonal
	X	X		Participates as member of a team
	X	X		Teaches others new skills
			X	Serves clients/customers
	X	X	X	Exercises leadership
		X	X	Negotiates
X	X	X		Works with diversity
				Information
	X	X	X	Acquires and evaluates info
	X	X	X	Organizes and maintains info
	X	X		Interprets and communicates info
	X		X	Uses computers to process info
				Systems
	X		X	Understands systems
X				Monitors and corrects performance
	X	X	X	Improves and designs systems
				Technology
X	X		X	Selects technology
X	X	X	X	Applies technology to task
	X			Maintains and troubleshoots equipment

Source: *School to Career Handbook* (VATEA funded project through the California Community Colleges, Chancellor's office, 1995).

Describing Skills

Remember that skills are the currency of the job market. The more you have and the better you are at describing them, the greater your opportunities will be.

- Review the list of transferable skills of a liberal arts major on page 103.

- As you read each skill under each category, think of a specific time when you developed or demonstrated that skill in school or during your leisure activities or during a past or present job.

- Jot down some notes to remind yourself how you used any of these skills, or create a file to save on your computer for future reference.

- Review these notes the next time you are writing a resume or interviewing for a job so that you can convincingly describe the skills you possess and how you demonstrated these skills.

- Your ability to communicate this critical information to employers will set you apart from the crowd in the interview process and help put you on top of any employer's list of candidates for hire.

---

you because you're cheerful!" However, once you have learned to identify your many job-specific skills and to summarize your experience in such a way as to make certain it relates closely to the job being discussed, you will have a much greater chance of succeeding if you are aware of and express your best self with interest, enthusiasm, and friendliness. Know and use your personal skills!

Summary

We all have our own special excellence. This excellence is most likely to be demonstrated in experiences that you consider to be achievements or life satisfactions. Your most memorable achievements usually indicate where your greatest concentration of self-motivator (motivated) skills exists. Analyzing several such achievements is likely to reveal a pattern of skills used repeatedly in making them occur. The more you know about your motivated skills, the better you will be able to choose careers that require the use of these skills. Using these skills gives you a sense of mastery and satisfaction. You will be happier, more productive, and more successful if you can incorporate your motivated skills into your chosen work. You will also find that your skills transfer to many different jobs.

Use past accomplishments to reveal skills.

If you have started reading about occupations by visiting a local library or college career center, you may find that some occupational information sources list the skills related to the specific career described. There are also computer programs such as EUREKA in California, SIGI Plus (System of Interactive Guidance and Information), CIS (Career Information System), and other systems that include lists of skills correlated with job descriptions. Check with your local college or computer store to learn about other skills analysis software. Be certain to review Exhibit 5.2 to identify how the SCANS skills relate to a variety of entry-level jobs. Now, complete the exercises that follow.

Skills Assessment

The following exercises will assist you in identifying your personal constellation of skills. Exercise 5.1 asks you to write about several major experiences in your life with enough detail so that you will be able to analyze each experience for the particular skills utilized. Exercises 5.2 and 5.3 ask you to list 10 accomplishments and then to describe a few of them in detail. Exercise 5.4 allows you to identify the skills used in the accomplishments described in the two previous exercises. Exercise 5.5 identifies your cluster of favorite skills. Exercise 5.6 helps you identify the extent of your experience related to the responsibilities of your ideal jobs. Exercises 5.7 and 5.8 serve to review and summarize your preferred and most often used skills.

> To answer these questions online, go to the *Exercise* module in Chapter 5 of the Companion Website.

Experiography

To explore your past experiences and relate them to your career plan, write an account of the significant experiences in your life—an *experiography*. The best way to go about this task is to think of three or four major experiences in each of the following categories and then describe each of them in writing in as much detail as you can. It is important to describe not only what happened but also your feelings (good or bad) about the experience or person and what you learned from the experience. The categories to include are:

a. work experience

b. activity experience—school, clubs, etc.

c. life events

d. leisure time

e. people in your life

f. life's frustrations

g. life's rewards

Remember, neither the chronology nor the order of significance is important. What is important is that you describe people or events that have had an impact on who you are right now. Keep in mind that the writing needs to be specific enough for you to be able to analyze these experiences for particular skills you have demonstrated.

Accomplishments

Make a list of up to 10 accomplishments. You may wish to look back at the ones you have already listed in the Values Grid in Chapter 3, but you do not necessarily have to include them in this list.

1. _____
2. _____
3. _____
4. _____
5. _____
6. _____
7. _____
8. _____
9. _____
10. _____

Description of Accomplishments

EXERCISE 5.3

Select one or two of the accomplishments listed above, and describe each of them. Use one sheet of paper for each. To be as detailed as possible in your description of the event, try to elaborate on *who* influenced you, *what* you did, *where* it happened, *when* it occurred, *why* you did it, and *how* you did it.

The Skills

EXERCISE 5.4

List the skills you used in the accomplishments described in Exercise 5.3:

_____

_____

_____

Your Favorite Skills

EXERCISE 5.5

Rank the following skills categories as they reflect your favorite skills (1 = favorite; 6 = least favorite):

_____ a. Help people, be of service, be kind

_____ b. Write, read, talk, speak, teach

_____ c. Analyze, systemize, research

_____ d. Invent, create, develop, imagine

_____ e. Persuade, sell, influence, negotiate

_____ f. Build, plant crops, use hand–eye coordination, operate machinery

Ideal Jobs

Write five ideal job responsibilities. Next to each one, write two or more examples of your experience in each of these areas (e.g., "writing—I wrote a 10-page report that was used to justify a grant application"). In areas where you have not developed extensive experience, you may want to create additional learning experiences to make yourself eligible for your ideal jobs. You can create learning experiences or gain experience by taking classes, by volunteering for extra work in your present job, or by finding another job closely related to your ideal jobs.

_____

_____

_____

_____

_____

_____

_____

_____

_____

_____

_____

_____

_____

_____

SCANS

Review the SCANS skills description on page 105. Identify up to eight volunteer, job, or homework activities:

1. _____
2. _____
3. _____
4. _____
5. _____
6. _____
7. _____
8. _____

On the worksheet on the next page, check the skills you used in these activities. Use the grid on page 108 as an example.

Exercise 5.7 Worksheet

Identify up to eight volunteer, job, or homework activities and check off which skills were used in each activity.

1	2	3	4	5	6	7	8	SCANS FOUNDATION

Basic Skills
Reading
Writing
Arithmetic
Listening
Speaking

Thinking Skills
Creative thinking
Decision making
Problem solving
Seeing things in the mind's eye
Knowing how to learn
Reasoning

Personal Qualities
Responsibility
Self-esteem
Cociability
Self-management
Integrity/honesty

SCANS COMPETENCIES

Resources
Time
Money
Material and facilities
Human resources

Interpersonal
Participates as member of a team
Teaches others new skills
Serves clients/customers
Exercises leadership
Negotiates
Works with diversity

Information
Acquires and evaluates info
Organizes and maintains info
Interprets and communicates info
Uses computers to process info

Systems
Understands systems
Monitors and corrects performance
Improves and designs systems

Technology
Selects technology
Applies technology to task
Maintains and troubleshoots equipment

Source: *School to Career Handbook* (VATEA funded project through the California Community Colleges, Chancellor's office, 1995).

Skills Review

List the skills that you have at present:

_____

_____

_____

_____

_____

Review your responses in the Assessing Your Skills activity on pages 100–101. What skills would you most like to use in your future career?

_____

_____

_____

_____

_____

Which of the above skills do you need to develop?

_____

_____

_____

_____

_____

How will you develop these skills?

_____

_____

_____

_____

_____

You have now identified your foundation—the areas in which you have been most effective and successful in your life. By examining these successes or achievements, you now know what you can do and what motivates you. It is especially important that you focus on skills you use and enjoy.

WWWebwise

For additional activities online, go to the WWWebwise module in Chapter 5 of the Companion Website.

Exercise Summary

Write a brief paragraph answering these questions.

What did you learn about yourself through these exercises? How does this knowledge relate to your career/life planning? How do you feel?

_____

_____

_____

_____

_____

_____

_____

_____

_____

_____

_____

_____

_____

_____

_____

_____

_____

_____

_____

_____

_____

_____

_____

_____

_____

_____

_____

_____

_____

_____

Go to page 207 of the chapter summaries and fill out the Chapter 5 exercise summary now.

The World of Work

CHAPTER 6
The World and You

CHAPTER 7
Information Integration

CHAPTER 8
Making Decisions

PART TWO

117

The World and You

Your assumptions, limitations, aspirations, dreams, and fantasies are all influenced by the spoken and unspoken rules and norms of the society in which you live.

In every society, even one as free as that of the United States, social and cultural traditions influence career choice. For example, it may still seem a little strange to us to hear the word *nurse* applied to a male health-care worker, even though both men and women are found in this profession. Old associations and stereotypes linger because of the many years during which societal limitations and expectations played a much greater role in determining career choices for men and women.

You have completed the personal assessment portion of your career fitness program. You have reviewed and analyzed your values, your interests, your personality, and your skills. Now you need to explore the world of work and assess where you best fit. In this chapter, you will learn about some of the important and exciting changes that are occurring in the workplace. These changes will affect the kinds of occupations available to you.

As you read about issues and trends in this chapter, think about your personal career profile and how it matches the opportunities that exist.

At the end of the chapter you will be able to . . .

- Identify personal beliefs and assumptions that will affect your career

- Recognize how social and cultural conditioning influences your career choice

- Identify trends that will affect your career planning through the next decade

- List changes in the workplace

- Recognize the skills employers expect in new employees

- Learn the value of a liberal arts degree

When one door closes,
another opens, but we often look
so long and regretfully upon the closed door,
that we do not see the ones which open for us.

ALEXANDER GRAHAM BELL

The first part of this chapter explores cultural norms, gender equity issues, cultural diversity, and ageism, as well as related factors that can constrict or expand your career options. The latter part of this chapter examines trends in the workforce as they relate to possible career choices. You will also explore careers for liberal arts and other nontechnical graduates and employer expectations of new hires, and you will complete some written exercises at the end of the chapter. The written exercises will help you to identify your own barriers, attitudes, and biases. This self-knowledge will assist you in better planning your future.

Societal Influences on Career Choices

Career planning does not happen in a vacuum. Your life situation influences the decisions you make and how you make them. The society in which you grow up, your background, your family, your peers, and the way you feel about yourself are all influences on the decisions you make. Sometimes these factors make it easier to choose and follow a career path. For instance, a friend or family member who encourages you in school and work efforts may help to build your confidence and therefore improve your chances of success in whatever field you choose. Or family support may allow you to devote full-time effort to schooling and thus more quickly complete your chosen degree.

However, social and cultural considerations, family, peers, and feelings about yourself can also act as obstacles to making and following through on decisions. For example, your time available for school may be limited by family responsibilities, or you may feel that the career you would like to pursue requires an advanced degree, or that it would not pay enough to support your family. Consider the following statements:

"I'm too old [or perhaps too far along in school] to start thinking about changing careers now."

"What I would really like to be is an engineer, but I've given up on that because I can't go to school full-time to get that kind of degree."

"I don't know whether I'm going to apply for that job or not. Besides, they're not going to hire a Latino."

"I'm not really qualified to do that kind of job, and my high school grades were weak. I was never good at schoolwork."

"Sure, I'd like to go back to school, but how could I get all the housework done, and who would look after the kids? There's no money for day care."

Do any of the preceding statements sound like some you have heard people say, or maybe even some you yourself have said or felt? They represent some of the most common obstacles that people face when making academic and career decisions. An obstacle to a satisfactory decision is anything or anyone who prevents you from adequately considering all the possible alternatives. For example, the people who say "I'm too old to start something new" when looking for a job will miss out by not even considering some positions for which they may be well qualified. Age stereotyping prevents these people from considering all the possible alternatives.

Striving for Equality in the Workforce

GENDER ROLES

As recently as 35 years ago, female students seeking career advice from school counselors were frequently encouraged to choose fields such as teaching and nursing. These choices were recommended both because they were "women's jobs" and because they fit best with the traditional female family role of mothering. It wasn't until the 1970s that newspapers no longer divided the classified employment ads into the categories of "men" and "women."

Within the past 30 years, school counselors began to recognize that female roles in society were expanding and that women could be doctors, engineers, and members of, in fact, any profession. Today, academic counselors are more aware of gender fairness issues (see the Equity Definitions box, below) and more often attempt to treat men and women similarly, without making judgments or assumptions about marriage and family roles.

As suggested above, many of our career and pay biases were based on the social norm of a "typical" four-member family in which the husband was the principal wage earner and the wife was primarily responsible for raising the children. Societal changes and evolutions have moved us away from these traditional roles and toward gender equity. Because many couples find it difficult, if not impossible, to manage a home and family on one income, both partners in today's "typical" marriage work outside the home. This major change has forced us (or permitted us) to rethink traditional male and female roles. Partners in a relationship are more likely to share home and child-rearing responsibilities.

Just as women's roles have changed over the past few decades, so too have men's roles undergone change. For example, some men may choose careers that don't require extensive travel or long work hours because they want and expect to assume an equal parenting role. Many women now play the role of primary breadwinner in a family. In some families, men are choosing to work or stay at home and take care of the children. Both traditional and nontraditional types of families face new challenges with each passing year. Finding reliable, affordable child care is a struggle for many parents, and this concern may influence career decisions and directions. Today, a great many families are single-parent households, in which the adult must combine the full-time job of earning a living with the all-consuming task of raising a family.

Equity Definitions

Affirmative action: Programs, policies, or procedures that attempt to overcome the effects of past discrimination, bias, and/or stereotyping.

Ageism: Any action or policy that discriminates on the basis of age, affecting employment, advancement, privileges, or rewards.

Americans with Disabilities Act (ADA): Legislation passed July 26, 1990, that prohibits discrimination on the basis of a disability.

Barriers: Anything that prevents a person from equal access to the use of goods, services, facilities, and so on. There are physical and architectural barriers (such as stairs) and there are attitudinal barriers (such as stereotyping).

Discrimination: Practices, policies, or procedures that are specifically prohibited by law; any action that limits or denies a person or group of persons opportunities, privileges, roles, or rewards on such prohibited bases as their sex, race, age, and so on.

Feminist: Any person (male or female) who believes that women should have political, economic, and social rights equal to those of men.

Gender bias: An attitude or behavior that r[...] adversely on a person or group because of g[...] but may not be covered under present legis[...] behavior resulting from the assumption that o[...] is superior to the other.

Gender fair: Practices and behaviors that treat[...] and females similarly; may imply separate but eq[...]

Gender role: Social behavior that is prescribe[...] defined for males and females according to tra[...] as contrasted with actual biological differences[...]

Gender stereotyping: Attributing behaviors[...] ties, interests, values, and roles to a person or[...] of persons on the basis of gender.

Nontraditional job: Working in a field or an[...] pation that typically employs 75 percent or m[...] the opposite gender (e.g., nursing employs [...] percent males; construction work employs [...] percent females).

Sexism: Any attitude, action, or institution tha[...] ordinates or assigns roles to a person or gr[...] persons based on gender. Sexism may be indi[...] cultural, or institutional; intentional or uninter[...] effected by omission or commission.

In an ideally unbiased society composed of 50 percent men and 50 percent women, it can be expected that most occupations would employ approximately 50 percent of each gender and would pay them like salaries for like work. However, in our society such equity is being achieved gradually. Exhibit 6.1 (later in the chapter) illustrates ongoing inequities in the types of jobs held by women and men.

Although you cannot predict the exact course of your life or your career, you can begin considering possible choices and how they relate to *you*. Take time now to anticipate challenges you may encounter in the future. Now is the time to plan. By setting objectives that lead toward accomplishment of a career goal, you may later avoid having to take a job just to pay the bills. It is now more important than ever to choose a career that truly reflects your interests and abilities, your values, your personality, and your life plan. The concept of gender equity means that everyone is free to explore a career of his or her choice.

AGE AND OPPORTUNITY

Ten years ago, there were 20 million people over age 65 in the United States. As we move into the 21st century, the figure is over 35 million, or 15 percent of the population. By 2020, the over-65 population could go as high as 53 million. There will be more single people older than 65, particularly women. Approximately 45 percent of all seniors are over 75. In fact, workers 55 and older are projected to increase from 12.9 percent in 2000 to 16.9 percent in 2010.

It should be noted that the number of people retiring at age 65 continues to decrease. Many victims of corporate downsizing are let go before becoming eligible for retirement pensions. And due to no-fault divorce laws and lack of retirement plans in the traditionally female occupations, many divorced women must continue to work long after their male counterparts have retired. If present trends continue, retirement-age single women will be the poorest segment of society.

Older workers competing in the workforce may face discrimination and the perception by employers that they are out-of-date or too old to learn. Although such ageism is illegal, it occurs. Young workers are valued for their energy, flexibility, and entry-level salaries. Some employers, however, may choose an older, more mature job candidate over a recent college graduate, in the belief that anyone, at any age, can display high energy and flexibility, but with age come maturity, reliability, problem-solving abilities, and a wealth of experience. As a prospective employee, it is your responsibility to know your assets, whether those of youth or maturity, and to highlight them at the right times with the right decision makers. The most effective way to deal with ageism (whether it's directed against your youth or lack of it) is to sell your present or prospective employer on how your age and particular experience are an asset to the job.

Many of today's retirement-age workers are finding satisfaction in the entry-level jobs once dominated by teenage workers, such as in fast-food and retail outlets. For some seniors, this work offers a social outlet, and the minimal pay is sufficient for workers whose income is supplemented by Social Security benefits.

People who live long, healthy lives may change careers frequently during their lifetimes, and their most satisfying and perhaps most financially rewarding career may come later in life: Novelist James Michener was first published after the age of 40; Colonel Sanders started Kentucky Fried Chicken after he was 50; Dr. Ruth became a celebrity talk-show sex therapist when she was 48; Sam Walton opened his first Wal-Mart at age 44; and Ted Turner started Cable News Network (CNN) at 42. Don't forget Margaret Mitchell, who won her first Pulitzer Prize, for *Gone with the Wind,* when she was 37; Senator Margaret Chase Smith, elected to the Senate for the first time when she was 49; Shirley Temple Black, named ambassador to Ghana at age 47; and Grandma Moses, who began a painting career at the age of 76!

Accentuate your assets

AFFIRMATIVE ACTION

Affirmative action has become a highly controversial and much-debated issue. Its advocates support policies and programs that increase opportunities for women, minorities, and other underrepresented groups. These

Women in the workplace

- In 1970 25 percent of women age 16 and over were in the labor force. Today, 60 percent of women work outside the home. Approximately 80 percent of women between 25 and 44 are in the workforce.

- In 1970, 30 percent of all mothers with children under 6 years old had paid employment. That figure has now increased to over 60 percent and is expected to rise to 75 percent within five years. Since 1970, households headed by women have increased 70 percent. Women are the sole earners in more than 18 percent of families. Of all families maintained by women, 27 percent are below the poverty level in income.

- Currently, a women earns, on average, 75 cents for every dollar earned by a man.

- Although percentages of women in nontraditional areas have increased, often the increase has occurred in the lower-paying jobs. About 25 percent of women work in what the U.S. Census labels "professional and technical jobs"; however, women are employed in only eight of the 50 job titles that comprise that area. Two-thirds of employed women hold clerical, service, nursing, and education jobs; these are traditionally low-paying occupations.

- Women make up over 48 percent of managers and 53 percent of professionals, including teachers and registered nurses. In the professions, women have made gains in the last 10 years and now comprise 30 percent of doctors and 20 percent of dentists. In such traditionally male jobs as pilots and navigators, women now make up 3.7 percent, up from 1.5 percent; among firefighters, women comprise 2.8 percent, up from 0.5 percent. Although women constitute 46 percent of the workforce, they fill only 10 percent of the top corporate positions.

- For women, the best paying jobs include pharmacist, lawyer, electronic and electrical engineer, computer systems analyst, and college faculty.

- Woman-owned businesses number approximately 10 million and employ more than 28 million people (35 percent more than all Fortune 500 companies employ worldwide). An estimated 40 to 50 percent of all woman-owned firms in this country are based in homes.

- Approximately 18 percent of military personnel are women.

WHAT DO YOU THINK?

1. Are these statistics true for women in the community where you live?

2. Why is it important to know these facts?

3. Why is it useful to know the best paying jobs for women?

4. How does knowing this information influence how you make your decision about your future career?

5. What challenges do women business owners face?

6. What suggestions would you give to help dual-income families handle the following:

   a. Housework

   b. Meal planning and preparation

   c. Child care

   d. Social activities

7. Name three successful women and explain what makes or made them successful.

Source: U.S. Department of Labor, Women's Bureau and Bureau of Labor Statistics, Report 960, May 2002 "Highlights of Women's Earnings in 2001."

 To answer these questions online, go to the *Facts and Figures* module in Chapter 6 of the Companion Website.

policies involve special consideration or set-aside positions for candidates who would—if hired, admitted, or promoted—increase the percentage of diverse members in a professional, academic, social, or business group. Many people oppose preferences or quota selection criteria and would prefer to see impartial screening of all candidates, regardless of gender, ethnicity, or socioeconomic status. A wide range of feelings and opinions exists on this issue. Compounding the controversy is a high demand for scarce resources that is pervasive in the fields of education, health and welfare services, and employment opportunities. Immigration, both legal and illegal, also complicates affirmative action decision making.

Recent decisions by state and federal courts have narrowed the scope of affirmative action by rejecting quotas or preferential formulas in favor of open and competitive criteria. These courts, however, have reversed unjustified discrimination in hiring, firing, and admissions and have also rejected forced early retirements due to age. Affirmative action remains a challenge in the 21st century.

OTHER CULTURAL CONSIDERATIONS: VALUING DIVERSITY

Today's workforce is more culturally diverse than ever, and this diversity will increase as the next wave of workers joins the workforce. To remain globally competitive, companies in the United States must improve training and advancement opportunities and use each employee's talent to the fullest. Stereotypes about and prejudices against particular ethnic or racial groups must be diminished and opportunities expanded for all workers.

Hispanics, African Americans, and Asian Americans are projected to make up approximately 30.8 percent of the workforce by the year 2005, with Caucasians declining to 69.2 percent. Moreover, projections for new workers entering the workplace indicate that in most urban centers, all minority group members together make up the majority of the entering workforce.

Legislation has also been enacted to eliminate discrimination against persons who have a disability. The Americans with Disabilities Act (ADA) prohibits discrimination on the basis of a disability and calls for the elimination of barriers, that is, anything that prevents a person or group of persons equal access to goods, services, and facilities. All places of employment must make reasonable accommodations for such otherwise qualified employees, including access to rooms and buildings, use of auxiliary aids, and services such as interpreters and hearing devices. Persons with disabilities should enjoy the same freedom of choice in making career decisions as those without disabilities, and this becomes more of a reality each year.

Companies are learning to respect diversity as an important component of the workplace. Just as many college campuses now require a course in diversity, firms are offering employee training in diversity to enable workers of differing backgrounds, educational levels, physical abilities, and cultures to accept and value one another. Whether in a social, political, academic, or economic context, we have begun to realize that our society will benefit from the fullest utilization of all its citizens and their many different talents.

The Changing Workplace

ifteen years ago terms such as the knowledge worker, global economy, computer literacy, learning organization, virtual workplace, small entrepreneurial business, woman-owned business, meeting customer needs, and temporary/leasing agencies would have been irrelevant in a book on career planning. But these terms represent trends, and the trends affect a large percentage of new entrants to the workforce. Therefore, it is to your advantage to understand the shifting nature of the workplace.

Manufacturing used to be the mainstay of the U.S. economy, but we are increasingly becoming a service-based economy, in which the majority of workers provide services (e.g., health care, retail, food preparation) instead of producing a commodity.

Many of today's jobs, such as Webmaster, diversity manager, and digital librarian, did not exist 15 years ago. There are more options for ways to perform your work, such as telecommuting or starting your own business. Today's worker faces less stigma associated with changing jobs or changing careers.

A further indicator of the changing workplace is shown in a 1999 California study. *The California Work and Health Survey* (of 2,044 California adults) (DiCamillo, 1999) found that only one-third of workers held traditional work schedules in which they worked eight-hour days five days per week. A quarter of the people did not work year-round, and 12 percent held multiple jobs. Three out of 10 were working at home at least part of the time. Four out of 10 workers said they had received a promotion or moved into a better job within the past year, with traditional workers more likely to be in this group. The poorly educated were far more likely to lose their jobs, as were those in traditionally high-turnover occupations such as clerical and sales. California is often considered the place where national trends begin. If this study is a prediction of the future, we are about to see a profound reorganization of work life that is influenced by such factors as the Internet, growth in home-based workers, and changing shopping patterns.

Implications

More job opportunities will be available at all hours of the day or night, any day of the week. Employees will have the option to work out of their homes or at the company workplace and will be expected to use technology to complete their assignments. Many workers will start as temporary employees and will need to prove their skills in order to be considered for long-term positions. More job opportunities will be available in the expanding service and information systems sectors. This is an exciting time to be looking for work, but it certainly requires that you understand the key trends shaping the workplace in order to find your niche.

THE NEED FOR KNOWLEDGE WORKERS

An employee becomes more valuable as he or she accumulates new skills. The challenge is to remain an outstanding contributor on the job (e.g., as a specialist) while learning new skills. As organizations downsize or flatten, employees must possess multiple skills, such as the ability to learn, use new technology, or sell a product. These people have an edge. They may, for example, be able to transfer from the training division, if it is reduced in size, to the sales division, and therefore remain employed.

There is still opportunity to move up. For example, Courtney got a job straight out of high school as a file clerk in a firm making shoulder pads. Learning new skills on the job, she began to manage the computer system and handle most payroll and personnel duties. Courtney is an example of a knowledge worker. A generation ago, the country shifted to a service-based economy in which fewer people produced industrial goods and instead provided services such as advertising or accounting or sold retail or wholesale products. Now we are in the midst of another shift toward a knowledge-based economy in which employees, like Courtney, will be expected to manage technology and information itself. The Bureau of Labor Statistics predicts in its occupational forecast for the year 2008 that the fastest-growing careers are all in high-skill, high-wage professional, managerial, and technical areas. This does not mean that service jobs will disappear. Industrial and service jobs such as autoworker and retail clerk will still be available. The fastest job growth, however, will be in those areas that involve the management and production of specialized knowledge.

Research the fastest growing careers

Sometimes it is necessary to spend time after work taking classes and studying job-related materials at home to get a head start. LaTricia was a public relations manager at a computer firm and had to spend as many as five hours a week on her own time becoming familiar with the company's new products. She also took a class in teaching English as a Second Language to become more sensitive to cultural diversity at a time when her business was becoming increasingly international.

Prepare for lifelong learning

Courtney and LaTricia are examples of workers continually learning new skills so they can be available for openings within their organizations and elsewhere. Remember, *luck is preparation meeting opportunity!*

THE IMPORTANCE OF NEW TECHNOLOGY

Technology is so much a part of everyday life that most of us don't stop to think about how much we depend on it. Think about what you did today since you woke up, and you will probably be able to name many activities that depended on technology. Just as it has affected our personal life, technology has revolutionized the kind of work we do, where we work, and how we complete our work. One in eight jobs is directly related to the field of high technology. Software engineer, CAD operator, computer programmer, and network administrator are probably familiar job titles. The real impact of technology, however, is on jobs that are indirectly related to technology. For example, today's travel agents must learn a special computer program in order to access information for their clients; ironically, these agents are becoming less crucial as clients make their own reservations directly over the Internet. Graphic designers rely on computer-aided drawings to produce high-quality, low-cost materials for clients. Even journalists are finding a niche online with the advent of Web-based magazines and news programs.

Technology has also affected where and how we do our work. Thanks to telecommuting, work does not need to happen in an office. Telecommuting means that you work from a home office, rather than at the company site, using phones, fax machines, modems, e-mail, and other communications tools to stay in touch with your coworkers and clients. Small businesses known as SOHOs (small office/home office) are being created and operated from home with the aid of technology.

A sample of the jobs that are able to accommodate telecommuting includes auto marketing consultant, reporter, investment adviser, investment research firm manager, online tutor, and virtual assistant. Cybercommuters, as some telecommuters are called, are becoming more common in all industries. Working anywhere will become even easier as cell phones, pagers, and other handheld devices become more powerful and less expensive. Additionally, all information required by a small business will be accessible over the Internet.

Think about technology and careers on a continuum. On one end are jobs that are directly related to technology, such as computer programmer. These are the jobs that produce the technology we use daily. These are the jobs of the new economy. The key industries that are expanding the fastest are those in which the main product or service is information. As you move along the continuum, jobs are less directly tied to technology. Somewhere in the middle of the continuum are administrative assistants who use various software packages for word processing as well as those jobs that are influenced by technology. For example, teachers have vast amounts of information available for research articles over the Internet. The distance education teacher who teaches using technology will be in increased demand as more people try to learn at any time and any place. Such a teacher must be able to adapt to the changes in teaching that require the use of technology. Many jobs will be affected by advances in technology, and those persons who are comfortable with and knowledgeable about computers may be the best job candidates regardless of where their jobs fall on the continuum.

At the opposite end of the continuum are the jobs that are least influenced by technology. These are the jobs of the old economy. Those in construction, transportation, general manufacturing, and retail stores are furthest from the

FACTS AND FIGURES

The new economy vs. the old economy

NEW ECONOMY:

High-tech equipment software
Computer services
Financial services consulting
Communications media
E-commerce
Distance education

OLD ECONOMY:

Construction/transportation
Utilities
Manufacturing
Wholesalers/retailers
Personal services/health care
Education

The World and You CHAPTER 6 129

technology end of the job continuum and must deal with real-time issues that affect the bottom line. These industries take longer to lower costs, develop new products, and increase profits. In manufacturing, new technology that reduces costs may also reduce the need for some employees, resulting in lay-offs. Furthermore, wages in these industries tend to rise with the cost-of-living adjustments rather than through company profits.

The contrast between the new and old economy can be seen in the salaries offered to new college graduates. According to recent data from the National Association of Colleges and Employers, starting salaries for accounting, information systems, and engineering graduates are approximately 25 percent higher than those of liberal arts graduates, as noted in Exhibit 6.4.

According to the "Digital Economy 2002" report by the Office of Policy Development, Economics, and Statistics Administration, average wages per worker in information technology (IT) industries are twice the national average. IT industry workers earn on average $73,800 compared with $35,000 for all workers engaged in private non-farm industries. (More than half of IT jobs are "high skilled" and require at least an associate degree.)

Information technology employment also provides self-employed and independent contractors the flexibility and mobility to work outside of a traditional organization. Although these temporary workers often earn less in wages and benefits and have less security than permanent workers, many IT workers prefer to be independent because they can command comparably high salaries and move from one employment situation to another with relative ease.

Implications

When choosing the industry that you wish to enter, the new economy provides both opportunities and challenges. For higher skilled workers, the new economy offers strong demand and high wages. Lower skilled workers, however, are seeing skill requirements rise. IT allows greater flexibility in working arrangements, letting employers quickly hire and release workers in response to changing market conditions and allowing workers to move more easily from job to job.

THE GLOBAL ECONOMY AND THE CHANGING CORPORATE STRUCTURE

A decade ago the United States was generating most of the world's technology; today that figure has diminished. The United States is striving to develop a more global economy by establishing trade agreements with other countries, such as the North American Free Trade Agreement (NAFTA). Global competition and multinational corporations will continue to influence the business world and our economy. Today it is not just the Fortune 500 companies, such as General Electric, IBM, and AT&T, that conduct business and have offices throughout the world. Employees wishing to advance in this new international economy must have the ability to speak more than one language and understand the cultural customs of other countries.

In today's global economy, NAFTA has created a need for multilingual talents. Asian investments in Latin America and Mexico are expanding. Many of the *maquiladora* (border) factories in Tijuana, for example, are run by Japanese, Chinese, and Korean corporations. Asian companies have invested billions in Mexico. Obviously, the ability to converse in several languages is an asset in the marketplace.

Today's organizations are flatter, leaner, more efficient

Success in the global economy requires innovative, high-quality, timely, customized, and efficiently produced products and flatter, leaner organizations. Successful companies need to have the following traits:

1. Maintaining a flat management structure that has shifted away from management-directed systems toward team-directed systems that require knowledgeable workers in each team, along with service providers and other self-supervising workers who are responsible for meeting the bottom line.

Virtual organizations are now more practical

2. Utilizing a virtual corporation by distributing design, marketing, and customer service operations across the globe through temporary partnerships that can focus on completing projects. Thus, many enterprises will ultimately become tripartite virtual partnerships. One unit will handle product development and engineering, another will cover marketing needs, and the third will do the production work. Increasingly, companies avoid building expensive, time-consuming in-house capabilities.

3. Creating even greater efficiencies. The production work is speeded up with computer systems called manufacturing execution systems that coordinate production. Such systems are able to cut assembly time by 80 percent!

4. Moving manufacturing plants to locations that offer availability of good educational institutions and low labor costs.

Outsourcing is on the rise

5. Purchasing product components from outside suppliers (outsourcing).

Use of temps is on the increase

6. Maintaining low numbers of permanent employees and using specialized teams of temporary employees on short-term projects.

7. Recruiting highly skilled workers worldwide who are knowledgeable about global issues.

Businesses are growing adaptable and flexible

8. Being able to evolve and adapt as a company. George Lucas' Industrial Light & Magic (ILM), one of the largest special effects film companies, started in a converted airplane hangar building models of battleships and clay miniatures for the original *Star Wars* movie and evolved to incorporate computers in office buildings and hundreds of ILM digital artists, modeling experts, and computer programmers working for months on "Episode II." ILM once thought it would be the electronic answer to all Hollywood projects but has found that it can be most profitable by focusing on larger and flashier projects. Similarly, such companies as Hewlett Packard and IBM have evolved from being large manufacturers to becoming service providers. One other factor requiring the need to adapt will be political trends in other countries. Most companies dealing in the global economy will be noticeably affected by international recessions and military conflicts.

E-commerce is increasing

9. Pursuing e-commerce. As businesses build websites to sell their goods and services to consumers, they are making it easier to transact business with their suppliers and distributors. Corporate information technology departments will shift their focus to Internet-based e-commerce products that increase corporate revenue and make customers happy. Some industry estimates show e-commerce spending quadrupled from about $12 billion in 1998 to $44 billion worldwide in 2002. Another research company pre-

dicted that e-commerce would add up to $1.3 trillion by 2003, accounting for 9.4 percent of total business-to-business sales. Although it is hard to imagine such large figures, consider that research by the U.S. Chamber of Commerce has shown that by March 2001, 26.6 percent of books, 23.4 percent of clothing and apparel, and about 20 percent of travel services were being sold by e-commerce. A report by the U.S. Commerce Department titled "The Emerging Digital Economy" concludes that information technology industries are growing at more than double the rate of the overall economy thanks to the acceptance and use of e-commerce.

10. Pursuing customization. Built-to-order products will proliferate. Just as Dell has been able to build customized computers that are ordered over the Internet, other industries, such as the automobile industry, are able to individualize orders. Web-based technology is contributing to this transformation.

11. Managing a mega-corporation effectively. The need for managers with a master's degree in business administration will continue to expand.

Implications

The main point for you to remember is that, in a global economy, the employee who helps the company remain competitive by being informed about technology, competition, and alternative ways to complete the job requirements will be the person who is most important to the company. Such employees will have the permanent jobs whereas others will be hired as temporary employees. The more skills that you can demonstrate to the employer, the more valuable you will be (as was mentioned in Chapter 5). For example, a software engineer at a telecommunications company who can also market her product to customers around the world will be considered a most valuable employee and most likely will be able to evolve with the expansion or changes that occur in her industry.

SMALL BUSINESSES

Small businesses are those companies that employ fewer than 500 employees. Fifty-two percent of all U.S. workers work in small businesses. More jobs are created by small businesses than by large corporations. During the 1970s, 9.6 million jobs were generated by firms with fewer than 20 employees; in contrast, the 1,000 largest firms created only 75,000 jobs. Between

---

FACTS AND FIGURES

Temporary work

In 1998, companies farmed out 15 percent of all manufacturing jobs. By 2000, they outsourced more than 40 percent. This means that contract employees held jobs formerly held by permanent employees. By 2002, 2 million people were estimated to be employed as temporary workers.

WHAT DO YOU THINK?

1. Why were manufacturing jobs being replaced?

2. Why do you agree or disagree with the following statements?

   - Temporary workers are replacing permanent workers.
   - It may be useful to start as a temp in order to get your foot in the door.
   - There are more temporary job ads and fewer full-time job ads in your own community.

3. Do you know anyone who started at a job as a temp?

4. Do you think that taking technology classes will improve your chances of getting hired?

 To answer these questions online, go to the *Facts and Figures* module in Chapter 6 of the Companion Website.

1981 and 1990, small firms created more than 20 million new jobs. If you want variety and responsibility and are results-oriented, a small business might be the place for you.

It is estimated nearly 50 million people have a home office with a personal computer. According to IDC/Link, a New York market research firm, 13 million Americans operated full-time businesses from their homes in the mid-1990s. It is estimated 14 million more have part-time home businesses and 8 million telecommute from home. The rest use their home office for work they bring from the outside office or for freelancing.

Small businesses strive to meet customer needs

Every day, small businesses are created to serve consumer needs. Did you know that the Home Shopping Network was created when a company that could not pay its bills instead gave its inventory to a TV executive? The executive needed to get rid of the inventory and announced the availability of the materials on his network. Everything sold within two hours!

WOMAN-OWNED BUSINESSES

It is estimated that more than 10 million companies are owned by women. It is also estimated that one in three American workers is employed in a woman-owned business. Between 40 and 50 percent of these companies are home-based, according to a study by the National Foundation for Women Business Owners. More than 70 percent of these businesses are concentrated in the services and retail trade. More than 60 percent of woman-owned businesses got their start as home-based operations.

TEMPORARY AGENCIES/ LEASING COMPANIES

Temporary employment agencies, in addition to their traditional business of providing secretarial and clerical professionals on a contract basis, now provide employees in such areas as accounting, health care, telemarketing, the paralegal field, and computers. Technical services contracting firms place a range of engineering and computer professionals as well as technicians and draftspeople in temporary positions. If this trend toward growing numbers of temporary employees continues as predicted, many people will find themselves working for an employee-leasing firm. Kelly Services, one of the largest temporary service agencies, expanded 800 percent in one five-year period.

Temporary employment is also a method of obtaining permanent employment. One multimedia graphic artist took temporary work through an agency and changed jobs four times in his first year, with a typical contract

---

FACTS AND FIGURES

Fastest growing small-business-dominated industries

Computer programming

Management consulting

Residential building construction

Job training services

Credit reporting and investment firms

Providers of day care

Counseling and rehabilitation services

WHAT DO YOU THINK?

Does knowing that these are the fastest growing small businesses influence your education and career decision making? What other factors must be considered?

Source: "U.S. Business Facts," U.S. Chamber of Commerce Statistics and Research Center, 2002.

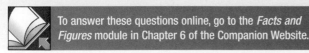

To answer these questions online, go to the *Facts and Figures* module in Chapter 6 of the Companion Website.

lasting about two months. Once he developed a reputation, however, potential clients began seeking him out, so he worked less through temporary agencies and agents. It has been reported that approximately 13 percent of the U.S. labor force are independent contractors, temporary workers, and self-employed individuals.

Trends: The Twenty-First Century

It helps to have a picture of tomorrow's opportunities when defining a reasonable job target. For example, you might guess that now is not the time to prepare for a lifelong job in an automotive assembly plant. Such positions will likely be phased out in the next decade by computerized robots. In fact, 80 percent of General Motors employees now work at jobs other than assembly.

Additionally, during a recession fewer college graduates secure college level jobs after graduation, and those without a degree may have to get experience as temps before they can get hired permanently. In this situation, many college graduates opt for graduate school, hoping that the recession will be over by the time they are again ready for the job market. The good news is that for the next two decades more people will be retiring than entering the job market. With 76 million "baby boomers" (people born between 1945 and 1960) predicted to retire in the next three decades and only 46 million people in "Generation X" (children of baby boomers) waiting to replace them, a shortage of 4 to 6 million workers is predicted by 2010.

Graduate school may be an option

These statistics take into consideration that large numbers may delay retirement for five to ten years due to cost of living expenses and not having saved enough for retirement. It is also assumed that some companies will be hiring back retired employees to fill vacancies. In fact, IBM Canada and Monsanto have pioneered the use of on-call retirees over the years. These options may slow the need for new permanent employees, but eventually, good temps will have a chance at securing these jobs.

However, the really good news is that in selected fields we are already hearing about shortages. There is a large demand for nurses, pharmacists, teachers, health care technicians, skilled contractors, electricians, plumbers, child care workers, firefighters, and law enforcers than people being trained in these fields. Additionally, the fields of accounting and auditing are expected to expand some 20 percent in the next decade. Finally, a very large number of workers are due to retire from all levels of government work.

Be aware of in-demand careers

LIBERAL ARTS MAJORS HAVE MARKETABLE SKILLS

Remember what you read in Chapter 5 about the value of a liberal arts major? Liberal arts refers to majors such as art, English, history, psychology, sociology, speech, or any degree that is considered a bachelor of arts (B.A.). Such majors are preparation for a variety of careers. Pursuing a liberal arts major enables you to develop skills such as problem solving, critical thinking, creative thinking, systems thinking, interpersonal savvy, resource management, communication, and the ability to deal with ambiguity, teamwork, research, and helps you learn how to learn! Employers will expect that you are able to scan information quickly and select what is relevant for your job. You will be

Meet Jessica

Jessica was a political science major who graduated from a small liberal arts college in Collegeville, Pennsylvania, in 2000. She had begun her education majoring in English, then switched to French before finally settling on political science. She loved learning everything and had a hard time narrowing her studies to one major. She finally settled on political science by using the College Career and Planning Center, taking some career assessments, and doing some information interviews. While visiting Washington, D.C., she visited with a French diplomat to the United States, and while visiting New York, she talked to a relative who worked for a big public relations firm. Additionally, Jessica was captivated by the excitement of touring Wall Street.

By graduation time, Jessica had used the College Career and Planning Center and gained multiple job offers from firms ranging from public relations to financial services and marketing. Fortunately the job market was expanding and she had choices. She had been counseled to consider graduate school and had taken the Graduate Record Exam and scored well, but she was tired of college. She took a job with the Vanguard Group, an investment company, and now helps employees of the firms' corporate clients manage their 401(k) retirement accounts. Vanguard provided her with six weeks of training, and Jessica was able to develop her job her own way (just as she had learned to do in her class assignments when she was in college). However, by 2002, the job was not as exciting as she had envisioned. Her industry was very stressful, and people actually grew upset with *her* whenever the stock market went down.

Jessica went back to her college's Career Center for Alumni and discussed her concerns. The career counselor suggested that she see if she could focus on some specialty industries at Vanguard in order to learn about other industries that might be part of her future direction. She found that she could add a specialty and selected the health care industry. When she met with clients in the health care industry, she actually interviewed them as well as giving them

expected to have a high level of reading comprehension and be able to prepare documents that are clear, concise, logical, and easy to understand. Such skills are necessary for this job market. You will be even better prepared for the 21st-century job market if you have also taken classes or developed skills related to business, computer software, or entrepreneurial thinking.

Although graduates with a degree in business, computer science, and engineering are often in greater demand because their curriculum has provided them with job-specific skills, there have always been employers who hire "liberal arts" graduates because their broad skills provide a strong foundation for job training in many fields. And such employers often find that liberal arts majors are excellent employees. One example is a political science major who graduated from a small liberal arts college. She had begun her education majoring in English, then switched to French before finally settling on political science. When she graduated she found a job with a financial services group. Vanguard provided her with six weeks of training, and she was able to continue to develop on the job. (See Meet Jessica.)

Develop transferable skills

Getting the right skills and education today will give you an advantage tomorrow. Over 80 percent of jobs require some postsecondary education assistance with their 401(k) retirement plans. She found that the issues facing hospitals really interested her. Additionally, some of her clients told her that there were great needs for her expertise in the human resources department, and if she had a master's degree in health care administration she could work in industry or government or be a consultant.

Jessica is now pondering going back to college for a master's degree and has her resume out to human resources departments at several hospitals and state and county health departments. Jessica is also happy that she has already scored well on the GRE and does not have to go back and study for it while she is under so much stress. Having taken the GRE has made her more open to graduate school, and she was happy to learn that she could attend graduate school after work and on weekends if she decided to go back to school. Having been out of college for two years and finding that her job was getting more stressful rather than more interesting, Jessica is now ready to consider graduate school.

1. Is your major related to any job that you have had?

2. Could you imagine yourself in a job unrelated to your field of study and experience?

3. Do you think Jessica made a good first choice out of college, or should she have done more investigation about the stresses related to her job?

4. What alternatives would you have explored that are not mentioned in this story?

5. What do you think about attending graduate school to expand your options?

 To answer these questions online, go to the *Real Stories* module in Chapter 6 of the Companion Website.

---

or training. Computer literacy and familiarity with several software programs are a necessity in many jobs. As discussed in Chapter 5, SCANS skills—such as reading, writing, communications, the ability to reason, problem solving, and the ability to learn on the job—will make you competitive in today's job market. If you are a college student, take advantage of the computer access that is available at school and learn as much as possible about using computers. Familiarize yourself with the Internet and learn to do your research online. When you get into the job market, you will find that many companies are relying on the Internet for their own internal communications.

LIFELONG LEARNING

More important than knowing what jobs will be available is being *flexible*—having the ability to adapt to this changing world of work. It is estimated that 40 percent of the jobs that will be available in the year 2010 have yet to be created. Thus you cannot obtain training specifically for every career change you may encounter, but you can develop learning skills that will prepare you for training in new job skills and applications. It is also possible that, due to advancing technology and other factors, you may change careers not just once but many times during your life. Even if this is not the case and you move along one career path throughout your life, you will need to continue educating yourself just to keep up with technological change. The trend toward lifelong learning is evidenced by the fact that several million people over age 40 were in college in 2000, compared to only 477,000 in 1970. Additionally, an increasing number of people are enrolled in corporate universities. Corporate universities and colleges range from company-run classes designed primarily for that company's employees to programs run by companies that confer credible degrees such as an associate's degree or a bachelor's degree.

Explore distance learning

The days when formal education ended after college or graduate school have disappeared. Now that people work at all hours to keep in touch with colleagues all over the world, continuing education must be available at times to fit into their busy schedules. The Internet is bringing such education to people whenever they have time for it. For example, one sales rep manager sometimes plugs in his laptop at midnight whether he is in a hotel room when away from home on business or at his home office (also known as the family room at other times of the day). He downloads lectures, submits papers, joins in student discussions, and even gets his grades over the Net.

Corporate universities offer options

Just 23 million Americans were enrolled in continuing education programs in 1984; that figure is closer to 80 million now and is predicted to be over 100 million by 2007, according to the National Center for Educational Statistics. About 400 company-run universities operated in the United States in 1988, but there are now more than 1,600, according to the Corporate University Xchange, a New York research and consulting firm. Thus, many adults are getting continuing education (also known as training classes) through their company's corporate university or training department. Motorola, for example, provides courses for 100,000 of its employees every year at 100 sites around the world. It is becoming the norm for those over age 25 to go to college. According to the National Center for Educational Statistics, 41 percent of those attending colleges and universities are over age 25. In addition, professionals who must take continuing education to renew their licenses are opting for Web-based classes.

The Internet has influenced the increase by providing a way for corporations to deliver training to their employees at any time of the day or night as well as anywhere the Web can be accessed. Additionally, prestigious universities are offering reputable degrees over the Net, thus encouraging more people to get their degrees than ever before. Whereas 710,000 U.S. students were in distance education in 1998 (about 5 percent of the approximately 15 million higher-education students), about 2.23 million out of 15.1 million students—15 percent—were online by 2002.

Implications

To maintain your currency in your career, you must get updated training throughout your life. Be sure that the training institution you choose is considered reputable by your employer before enrolling for a program of study. Make sure that you have the time management skills and self-discipline to

Multimedia Revolution Ignites Creative Industries

Film, animation, entertainment, fashion, graphic design, publishing, architecture, and other media-related fields are creating a new surge of employment opportunities. The evolution of this trend is closely related to the development of computer software and hardware.

Digital Domain, which produced special effects for the movie *Apollo 13,* employs artists, digital designers, and technicians. From film special effects, this firm has expanded to commercials, music videos, CD-ROM games, and theme park attractions—with additional plans to be involved in high-resolution, interactive programming delivered over cable.

Although multimedia may best be known for the CD-ROMs and DVDs that combine text, sound, pictures, and video, the technology is advancing into new forms. One form is virtual reality, in which special glass-es or headsets allow a person to perceive an experience as if it were real. Another form of multimedia technology created "smart" cameras that recognize faces and facial expressions in order to identify people for security systems. Another application of the technology is evident in incorporating animation into live-action film. The film industry labels this animation *digital effects.* It can be seen regularly in commercials (e.g., cola-drinking polar bears, flirtatious M & Ms, and an athletic Pillsbury doughboy) and in movies such as *Stuart Little* and *The Lord of the Rings.* Employers emphasize they are looking for good technicians who have developed artistic talents and technological skills. The digital designer must understand lighting, texture, and motion. Such professionals are rewarded with salaries ranging from $40,000 to over $150,000.

---

complete the required studying and research if you choose to take classes on the Web.

As it gets easier to study anytime and anywhere and to earn college credit for such work, more people will be getting college degrees. Already some say that as more people get degrees, jobs that did not require a degree in the past will require a degree in the future. This trend means that you will have to earn a college degree in order to remain competitive in the future job market.

Many of the best job opportunities during the next decade will demand that applicants have cross-functional training to broaden their qualifications. Dual majors, interdisciplinary programs, and foreign languages can make a difference in the competitive, increasingly global job market. Job applicants are also being informed they need both people skills and technical skills in order to be competitive. Today's college graduates are finding that, to compete for the best jobs, they must commit to lifelong continuing education to bolster their job skills and prepare for career changes.

JOB GROWTH TRENDS

If you aren't interested in a career that requires a four-year degree, there will always be a need in society for people selling merchandise, running businesses, maintaining homes, caring for children, working in restaurants, attending to health and fitness needs, and working in a variety of trades that may or may not require training beyond high school. Many of these fields are experiencing greater demand due to the important sociological changes

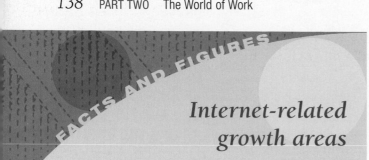

Internet-related growth areas

1. Webmaster, webpage designer

2. Internet security

3. Cybrarian (or cyber-librarian)

4. Geographic Information Systems (GIS)

5. Multimedia designer (art and computer backgrounds); virtual set designer

6. Intellectual property lawyer

7. Online content developer

8. Artificial intelligence programmer

mentioned previously in this chapter and the increase in the number of two–wage earner households. Many of the jobs listed in the box titled "Job Growth Throughout the Next Decade," and later in Exhibits 6.5 and 6.6, do not require a bachelor's degree.

The last section of this chapter includes exhibits indicating the fastest-growing jobs and the largest job markets. Again, it must be emphasized that many of these jobs require only one or two years of postsecondary education, and many are in the fields of health, computers, law (e.g., prison guards, paralegals), and education. However, the number of new jobs open to college graduates will rise twice as fast as the number of jobs requiring short-term training. And jobs requiring master's degrees are predicted to grow 30 percent over the next decade!

Finally, many of the fastest-growing occupations that require a college degree are related to the following titles: systems analysts, computer engineers, physical therapists, managers, human services workers, and educators.

Please note Exhibits 6.5 through 6.9 describe two different categories of job growth: "fastest growing" and "largest job growth." The *fastest growing occupations,* such as computer software engineer, are growing in terms of percentage of total number of current jobs, e.g., growth from 380,000 to 760,000 in 2010 is 100 percent growth for this occupation. The *largest job growth* is stated in terms of how many people are currently in this occupation and how many more will be in this occupation by 2010, e.g., retail salespersons numbered 4,109,000 in 2000 and will number 4,619,000 by 2010, so it is one of the largest job growth categories in terms of absolute numbers even though it is expanding only 12 percent.

Although it is helpful to take growth trends into consideration as you explore your options, it is not necessary to choose a career path only in the areas most likely to have openings. In fact, as will be discussed in the job search strategy section of this book, the best direction to follow is most often *directly toward what you really want to do*. The key is *desire*. Desire plus talent and perseverance gets people jobs in even the tightest job markets.

Finding Your Place in a Changing World

How do all these social and cultural changes affect you? Your expectations about your future are influenced by your early socialization and by the culture that surrounds you. (Look back at Super's theory in Chapter 1.) Career opportunities can be discovered and pursued through family, childhood play, school experiences, volunteer work, and early work activities. *The degree of satisfaction you*

Job Growth Throughout the Next Decade

- **Health services.** Demand will be especially great for primary-care workers such as nurse practitioners, nutrition counselors, gerontological social workers, radiology technicians, respiratory care technicians, home health-care aides, and health service administrators.

- **Hotel management and recreation.** This category includes restaurants, resorts, and travel services, as well as opportunities in conference planning.

- **Food service.** Managers and chefs will be in demand for all those restaurants and hotel kitchens, as well as for food processing plants and labs. Specialty restaurants will continue to expand.

- **Engineering.** Specializations in high demand will include robotics, aviation, biotechnology, manufacturing technology, and civil engineering.

- **Environmental sciences.** Specializations include hazardous waste management, environmental impact research, conservation and environmental preservation, and alternative fuels.

- **Basic science.** Biogenetic engineering will be an important field in the next decade, as will chemistry (especially food science) and fiber optics.

- **Computer science, information systems.** Opportunities will continue to be strong in design, engineering, programming, networking, and maintenance.

- **Business services.** Growing fields will be accounting, forensic accounting, statistical analysis, and payroll management. Many jobs will be filled by temporary workers. In management, managers of telecommunications, environmental protection, and security systems will be in demand.

- **Human resources and personnel.** The field of employee management continues to grow as a result of legislation concerning employee rights, new payroll requirements, and new compensation options. Specialists are needed to handle such responsibilities as job evaluation, hiring and firing, benefits planning, and training.

- **Financial services.** This field includes financial planning and portfolio management. An increased demand for temp employees and employees specializing in retirement and estate planning is expected.

- **Educational services and products.** Demand is growing in the school system, where both teachers and administrators will be needed to meet the changing needs of immigrants and the baby boomers' children (and grandchildren!). Corporate America will be hiring educators and trainers to teach literacy skills such as English. High-demand subjects include math, science, computer software, interactive learning modalities, and foreign languages such as Spanish, Japanese, and Chinese. The latest need for educational products is on the Internet, where new interactive products are being introduced daily.

- **Maintenance and repair.** These are the people who will take care of all the equipment that will keep tomorrow's world running, e.g., electricians, plumbers, and network maintenance personnel.

- **Artistic/multimedia.** Writers, entertainers, party planners, artists, digital designers, animators, and graphic designers will have good prospects but must be entrepreneurial types.

For specific predictions regarding growing job fields, see Exhibits 6.1 through 6.9 at the end of this chapter. Because data are presented from several sources, figures may differ from exhibit to exhibit for the same profession and are meant to be representative.

find in work and in life depends on your finding opportunities to develop and use your abilities, interests, values, and personality traits.

Unfortunately, opportunity is not distributed equally throughout society. You may feel limited economically, academically, or by family responsibilities. Opportunities may be limited by gender stereotyping, by educational requirements, by discrimination, or by the changing economy. However, as perceptions change, as laws change, as the economy becomes more global and requires employers to appreciate and utilize diverse human talents, all women and men should feel free to choose and train for the type of career that best suits their interests and talents.

If you are experiencing (or worrying about) limitations of one type or another, seek help in overcoming them. Talk to a career or academic counselor, or seek help from a support group or your family. As you read this book, you are preparing for the career that best fits you. Don't let the world set unnecessary limitations on your plans and goals. Instead, use this oppor-

EXHIBIT 6.1   *Nontraditional occupations for women.* (Numbers in thousands.)*

OCCUPATIONS	EMPLOYED BOTH SEXES	EMPLOYED FEMALE	PERCENT FEMALE
Guards and police, excluding public service	786	189	24.0
Sales representatives in mining, manufacturing, and wholesale	1,480	351	23.7
Architects	214	50	23.4
Correctional institution officers	323	73	22.6
Supervisors, guards	62	14	22.6
Atmospheric and space scientists	14	3	21.4
Sheriffs, bailiffs, and other law enforcement officers	169	36	21.3
Drafting occupations	220	44	20.0
Dentists	170	34	20.0
Agricultural and food scientists	35	7	20.0
Supervisors, production occupations	1,076	212	19.7
Electrical and electronic technicians	475	93	19.6
Forestry and conservation scientists	26	5	19.2
Broadcast equipment operators	52	9	17.3
Managers, horticultural specialty farmers	247	4	16.7
Purchasing agents and buyers, farm products	12	2	16.7
Motion picture projectionists	6	1	16.7
Auctioneers	7	1	14.3
Police and detectives, public service	574	81	14.1
Surveying and mapping technicians	68	9	13.2
Meter readers	55	7	12.7
Announcers	49	6	12.2
Sales workers, motor vehicle and boats	329	33	10.0

tunity to reach beyond those limitations and take advantage of all possible opportunities. You will find that as you form definite plans and objectives, it becomes easier to move forward and to anticipate and avoid obstacles.

Facts and Figures

The exhibits that follow provide a cross-section of information about salaries, including pay equity across gender and race, and about occupations projected to experience good job growth. The exhibits are intended to provide general information of interest to you as you consider various career options. Although numerical data give the impression of being hard facts, remember that such information should be considered approximate. The future is only partially predictable, but it's a good idea to be informed!

Continued.

EXHIBIT 6.1

OCCUPATIONS	EMPLOYED BOTH SEXES	EMPLOYED FEMALE	PERCENT FEMALE
Supervisors, police and detective	111	11	9.9
Fishers, hunters, and trappers	42	4	9.5
Supervisors, mechanics and repairers	261	23	8.8
Groundskeepers and gardeners	876	69	7.9
Forestry and logging occupations	90	7	7.8
Physicists and astronomers	26	2	7.7
Garage and service station related occupations	173	13	7.5
Supervisors, related agricultural occupations	179	13	7.3
Air traffic controllers	28	2	7.1
Sales engineers	31	2	6.4
Garbage collectors	56	3	5.4
Truck drivers	3,156	167	5.3
Mechanical engineering technicians	19	1	5.3
Mechanics and repairers, excluding supervisors	4,547	214	4.7
Airplane pilots and navigators	136	5	3.7
Firefighter occupations	250	7	2.8
Supervisors, firefighting and fire protection	39	1	2.6
Construction trades	6,253	153	2.4
Tool programmers, numerical control	18	<1	<1.0
Roasting and baking machine operators, food	5	0	0

*Statistics are from 2001. Nontraditional occupations are those in which women make up 25 percent or less of the total employed.

Source: U. S. Department of Labor, Women's Bureau, February 2002.

6.2 *2001 median weekly earnings of the nation's full-time workers over 16.*

| | Weekly Median Income | |
Type of Worker	Women	Men
Caucasians:	$ 521.00	$ 694.00
African Americans:	451.00	518.00
Hispanics:	385.00	438.00

- Median weekly earnings of all workers: $ 591.50

- Women's earnings as percent of men's earnings: 76%

Source: U.S. Department of Labor, Bureau of Labor Statistics, May 2002.

6.3 *Median earnings in 2000.*

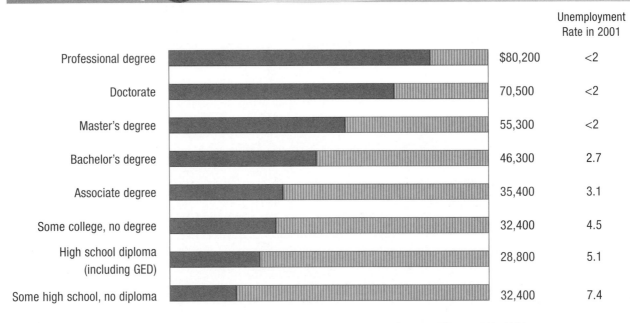

	Median earnings	Unemployment Rate in 2001
Professional degree	$80,200	<2
Doctorate	70,500	<2
Master's degree	55,300	<2
Bachelor's degree	46,300	2.7
Associate degree	35,400	3.1
Some college, no degree	32,400	4.5
High school diploma (including GED)	28,800	5.1
Some high school, no diploma	32,400	7.4

Source: U. S. Department of Labor, Bureau of Labor Statistics, *Occupational Outlook Quarterly,* Winter 2000–2001.

HOW MUCH IS A DEGREE WORTH? Earning a professional or doctorate degree could be worth millions in added income over 40 years.

Degree	Income
Professional or doctorate degree	$2.8 million
Master's degree	$2.3 million
Bachelor's degree	$2 million
Two-year associate degree	$1.5 million
High school diploma	$369,818

Source: Data from *Human Resources Review,* May 2002.

Representative starting salaries for college graduates, 1999 and 2003.   EXHIBIT **6.4**

ASSOCIATE DEGREE	1999, RANGE
Business Management	$21,600–69,600
Computer Maintenance Tech	$14,040–31,280
Registered Nurse	$15,600–51,960
Radiology Tech	$32,148–53,316
Respiratory Tech	$18,000–34,836

Source: EUREKA, California Entry Salary 1999.

BACHELOR'S DEGREE		2003
Engineering	Electrical	$50,615
	Computer	$52,722
	Mechanical	$48,115
	Civil	$41,541
	Chemical	$51,301
	Computer Science	$44,678
Business	MIS	$40,566
	Business Administration	$36,634
	Marketing	$35,698
	Accounting	$42,005
	Economics/Finance	$40,413
Humanities/	English/Liberal Arts	$29,586
Social Science	Psychology	$27,194
	Political Science	$35,594

Source: NACE (National Association of Colleges and Employers), Winter 2003 press release summarizing Winter 2003 Salary Survey.

6.5   *Fastest-growing occupations, projected between 1998 and 2008 by level of education and training.**

EDUCATION/TRAINING CATEGORY	FASTEST-GROWING OCCUPATIONS	
First professional degree	Veterinarians Chiropractors Physicians	Lawyers Clergy
Doctoral degree	Biological scientists Medical scientists	College and university faculty Physicists and astronomers
Master's degree	Speech-language pathologists and audiologists Archivists, curators, and conservators Physical therapists	Urban and regional planners Counselors
Work experience plus bachelor's or higher degree	Engineering, science, and computer systems managers Medical and health services managers Advertising, marketing, and public relations managers	Artists and commercial artists Management analysts
Bachelor's degree	Computer engineers Computer systems analysts Database administrators	Physicians assistants Residential counselors
Associate degree	Computer support specialists Paralegals and legal assistants Health information technicians	Physical therapy assistants and aides Respiratory therapists
Postsecondary vocational training	Data processing equipment repairers Surgical technologists Central office and PBX installers and repairers	Emergency medical technicians Manicurists
Work experience in a related occupation	Private detectives and investigators Detectives and criminal investigators Instructors, adult (nonvocational) education	Lawn service managers Office and administrative support supervisors
Long-term on-the-job training (more than 12 months)	Desktop publishing specialists Correctional officers Sheriffs and deputy sheriffs	Police patrol officers Telephone and cable TV line installers
Moderate-term on-the-job training (1–12 months)	Medical assistants Social and human services assistants Electronic semiconductor processors	Dental assistants Models, demonstrators, and product promoters
Short-term on-the-job training (up to 1 month)	Personal care and home health aides Bill and account collectors Ambulance drivers and attendants, except emergency medical technicians	Adjustment clerks Teacher assistants

*Keep in mind that the term *fast-growing* may be misleading in the sense that if the occupation employs small numbers of people to begin with, even a 100 percent growth would still mean few overall employment opportunities. See Exhibit 6.6 for occupations with largest overall job growth, in other words, the occupations that employ large numbers of people and have good job growth.

Source: U.S. Department of Labor, *Occupational Outlook Handbook,* Bureau of Labor Statistics.

6.6

High paying, fast-growing job openings for new entrants in occupations that usually require postsecondary education or more than one year of training, projected 2000–2010.

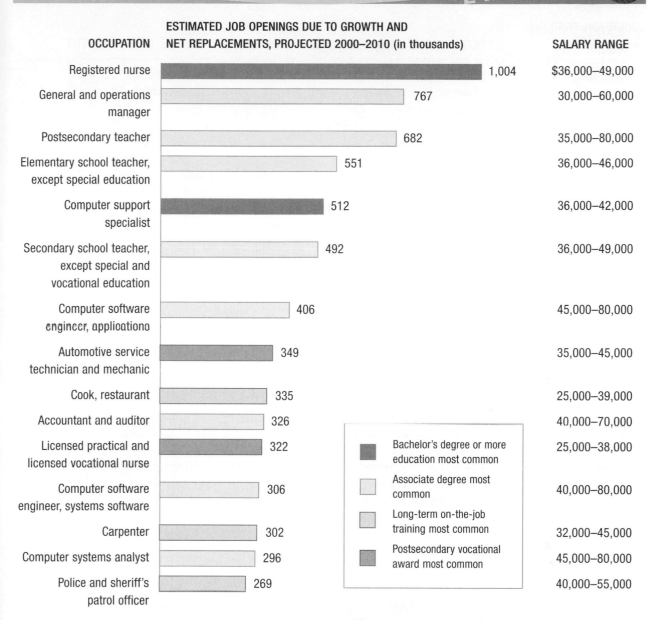

OCCUPATION	ESTIMATED JOB OPENINGS DUE TO GROWTH AND NET REPLACEMENTS, PROJECTED 2000–2010 (in thousands)	SALARY RANGE
Registered nurse	1,004	$36,000–49,000
General and operations manager	767	30,000–60,000
Postsecondary teacher	682	35,000–80,000
Elementary school teacher, except special education	551	36,000–46,000
Computer support specialist	512	36,000–42,000
Secondary school teacher, except special and vocational education	492	36,000–49,000
Computer software engineer, applications	406	45,000–80,000
Automotive service technician and mechanic	349	35,000–45,000
Cook, restaurant	335	25,000–39,000
Accountant and auditor	326	40,000–70,000
Licensed practical and licensed vocational nurse	322	25,000–38,000
Computer software engineer, systems software	306	40,000–80,000
Carpenter	302	32,000–45,000
Computer systems analyst	296	45,000–80,000
Police and sheriff's patrol officer	269	40,000–55,000

Legend:
- ■ Bachelor's degree or more education most common
- □ Associate degree most common
- □ Long-term on-the-job training most common
- ■ Postsecondary vocational award most common

Among occupations that usually require at least a bachelor's degree, those expected to have the most openings for new entrants are general and operations manager (767,000), postsecondary teacher (682,000), and elementary school teacher (551,000). Postsecondary teachers include community college professors, who need at least a master's degree, and college professors, who need a doctorate in a specialty.

Carpenter and restaurant cook are projected to top the list for occupations that usually require long-term or on-the-job training, with a combined total of 637,000 openings for new workers. Of occupations that usually require a postsecondary vocational degree, automotive service technician and mechanic and registered nurse will have the most openings; combined, these account for more than 1 million openings.

Source: U.S. Department of Labor, *Occupational Outlook Quarterly,* Summer 2002 (Vol. 46, Number 2), Bureau of Labor Statistics (www.bls.gov/opub/ooq/oochart.htm).

6.7 *Occupations with largest increase, 1998–2008.*

EDUCATION/TRAINING CATEGORY	OCCUPATIONS HAVING THE LARGEST NUMERICAL INCREASE IN EMPLOYMENT	
First professional degree	Physicians Lawyers Clergy	Veterinarians Pharmacists
Doctoral degree	College and university faculty Biological scientists	Medical scientists Physicists and astronomers
Master's degree	Counselors Physical therapists Speech-language pathologists and audiologists	Psychologists Librarians
Work experience plus bachelor's or higher degree	General managers and top executives Engineering, science, and computer systems managers Advertising, marketing, and public relations managers	Management analysts Financial managers
Bachelor's degree	Computer systems analysts Computer engineers Teachers, secondary school	Social workers Teachers, elementary school
Associate degree	Registered nurses Computer support specialists Paralegals and legal assistants	Dental hygienists Electrical and electronic technicians and technologists
Postsecondary vocational training	Licensed practical nurses Automotive mechanics Hairstylists and cosmetologists	Emergency medical technicians Data processing equipment repairers
Work experience in a related occupation	Office and administrative support supervisors Marketing and sales worker supervisors Blue-collar worker supervisors	Food service and lodging managers Teachers and instructors, vocational education and training
Long-term on-the-job training (more than 12 months)	Corrections officers Maintenance repairers, general utility Police patrol officers	Cooks, restaurant Carpenters
Moderate-term on-the-job training (1 to 12 months)	Social and human services assistants Instructors and coaches, sports and physical training Packaging and filling machine operators	Medical assistants Dental assistants
Short-term on-the-job training (up to 1 month)	Retail salespersons Truck drivers, except driver/sales workers Personal care and home health aides	Office clerks, general Cashiers

Source: U.S. Department of Labor, *Occupational Outlook Handbook,* Bureau of Labor Statistics.

Employment projections: The 15 fastest-growing occupations 2000–2010.   EXHIBIT 6.8

(Numbers in thousands of jobs)	Employment		Change		Quartile rank by 2000 median hourly earnings*	Education and training category
Occupation	2000	2010	Number	Percent		
Computer software engineers, applications	380	760	380	100	1	Bachelor's degree
Computer support specialists	506	996	490	97	2	Associate degree
Computer software engineers, systems software	317	601	284	90	1	Bachelor's degree
Network and computer systems administrators	229	416	187	82	1	Bachelor's degree
Network systems and data communications analysts	119	211	92	77	1	Bachelor's degree
Desktop publishers	38	63	25	67	2	Postsecondary vocational award
Database administrators	106	176	70	66	1	Bachelor's degree
Personal and home care aides	414	672	258	62	4	Short-term on-the-job training
Computer systems analysts	431	689	258	60	1	Bachelor's degree
Medical assistants	329	516	187	57	3	Moderate-term on-the-job training
Social and human service assistants	271	418	147	54	3	Moderate-term on-the-job training
Physician assistants	58	89	31	53	1	Bachelor's degree
Medical records and health information technicians	136	202	66	49	3	Associate degree
Computer and information systems managers	313	463	150	48	1	Bachelor's or higher degree, plus work experience
Home health aides	615	907	291	47	4	Short-term on-the-job training

*The quartile rankings of Occupational Employment Statistics annual earnings data are presented in the following categories: 1 = very high ($39,700 and over), 2 = high ($25,760 to $39,660), 3 = low ($18,500 to $25,760), and 4 = very low (up to $18,490). The rankings were based on quartiles using one-fourth of total employment to define each quartile.

Source: U.S. Department of Labor, *Monthly Labor Review,* November 2001, Bureau of Labor Statistics (www.bls.gov/emp/emptab3.htm for updates).

Employment projections: The 15 occupations with the largest job growth, 2000–2010.

| (Numbers in thousands of jobs) | Employment | | Change | | Quartile rank by 2000 median hourly earnings* | Education and training category |
Occupation	2000	2010	Number	Percent		
Combined food preparation and serving workers, including fast food	2,206	2,879	673	30	4	Short-term on-the-job training
Customer service representatives	1,946	2,577	631	32	3	Moderate-term on-the-job training
Registered nurses	2,194	2,755	561	26	1	Associate degree
Retail salespersons	4,109	4,619	510	12	4	Short-term on-the-job training
Computer support specialists	506	996	490	97	2	Associate degree
Cashiers, except gaming	3,325	3,799	474	14	4	Short-term on-the-job training
Office clerks, general	2,705	3,135	430	16	3	Short-term on-the-job training
Security guards	1,106	1,497	391	35	4	Short-term on-the-job training
Computer software engineers, applications	380	760	380	100	1	Bachelor's degree
Waiters and waitresses	1,983	2,347	364	18	4	Short-term on-the-job training
General and operations managers	2,398	2,761	363	15	1	Bachelor's or higher degree, plus work experience
Truck drivers, heavy and tractor-trailer	1,749	2,095	346	20	2	Moderate-term on-the-job training
Nursing aides, orderlies, and attendants	1,373	1,697	323	24	3	Short-term on-the-job training
Janitors and cleaners, except maids and housekeeping cleaners	2,348	2,665	317	13	4	Short-term on-the-job training
Postsecondary teachers	1, 344	1,659	315	23	1	Master's/doctorate degree

*The quartile rankings of Occupational Employment Statistics annual earnings data are presented in the following categories: 1 = very high ($39,700 and over), 2 = high ($25,760 to $39,660), 3 = low ($18,500 to $25,760), and 4 = very low (up to $18,490). The rankings were based on quartiles using one-fourth of total employment to define each quartile.

Source: U.S. Department of Labor, *Monthly Labor Review,* November 2001, Bureau of Labor Statistics (www.bls.gov/emp/emptab4.htm for updates).

The World and You

It is our hope that you will develop your own personal objectives, believe in yourself, acknowledge stereotypes pertaining to life and work, and develop a clear strategy for entering the career of your choice. Whether you have directly experienced bias or other barriers to employment or have had the good fortune not to, we would like you to use the following written exercises to reflect upon your personal, social, and cultural opinions and biases. Exercise 6.1 helps you become aware of how you may react to roles and events that differ from those to which you are accustomed. Exercise 6.2 asks you to explore your own stereotypes. Be spontaneous with your answers; do not censor yourself because you fear your answer is wrong. Exercise 6.3 asks you to list the advantages and disadvantages of belonging to one or more distinct groups. Exercise 6.4 helps you become aware of your knowledge of various groups of people. The more difficult it is for you to identify names for this exercise, the more likely it is that you have led a life that excludes other cultures. Stereotypes and barriers tend to develop when we stick to our own groups. Exercise 6.5 asks you to think about the small businesses you use regularly. Exercise 6.6 asks you to consider the impact of globalization. In Exercise 6.7, you are to list jobs technology has recently created.

To answer these questions online, go to the *Exercise* module in Chapter 6 of the Companion Website.

First Impressions

EXERCISE **6.1**

Think about each of the following situations. What are your first impressions?

a. You are applying for a job. A male receptionist ushers you into an office where you are greeted by a female vice president who will conduct the interview.

b. You are flying to Chicago. A male flight attendant welcomes you aboard the plane; later a female voice says, "This is your captain speaking."

c. You go to enroll your four-year-old in a nearby nursery school and discover all three teachers at the school are male.

d. You are introduced to a new couple in the neighborhood and discover the man stays home all day with two small children while the wife works outside the home.

e. You are African American and live in a neighborhood that is all Caucasian.

f. You have a conference with your child's teacher, who grew up in Taiwan.

g. You are in a class with many students who speak a different language.

h. You move into an apartment and learn your neighbors are homosexual.

i. You are temporarily disabled, must use a wheelchair, and have found a wonderful job opening. You haven't yet told the interviewer about your disability (and the room is on the second floor, with no elevator).

j. You arrive at your new dentist's office and find she has green-and-orange spiked hair.

k. You are referred to a hospital known for excellence in surgery, and your team of doctors is all Latino.

l. You go to court and find every jury member is African American.

m. You go to a job interview and find yourself facing a panel of younger men and women.

n. You find yourself in a statistics class in which all the students are Asian American.

o. You are on an airplane, and the flight attendant is older than your grandmother.

Gender Roles Questionnaire

EXERCISE 6.2

In order to explore your own stereotypes, complete these sentences with the first thought that comes to mind. Don't censor yourself.

1. Women are happiest in careers when _____

2. Men are happiest in careers when _____

3. The most difficult emotion for a man to display is _____

4. The most difficult emotion for a woman to display is _____

5. Women tend to be better than men at _____

6. Men tend to be better than women at _____

7. Men get depressed about _____

8. Women get depressed about _____

9. Men are most likely to compete over _____

10. Women are most likely to compete over _____

11. Men tend to get angry about _____

12. Women tend to get angry about _____

13. As a man/woman, I was always taught to _____

14. Men feel pressured on the job when _____

15. Women feel pressured on the job when _____

Pros and Cons

EXERCISE 6.3

List advantages and disadvantages of being any of the following:

1. Female _____

   advantage _____

   disadvantage _____

2. Male _____

   advantage _____

   disadvantage _____

3. Caucasian _____

   advantage _____

   disadvantage _____

4. African American _____

   advantage _____

   disadvantage _____

5. Latino _____

   advantage _____

   disadvantage _____

6. Asian American _____

   advantage _____

   disadvantage _____

7. Native American _____

   advantage _____

   disadvantage _____

Famous People

For each of the groups listed above, name five famous people (may be currently living or a historical figure).

_____

_____

_____

_____

_____

_____

_____

_____

_____

_____

Small Businesses

List three small businesses whose services or products you use:

1. _____

2. _____

3. _____

Name one business that is operated out of a home:

_____

Globalization of the Work World

List five impacts of globalization on the workplace:

1. _____

2. _____

3. _____

4. _____

5. _____

Changing Nature of Work

Think about jobs that you, your friends, and family have had. Name three jobs that did not exist 10 years ago:

1. _____

2. _____

3. _____

WWWebwise

For additional activities online, go to the WWWebwise module in Chapter 6 of the **Companion Website.**

Exercise Summary

What about you? How do you think gender, race, age, sexual orientation, or physical disability could affect your ability to get a job? While doing these exercises, did you discover anything about your stereotypes of people? Have affirmative action policies affected you or anyone you know in applying for college or a job? Summarize your feelings about what you have learned.

_____

_____

_____

_____

_____

_____

_____

_____

_____

_____

_____

_____

_____

_____

_____

_____

_____

_____

_____

_____

_____

_____

_____

_____

_____

_____

_____

_____

Go to page 207 of the chapter summaries and fill out the Chapter 6 exercise summary now.

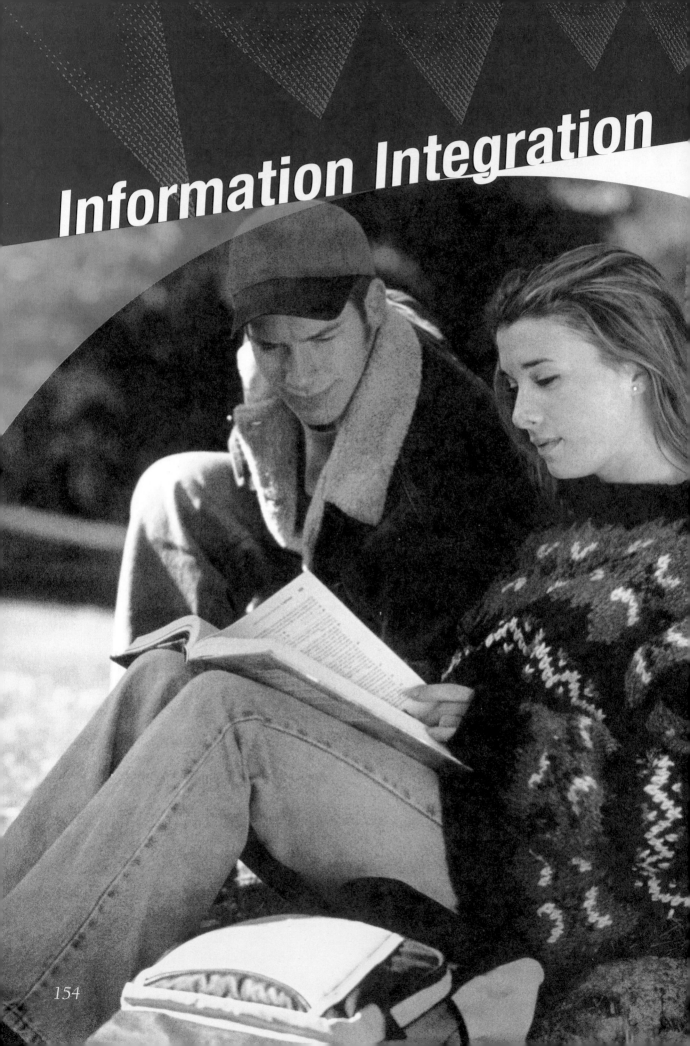

Information Integration

By now, you probably have one or several career areas in mind. This chapter will help you get more specific. It will enable you to review, clarify, and integrate the information you've collected about your needs, desires, values, interests, skills, and personal attributes. It is important to put these pieces together to identify some specific occupational areas that you can begin to research.

Sometimes the hardest part of making a career choice is knowing what kinds of jobs exist. As you learned in the last chapter, the work world is changing so rapidly that it is difficult to stay current regarding all the kinds of jobs that are available. This can be complicated if you have been out of the workplace for a period of years, are looking for your first job, or are uncertain about how your academic background has prepared you for work.

This chapter will introduce you to the written and electronic resources available in libraries, in college career centers, and on your home computer when you are connected to the Internet. By using these references, you will have the information necessary to clarify and confirm your tentative career choices. Then, in Chapter 8, you will be encouraged to make a tentative career decision.

LEARNING OBJECTIVES

At the end of the chapter you will be able to . . .

- Brainstorm possible career options based on information you learned about your attitudes, beliefs, interests, personality, and skills

- Adopt a strategy to approach occupational research that will enhance your efficiency and effectiveness

- List printed and computerized sources of information to use in further clarifying your career choices

- Use your skills to gather information about specific occupations and career-related opportunities by using library materials and computerized resources

- Confirm or revise your first impressions about your top career choices

Even the lowly woodpecker
owes his success to the fact that
he uses his head.

In case you get stuck or blocked in listing specific occupations, try using the guided fantasy (Exercise 7.8). Start by quickly reviewing all the written information that you've recorded (in the Chapter Summaries section, beginning on page 203). Then close your eyes and visualize yourself in your perfect career. Mental visualization can sometimes focus your thoughts on areas that suit you perfectly. This technique helps you tap into and integrate the wealth of information, intuition, and wisdom that you already have about yourself. It is only natural to feel hesitant and even fearful about committing yourself to a career decision. These are the feelings that block you from making a decision and getting specific. Mental visualization is a technique to help your mind "wander" into a career choice.

Brainstorming Career Options

Before you can begin researching career options, you need to know what you are looking for. Many job searchers find this very difficult because they simply do not know very much about the kinds of jobs that are available, especially if they are changing careers. Other times, job searchers will make a decision about a career without knowing very much about it. At this phase in your career decision making, you should emphasize generating many different *possibilities*. In a later section of this chapter you will learn how to research these possibilities with written and electronic resources. That process provides the information you will need in order to make decisions about your career choices.

Your personal career profile from Part One is a good place to begin. The exercises you completed at the end of each chapter may give you ideas about your skills, interests, personality, and values as they relate to the world of work. For example, think about one of your interests you identified in the exercises at the end of Chapter 4. How could you teach people about this interest? How could you sell something related to this interest? What kind of service could you perform related to this interest? Suddenly your interest has become an important occupational consideration.

Obviously, the point of this exercise is to help you identify the relationship between your personal career profile and different occupations. Each element of your profile is something that you want to try to satisfy in order to be happy in your work. You are more likely to enjoy your job if you find the work interesting and you are using your skills. Your personal preferences provide insight into your preferred work style. You want to find a job that is consistent with your values so that you are satisfied with your daily work and feel that your occupation is important. Each of these areas needs to be satisfied every day at work, not just once a month or once a year. Exploring a large number of career options is the best place to begin to find satisfying work.

At the end of this chapter, you will find a series of exercises that will help you brainstorm a large number of job titles that you will use as you begin your research using the written and electronic resources presented later in this chapter. These exercises present a variety of techniques for brainstorming career ideas, and not every technique will appeal to you. Stick with these exercises, even those that seem wacky. Each one will challenge you to think differently about all the various jobs you might do. You simply want to generate a list of many, many different career possibilities and not eliminate anything yet that seems unrealistic. The ideas you generate in these exercises will be necessary for you to complete this chapter.

As you complete these exercises, keep a few thoughts about brainstorming in mind. Brainstorming is a creative process to produce as many ideas on a particular topic as possible—career ideas, in this case. It is a very useful way to begin thinking beyond all of the obvious ideas, those career options you have considered over and over again. In order for brainstorming to work, however, you need to remember two very important rules. First, at this point you should be more concerned with quantity than quality. Your goal should be to come up with a very long list of occupational ideas and pare it down later. Second, consider even the most outrageous ideas. Maybe being a lion tamer in the circus is not a realistic occupational goal, but it might spark another idea that is realistic.

You might look back at the exercises in Chapter 4 that made you think about jobs (e.g., the classified ads exercise). Using some of the websites suggested at the end of this chapter, you will be seeing some of this information in a new light. Be sure to use some of the websites found in the Chapters 6 and 7 Web links on the Companion Website to generate ideas. For example, the University of North Carolina career majors site has a "What can I do with a major" heading that is excellent for finding jobs related to majors.

Brainstorm your way to a career choice

Understanding Career Paths and Common Organizational Divisions

Sometimes a greater awareness of the job market can be gained by researching career paths or career ladders in a specific industry. Most career centers and libraries have books that outline career paths. Once you've assessed where you currently fit in, you can start preparing to move up the ladder. If you are presently working, your immediate supervisor and the human resources department can provide information about routes for advancement, for example, in-house workshops, institutes, on-the-job training, community college associate degrees and certificates, and bachelor's degrees.

Although the world of work includes a number of broad fields such as business, education, government (including the military), health care, and non-profit agencies, all of these fields share certain common functional needs and have some common organizational units. As an example, many fields need the accounting functions of payroll computation and disbursement, budgeting, and servicing of accounts payable and receivable. Administration, finance, human resources, marketing, public relations, management information systems, and research and development are departmental functions common to almost all work fields. The following list explains the general functions of these and other departments in typical businesses; however, you will find identical or very similar organizational units performing very similar functions in the fields of education, government, nonprofit agencies, and health care.

If you have been concentrating on specific industries in your search for job possibilities, you can gain a fresh perspective by selecting functions that may be interesting to you and then researching jobs within those functions, but among various industries.

Be aware of common organizational elements

Administration. An organization's top executive officers and other managers, secretarial and word processing personnel, and human resources staff are included in this function.

Corporate relations. Responsible for advertising, public relations, and community relations.

Distribution. Sometimes called the transportation department; oversees warehousing and shipping of the company's products.

Engineering. Product design and modification; often oversees manufacturing of products (process engineers).

Finance. Accounting functions, including payroll, budgets, and accounts payable and receivable.

Sales. Responsible for initiating and maintaining customer accounts, selling the company's product; sometimes includes marketing function.

Remember that some companies are restructuring so that jobs may not be part of career paths. They may hire a coordinator with cross-functional skills: that person develops and tracks the project, motivates the team, assists the team in marketing the project/product, and also keeps track of the budget. The project may last six months or so, and then the coordinator is assigned to a different project with either similar or different duties. This type of organization is called a *web*. Another type of web is a situation in which a specialist works for *several* companies, such as an accountant who does the books for a designer, publisher, educational consultant, and marketing specialist.

Learn about web organization

Your research should reflect the location of your chosen path(s). Do you hope to work somewhere as a *generalist* and be adept in many areas in the web? Or do you prefer to be part of an organization as a *specialist,* such as an accountant? See Exhibit 7.1 for examples of career paths in business fields.

Now that you have a clearer idea of the jobs that best suit your personality, it is necessary to research the actual requirements of the jobs. There are two primary ways to obtain job information: searching through written or computerized materials in the library and contacting people who already work in your area of interest. This chapter focuses on written and computerized materials, whereas Chapter 9 focuses on people and contacts. Your local library or college career development and placement center should be able to provide you with some or all of the following resources.

SALES AND MARKETING

Vice President, Sales and Marketing ($150–750)

National Sales Manager ($150–250)

Regional Sales Manager ($125–175)

District Sales Manager ($80–120)

Marketing/Sales Representative ($35–70)

Marketing Director/VP ($80–175)

Marketing Manager ($40–100)

Marketing Communications Manager ($30–60)

Marketing Assistant ($27–35)

ADVERTISING

Executive Vice President ($180–500)

Account Supervisor ($75–120)

Senior Account Executive ($48–70)

Account Executive ($35–41)

Account Coordinator ($28–31)

Assistant Account Coordinator ($24–30)

RETAILING

Vice President, Merchandising ($225+)

Store Manager ($75–175)

Buyer-Planner/Buyer ($36–80)

Assistant Buyer ($30–35)

Management Trainee ($26–30)

General Merchandise Mgr. ($60–200)

Merchandise Manager ($50–70)

Group Sales Manager ($40–60)

Sales Manager ($30–35)

INTERNATIONAL

V.P. International Operations ($90–250)

Sales Manager International ($80–150)

Export Manager ($60–100)

Contracts Administrator ($50–100)

Export Administration ($25–60)

Strategies for Researching Career Options

The best place to begin your research is not in the library, but with a strategy. This will help you focus your efforts, know what to look for, and not waste time on dead-end research.

1. Decide which occupations you are going to research. After completing the exercises at the end of this chapter, you should have a very long list of occupational possibilities. It is unrealistic to suggest that you should research every job you brainstormed. There are probably some jobs on your list that you can remove right away. Review your list and prioritize your ideas. If you still have a long list, try grouping your ideas according to industry or function. For example, if you have five occupational ideas related to writing and journalism, you might group them for purposes of research in a category called "communication careers." You should identify a realistic number of occupations or occupational areas about which you would like to learn more.

2. Research the industry and functional areas. Once you have decided what you are going to research, your next step is to conduct broad research on the industry and field. It is best to start with resources that can give you enough information in a small space to decide if a particular occupational area is interesting. Some of the U.S. Department of Labor publications discussed in this chapter will be your best tools.

3. Learn about current events affecting your areas of interest. Magazines and newspapers, especially publications that focus on business such as *Fortune, Business Week,* or the *Wall Street Journal,* are rich resources for information about current industry trends, relevant new technology, key companies and organizations, and job growth. You can easily find the most current publications by completing a key word search on most library databases.

4. Identify relevant professional and trade associations. Most industries have a professional organization. These are associations that bring together professionals in a particular industry for networking and continuing education. These organizations exist to disseminate information about a particular industry. Professional and trade associations also publish journals and newsletters that can give you insight into the industry's current issues, types of employers, and common vocabulary.

The Encyclopedia of Associations and Chamber of Commerce publications are the best resources for this information. As you research occupations, develop a list of relevant

---

SUCCESS STRATEGIES

Questions to Ask When Researching a Job

- What are the job duties and responsibilities?
- What qualifications are needed in terms of college degrees, skills, or work experience?
- Are you likely to receive on-the-job training in this field?
- What is a typical career path in this field?
- What is the employment outlook for this industry?
- What is the average salary for someone entering this field? What are the top salaries in this field?
- Who are typical employers in this field?
- What are the key professional and trade associations for this field?
- What is the work environment like for this field? Is traveling required?
- Is relocation to a specific geographic location required?

professional associations to which you can write to request additional career information.

5. Locate useful websites on the Internet. The Internet brings a wide range of information about different industries, professional associations, and employers literally to your fingertips. The World Wide Web has become such a valuable tool that many libraries offer Internet access to their patrons. By using your industry as a key word in any of the different Internet search engines, you can identify many useful websites that provide the most up-to-date information. A complete discussion of computerized job search resources, including tips for people unfamiliar with the Internet, begins on page 170.

6. Identify key employers. The last step is to compile a list of typical employers, noting all kinds of employers (e.g., nonprofit, government, or business) and actual organization names. Several of the directories listed in Exhibit 7.2 can provide you with lists of companies that hire people for a particular industry.

Local government

According to the Bureau of Labor Statistics, more than 18 million people are employed by states, counties, cities, and towns.

WHAT DO YOU THINK?

1. What kind of local government job might interest you?
2. If you know someone working for local or state government, what is the job and how did the person get the job?
3. What are the advantages and disadvantages of working for government?

To answer these questions online, go to the *Facts and Figures* module in Chapter 7 of the Companion Website.

Government Employment Opportunities

State and local governments hire the majority of people in public work. Local government alone hires over 50 percent of all public employees. In addition, the federal government hires hundreds of people each day across the United States. When private industry is cutting back on hiring, government often seems like it is the best place to find a job. In fact, within five years, almost half of the federal government's current employees will be eligible to retire.

Government listings offer opportunities

Information regarding employment with local and state government offices is typically available at state or local One Stop Career Centers. Federal and state employment information is often available on the Internet through computers at colleges and One Stop Career Centers. (For more information about surfing the Web, see the Internet section of this chapter.) For those who don't have access to these locations, state personnel offices offer applications, tests, job descriptions, and occupational outlook data for that state. For example, California publishes "A Guide to the Use of Labor Market Publications" to help prospective employees research job opportunities. It is important to consider that it may take six to nine months to complete the application, test, interview, and hiring process for state government jobs. This is not a good option for someone who needs immediate employment; however, many people find it possible to complete the process while employed elsewhere. Also, many college students begin the application and testing process during their senior year in college, enabling them to interview for jobs before they graduate.

Excluding the postal service, the federal government employs almost 2 million workers. There may be 15,000 vacancies on any given day. No one in the federal government knows all the positions vacant on a particular day, week, or month, and you must contact the personnel office of each agency for a complete listing of vacancies in that agency. If you have access to the Internet, you may want to check out America's Job Bank (www.ajb.dni.us) or Federal Jobs Digest (www.fedjobs.com). These services are updated daily and have links to many other employment options. At the end of this chapter, several other career information services available on the Internet are listed. These sources also link to federal and state employment information. One other website worth visiting is www.careersingovernment.com.

You can also find information about federal jobs in publications such as *Federal Careers Opportunities,* a biweekly publication containing more than 4,000 job listings representing vacancies in the executive branch on congressional and judicial staff as well as in the United Nations. Also check with the Government Printing Office, your nearest branch of the Office of Personnel Management, and www.usajobs.opm.gov. Exhibit 7.2 lists some of the many federal employment opportunities.

Federal job information centers may also have access to a national computerized job bank. This is especially useful for people who want to know about job opportunities located some distance away.

DOT entry for copywriter

Writes advertising copy for use by publication or broadcast media to promote sale of goods and services. Consults with sales media and marketing representatives to obtain information on product or service and discuss style and length of advertising copy. Obtains additional background and current development information through research and interview. Reviews advertising trends, consumer surveys, and other data regarding marketing of specific and related goods and services to formulate presentation approach. Writes preliminary draft of copy and sends to supervisor for approval. Corrects and revises copy as necessary. May write articles, bulletins, sales letters, speeches, and other related informative and promotional material.

U.S. Department of Labor Publications

The Occupational Information Network (O*NET) is a relatively new interactive tool devised by the U.S. Department of Labor. The program is an easy-to-use computer database that collects, analyzes, and disseminates skill and job requirement information. It is designed to replace the *Dictionary of Occupational Titles* (DOT) and *Occupational Outlook Handbook* (OOH).

Most libraries, college career and placement centers, One Stop Career Centers, and high school career centers have copies of the DOT and OOH. You may use the on-line services, CD-ROM copies, or hard-copy publications.

The *Dictionary of Occupational Titles* (www.oalj.dol.gov) lists more than 35,000 job titles and more than 21,000 different occupations. This resource has been mentioned in previous chapters and will be referred to in Chapter 10 as a tool to use in writing a resume. It is especially useful because it lists specific tasks to be done on a job, as in the entry for copywriter.

Sample federal employment opportunities.

EXECUTIVE DEPARTMENTS

Agriculture	Health and Human Services	Labor
Commerce	Housing and Urban	State
Defense	Development	Transportation
Education	Interior	Treasury
Energy	Justice	Veterans Affairs

SAMPLE FEDERAL EMPLOYMENT POSITIONS COVERED BY ANNOUNCEMENTS

Accountant	Forester	Occupational therapist
Architect	Geophysicist	Oceanographer
Astronomer	Hospital administrator	Patent examiner
Attorney	Hydrologist	Pest controller
Bacteriologist	Illustrator	Pharmacist
Biologist	Internal revenue agent	Prison administrator
Chemist	Librarian	Social worker
Dietitian	Mathematician	Soil conservationist
Education officer	Meteorologist	Special agent
Engineer	Nurse	Teacher

MAJOR INDEPENDENT AGENCIES

Central Intelligence Agency	National Archives and Records
Environmental Protection Agency	Administration
Equal Employment Opportunity	Nuclear Regulatory Commission
Commission	Office of Personnel Management
Federal Deposit Insurance Corporation	Small Business Administration
Federal Emergency Management Agency	Smithsonian Institution
Foreign Service of the United States	Tennessee Valley Authority
General Services Administration	U.S. Information Agency
International Monetary Fund	U.S. International Development
National Aeronautics and Space	Cooperative Agency
Administration	U.S. Postal Service

The *Occupational Outlook Handbook* (OOH) (www.bls.gov/oco) includes information on job descriptions, skills, places of employment, training, educational requirements, personality traits, and values that might be important in a particular field, as well as salary ranges. It is updated every other year and represents a national survey of occupations. Salary information should be compared with local salaries and local cost-of-living factors. For example, Los Angeles employers tend to pay $1,000 to $2,000 more per year than many of the generalized estimates shown in the OOH.

Between editions of the OOH, the *Occupational Outlook Quarterly* provides updates of occupational projections as well as compensation ranges and cost-of-living comparisons throughout the United States.

The *Guide for Occupational Exploration* (GOE) provides detailed information about the interests, aptitudes, skills, and job activities of various occupational groups. The data in this publication are organized into 12 interest areas, 66 Worker Trait Groups, and 348 subgroupings. More detailed information regarding the GOE was provided in Chapter 4.

Employer Directories

Employer directories provide information about specific companies, such as those in your field with current job openings.

Information about a variety of enterprises, from foundations to corporations, can be found in directories. Directories list an employer's name and address, product, and geographic location, as well as other information including size in terms of volume of sales, number of employees, and names of top-level executives. Don't forget to use your local telephone directory. The white (or blue) pages list government agencies and departments, and the yellow pages list other places of employment.

Let your fingers do the researching

The yellow pages are available on the Internet. A benefit of this resource is that small businesses are listed. At the address line, simply type "yellow pages" and then key words pertaining to your job interest. If you are thinking about starting a landscape business, determine the competition in a specific geographic area by typing "yellow pages landscape businesses." At the prompt, click on **Yellow Pages.** If you would like to work in a certain city, for instance, to get experience before opening your own business, a phone call to the businesses listed in the yellow pages may provide you with information about a job or when one might be available.

As you review the directories listed in Exhibit 7.3, look for the following types of information:

- A geographic list of companies in a specified field
- Small, growing companies
- A company with international positions
- Names and addresses of corporate officers

Note which directories give information about trade publications. These offer insider information about companies doing well, job openings in specific fields, and firms that may not be listed in any other directory. Again, a simple phone call will provide you with valuable information.

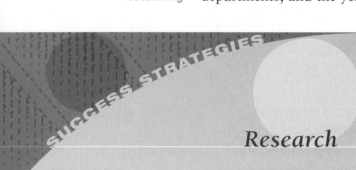

SUCCESS STRATEGIES

Research

Research helps you to accomplish the following:

- Locate high-level company information (such as names of executives)
- Obtain telephone numbers and addresses
- Locate company webpages
- Research company financial information
- Monitor company news and periodicals
- Review public opinion about a company
- Learn about an industry
- Learn to use business and financial websites
- Locate professional associations
- Find career-related conferences and seminars
- Research nonprofit organizations
- Identify international business resources

The Almanac of American Employers. Lists 500 companies with one page per firm, which includes the following information: recent financial performance, salaries and benefits, regional offices, brands, and divisions.

California Manufacturers Directory. Lists companies by location and product, with an additional section on companies that have import/export business.

Directory of American Firms Operating in Foreign Countries. Lists about 3,000 American corporations with factories and branch offices covering more than 36 countries. Also lists key personnel, but because it is not published annually, such information may be out-of-date.

Dun and Bradstreet Million Dollar Directory. Lists 160,000 companies in five volumes. Largest directory of its kind, indexed in a variety of ways. Includes subsidiaries not mentioned in other directories and is especially useful for direct-mail campaigns (see Chapter 9).

Dun's Employment Opportunities Directory. Lists 11,000 companies throughout the United States. Includes information about educational specialties the company values, most promising areas of employment, and a brief description of the company's insurance plans. Is divided into geographic and industry sections.

Encyclopedia of Associations. Lists 15,000 associations in every field, with names of officers, telephone numbers, and brief descriptions of orientation and activities.

Encyclopedia of Business Information Services. Lists source materials on businesses.

Gale Directory of Publications and Broadcast Media. Lists every newspaper, magazine, and radio station in the United States. Information found by region or industry groups (e.g., retailing, restaurants). Excellent source of information about trade publications.

Guide to American Directories. Describes 3,300 directories subdivided into 400 topical areas.

Hoover's Handbook of American Business. Its industry master list has more than 300 industries and 4,000 detailed company profiles, including a very thorough overview of what each company owns, how it is structured, key personnel, and company performance. Shows how employment prospects compare (e.g., top 100 companies in employment opportunities).

INFOTRAC. A computer-based program providing up-to-date directory information.

Regional and community magazines. Published by most large cities and metropolitan areas and focus on business, industry, education, the arts, and politics; states and regions also have their own magazines.

Standard and Poor's Register of Corporations, Directors, and Executives. Lists about 55,000 public and private companies in three volumes. Volume one covers basic information; volume two includes summaries about key executives; volume three indexes companies according to industry classification.

Standard Periodical Directory. Describes 50,000 periodicals and directories.

Standard Rate and Data Business Publications Directory. Lists names and addresses of thousands of trade publications.

State directories. Directories of trade and industry published by each state. If one is not in your library, contact the local or state chamber of commerce, or write to U.S. Chamber of Commerce, 1615 H Street NW, Washington, DC 20006 or to to www.uschamber.com.

Thomas's Register of American Manufacturers. Lists 100,000 manufacturers by location and product.

Who's Who in Commerce and Industry. Gives names and biographical sketches of top executives.

Other Written Sources of Information

NEWSPAPERS

Check out all the newspapers in the geographic area in which you are interested in working. Read the help-wanted section for openings as well as for local wage and fringe benefits information. There may be a separate business section that advertises professional jobs. Read everything in terms of your own job target and keep a file, but be aware that only 15 percent of job openings are listed in want ads. Therefore, note other areas of the paper, such as articles that announce business expansions, personnel changes, and new ideas. Planning commission announcements usually mention new industrial parks and the expected number of employers to be located there. Marriage announcements usually list the bride's and groom's occupations and may give you the name of an important executive of a firm that interests you. Lifestyle sections may profile leaders in the community; gossip columns may suggest where to find trendsetters.

Want ads = only 15% of job openings

TRADE JOURNALS

Almost every trade and profession has at least one regularly published journal. The business section of your library should have references. A book or pamphlet on your chosen career may list names of related associations and trade journals. Your library or career center may also have computerized retrieval systems (see Computerized Information Sources later in this chapter) to access trade journal information. The following resources are useful in tracking down particular trade journals: *Ulrich's International Periodical Directory,* the *Encyclopedia of Business Information Services,* the *Gale Directory of Publications and Broadcast Media,* and the *Encyclopedia of Associations.* Use these trade journals to locate job ads and to familiarize yourself with the people, products, current trends, and specific vocabulary of a field.

MAGAZINES

The *Reader's Guide to Periodicals,* available at any library in either printed or electronic form, can be used both to locate names of magazines and to find titles of informative and useful articles about any field you wish to research. Do you want to learn the latest in animation careers, the outlook for engineers in the western United States, opportunities for liberal arts graduates? It's been covered in some magazine recently! Business magazines also provide profiles of both businesses and their executive officers, which is information you might use in comparing companies.

Ask the librarian for the *Business Periodicals Index.* It accesses trade journal articles and has citations for hundreds of publications. The articles are arranged according to subject; broad subjects are divided into more specific categories. University business/management libraries are more likely to hold publications listed in the *Business Periodicals Index;* they are less likely to be found in local libraries.

SAMPLE USEFUL MAGAZINES FOR BUSINESS INFORMATION

Black Entrepreneur	*High Technology Careers*
Business Week	*Inc.*
Entrepreneur	*National Business Employment Weekly*
Executive Female	*Success*
Fast Company	*Wall Street Journal*
Fortune	*Working Woman*
Business 2.0	

SPECIALIZED MAGAZINES FOR COLLEGE STUDENTS AND GRADUATES

Black Collegian

Business Week's Guide to Careers

Business World (a career magazine for college students)

College Placement Annual (check with college placement office)

Hispanic Times Magazine

Saludos Hispanos

Women's Careers

IN-HOUSE BULLETINS AND ANNOUNCEMENTS

Personnel offices in virtually every business, agency, school, and hospital post jobs as they become available. Job posting best serves the people already employed at such places; however, some of the job listings may be open to anyone.

Large corporations such as Bank of America and General Electric publish in-house job announcement newsletters monthly or quarterly. Most of these newsletters are not intended for public use but are circulated among all employees to encourage internal job mobility. The job announcements list required skills, degrees, and relevant experience. Such in-house newsletters are an excellent way to explore current needs within large companies and to learn more about the types of job skills being sought.

Computerized Information Sources

 omputerized information can often be more quickly accessed and may be more complete than that found in traditional sources. Contact your library or campus career center for assistance in locating the sources described here—and for others.

SELECTED COMPUTERIZED SOURCES

Probably the largest resource on occupational information is the Career Information System (CIS; also known as EUREKA in California). This software provides occupational information, including job descriptions, locations for training such as vocational schools and colleges, and financial aid information, specific to the state in which it is located. Another compo-

Meet Jackie

Jackie, a single mother with two children, is working as manager of the gift shop in the Los Angeles Hilton Hotel. Her days are long and her pay is not enough to support herself and her children. Her child support helps, but she is always short at the end of the month. Her boss is not the most understanding woman in the world, and Jackie knows she has to make a change. Her mother tries to tell her that having a job, any job, is important in this economy, but she can't imagine staying at this job for much longer.

Jackie attended community college several years ago and she has completed her general education classes. She wonders how long it will take her to obtain a degree, and decides to make an appointment with a counselor. When the counselor asks Jackie what she wants to do when she receives her AA degree, Jackie can't come up with one thing. Jackie worries that the counselor might feel she is wasting his time, but instead he asks, "Why don't you take a career planning class? It will help you learn about yourself and careers that might suit you." Since the class meets on Jackie's day off, she decides to do it.

Jackie likes the class and she learns a lot about herself. From the interest inventory she takes, she learns that she likes the helping professions and that she is interested in physical fitness, science, and nutrition. She also learns that she values freedom, accomplishment, and creativity and that she prefers working with people and has an organized, logical mind.

When Jackie looks over the occupations that match her assessment results, she discovers physical therapist, personal trainer, and occupational therapist. Jackie does not know much about each occupation, so she uses the Career Center's resources to do some research. She begins with the Chronicle Guides and the Vocational Biographies, and she also uses Eureka, a computerized information system. Her research gives her information on education, training, job outlook, salary, and job search techniques. Jackie also interviews people working in those fields to get a sense of what the daily routine of the job is like.

After all her research, Jackie decides to study physical therapy and sets about figuring out how she is going to do it. Jackie makes a plan. First she looks over the next semester's schedule and arranges all her classes in late afternoon and evening, then she goes to her employer and asks if she may work part-time. She asks her ex-husband if he can increase his

nent of CIS, called QUEST, helps users identify the work characteristics that are common to certain occupations. A second program, SIGI PLUS (System of Interactive Guidance and Information plus more), is designed to clarify your values and to match your values, interests, and skills with occupations. A third program, GIS (Guidance Information System), acts as a source of national occupational information. The program DISCOVER identifies career sources and includes vital information on decision making. A commercial program available on CD-ROM, Discovering Careers, contains the *Occupational Outlook Handbook*, *Dictionary of Occupational Titles*, current trends, projected job growth, wages and salary information, licensing rules, related publications (e.g., trade journals), associations, and potential employers. Most of this information can now be found by going to www.ajb.dni.us and O*NET.

child support, then she applies for financial aid through the college. Finally, she asks her mother if she will watch her kids in the evening so she can save money on babysitting.

With a little luck, she can survive. The first year is a struggle but her money management is not the biggest problem. Jackie passes only 12 of the 24 units she attempts. She hadn't realized how difficult the science classes would be, and she also hadn't realized how rusty her English and math skills are. Discouraged, she makes an appointment with her advisor. He is sympathetic, but he feels that Jackie needs to be realistic about her career choice and about her chances of completing her program of study and transferring to the university in the time she has planned. After much discussion, Jackie decides to give herself two additional semesters, but after the first semester, she knows even with the extra time it will be impossible.

When Jackie sees the counselor again, he says that he might have a solution: The college is planning to add a Recreation Fitness Certificate Program to the curriculum. Students with the certificate will be able to work in recreation programs for children and adults, and with a higher degree they can become supervi-

sors. The counselor tells Jackie that she can speak with the department head for more specific information. Jackie makes an appointment and discovers that the field holds many opportunities, some of which she can take advantage of right now. With this news, Jackie feels better. She decides to talk again with her counselor and make a new plan of action.

1. What strategies would you use to overcome the situation that Jackie faced?

2. Was Jackie too optimistic in the beginning? Would you have developed a different plan?

3. Was Jackie too pessimistic at the end? Would you have taken a different direction?

4. Give several reasons for quitting a job before you have another one.

5. Is college always the answer to a better life? Give examples of ways that you can improve your life or your career without attending college. Identify five jobs that pay well and don't require a college degree

 To answer these questions online, go to the *Real Stories* module in Chapter 7 of the Companion Website.

In many colleges, computers located in counselors' offices or in the career center use software to help students explore occupations related to their college major. For students seeking help in selecting a major, 3,000 college majors can be scanned by a computer in three to five seconds to locate the ones that match the student's interests. Often this software includes a file with information on all two- and four-year colleges in the United States, which can assist students in choosing a school, preparing for admission, and planning a course schedule.

Many college career planning and placement offices have online or CD-ROM resources that provide employment information about some of the largest companies in the United States. For example, Moody's Corporate Profiles on Dialog lists more than 5,000 publicly held companies with information such as business analysis, annual earnings, and financial data.

FlipDog.com provides company profiles in its "Resources" section, while Fortune.com has a company profiles section including descriptive information on the "Fortune 500," "Small Business 100," and 100 fastest-growing companies. Another place to find such information is the business section of your campus library or most city libraries. Finally, if your family or a friend subscribes to an online service such as America Online, company/job information can be obtained from the business/financial sections, the career sections, or various bulletin boards, or from other Internet sources such as those listed in the next section and in Chapter 9 (see Selected Online Employment Databases, page 238).

THE INTERNET

The information superhighway offers immediate access to unlimited sources for both job descriptions and company information. If you don't own a computer or haven't subscribed to an Internet service provider, access is possible through libraries, colleges, universities, quick print centers, and even some coffeehouses. The local library is a great place to try out the Internet.

Library Resource Centers

Librarians, as information specialists, may be available to help you both conduct your search and use the library's information-retrieval tools to access indexes, abstracts, and (in some cases) the full text of thousands of newspapers, magazines, and journals. The library's Internet connections (called T-lines) are significantly faster than the typical family modem, allowing users to search through hundreds of thousands of references.

Libraries subscribe to powerful research index services such as Nexus, Dialog, and Infotrac and have access to databases containing hundreds of periodicals. Library Internet access can simplify the search for information and articles. You may be able to tap into the library's indexes through your home computer; however, you'll probably have to *order* copies of articles rather than download them. (It may be possible to retrieve your college library documents at home or in the office, if your school allows such an arrangement.)

Career Sites

To explore careers and the job market, online resources are available for every phase of the job search: identifying opportunities, researching specific industries and companies, posting resumes online, and making contacts with potential employers. Information on job search and resume resources is located in Chapter 9, Targeting Your Job Search, and Chapter 10, Preparing a Winning Resume.

Job Market Research Sites

To begin your online search, go to the Chapter 7 section of the Companion Website, where you can click on some of the websites listed below.

Monster Board www.monster.com This is one of the largest sites on the Web, with an excellent "career center." It includes a Resources section that has information for new job seekers, career changers, and people making military transitions. Additionally, you can search for information on industries, franchises, salary statistics, resume writing, and interview techniques. Monster is also known as the largest database for job listings.

Monstertrak www.monstertrak.com This site has great career information for students, and many colleges post their job listings here. Be sure to look for the Career Guide when checking out this site.

Flipdog www.flipdog.com This popular website offers a wide range of job listings. Subscribe to the newsletter for weekly job-finding tips and interesting and different jobs. The Resource Center offers resources including company research, stress management, personal finance, resume tips, and interview strategies. Especially useful at this stage in your exploration is the section titled "Research Employers," which allows you access to Wetfeet and Hoover's company research.

Black Voices www.blackvoices.com This site includes job search and many other helpful features for African Americans. Another helpful site is www.blackcollegian.com, where many of the links lead to discussions of barriers to employment. This site also includes information about the best companies for African Americans.

Wemedia www.wemedia.com This site focuses on workplace and lifestyle issues facing the disabled.

Hire the Deaf Network www.hiredeaf.com This is the number one website for individuals who are hearing impaired to find jobs.

Hispanic Business www.hispanicbusiness.com This site offers up-to-date stories, links to business-related articles, and information about the top 500 Hispanic-owned companies in the United States.

America's Job Bank (www.ajb.dni.us) is a valuable site during a job search. If you are interested in federal government jobs, look at *Fed World* (www. fedworld.gov) and www.studentjobs.gov (beware: if you type studentjobs.com you will get Canadian job information!). You may find access to your state employment service most easily through *America's Job Bank*. At your state site, you will have access to skill requirements for many of the state's jobs.

About (www.about.com) has a section titled "Jobs & Careers" that provides helpful information on general job hunting and topics related to starting a business. It includes advice on developing effective resumes and cover letters.

Classified ads from several major newspapers can be found at www.careerbuilder.com. Or, type "resume and interview advice," "labor market information," or "career information" into a search engine to find a number of possible sites to visit.

Interested in working overseas? (www.overseasjobs.com) may help you locate a position. It contains 1,500 overseas job vacancies, which can be searched by key word. It also offers hundreds of resources in more than 40 countries. In addition, it has an online bookstore with titles such as *Finding a Job in Australia*.

Industry Searches

If you are interested in financial services such as investment banking and retail banking, use the following search method: in your browser's search box, type "financial services." Narrow your search by adding key words, such as "banks," to the search box. From the results of this search you can investigate specific companies. To learn more about the banking business, visit several banking sites on the Web and return periodically to follow developments in each business. Firms often announce new departments, services, and products first on the Web.

Trade Journals

Earlier in the chapter, we mentioned industry trade journals. Sometimes these journals have websites. For example, *Advertising Age* is located at www.adage.com. Journals such as this provide the latest information about trends in an industry. You may be able to add your name to an e-mail list, which will allow you to receive information about current industry issues. Most magazines and trade journals print their e-mail and website addresses in the front of the publication. One website, www.bizjournal.com allows you to search for articles from more than 40 local business journals across the United States.

Sometimes a business magazine such as *Business 2.0* (www.business 2.com) or *Fortune* (www.fortune.com) provides links to many businesses. Business 2.0's website offers a "webguide" (www.business2.com/webguide). When you go to this site, click on "Careers by Industry," then select one, for example "Advertising and Marketing." There you will find these topics: *Category Path, Related Categories* (company career pages, recruiters, job search sites), and *Links* (Career Advisor, Thinking of a Career in Advertising, and Work in PR).

The computer resources available to you will vary from location to location. Check with your local library, college career center, college adviser, and computer store to explore how computers can help you obtain information that will aid in your career planning.

Information Integration

The following written exercises will help you digest the contents of this chapter. You can complete them by using your local library or college career center to explore some of the resources mentioned in this chapter. Exercise 7.1 asks you to list 10 tempting jobs. In Exercise 7.2, you are asked to write about a job based on your interests. Exercise 7.3 has you list five favorite jobs that people you know currently hold. Exercise 7.4 requires that you investigate resources utilizing the local library, college library, and local newspaper. Exercise 7.5 asks that you learn what kinds of information and assistance are available from your college career center, local state employment office, and other employment offices. Exercise 7.6 gives you a format for gathering facts about three jobs.

> To answer these questions online, go to the *Exercise* module in Chapter 7 of the Companion Website.

A Tempting 10

EXERCISE 7.1

Identify one industry that you find interesting, such as entertainment, business, or education. In the space below, write 10 different jobs related to that industry. When you have completed this, prioritize the job titles in order of how interesting they sound to you, and list them in the space below. Repeat this exercise with two to three different industries. Use www.yahoo.com or the webguide on www.business2.com.

1. _____   6. _____
2. _____   7. _____
3. _____   8. _____
4. _____   9. _____
5. _____   10. _____

I'd Do This Even If I Didn't Get Paid

EXERCISE 7.2

Pretend that you do not have to work for a living but instead can do whatever you enjoy all day. Write some ideas in the space below. When you are finished, identify a likely job title for your activities and the relevant industry. For example, if you thought that you would enjoy spending your time painting, you might give portrait artist or graphic artist as your job title and art as your industry.

_____
_____
_____
_____

The Grass Is Always Greener

In the space below, write the names of five friends or family members who hold jobs that interest you. Next to each name, write a key phrase to explain what interests you about the job. Prioritize the jobs and industries you find interesting.

1. _____

2. _____

3. _____

4. _____

5. _____

Job Research

1. Which directories could be most helpful to you now, and what do you need to know? Where are these directories found?

   _____

2. What are the names of three trade journals related to your field of interest? Where are they found?

   a. _____

   b. _____

   c. _____

3. What are some of the current trends reflected in these journals?

   _____

4. Name one professional association related to your field. List where and when local meetings are held. (What about the national conference—can you attend or join as a student?) For example:

   American Society of Women   Your field: _____

      Accountants (ASWA)   Association: _____

   Local contact: Joan Smith—   Contact: _____

      phone: 805-555-1213   _____

   Meeting time & location: 3rd Thursday   Meeting: _____

      of each month, 7 P.M. (dinner),   _____

      Colonial House Restaurant, Oxnard   _____

5. Study a local daily newspaper for three weeks, and make a scrapbook or database of articles that relate to your field. (Include want ads, feature articles, meetings, networking groups, and names of executives in your field who were mentioned anywhere in the paper.)

Local and Internet Resources

1. Investigate local career and placement centers. Ask if they place people in your field or if they can refer you to others who do.

2. Visit the state employment office as well as private employment or temporary agencies to find out how they place people and how long it may take to get a job.

3. Find a local job opportunity on the Internet.

4. As you collect information, create a folder on your computer titled "Research." In this "Research" folder, create subfolders entitled "Associations/Conferences," "Company Profiles," "Job Search Strategy," "Industry Specific," "Labor Market Information," and "New Articles." Keep the information you gather organized in these folders.

Gathering the Facts

Following the format below, research three jobs in a library or career center. You may select either three different jobs (e.g., public relations specialist, social worker, manager), three jobs that are related (e.g., lawyer, paralegal, legal secretary), or three that represent the same field but vary in the nature of the work (e.g., marketing executive, graphic artist, display assistant).

Once you identify job titles of interest to you, gather the following information for each one:

Title of career: _____

Salary: _____   _____

Hours: _____

Benefits: _____

Outlook (whether there will be jobs in the future): _____

_____

Educational requirements—minimum training necessary: _____

_____

If college is necessary, what types of programs are available locally? _____

_____

_____

Schools or colleges offering the training: _____

_____

Personal requirements: _____

_____

Physical demands: _____

_____

Work description (attach a copy of the DOT description): _____

Working conditions: _____

_____

Location: _____

_____

Opportunities for advancement: _____

_____

Related occupations with the following educational requirements:

No additional training needed: _____

Some college needed: _____

B.A. or B.S. degree needed: _____

Other training (e.g., master's degree or special license): _____

_____

Sources (may include resources in the career center and names of local people working in this field; include Internet addresses where you might find related information):

_____

_____

_____

After researching the specifics, are you still interested? How well does this occupation mesh with your vision of a lifestyle?

_____

_____

_____

If, after reading about three different careers, you are still confused about how to choose one, try Exercise 7.8, a guided fantasy. Visualize yourself in each career. Which one feels most comfortable, most consistent with who you are?

Chapter Eight will help you narrow your focus and decide among different careers.

EXERCISE
7.7

WWWebwise

 For additional activities online, go to the WWWebwise module in Chapter 7 of the **Companion Website**.

Exercise Summary

Here is a guided fantasy. Close your eyes, take a few deep breaths, and relax. Remove all feelings of tension from your body, and erase all previous thoughts and worries from your mind. . . .

Imagine that you are getting up on a typical workday about five years from now. You're sitting on the side of your bed trying to decide what you are going to wear. Take a moment and look over your wardrobe. . . . What type of clothing do you finally decide to wear? . . .

Imagine yourself getting ready for work. Any thoughts about the day to come while you're getting ready? . . . What kind of feelings do you have as you look forward to your workday? . . . Do you feel excited? Bored? Apprehensive? . . . What gives you these feelings? . . .

It's time for breakfast now. Will you be sharing breakfast with someone, or will you be eating alone? . . .

You've completed your breakfast now and are headed out the door. Stop for a moment and look around your neighborhood. What does it look like? . . . What does your home look like? . . . What thoughts and feelings do you experience as you look around? . . .

Fantasize now that you're heading toward work. How are you getting there? . . . How far is it? . . . What new feelings or thoughts are you experiencing? . . .

You're entering your work situation now. Pause for a bit and try to get a mental picture of it. Think about where it is and what it looks like. Will you be spending most of your time indoors or outdoors? . . . How many people will you be working with? . . .

You are going to your specific job now. Who is the first person you encounter? . . . What does this person look like? . . . What is this person wearing? . . . What do you say to this person? . . .

Try to form an image of the particular tasks you perform on your job. Don't think about it as a specific job with a title, such as nurse or accountant. Instead, think about what you are actually doing, such as working with your hands, adding figures, typing, talking to people, drawing, thinking, etc.

In your job, do you work primarily by yourself or mostly with others? . . . In your work with others, what do you do with them? . . . How old are the other people? . . . What do they look like? . . . How do you feel toward them? . . .

Where will you be going for lunch? . . . Will you be going with someone else? Whom? What will you talk about? . . .

How do the afternoon's activities differ from those of the morning? . . . How are you feeling as the day progresses? Tired? Alert? Bored? Excited? . . .

Your workday is coming to an end now. Has it been a satisfying day? . . . If so, what made it satisfying? . . . Was there anything about the day that made you less happy? . . . Will you be taking some of your work home with you? . . .

Consider sharing some of your guided fantasy with a classmate and significant others in your life. How compatible is your fantasy with theirs?

_____

_____

_____

_____

_____

Go to page 208 of the chapter summaries and fill out the Chapter 7 exercise summary now.

Making Decisions

Career decisions are the Olympic trials of your career fitness program. They give you an opportunity to integrate and test out all the components of your career fitness program—your attitudes, values, skills, interests, and biases. For most of us, it is safe to assume that whatever decisions we make are the best we can make given the information, circumstances, and feelings of the moment. However, we can all improve our decision-making performance by examining some of the assumptions and strategies that other people have used in the decision-making process.

This chapter will review decision-making strategies that are potentially limiting and those that are potentially empowering and success-oriented. The primary focus of this chapter is on explaining a decision-making model that involves setting *realistic goals*. To bring about change, you must set *specific goals with specific time frames*. They must be realistic for you, and you must maintain an attitude that you are deserving and capable of reaching these goals.

In most of the previous chapters, you completed exercises at the

LEARNING OBJECTIVES

At the end of the chapter you will be able to . . .

- **Describe and explore your own decision-making process**

- **Apply the principles of decision making to your career search**

- **Identify psychological barriers to decision making and develop alternative strategies for success**

- **Write a clear objective**

- **Summarize insights gained from past chapters and identify potential occupations**

- **Make tentative career/education/ training choices**

- **Define and use stress management techniques**

179

Shoot for the moon.
Even if you miss it,
you will land among the stars.

end of the chapter. This was done to help you solidify and integrate what you had read in the entire chapter. In this chapter on decision making, you will be asked to complete some of the chapter-end exercises as you read. This will help you begin to test your aptitude for using various aspects of the decision-making model directly after they are presented in the chapter.

Overcoming Barriers to Decision Making

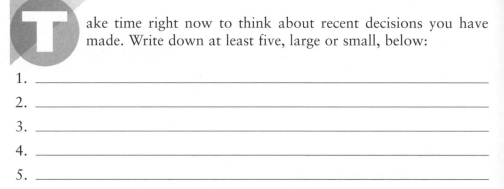

ake time right now to think about recent decisions you have made. Write down at least five, large or small, below:

1. _____
2. _____
3. _____
4. _____
5. _____

Because you are reading this book, you undoubtedly want to improve your life and increase your career options. Attitude has already been identified as an important internal factor in making decisions. Essentially, your attitude controls your ability to use your skills and potential to the fullest. Our attitudes are gut-level feelings that indicate what we expect of ourselves. If we are aware of our attitudes and habits, we can enhance our daily effectiveness. Again, if we believe we can, we can!

Much of human behavior is based on attitudes that are limiting. People often make decisions with limited conscious involvement or sense of personal responsibility, sometimes in an effort to simplify or accelerate the decision-making process. As you read the following sections, think about the process you followed in making the decisions you listed above.

Decision-Making Strategies (Good and Bad)

he box on the following page, "Ways to Make Decisions (Strategies)," describes some of the ways people go about making decisions. Read it now, then read the story in the box titled "Meet Art." Try to determine what decision-making strategies Art used.

Ways to Make Decisions (Strategies)

- **Planning.** "Weighing the facts." Consideration of values, objectives, necessary information, alternatives, and consequences. A rational approach with a balance between thinking and feeling.

- **Impulsive.** "Don't look before you leap." Little thought or examination; taking the first alternative.

- **Intuitive.** "It feels right." Automatic, preconscious choice based on inner harmony.

- **Compliant.** "Anything you say." Nonassertive; let someone else decide; follow someone else's plans.

- **Delaying.** "Cross that bridge later." Procrastination, avoidance, hoping someone or something will happen so that you won't have to make a decision. Taking a moratorium; postponing thought and action.

- **Fatalistic.** "It's all in the cards." What will be will be. Letting the environment decide; leaving it up to fate.

- **Agonizing.** "What if? I don't know what to do." Worrying that a decision will be the wrong one.

Getting lost in all the data; overwhelmed by analyzing alternatives.

- **Paralytic.** "Can't face up to it." One step further than "what if"—complete indecision and fear. Accepting responsibility but being unable to approach it.

WHAT ABOUT YOU?

1. Which of these approaches to decision making do you use most and least often?

2. Which would you like to use more often? Which would you like to avoid? Why?

3. Consider a current decision in progress (e.g., one you wrote at the beginning of this chapter). Think it through using several of these approaches. Which prove to be most useful?

Apply your answers here to the Exercises at the end of this chapter.

Choosing a career is a life development process. At different points during the process, different issues must be decided. Thus, planning (the first of the strategies listed) is the key to reaching your goals. It implies gaining control of your life. You might glance back at the lifeline you completed in Chapter 1. Analyze which strategy you used most often in making decisions. Then note the other strategies you used. Planning and intuitive strategies are the only two positive strategies listed. The others contain a hint of fear: fear of failure, fear of imperfection, fear of rejection, fear of ridicule. Such fears are based on "internal factors" related to how you feel about yourself.

When you feel stuck or unable to make a decision, try asking yourself the following questions:

1. What are my assumptions (attitudes)?
2. What are my feelings?
3. Why am I clinging to this behavior? (What are the rewards or payoffs?)

Ask yourself questions to get unstuck, gain control

1. What are my assumptions?

Many of us assume that if we could only make the one right decision about the matter at hand, everything else would fall into place. In fact, most decisions do not have such power over our lives. Decisions are not typically black-and-white in terms of their consequences but simply move you in one direction rather than another. Decisions open up some options and close off

There is no "right" decision

Meet Art

Art was born and raised in California. When he was a child he and his family loved to hike in the mountains, surf, and scuba dive. After graduating from high school, Art attended state college, where he earned a degree in graphic design. After Art had spent several months job hunting, a friend of Art's from Ohio told him that he and his father were starting a new company and they felt Art would fit right in. The company was going to specialize in designing packaging for educational materials. Art's friend said that they needed someone to help with sales and develop new design concepts.

Art was very excited until he learned that they needed start-up money and wanted Art to put up $5,000. Art's friend and his father told Art that the bank was willing to loan them half of the money they needed and that from all the feedback they received from financial and business consultants, the business was a solid idea with a good chance for success. They said that the cost of living in Ohio was less than in California, so Art could find affordable housing and insurance. Art's friend also promised that Art's investment would be repaid within the first two years.

Art had a trust account from his grandmother that he was planning to use to return to school and get his master's degree. Without telling anyone, Art withdrew the money. The business did fairly well the first year, and Art began to make a life in Ohio. He met a girl and soon they were married. Joan was in her last year of nursing school, working part-time in a nursing home, and she had excellent prospects of work after she graduated.

Six months later, Art's friend declared bankruptcy. Depressed and embarrassed, Art didn't know what to do. The job market in Ohio was not strong in Art's field, so Art and Joan decided that Art would go

---

others. If you assume that most decisions can be changed or altered—that most decisions do not, in fact, signify life or death—then you will not be so hesitant to make a decision, act on it, assess the implications as they occur, and make adjustments (or new decisions) as necessary.

2. What are my feelings?

Avoid either/or ultimatums

Some people create unnecessary stress about making decisions because they give themselves an either/or ultimatum. Neither option really feels right, but they panic and impulsively choose one just to ease the anxiety, or they become paralyzed and don't make any choice, allowing circumstances to decide for them. When you are feeling pressured or paralyzed about making a decision, stop, take several deep breaths, and begin to generate some additional alternatives. A friend, counselor, or skilled listener can often help with this process. As you gain more information about your options, you will realize which decision is best for you.

Other people cry over spilled milk; in other words, they think back over past decisions and lament not having decided differently. This psychological stance wastes time and energy and can be destructive to the self-image. When you begin to feel self-doubt or regret about past decisions, remind yourself that you made the best decision you could, given the time, circumstances, and information available.

back to California and Joan would finish nursing school and then join him.

With only phone calls and e-mails, Joan and Art found their relationship was in trouble. Art found work, but it was not what he wanted to do and the money was barely enough to support one person. Joan graduated and was offered a good job in Ohio. She encouraged Art to come back, but he knew that he could not make a good living there and he didn't want Joan to be the primary wage earner. Art tried to get Joan to come to California, but she felt comfortable in Ohio and was reluctant to make the move. After three months, Joan told Art that she didn't think the marriage was going to survive and asked for a divorce.

1. How would you evaluate Art's decision-making skills? What would you have done differently if you were Art?

2. What alternatives were available to Art in relation to his job search decision?

3. How would you evaluate Joan's response to Art's request?

4. What assumptions did Art and Joan make in choosing to pursue careers in different geographical areas? Were there any issues they could have discussed before making their decision?

5. If you were Art, what research would you have done before you took the job in Ohio?

6. What strategies or resources could Joan and Art have used to save their marriage?

7. How can people learn decision-making skills?

 To answer these questions online, go to the *Real Stories* module in Chapter 8 of the Companion Website.

3. Why am I clinging to this behavior?

Acknowledging that you are causing this indecisiveness may generate a different point of view. For example, sometimes people cling to old, nonproductive behaviors because they are the safe ways to act; they don't have to deal with the unknown or the possibility of making mistakes (also known as taking risks). However, without risk, there is no challenge and no growth.

Old habits can limit you

We usually find it difficult to change habits because they have given us some form of positive payoff or reward. A person who enjoyed the status and praise gained by being an excellent and achieving student might find that superior achievement in a work environment alienates others on the job. It is important to recognize when the old, comfortable ways of doing things no longer provide the payoffs they once did.

Visualize yourself at your best

Are you a risk taker? Whether you consider yourself a risk taker or not, it is important to remember that you have, in fact, taken many risks, just as we all have. What has been your greatest risk? What risk have you taken in the last two weeks? In its most basic sense, risk taking means moving from the safe and familiar to the unknown and scary. Most of us are fairly conservative risk takers in that we want the odds to be at least 50–50 before we jump in. Yet millions of people play the lottery, start businesses, and get married even when the odds are clearly not in their favor. Why? Because

Take calculated risks

regardless of the probability of success (the odds), people sometimes take risks based on the *desirability* of the successful outcome.

In a lottery, the probabilities are a million to one against winning, yet people continue to gamble because of the high desirability of the positive outcome of winning. You are in the best position to take a calculated risk when you assess both the probability and desirability of an outcome and weigh it against other possible outcomes. Failure to consider outcomes in this fashion is the most common cause of unsuccessful risk taking. For example, most people are afraid to take the risk of changing careers or even changing jobs. They immediately think of the worst possible outcome: "I'll fail" or "I will never find another job if I quit this one." They don't ask themselves how probable or desirable the best possible outcome would be. The probability of their worries actually materializing (i.e., the likelihood of a highly negative outcome) is very low.

Generate other possible outcomes

Many people paralyze themselves with this "worst possible consequence" thinking, decide not to risk it, and consequently feel trapped. What they haven't done is generate other possible outcomes that are more probable and more desirable. What are some of these? A new job that is more energizing and financially rewarding, a new career with an opportunity to grow and develop, a chance to get retraining. The probability and desirability of these outcomes are, in fact, much higher; therefore, the decision is less risky. Yet many people miss opportunities because they fail to generate and assess all possible outcomes. This process often takes the assistance of another person who can help identify negative or limiting thinking, as well as some realistic and positive outcomes.

Conditions for Change

Decisions = opportunities

Decisions provide an opportunity to experience life in new ways, to learn and find out who you are and what you would like to do. Each path is filled with opportunities. Just imagine: by making good decisions, renewal and growth are within your reach. By engaging in affirming self-talk, positive change is possible.

It has been said that three conditions must be present to trigger change. First, there must be a real dissatisfaction with what is, and then there must be a concept of what would be better; last, there must be a belief that there is a way to get there. This whole process rests on the premise that the benefits of the change outweigh the costs of making the change. Affirmations help you believe that change is possible.

The following questions relate to obstacles that may be interfering with the achievement of your desires:

- How much determination do you really have?
- What identity would be threatened by achieving your goal? For example, would a better job make you too independent or enable you to earn more than your mate? Would it demand more time, giving you less time as mother, husband, or partner?
- Do you secretly feel you don't deserve to attain your desires?
- Are you proving to anyone else that you can't change?
- Is it (the work, concentration, time) worth it to you?
- Are you following all the steps suggested?
- Is it what you really want?

A Decision-Making Model

Exhibit 8.1 offers a model for making informed decisions. The five steps necessary to make an informed decision are the following: *defining your goal, assessing your alternatives, gathering information, assessing the consequences (both probable and desirable)*, and *establishing your plan of action or the steps needed to achieve your goal*. Read through Exhibit 8.1 now.

Rational/Linear Decision Making

Planning is also known as the rational, or linear, approach to decision making. Decisions involve prediction. Prediction involves uncertainty. And uncertainty makes most people uncomfortable. Planning is one approach that decreases the amount of uncertainty and discomfort and increases your chances of achieving your designated goals.

Rational decision making uses the talents of the left brain, which is analytical and logical and deals with deductive thinking. It ideally follows the sequential, step-by-step procedure described in Exhibit 8.1. Please note that the arrows go in both directions to allow for new information and insights along the way.

Intuitive Decision Making

People who prefer the intuitive approach tend to be more creative and artistic. Intuitive decision makers look for the direction that feels right. They use their right brain, which thrives on imagination and creativity and adapts to change spontaneously. They feel confined when asked to write out a step-by-step process.

When faced with career planning and a job search, such individuals tend to engage in research until they have several alternatives that they believe would satisfy them equally. They like to get a feel for the overall, global picture and then decide where they fit in. Once they have researched several options, talked to people in the field, and walked around the work environment, they tend to know if it's right for them. Call it intuition or a hunch, but it is based on the cumulative insight that fits their personality. Intuitive decision makers are most apt to say they were lucky in finding the

FACTS AND FIGURES

Decision styles

Personality/temperament studies have estimated that up to 75 percent of the population prefer and use the rational decision-making approach. These studies also suggest, therefore, that 25 percent of the population prefer to use the strategy known as intuitive. Review your personality type results in Chapter 4 and list them here:

———— ———— ———— ————.

1. If you are intuitive, do you feel that many people do not understand your decision-making style?

2. If you are intuitive, what is your biggest challenge or concern when making a decision?

3. If you feel confined when asked to write a step-by-step answer to questions in this book, what would be your alternative method to show that you are understanding the information you are reading?

4. If you are a rational thinker, what is your biggest challenge in making a decision?

5. If you are a rational thinker, do you prefer to make a decision and get it done, or do you find yourself procrastinating by thinking about everything over and over again?

 To answer these questions online, go to the *Facts and Figures* module in Chapter 8 of the Companion Website.

8.1   *Choice, not chance: Decisions are in our power.*

1. Define goal or objective
   - Can you change part of the problem into a definite goal?
   - What do you want to accomplish by what date?
   - Can you state your objective now?
2. Assess alternatives
   - What are your alternatives or options?
   - Are your alternative choices consistent with your important values?
   - Can you summarize your important values in writing?
   - What is a reasonable amount of time in which to accomplish your alternatives?
3. Gather information
   - What do you know about your alternatives?
   - What assumptions are you making that you should check out?
   - What more do you need to know about your alternatives?
   - What sources will help you gather more information about your alternatives?
   - What sources will help you discover further alternatives?
4. Assess outcomes or consequences
   - Probability:
     What is the probability of the success of each alternative?
     Are your highest values part of each alternative?
   - Desirability:
     Can you eliminate the least desirable alternatives first?
     When you consider the best possible alternative, how much do you want it?
     What are you willing to give up in order to get what you want?
5. Establish a plan of action
   - Weighing everything you now know about your decision, what is your plan of action?
   - What dates will you start and complete your plan of action?
   - Does your plan of action state a clear objective?
   - Does your plan of action specify the steps necessary to achieve its objective?
   - Does your plan of action specify the conditions necessary to achieve its objective?

Until you start your plan of action, you haven't really made a decision. So start now. Make systematic decision making an adventure!

right job, the right major, or the right college. However, their luck is actually "preparation meeting opportunity." Intuitive decision makers are highly adept at finding opportunities. Thus, it is very important that such people be truly familiar with their values, interests, skills, and personalities as they explore careers.

Sometimes, the best approach for the intuitive decision maker is to fantasize and describe an ideal occupation, or to give examples of people who have an appealing career. Intuitives tend to be able to fantasize, daydream, and create verbal or written pictures of what they think is appealing. Thus a collage of images depicting a career plan may be as useful as the written action plan created by a rational decision maker. Intuitive decision making may work for some people; however, for the majority of us, a logical, step-by-step approach will yield better results.

Luck = preparation meeting opportunity

Goal Setting

Your goals and objectives are the road signs that lead you to what you want to attain in life. It is important, therefore, that a goal be distinguished from an objective.

Goals are broad statements of purpose. They are general and long-range. They refer to an ongoing process, a challenge that's meant to stretch our limits. If you have trouble defining your goals, try listing the dissatisfactions and problems in your life that are bothering you. Now ask yourself what you can do about them. You have just defined a goal. Thus, if you have been analyzing yourself while reading each chapter, you may have concluded that your problem is that you are not working in a field that utilizes your values, interests, attitudes, and skills. The goal would be to find a career that best allows you to utilize your talents. (At this point, complete Exercises 8.2 and 8.3. Exercise 8.2 will help you identify and rank some long-term goals that have importance for you. Exercise 8.3 will help you assess how ready you are to begin working on your goals.)

A career that meshes with your values, interests, attitudes, and skills but that requires five or more years of training can be considered your long-range career goal. The entry-level jobs that can prepare you for this

> ### SUCCESS STRATEGIES
>
> ## *Sample Goal and Objectives*
>
> **GOAL**
>
> To explore career alternatives to teaching by July of this year.
>
> **OBJECTIVES**
>
> 1. By February, I will start reading *The Career Fitness Program*.
> 2. Each week, I will read one chapter & do the exercises; I will finish the book by June 1.
> 3. By May, I will determine the strategies I will need to identify three jobs that use my talents.
> 4. By May, I will attend a job search workshop at the college.
> 5. By June, I will research three jobs by reading about them in the career center or library & by identifying three or more people working in those jobs locally.
> 6. By July, I will visit three of those people at their jobs.

career can be considered your short-term career goals. Thus, becoming a manager or executive would be the long-range career goal, whereas working toward a bachelor's degree in business management and/or becoming an assistant manager would be short-term goals.

Understand long-range career goal vs. short-term career goal

Objectives are the specific and practical steps used to accomplish goals. Objectives are short-term "baby steps." They are visible and measurable signposts that indicate where we are relative to reaching a goal.

The more specific our objectives are, the higher the probability that we will accomplish them. A specific objective has some indication of the action, conditions, and amount of time it will take to achieve it. Most of us have said, "I'm going to lose weight." That's an example of a nonspecific objective. We know what the action is, but we don't know how, when, and to what extent it will be accomplished. We rarely follow through with an unclear objective. Occasionally you will hear someone say, "I'm going to lose one pound this week by cutting out all bread, butter, and sweets from my diet." That's an example of a specific objective; the action, losing weight, is made specific with information on how much, when, and how it will be accomplished.

Four points should be remembered in setting goals. First, *consider what you are willing to give up* to get what you want. When most people make career changes, life in general changes for them. You may need to give up free time to take special courses. You may need to take a cut in pay (temporarily or permanently) to obtain better fringe benefits, security, and a potential chance for growth in another field, or you may need to give up being the old-timer and become the new kid on the block (and need to prove yourself again as a competent worker).

Develop a timeline

Second, *give yourself a realistic timeline* to reach your goal. If you've incorporated "baby steps" (objectives) into your timeline, you are more likely to achieve your goals. A timeline is just a way of listing in chronological order all the objectives needed to accomplish your goal.

Once you've developed a timeline, it's a good idea to show it to a close friend or counselor and to sign and date it as if it were a contract. In actuality, this is a contract with yourself. At best, you will achieve your goals; at worst, you will need to revise them and alter the timeline. At this point, complete Exercise 8.17 to reinforce your ability to formulate specific objectives.

Third, *set your goals high*. Of course, the goal must be realistic enough to be achievable. Remind yourself that you are deserving and capable; if your initial steps are specific, clear, and small enough, you will achieve them. The example provided in the box titled Sample Goal & Objectives illustrates that each objective must have importance in itself and must help lead to the overall (larger) goal.

Finally, the fourth point about setting goals is quite simple indeed: *Reward yourself after completing each objective and after reaching each goal*. Some say that the mere accomplishment of the goal should be reward enough. However, most of us tend to be more motivated toward success when we have both internal and external reward systems. The internal

Time Management Strategies

SUCCESS STRATEGIES

1. Plan and set priorities each day.
2. Prioritize specific tasks.
3. Eliminate unnecessary work or tasks.
4. Have confidence in your judgment.
5. Work on your concentration.
6. Listen actively.
7. Focus on the present.
8. Accept the help of others.
9. Set firm deadlines.
10. Schedule relaxation time.
11. Build on successes.
12. Do something; get started!
13. Ask: What is the best use for my time now?

reward is the feeling of success; the external reward is something outside of ourselves (e.g., crossing the objective off the checklist, a grade on a paper, recognition from a group of friends, dinner at a special place, or splurging on those athletic shoes you wanted). How do you reward yourself when you attain an objective or reach a goal?

One way that you can reward yourself is by learning to manage your time so that you can create the best possibilities for success. People who are successful in reaching their goals know how to manage their time. (Refer to the "Time Management Strategies" box on the previous page for hints on how to be more successful.) Many recent high school graduates and reentry students face new unstructured situations in college and need to schedule their time carefully to allow for study, work, leisure, and other responsibilities.

Manage your time

Stress Management

Sometimes the biggest obstacles that you will encounter in your job search and decision making are those that you put in place yourself. Learn how to look out for one of those landmines that can explode and destroy your best efforts: stress.

One of the greatest sources of stress is change, even when it is positive and planned, such as the change associated with finding a new job. Two researchers studying the relationship between stress and change in the late 1960s developed the Social Readjustment Rating Scale, which listed significant life change events and a corresponding stress score. The scale includes 43 life change events that might be considered stressful, such as death of a spouse, a divorce, or a jail term. The Social Readjustment Rating Scale also included several items that are related to work and the job search, including being fired at work, a change to a different line of work, and a change in responsibilities at work.

Some stress can be positive, associated with high motivation, high energy, and sharp perception. Negative stress, however, can reduce your effectiveness in your job search in many ways. Stress may produce psychological results, such as anxiety, frustration, apathy, lowered self-esteem, aggression, and depression.

You will need to develop strategies to cope when you encounter these obstacles so as to not erode your self-esteem or motivation to find work. To find work does not mean, however, that you need to give up your identity, sell out, or compromise on issues important to you. It is also not your responsibility to change

SUCCESS STRATEGIES

Stress Management Techniques

- **Take time for yourself:** Do nice things for yourself and pay attention to your personal needs and enjoyment.

- **Maintain or start a realistic exercise schedule:** Participate in activities you enjoy that will also get you moving. Exercise is one of the best remedies for stress.

- **Socialize with friends and family:** Your support network can help you keep your job search in perspective.

- **Remind yourself about the things you are good at:** Some people find it reassuring to have a list of things they do well to give themselves a motivational boost when the job search becomes overwhelming.

- **Encourage a sense of humor:** A good healthy laugh is a great way to keep perspective on all the changes in your life.

- **Keep your eye on the goal!** Remember why you are job searching and how good it will feel when you finally find an occupation that you know you will really enjoy. All the hard work pays off in the end.

Tomorrow

She was going to be all she wanted to be . . .
tomorrow.

None would be smarter or more successful than
she . . . tomorrow.

There were friends who could help her—she knew,

Who'd be only too happy to see what they could do.

On them she would call and pay a visit or
two . . . tomorrow.

Each morning she stacked up the letters she'd
write . . . tomorrow,

And thought of the things that would give her
delight . . . tomorrow.

But she hadn't one minute to stop on her way,

"More thought I must give to my future," she'd
say . . . tomorrow.

The greatest of workers this gal would have
been . . . tomorrow.

The world would have hailed her—had ever she
seen . . . tomorrow.

But, in fact, she passed on, and she faded from view,

And all that was left here when living was through

Was a mountain of things she intended to
do . . . tomorrow!

—*Unknown*

the work world. Employers who want to hire successfully from a diverse worker pool also have an obligation to help eliminate obstacles for recruiting and retaining quality employees. Some employers who have had little experience hiring for diversity may welcome your willingness to discuss your work needs and expectations.

Recognize priorities

Decision making requires all the elements of positive affirmations and coping with stress when you are seeking an interview or starting a new position. Strategies for improving your overall attitude and managing stress are essential in establishing priorities for success. Some of these techniques are listed in the box "Stress Management Techniques" on the previous page.

Deciding on a Major

At this point you should be focusing your thoughts regarding your values, personality, interests, and skills toward either a college major or a few occupations that will express your career goals.

If you are thinking about a major, you will need to gather information about how jobs are related to college majors. The last chapter explained how to gather written information about careers; some resources may mention majors related to specific careers. Whenever you meet people who have interesting jobs, do your own research by asking them if they have a degree and in what major. Because many people have majored in subjects seemingly unrelated to their jobs, your big choice will be to decide whether you should choose a major closely related to an interesting area of work (for example, a business major to become a manager), or if you should select a major that seems most interesting to you at this time in your life (for example, communications or psychology). The fact of the matter is that either major can lead you to a successful business career.

If all of your personal assessment does not suggest a specific major, you may need to sample some introductory courses to see if they appeal to you; for example, you might want to take a course providing an introduction to interior design, an introduction to management, or an introduction to engineering. It is better to sample several majors during one or two semesters than to choose one prematurely only to find out after several semesters that you don't really like that field.

Remember, many occupations do not have a strong relationship to a specific college major. Employers are looking primarily for candidates who are well-rounded individuals and who have done well in college no matter what their major. Therefore, identify a major that interests you and in which you can excel and enjoy the learning experience.

Deciding on Training

If you are not interested in attending or completing four years of college but want to select a job that can best fulfill your career goals as soon as possible, then you have at least two issues to address: (1) job information and (2) training requirements. If the job information you have collected indicates that you are ready to enter the field, then you are also ready to read the chapters on job search strategy. If the job you want requires that you obtain further training, you will need to find out where to obtain it. Possible resources to use in obtaining this information were discussed in Chapter 7. Using personal contacts or the yellow pages, you can call people working in the field of your interest, or the professional or trade association for that field, to obtain information on credible training centers. Usually people who work in a field know which schools have the best reputation. Public community colleges, technical junior colleges, and adult and proprietary schools also offer a variety of training programs. Be sure to compare the courses that you will be required to take with the preparation and skills necessary to perform the job. Making informed decisions is dependent on acquiring accurate information.

Define your goals and know how to reach them

Deciding on Change

If you are exploring career opportunities as a result of company downsizing or family changes, the need for competent decision-making skills is perhaps even more imperative. All that you have learned about yourself thus far should give you the incentive and confidence to apply the decision-making skills discussed in this chapter. The exercises that follow will give you additional decision-making practice.

Summary

uccessful career planning involves two processes related to goals: (1) defining your goals and (2) knowing how to reach them. The more completely you plan out your objectives, the more likely you will be to achieve your goals. The key to the process is overcoming the hurdle of negative thinking. Block out the tendency to be self-critical. Dare to put aside your anticipation of failure, your fears and excuses, and your past habits. Allow yourself the right to create goals that energize you and take you beyond your past efforts.

The following exercises are designed to help you become aware of steps in the decision-making process and to encourage you to set some career and life goals. For example, you will be asked to decide what you want to do by the end of the current year and then one year from now. This can mean acquiring new skills or improving current skills, moving toward career advancement or career change, or staying where you are. Remember to try to picture in your mind what you want in your work life (e.g., type of work, responsibility, surroundings, salary, management relationship), and then focus on the exact steps necessary to reach your goals. If you can't picture the necessary steps, you need to gather more information (e.g., from people who have been in similar positions or from written materials about the field) so you can make attainable career decisions.

Following the outline in the decision-making model (see Exhibit 8.1), choose from alternatives, select the one that has the best possibility of success for you, create a plan of action, set specific objectives, and take action. As you attain objectives that move you toward your goal, reassess your decisions by taking in and processing information about how you feel in moving toward this goal. Be flexible, have alternatives, and understand that change may provide you with options (and challenges) that you never expected. Be honest with yourself. If you feel uncomfortable with your goal or your plan of action, enlist the help of a career guidance professional to assist you in formulating a goal that you can successfully attain.

Making Decisions

The written exercises that follow help increase your awareness about how you make decisions. Exercise 8.1 asks that you rank yourself on two dimensions of decision-making style. There are no right or wrong answers. This is a chance to become aware of your personal style of decision making. Exercises 8.2 and 8.3 review goal setting. Exercises 8.4 to 8.7 assess whether you actually do what you say is important to you. Exercises 8.8 to 8.15 should clarify other factors that can affect your decisions. Exercise 8.16 asks you to think about some alternatives to your current life choices. Exercise 8.17 indicates your ability to recognize and state clear objectives (there are right and wrong answers). Exercise 8.18 encourages you to look for creative solutions. Exercise 8.19 asks you to list your time-savers. Exercise 8.20 asks you to choose a long-term goal along with clear short-term activities that will start you toward the long-term goal now.

To answer these questions online, go to the *Exercise* module in Chapter 8 of the Companion Website.

Ranking Yourself

Place a check (✓) on each of the scales below to indicate your style of decision making:

cautious										risk taking
intuitive										logical
dependent										independent
influenced by others										self-motivated
feeling/emotional										rational
passive										active
quiet										assertive

Reviewing Goal Setting

In Chapter 2, we discussed long-term goals. Now let's try to become much more specific. List three specific long-term goals. Use additional paper if you have more than three.

1. _____

2. _____

3. _____

Let's assume you knew that you would not survive an earthquake six months from now. Would your short-term goals be any different? List at least three goals that relate to how you would live the next six months:

1. _____

2. _____

3. _____

Now you have a list of long-term and short-term goals. Deciding which ones are most important to you is the next step. This is called *setting priorities*. To do this, mark with the letter A those goals that are of most importance or value to you. Those of medium importance, mark with a B, and those of low importance, with a C. Let's look at the A goals first. With more than one A goal, you will want to rank them, for example, A_1, A_2, and A_3, with the A_1 goal being the most important to you at this time. Do the same for your B and C goals. Now rank your long- and short-term A, B, and C goals.

Activities are those actions we take to accomplish our objectives, which in turn get us closer to accomplishing our long-term goals. Take a separate sheet of paper for each of your three long-term goals, and list as many activities as you can think of to get you close to the goal. Don't question or judge the activities that come to mind; just list whatever they are. After you've listed these activities, ask yourself this question: Am I willing to commit five minutes in the next week to working on this activity? If your answer is no, then draw a line through the activity. It's okay if you don't want to spend the time on the activity; you don't have to make excuses. Your choice of the activities you're willing to commit five minutes to will enable you to choose the high-priority tasks. Now rank those activities you will do in the next week (A_1, A_2, A_3, etc.). Your activities are now organized. You're on your way toward meeting your goals. Make it an adventure and enjoy your accomplishments along the way.

Write a Goal Statement

1. Write a goal statement, describing either a short-term or a long-term goal:

   _____

   _____

   _____

2. Can you answer yes to the following questions about this goal?

   Did I choose it personally?

   Am I ready to make a written commitment to this goal?

   Am I setting a deadline?

   Is it within my control?

   Have I thought through the consequences?

   Is the goal based on my values?

   Can I visualize it in considerable detail? (Is this goal specific?)

   Will I work toward it?

   Am I taking responsibility for this goal?

   Is this goal measurable?

Task Identification

Spending a maximum of five minutes, write down all the tasks you need to do in the next week.

_____

_____

_____

_____

_____

_____

_____

One Year to Live

If you had only one year to live, which of the tasks listed would still be important to you?

_____

_____

_____

Meeting Your Needs

How much of a week's work is spent reaching your own personal goals versus meeting others' needs?

_____

_____

Your Energizers

What percentage of your daily activities gives you energy? List your energizing activities.

_____

_____

_____

_____

_____

Recent Decisions

What are some decisions you have made recently?

_____
_____
_____
_____
_____
_____
_____

Priorities

Were some of these decisions more important than others? Why?

_____
_____
_____
_____
_____

Irrevocable Decisions

Give an example of a decision you made or might have to make that could be extremely difficult to change.

_____
_____
_____

Harmful Decisions

Give an example of a decision that might be harmful to you or someone you care about in some way.

_____
_____
_____

Limiting Decisions

Give an example of a decision you could make that might keep you from doing something you want to do.

_____

_____

_____

Contingent Decisions

Give an example of a decision that would have an effect on other decisions.

_____

_____

_____

Values

What value or values were important to you in making the decisions listed in Exercises 8.10 to 8.13?

_____

_____

_____

_____

_____

_____

Factors Adversely Affecting Decisions

The purposes of this exercise are to investigate factors that may unfavorably influence decision making and to determine whether any patterns are evident. First, on the lines provided, write down three decisions you have made. Then, using the chart that follows, indicate which of the factors influenced you in making each decision, and to what extent they were present. To do this, use a ✓ to represent decision 1, an X for decision 2, and an O for decision 3. (Some sections of the chart may contain two or three symbols when you are done.)

Decision 1 (✓) _____

Decision 2 (X) _____

Decision 3 (O) _____

External Factors	Slightly Present	Moderately Present	Strongly Present
1. Family expectations			
2. Family responsibilities			
3. Cultural stereotypes			
4. Male/female stereotypes			
5. Survival needs			
6. Other (specify)			
Internal Factors	Slightly Present	Moderately Present	Strongly Present
1. Lack of self-confidence			
2. Fear of change			
3. Fear of making a wrong decision			
4. Fear of failure			
5. Fear of ridicule			
6. Other (specify)			

After filling in the chart, look for patterns that may appear:

1. Do you experience more feelings related to internal or external factors as obstacles to making satisfying decisions?

_____

_____

_____

2. If a particular factor is strongly present only once, but another factor is moderately present in two or possibly all three of your decisions, which of the two factors do you think is more significant in affecting your decision making?

_____

_____

_____

_____

_____

What If . . .

1. Suppose you have lost all sources of support (e.g., you have been laid off or your family has withdrawn support of your schooling). List three things you could do:

a. _____

b. _____

c. _____

2. How satisfying would these alternatives be to you?

_____

_____

3. Suppose you have one year before losing the support. With one year to prepare, what would you do?

   a. What alternatives might you choose?

   b. What information would you need about your chosen alternatives?

   c. What action would you take?

   d. How satisfying would your one-year plan be?

Specific/Nonspecific Objectives

The following statements are objectives. Read each objective and decide whether the objective is specific or nonspecific. These are statements anyone might make; they don't necessarily apply to you. Imagine that someone is standing in front of you in a line making each of these statements. With that in mind, mark each objective as "S" (specific) or "N" (nonspecific) to the left of the statement.

_____ 1. I want to explore my interests.

_____ 2. I want to get a good job.

_____ 3. I'd like to get an idea of the job I'm best suited for.

_____ 4. I'd like to take Spanish 1 next semester and for at least two years more, so I'll have another skill to use as a teacher.

_____ 5. When I leave school, I want to get a job that pays at least $10 an hour.

_____ 6. Tomorrow I'm going to make a one-hour appointment to see Ms. Rogers in her office.

_____ 7. I want to get at least a B on every history exam and earn a B as my final grade this semester.

_____ 8. I'm going to ask Teresa to help me find some information about health careers in the Career Development and Placement Center right after class.

_____ 9. I plan to move to an area where there are lots of jobs.

_____ 10. I want to be accepted by the state university when I graduate.

_____ 11. I want to find out more about myself.

___ 12. I want to get along better with other people at work.

___ 13. Next week I'm going to see my friends more.

___ 14. I'm going to read one good book about social service careers tonight.

___ 15. I want to get a good education.

(See page 202 for answers.)

Test Your Assumptions

EXERCISE 8.18

1. Try to connect the dots below with only four straight lines and without lifting your pen.

• • •

• • •

• • •

2. Make a 6 out of IX by adding one line.

IX

(See page 202 for answers.)

Time-Savers

EXERCISE 8.19

List three things you do to save time:

_____

_____

_____

Short- and Long-Term Goals

EXERCISE 8.20

Write down a long-term goal, and list two activities you can do in the next two weeks that will contribute to it.

_____

_____

_____

EXERCISE
8.21

WWWebwise

For additional activities online, go to the WWWebwise module in Chapter 8 of the Companion Website.

EXERCISE
8.22

Exercise Summary

Write a brief paragraph answering these questions.

What did you learn about yourself from these exercises? How does this knowledge relate to your career/life planning? How do you feel? Go back to the decisions you listed in Exercises 8.4–8.14. Has your thinking changed regarding these decisions?

_____

_____

_____

_____

_____

_____

_____

_____

_____

_____

_____

_____

_____

_____

_____

_____

_____

_____

_____

_____

_____

_____

_____

_____

_____

_____

_____

_____

Go to page 208 of the chapter summaries and fill out the Chapter 8 exercise summary now.

Answers to Exercise 8.17:

1. N	4. S	7. N	10. N	13. N
2. N	5. N	8. S	11. N	14. S
3. N	6. S	9. N	12. N	15. N

Answers to Exercise 8.18:

1.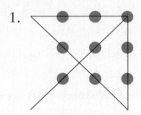

(The directions did not indicate that you must keep the lines *within* the pattern of dots.)

2. # SIX

(The directions did not mandate a *straight* line.)

Chapter Summaries

Putting It All Together
to Reach a Tentative Career Goal

The summary section on the following pages will be helpful to you as you progress through *The Career Fitness Program* and as you prepare to begin Part Three of the text.

First, as you complete each chapter, we encourage you to fill in the appropriate chapter summary here. Be as thorough as you can.

Second, when you reach this part of the text after completing Chapters 1 through 8, review all your responses carefully. If your responses today are different from those you recorded when you initially read the chapter, record your current responses now.

Third, complete the exercises on pages 209–212, which will help you integrate all of this information and set a career goal.

Exercise Summary

CHAPTER **1**

Refer back to original Chapter 1 answers.

1. I am _____

_____

_____

2. I need _____

_____

_____

3. I want _____

_____

_____

(continued)

4. My current life stage in selecting a career could be summarized as

_____

_____

_____

5. The Holland Type most like me is:
   - ○ Realistic   ○ Investigative
   - ○ Artistic   ○ Social
   - ○ Enterprising   ○ Conventional

6. Five adjectives that best describe me are _____

_____

_____

_____

7. My favorite school subjects include _____

_____

_____

_____

8. Five high-status occupations are _____

_____

_____

_____

_____

Exercise Summary

CHAPTER 2

Refer back to original Chapter 2 answers.

1. I am proud that _____

_____

_____

2. Five positive attitudes I bring to the job are _____

_____

_____

_____

3. I admire the following characteristics in people: _____

_____

_____

_____

4. I am working on developing the following qualities: _____

_____

_____

5. My affirmations are _____

_____

_____

_____

_____

Exercise Summary

CHAPTER

3

Refer back to original Chapter 3 answers.

1. I highly value _____

_____

_____

2. A problem in society that really concerns me is _____

_____

_____

3. My most important considerations in a job are _____

_____

_____

4. I am energized by the following types of activities (from my past jobs, volunteer experiences, or hobbies):

_____

_____

_____

5. My ideal job would be (if you don't have a title, list the job tasks or activities)

_____

_____

_____

Exercise Summary

CHAPTER 4

Refer back to original Chapter 4 answers.

1. Circle the term in each of the following pairs that best describes your personality type:

    extravert / introvert   sensing / intuitive   thinking / feeling   judging / perceiving

2. Circle your top three Holland Interest Environments from Chapter 4:

    realistic   enterprising   investigative
    conventional   artistic   social

3. List the results of any assessments or inventories you have taken during the past year. For example:

    a. Strong Interest Inventory: Code letters ___ ___ ___ General Occupational Themes:

        _____

        Three highest Basic Interest Scales:

        _____

        _____

        Very similar/somewhat similar occupational scales (job titles). List five:

        _____

        _____

        _____

    b. Career Occupational Preference Survey (COPS), U.S. Interest Survey, or other interest inventory:

        _____

        List your three highest occupational groups from this survey or from any other interest inventory used:

        _____

        _____

        List five related job titles that sound interesting:

        _____

        _____

        _____

4. After reviewing your interests, list your three career choices:

    _____

    _____

    _____

Exercise Summary

CHAPTER 5

Refer back to original Chapter 5 answers.

1. Fill in the percentage of time during the day you would like to work with data, people, and things.

   _____ data   _____ people   _____ things

2. Three of my accomplishments are _____

   _____

   _____

3. A summary of the skills I most enjoy using: _____

   _____

   _____

4. The skills I want to use in my future career are _____

   _____

   _____

5. The skills I hope to develop in the next few years are _____

   _____

   _____

Exercise Summary

CHAPTER 6

Refer back to original Chapter 6 answers.

1. The advantages of my age, sex, and background in looking for a job or working toward my career goal are _____

   _____

   _____

2. The disadvantages of my age, sex, race, or physical limitations in looking for a job or working toward my career goal are _____

   _____

   _____

3. Occupations that interest me (based on the trends described in Chapter 6):

   _____

   _____

   _____

Exercise Summary

CHAPTER 7

Refer back to original Chapter 7 answers.

1. List one job from Exercise 7.6: _____

2. Choose a job you researched and list the titles or names of sources used in each category:

   a. Newspapers, bulletin boards, magazines _____
   _____

   b. Trade journals (name one) _____

   c. Directories (name one) _____

   d. Internet addresses _____
   _____

   e. Career and placement centers _____
   _____

Exercise Summary

CHAPTER 8

Refer back to original Chapter 8 answers.

1. I use the following decision-making strategies: _____
   _____

2. My limiting beliefs include _____
   _____

3. My belief about the future is _____
   _____

4. The best use of my time right now (according to time management strategies) is
   _____

5. A long-range goal related to my career is _____
   _____

6. A short-term goal related to my career is _____
   _____

7. External factors that can affect these career decisions include ____
   _____

8. Internal factors that can influence these career decisions include __
   _____

Now complete the following exercises to integrate this information and set a tentative career goal.

Quick Impressions

R ead each category and respond quickly by recording the first three thoughts that come to mind in each one. Then list short- and long-term career goals.

Career Values _____

_____

_____

Career Interests _____

_____

_____

Career Skills/Abilities _____

_____

_____

Possible Careers _____

_____

_____

Career-Related, Leisure-Time Pursuits _____

_____

_____

SHORT-TERM CAREER GOALS AND OBJECTIVES	LONG-TERM CAREER GOALS AND OBJECTIVES	SUPPORTIVE PEOPLE TO HELP ME IMPLEMENT MY CAREER GOALS
1. _____	1. _____	_____
2. _____	2. _____	_____
3. _____	3. _____	_____
4. _____	4. _____	_____
5. _____	5. _____	_____

Review your Quick Impressions with three supportive people in your life. Ask for their input and help in working toward your goals. As a final step in confirming your career goal, complete the next exercise, Information Integration and Goal Setting. Refer to the sample on page 211 if you need a sample to help you.

Information Integration and Goal Setting

Complete the form below using the sample on the following page as a guideline.

Long-range career goal: _____

Present short-range career goal (one- to five-year goal):

I look forward to *majoring* or *getting training* in _____

so that I can become _____

because I *value* _____

_____

and my *interests* include _____

_____

and this career would allow me to _____

_____

Summary of strengths and weaknesses related to goal:

Personal strengths ("your type")

_____

_____

_____

_____

Personal weaknesses (need to improve)

_____

_____

_____

_____

Favorable external conditions
related to career choice

_____

_____

_____

_____

Unfavorable external conditions
related to career choice

_____

_____

_____

_____

Strategies to reach goal

_____

_____

_____

_____

Resources available to help reach goal

_____

_____

_____

_____

Alternative short-range career goals that would be equally satisfying: _____

_____

_____

Training needed to enter this career alternative: _____

_____

Information Integration and Goal Setting

Long-range career goal: <u>To enable people to use their resources.</u>

Present short-range career goal (one- to five-year goal):

I look forward to *majoring* or *getting training* in <u>Psychology</u>

so that I can become <u>a social worker or counselor</u>

because I *value* <u>helping others, serving people, being resourceful, variety, creativity, and continually learning.</u>

and my *interests* include <u>communication, holistic health, adult development, higher education, and career counseling.</u>

and this career would allow me to <u>share, keep informed, serve people, be an expert</u>

Summary of strengths and weaknesses related to goal:

Personal strengths ("your type")

<u>Have a B.A., willing to study, quick learner, self-confident, able to present before groups, eligible for credential programs, have already volunteered</u>

Personal weaknesses (need to improve)

<u>Impatient, lack money for further education, fear taking the Graduate Record Examination, need time management instruction</u>

Favorable external conditions
related to career choice

<u>Many education programs available, many counselors retiring in next 3 years, already working, volunteer experiences are available, graduate programs exist</u>

Unfavorable external conditions
related to career choice

<u>Not many openings now, not many paid positions available now, many people with this degree out of work</u>

Strategies to reach goal

<u>Talk to graduate advisor, obtain application to graduate school, discuss alternatives with adviser, identify volunteer opportunities, volunteer, seek part-time job related to counseling (e.g., teacher's aide)</u>

Resources available to help reach goal

<u>Faculty, counselors, college career and placement centers</u>

Alternative short-range career goals that would be equally satisfying: <u>Work in the Student Activities Club as a Club Organizer or be a Student Affairs Assistant in the Career Center helping students find resources, leading orientations, and organizing outings to industry.</u>

Training needed to enter this career alternative: <u>Working in Student Affairs or the Career Center while in college.</u>

If you are still confused about which career to focus on, start with the one that is most easily attainable. Work through your job search strategy in Part Three of this book using that career as your focal point. Once you understand the job search process, you can use it to explore additional career goals.

Now that you have selected a career goal and identified your strengths and weaknesses, answer the following questions:

1. What can you do now (or in the next six months) to address one or two of your weaknesses? List one weak area here (e.g., test anxiety), and list one method to help you improve (e.g., see a counselor to learn how to reduce anxiety).

   Weakness: _____

   _____

   _____

   _____

   How to improve: _____

   _____

   _____

   _____

2. What can you do now (or in the next six months) to start working toward your career goal? List three activities you can do to move you closer to your goal (e.g., see a counselor to find out requirements for the major; sign up for major-related classes).

   To do:

   a. _____

   b. _____

   c. _____

Job Search Strategy

CHAPTER 9
Targeting Your Job Search

CHAPTER 10
Preparing a Winning Resume

CHAPTER 11
Interviewing Successfully

CHAPTER 12
Future Focus

PART THREE

213

Targeting Your Job Search

LEARNING OBJECTIVES

**At the end
of the chapter
you will be able to . . .**

- Identify the components
  of a successful job search

- Begin the process of
  searching for a job

- Explain how to find the
  hidden job market

Congratulations! You have finished the personal assessment and world of work portions of your career fitness program. You have reviewed and analyzed your skills, your interests, your personality, and your values, and you have tentatively selected some career options. They are tentative because you may find reason to alter your decisions as you continue to gather information. Just as adjustments occur in a physical fitness program based on your body's responses, so must adjustments occur in your career fitness program based on your gut-level responses. The next step is to begin to design your job search strategy, which represents the third part of the career-planning process. Job search strategy involves the long-term process of acquiring the training, background, and experience needed to be competitive in the job market associated with your anticipated career goal. Simultaneously, you need to begin to identify potential employers for your skills and to develop a resume that reflects your background and your particular career goal. Finally, you need to learn how to present yourself in the best light in job interviews.

Experience is not what happens to you.
It is what you do with what happens to you.

Your job search must be conducted consistently over a period of time. Studies indicate that it can take as long as four months or more of searching to obtain the job you are seeking. Regardless of how certain or tentative you are currently feeling about your career alternatives, you must have a specific occupation in mind in order to benefit from the remainder of this book. The goal of this chapter is for you to choose one of the occupations you have been considering. Then keep it in mind as you read and work through the following chapters.

The rest of this chapter will provide you with the information and skills to enable you to gain control in a competitive job market. In other words, you will learn many techniques to put yourself in the right place at the right time and to present yourself as the best candidate for your desired job. The underlying and most important concept, however, is focusing on what you want. Without this concentration, you run the risk of being swayed by random opportunities and jobs that don't live up to your expectations. *Focusing* means evaluating and comparing all new information with your needs, values, interests, and skills. Remember, the first job you seek should not be considered an end in itself. It is one job on the way to several more that will compose your total career. As the dictionary defines *career,* it is a "pursuit of consecutive progressive achievement in public, professional, or business life." Additionally, career experts predict that the average worker can expect to make three to five career changes in a lifetime.

This approach assumes that you have identified a job objective for which you feel *100 percent enthusiasm,* that you will go after with *100 percent determination,* and that you will interview for with *100 percent of your heart.* This approach charges you with the responsibility to make things happen!

Your Comprehensive Job Search Strategy

1. Commit 100 percent to your job objective.

2. Compare the tasks and responsibilities required in your chosen job at different companies and organizations.

3. Get involved in voluntary and entry-level jobs related to your ultimate goal.

4. Identify the hidden job market through personal contacts and professional associations.

5. Use the Internet.

6. Utilize professional assistance, if necessary.

7. Conduct information interviews with people who are in a position to hire you. Approach all contacts with enthusiasm and sincerity and send thank-you letters to all contacts.

8. Network: let everyone know you are looking for a job (friends, neighbors, dentist, etc.).

9. Identify the needs of the organization. If the exact position you would like is not available, your task is to define a problem within the organization that you can help to solve with your unique skills.

10. Convince an employer that you have the skills he or she needs.

Designing a Comprehensive Job Search Strategy

A comprehensive job search strategy involves much more than just researching to decide what your ideal job is, or simply identifying areas of employment in which you expect to find such jobs. It encourages you, once having made these basic decisions, to be assertive in locating and actually becoming employed in your ideal job. A comprehensive job search strategy stimulates you to consider a variety of aspects related to attaining your ideal job goal, such as whether you are likely to find your job in the geographical area where you live or want to live, and what sorts of activities and experiences will better qualify you for your career objectives. Equally important, job search strategy helps you to select and become involved in volunteer and entry-level activities that are the vital first steps toward your ultimate career goal. You can't always start right out in your ideal job, but guided by job search strategy, you can almost always start out in jobs and activities that will lead to your goals. Assuming that you have adequate skills and background and that you have identified a job for which you are 100 percent enthusiastic, the following approach will work for you.

Go for the job you really want!

First, you must make a contract with yourself to complete all the tasks necessary to get the job. Next, you must become totally informed about the tasks and responsibilities of the job you are seeking. Much of this information can be gained from the written and electronic materials previously cited. Additionally, you will need to amplify the written information by making personal contacts with insiders.

Once you have identified your ideal job situation, an important part of your job search strategy is to investigate activities that may be indispensable first steps toward your goal. Such activities may be temporary, volunteer, or entry-level jobs in your chosen field. They can be very important in adding to your experience and making you a better candidate for your preferred job. For example, a student who wanted to move into the advertising business took a job as a receptionist in the executive suite of an advertising agency in New York. Of course, he had brushed up on his office skills to get this entry-level job, but he didn't plan to remain at that level for long. He kept his eyes and ears open for ways that he could contribute to the efficiency of the business. Within six months he had learned enough about the advertising business to interview at a competing firm and become assistant to an executive account manager.

Identify your ideal job situation

One final suggestion before you conduct further research: You may find that your ideal job is years of education and experience away from you, or that you don't have the dedication or talent to make it in your ideal field. If so, you may be just as satisfied if you work in some job *related* to the career of your dreams. For example, behind every president of the United States there are advisers, speech writers, guards, secretaries, chefs, press representatives, and chauffeurs. Behind every rock musician there are disc jockeys, public relations representatives, recording technicians, piano tuners, album cover designers, sound editors, cutting designers, concert coordinators, costume and makeup artists, and background musicians.

Begin with an entry-level job related to your ideal

There is some merit to the idea that if you stay around the field, constantly adding to your experience, you may be at the right place at the right time and get the job of your dreams. Every understudy in a play or musical has the chance to become a star some day!

Your Job Search: Getting Started

To improve the chances of getting your dream job, use a variety of strategies. Typical resources include reading newspaper want ads and trade journals, using the Internet, sending resumes to potential employers through the mail and by e-mail, using permanent or temporary employment agencies, and volunteering or interning while in school. In addition, many hidden resources exist. The first section of this chapter focuses on common employment resources; the latter part suggests ways to tap into those that are less apparent.

UNDERSTANDING AND USING CLASSIFIED ADS

Employment or classified ads are found in local newspapers, newspapers from your desired geographical area, trade journals, a supplement from *The Wall Street Journal,* and association magazines, as well as on the Internet. Most newspapers have classified advertising sections with separate employment sections. Other job listings are found in the state employment department, county and city personnel offices, college placement centers, private employment offices, and the personnel offices of individual organizations.

Only 15–20% of all available jobs appear in employment ads

Regularly reviewing the want ads, especially in larger cities, over several months can lead to meaningful employment leads. Although it has been estimated that only 15 percent of jobs are found through ads, thousands of ads are published in large newspapers. You can increase your chances of obtaining a job by applying for a variety of job titles. People with accounting degrees may be eligible for junior accountant, management trainee, accounts payable, auditor, and securities broker, in addition to accountant.

Another way to increase your chances of finding a good job involves combining a newsprint want ads search with your active accumulation of Internet information about companies. When you see a job opening at a firm that you've already visited, you should have a contact in that company to call and ask for more information about the opening. You may find that the ad is written with absolute qualifications but that the specific department will accept alternative experiences in lieu of some of the specific qualifications. Only people who have personal contacts would know such information.

PROMOTING YOURSELF THROUGH MAIL AND E-MAIL

If you fail to find your ideal job in employment ads, you might try promoting yourself via mail. You may use the more traditional form of mail, or you may choose to communicate electronically via the computer.

Postal mailings are quickly becoming outdated; they are expensive and usually result in low response. Some career fields lend themselves to this type of self-promotion better than others. For example, if you are a graphic artist or a freelance editor or writer, your potential employers may be more likely to peruse mailed-in resumes and sample work than employers in fields such as accounting and education. If creative promotion would be a plus in your field, then a direct-mail campaign may be an important part of your job search.

In the case of postal mailings, you will probably limit your campaign to those companies and organizations most likely to employ people in your career field, due to the expense of blanket mailings. No matter what your field, devote time and energy to coming up with your list of target employers. (Use the sources of information we discussed in Chapter 7, and also rely heavily on local business directories and even telephone directories.) To encourage response, include a stamped, self-addressed postcard for employers to use. Your postcard might include check-off statements such as "Sorry, no openings" and "Opening available; please contact _____," as well as blanks for the name, address, and telephone number of the organization.

In the case of electronic mailings (e-mail), you will be able to cover much more ground (for less money). Using the online programs available today, you can send your resume or other promotional material to specific groups and organizations, as in postal mailings. You can gain access to electronic mailing lists, lists of interest groups and discussion forums, and other means of targeting your promotion. Many resources explaining how to make good use of the electronic resume are available; refer to Chapter 10 for more information. Additionally, refer to the box titled "Selected Online Employment Databases" at the end of this chapter.

Accentuate your assets

UNDERSTANDING AND USING EMPLOYMENT AGENCIES

Before you register with an agency, check carefully on its fees, the types of positions it handles, and its reputation. There is some controversy over the merits of a system that makes a profit by simply placing you on a job with limited concern for your satisfaction. However, there are good agencies that are very concerned about matching people with jobs that suit them.

Temporary employment agencies provide excellent ways to get back into the workforce or to test the climate in a variety of companies. The jobs available are no longer just clerical or entry-level. Many temporary employment agencies specialize in specific fields such as accounting or nursing. Some agencies place people part-time; some place people for short-term assignments. Agencies are placing even chief executive officers and college presidents in temporary, as well as full-time, employment.

For energetic, industrious workers, part-time and temporary assignments may lead to full-time employment and the opportunity to move up to better positions. Any job you hold may be the first step in a career. Exhibit a positive attitude, and do your best no matter what the position. However, you will probably be under contract to the temporary agency for a specified period of time, and thus cannot be hired by the employer until the contract expires.

VOLUNTEERING

The importance of getting job-related experience cannot be overestimated. As can be seen in Xiao-ying's story, her volunteer experience supplemented her previous training. Many people have negative images of volunteering. They think volunteering means doing paperwork or "go-fer" work. However, you can create meaningful volunteer positions for yourself rather than taking whatever is available. To optimize your chances for obtaining such useful

Meet Xiao-ying

Xiao-ying is tired of going to college. As she is beginning work in a master's degree program in anthropology, she realizes that studying native tribes in the wilds of Africa will not enable her to make the personal contribution to other people's lives that she feels necessary for her own job satisfaction. With the help of a career counselor at the local YWCA and by talking with people working in her ideal setting, she becomes aware that working in a family-planning clinic will best suit her personal needs. Xiao-ying volunteers for one year in a clinic and, in addition, conducts some studies on pregnancy and childbirth. Within a year she has a full-time job in the education department of Planned Parenthood.

Once she has committed to a full-time job at Planned Parenthood, Xiao-ying realizes that she is no longer interested in pursuing a master's degree in anthropology. She finds that, instead, she can be accepted to an evening graduate pro-

experience, go through a community voluntary action center, a college volunteer services office (sometimes part of the college placement office), a college cooperative education office, or a service learning office.

An even more intense volunteer experience for those who have the time and resources may be through the U.S. Peace Corps, VISTA, or the UN Volunteers. Such volunteer work requires a commitment of one to three years and provides room, board, benefits (including government service experience), and a living allowance.

The Peace Corps recruits individuals with varied academic backgrounds; for example, recruits may teach math and English in developing countries. Engineering graduates are especially valuable in the Peace Corps, with their math and science expertise, and civil engineers are needed to build water purification plants and roads.

Volunteering adds visibility and experience to your job search. However, volunteering does not relate only to jobs. Think about becoming a student member of a professional association. Student membership usually offers all the same benefits of regular membership but costs much less. Once in an organization, *volunteer* for committees and leadership positions, and gain visibility and recognition. The people in these organizations will soon be your peers. This is also an excellent method of making contacts for both jobs and letters of recommendation.

INTERNING

Your college or university may help to arrange *internships* in some fields of study. Internships may be paid or unpaid and are usually restrict-

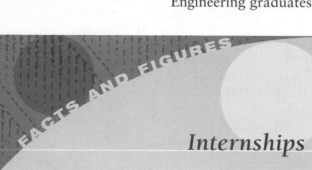

FACTS AND FIGURES

Internships

The book *Internships 2003,* published by Peterson's (Princeton, NJ, 2003) includes detailed information on more than 2,000 organizations offering 50,000 internships in the business, nonprofit, and government sectors. Arranged by career field, it includes short-term positions with businesses such as *The Wall Street Journal,* Procter & Gamble, 3M, Aetna Life and Casualty, Sierra Club, and the U.S. Department of Energy.

gram in counseling at the same university. This allows her to work full-time and complete a master's degree in counseling within three years. At that time, Xiao-ying becomes a counselor for Planned Parenthood and begins a private practice on the side.

1. How did Xiao-ying decide that her master's degree studies were not leading to her ultimate job satisfaction?

2. How did her volunteer experience help her?

3. What kind of volunteer experience, internship, or service learning assignment could help you choose or confirm your career goals?

 To answer these questions online, go to the *Real Stories* module in Chapter 9 of the Companion Website.

---

ed to students who have studied in the subject area of the internship. For example, a history major or a political science major may be given the highest priority among applicants for an internship in local or state government; a graphic arts, English, or communications major may be given priority for an internship in an advertising agency.

Some colleges have internship offices or experiential education offices that arrange internships of different types, including *fieldwork,* which involves work required as part of a major. (Prospective teachers usually must student teach, for example, to earn their degree or certificate.)

Internships can be used to build extremely valuable experience and contacts. At Keuka College in New York, one political science major had *three* government internships before graduation. At that campus, each political science major takes a four-week field period either in January or during the summer. Students have worked for state assemblypersons, the lieutenant governor, and the Democratic Senatorial Campaign Committee in Washington, for example.

At Concordia College in Minnesota, students alternate semesters of work and study or work part-time while continuing classes in the school's cooperative education program. This gives them longer-term connections with an organization and allows them to learn more about the workplace and professional environments. Ramapo College in New Jersey provided one of its students with overseas experience at a marketing firm in England. When she graduated, she got a job as an assistant account executive at the New York office of Lloyds Bank PLC, the British bank chain.

The Princeton Review Online: *America's top internships*

Want to intern with the Academy of Television Arts & Sciences? How about the White House? The *Princeton Review* carries descriptions and application information for some of the best internship programs in the country. Its website describes the positions, requirements, compensation (they're not all unpaid), duration, deadlines, and other important info.

The *Princeton Review Online* can be found at www.review.com. Click on **Career Internships.**

Meet Felipe

As a business student, Felipe wanted to focus on human resources development and training in industry. So he joined the American Society for Training and Development (ASTD). He volunteered to chair the student recruitment subcommittee and joined the Career Development Special Interest Group. Two years later, when interviewing for a job as assistant to a director of training, he found he knew people who had worked with the director, was able to learn about the firm from former employees who were ASTD members, and made an excellent impression in his interview.

FACTS AND FIGURES

Employers rate experience

(5 = extremely important / 1 = not important)

Relevant Work Experience	4.00
Internship Experience	3.82
Any Work Experience	3.69
Cooperative Education Work Experience	3.32

Source: Annual employer survey by NACE, 2002.

WHAT DOES THIS MEAN TO YOU?

1. Do you have work or volunteer experience?
2. How can you get an internship or volunteer experience related to your identified goals?
3. Who are the people or what are the resources you can use to find experience related to your goals?
4. If you are a student, have you investigated cooperative education at your college? What is preventing you from enrolling in this program?

To answer these questions online, go to the *Facts and Figures* module in Chapter 9 of the Companion Website.

Explore internship listings on the Internet

Interns are generally closely supervised by college professors to help ensure they gain educational experience and benefit from the internship personally, while they provide services for the employer. Ideally, interns working as part of a college program enjoy a meaningful learning experience that provides them with skills that could not be learned from a book.

Another way for college students to get experience that may lead to a full-time position is through cooperative education programs. (At some schools, the terms *internship* and *cooperative education* are used synonymously, but others make distinctions between the two programs.) The Cooperative Education Association publishes a list of participating colleges and universities that have official co-op programs.

The Princeton Review Online site (www.review.com/careers/) is typical of many websites related to published materials. These sites are advertisements for related books but contain a variety of career resources. Another way to get similar information is to go to websites of associations where information about paid and unpaid positions can be found. For example, the National Multimedia Association of America (NMAA) job bank can be found at www.nmaa.org. You can also find this site by using a search engine such as Yahoo! (http://search.yahoo.com) or Magellan (http://searcher.mckinley.com); search for "career multimedia internship." (When you use search engines, you may get thousands of listings, many of which may be unrelated. Use more key words to narrow your search.)

Starting Your Own Business

One more way to get a job, of course, is to start your own business. In recent years, college students faced with limited job prospects have been starting businesses in record numbers. A reduction in corporate recruiters pitching jobs for graduates has led to new entrepreneurial pursuits and the rise of students *inventing* their own careers. Some examples include a myriad of Internet-related companies, organized walking tours in major cities with bilingual materials for foreign visitors, specialized photography to enhance pictorial magazines, and networks for improved services for persons with disabilities.

Become your own boss

HOME BUSINESSES

The U.S. Bureau of Labor Statistics counts more than 9 million Americans out of more than 14 million self-employed who are working at home in a wide variety of careers. These numbers are growing each year as computer and Internet sites continue to expand. Approximately 25 percent of these home businesses are in the field of marketing and sales, with contracted services, professional jobs, and technical jobs accounting for another 25 percent. A potential consumer population with huge and diverse needs encourages this trend in home businesses. Among home business owners, 45 percent are college graduates and 85 percent are married, with half having dependent children. The average household income is approximately $55,000 annually.

Explore freelance opportunities

According to the Associated Press, freelancing, long associated with artists, writers, and performers, is a career option for people in all fields these days. Freelance opportunities are growing for specialists in accounting, marketing, management, and other traditional business functions. These growing opportunities are largely due to technological advances of the last decade or two; the proliferation and increased affordability of fax machines, cellular telephones, personal computers, and desktop/multimedia publishing capacities enable small businesses to compete for and service clients in a manner previously possible only for large businesses.

GETTING HELP TO START YOUR OWN BUSINESS

Career centers, libraries, and the Internet have useful information on starting a business. The Small Business Administration (www.sbaonline.sba.gov) provides seminars and low-cost materials within local communities. A group called SCORE (Service Corps of Retired Executives) is composed of local retired businesspeople

---

FACTS AND FIGURES

Women-owned firms

According to the Center for Women's Business Research, between 1997 and 2002 women-owned firms increased by 14 percent nationwide—this was twice the rate for all firms.

WHAT DO YOU THINK?

1. Why do you think women-owned firms are increasing at twice the rate for all firms?
2. If you find this fact encouraging, explain why.
3. Do you know any women who have opened businesses in your community? If so, what do they own?
4. In general, what types of businesses do women own?
5. Does this information help you to make your career choices?

To answer these questions online, go to the *Facts and Figures* module in Chapter 9 of the Companion Website.

who lead low-cost workshops and offer free technical advice. Contact your local chamber of commerce for information about these resources. Also, a local community college or the extension/continuing education division of a local university may offer courses in small business administration or marketing. If colleges offer such courses, they may also have students available who get college credit by giving free technical assistance to newly formed small businesses.

If you would like to explore the possibility of beginning your own business, either home-based or traditional, do thorough market research about the need for your service. You will benefit greatly from consulting SCORE, statewide Small Business Development Centers, your local chamber of commerce, and Internet sites (which you can find by typing "small business" and "careers," or "entrepreneurs" and "careers," into a search engine). Finally, a healthy savings account will be needed to get you through many months until you can count on regular income from your enterprise. Better yet, try to begin building your new business while you are still employed (at least part-time) to ensure some income.

Related websites are www.inc.com and www.ideacafe.com. The first is the site of *Inc.,* a magazine dealing with starting small businesses, and the second specializes in helping small business owners with marketing, market research, starting businesses, legal information, operations, accounting, and more. A useful government site can be found at SBA Online: www.sbaonline.sba.gov/gils/. A site that specializes in youth development and entrepreneurial leadership programs can be found at www.entreworld.org.

FACTS AND FIGURES

Franchise information

Here are a few sources of preliminary information about franchises:

- *The Worldwide Franchise Directory,* published by Gale Research, is available at most libraries.

- A "Franchise Opportunities Guide" is available from the International Franchise Association.

- www.frannet.com

- www.sbaonline.sba.gov/workshops/franchises

Franchising

Franchising offers another means of owning and operating your own business. Franchising may appeal to individuals who have worked for large companies and those not quite ready to be full-fledged entrepreneurs. When you buy a franchise, you become part of a larger structure; thus, you must do extensive research to ensure that your personality fits well with the goals and operations of this larger company.

Using Career Planning Services

No matter what year you are in, there is much you can do to advance your career while still in college. First-year college students and sophomores should be taking courses in career exploration, exploring academic alternatives, setting goals, and making choices. Students further along in school should be pursuing internships, doing volunteer work, networking, and doing informational interviewing. Finally, you should be working with your school's career planning and placement office at all stages of your career exploration!

Even though fewer companies are recruiting on college campuses these days, many new college graduates still find jobs via this method. If you have researched your career, done related volunteer work, completed an internship, held a part-time position, or done well in your field academically, your appeal to these recruiters and other employers will be enhanced.

If the career planning office offers job search workshops covering resume writing and interviewing techniques, or the opportunity to videotape practice interviews, sign up for these services. Explore alumni contacts in the field you hope to pursue. While it is still easily accessible to you, use your college library to research career opportunities.

Be prepared to be flexible when considering job offers. Especially during tight economic times, college graduates may find it difficult to find their ideal first job and may have to lower their expectations regarding starting salary. Read and inform yourself about today's opportunities and current salaries in your geographical area.

Remember, a job that seems less than ideal may lead to one at which you can truly excel. For example, one university fine arts student became a recruiter at Prudential Life Insurance Company. Later, that art graduate's job involved purchasing art for Prudential Regional Headquarters!

During tight economic times, college graduates may decide that graduate school is the best bet and enter medical or law school or graduate degree programs in science, education, or business. If, when the time comes, you are genuinely interested in an advanced degree and the knowledge it will give you, this may be a good option for you. However, if you find you are considering graduate school simply to avoid the "real world" and put off job hunting, consult a career counselor. The job market may or may not be better in two or three years. It would be wiser to devote your energies to finding out more about what you want to do and how you can accomplish your goals than to invest additional years in school.

FACTS AND FIGURES

Job hotlines

- Many companies and government agencies have job openings hotlines. A book titled *Job Hotlines USA* identifies more than 1,000 telephone numbers. Numbers and organizations are listed both alphabetically and by geographic location.

- Try America's Job Bank: www.ajb.dni.us.

- In California, use www.jobstar.org.

Interviewing for Information

Survey after survey on job hunting confirms a basic fact about job search strategy—namely, that the one best way to find out about a job and to get a job is through *people*. Now that you have reviewed the written sources of information on jobs, you are ready to begin conducting *information interviews*. These interviews help you develop contacts, sources of knowledge, and guides to meeting other people in a particular field. This network of people will keep you informed and connected to possible job openings. Once you gain some experience through information interviewing and networking, you will be ready to master the techniques involved in interviewing for a job.

Cultivate contacts

INFORMATION INTERVIEWING—THE PURPOSE

Information interviewing involves identifying people who are doing what you want to be doing and asking them questions related to their current jobs. Information interviewing serves several purposes. It helps you further refine your knowledge and understanding of the field you are exploring. It enables you to develop social skills related to feeling comfortable and knowledgeable while you are being interviewed. Information interviewing creates the setting to develop contacts. These contacts are often helpful to your specific job search. The people you interview may themselves be in a position to hire someone like you for a job, or they may simply hear about a job opening and pass the information on to you. Remember that your specific purpose in information interviewing is *not* to look for a job but to confirm your information about the field and to develop contacts that may be helpful in the future. When involved in an information interview, *you are asking* the questions. When on a job interview, *you are being asked* the questions.

Information interviewing is based on the premise that you have already read much of the written information related to a specific type of job and now need confirmation from people who are already doing that job. You want them to tell you basically what the field is really like before you commit your time, effort, and finances to the pursuit of a new field. Or, if you are already in the field, you want to know if one employer's environment would be more appealing to you than another's. Other information you can gain from such an interview involves much more than simply confirming the skills needed and the salary range. On one hand, you can find out if you like the people, if the atmosphere feels comfortable, or if the people are friendly and helpful. On the other hand, you may find that no one has time to talk to you, they keep you waiting, they let the telephone constantly interrupt your interview, or they work in noisy cubicles. This information is available only through an on-site visit. Thus, the overt goal of information interviewing is to collect information, but an additional goal is to make contacts and determine whether you have made an appropriate match between your personal needs and your career goal.

INFORMATION INTERVIEWING—THE PROCESS

The first step in the process of information interviewing is to identify people who are working in the fields that you've decided are interesting to you. It's especially helpful if you know a relative, friend, or neighbor involved in the field or at least someone who can refer you to a potential contact; it's always easier to talk to someone whose name is familiar. The hardest step is making the first phone call to a stranger or, even worse, a strange firm and asking for the name of a person doing that interesting job! Strangers will be more receptive to talking to you if you do the following:

Identify people who are doing what you would like to do

1. Indicate that you are seeking personalized information about their field before you decide to enter it.
2. Confirm the person's job title by asking.
3. Sound enthusiastic and delighted to have reached this person.
4. Refer to the research you've already reviewed about this field or company.

5. Ask if you can have a specific amount of time to interview this person (e.g., 15 to 20 minutes).

6. Try to arrange the interview at the person's work site, so you can determine firsthand how it might feel to work there.

7. Keep to your agreed-upon time frame.

8. Thank your interviewee, and follow up with a thank-you note.

As we noted, it's tough making that first phone call. Here are some specific examples of telephone lead-ins to help you get started. Remember to identify yourself, state your purpose, and ask for an appointment with the appropriate person. This straightforward approach is generally effective.

Example:

Hello, Mr. Jones, I am Diane Smith from Moorpark College. I'm doing some research in the field of houseplant maintenance service, and I'd like to stop by at your convenience to ask you a few questions. I'd appreciate about 15 to 20 minutes of your time. When may I stop by? Is Thursday at 2 p.m. all right?

or:

Hello, Ms. Smith, this is George Brown. This morning I talked to Dr. Green about the opportunities in food supplement marketing, and he spoke very highly of you. I'm calling to find out when you might have a few minutes to see me. Would it be convenient to meet with you in the morning or afternoon?

INFORMATION INTERVIEWING OUTLINE

Once you have located your contacts and made definite appointments to interview them, you need to consider in specific detail the best questions to ask to gain the maximum useful information as quickly and pleasantly as possible. Remember, you will be talking to busy people with many demands on their time; they will expect you to be, and it's to your advantage to be, as businesslike as possible. Finally, having made the telephone contact and set the date to meet, you should send a note confirming the information interview appointment.

Here is a framework to help you design your interview for an information field survey. You may think you already have answers to some of the questions, but personal interviews should help flesh out details and possibly fill in some gaps in your information that you don't realize are there. Try to choose your questions from the general categories of type of business, position classifications, position descriptions, work environment, benefits, and entrance requirements, as follows:

- **TYPE OF BUSINESS**

  What are the services, products, or functions of the organization?

  Who utilizes the organization's services or products?

  Who are the competitors in this field?

  What sets the company apart or distinguishes it from others in the same industry?

  What are the projections for future development or new directions?

- **POSITION CLASSIFICATIONS**

  In each major corporate division, what types of positions are available?

  What are the qualifications for entry-level and experienced positions? (Consider education, skills, abilities, etc.)

- **POSITION DESCRIPTIONS**

  What duties and responsibilities are performed in the area in which you are interested?

  What are some examples of projects currently under way and problems currently being solved?

  What is a typical day like?

  What contacts would there be (e.g., personal, telephone, e-mail) with other organizations?

- **WORK ENVIRONMENT**

  What type of physical localities are involved: outdoors, indoors, travel? Is there pressure? Routine? Variety? How much supervision is there? Do flexible work schedules exist? Is overtime typical or atypical?

- **BENEFITS**

  How does compensation compare to education and ability level?

  What are the opportunities for advancement, promotions, or lateral mobility?

  What opportunities are available for advanced training, on-the-job training, or academic course work? Is there a tuition reimbursement plan?

  What other benefits are available? Possible benefits might include:

Medical/dental insurance	Profit sharing
Life, disability insurance	Retirement
Vacations, holidays	Preretirement planning
Expenses for moving, travel	Employee assistance programs
Outplacement	(counseling for work-related
Recreation, personal health	problems)
services	Job placement assistance (for
Child-care facilities	your spouse, when relocating)

- **ENTRANCE REQUIREMENTS**

  What suggestions do you have for an individual wishing to enter this field of employment?

  What other companies might employ individuals to perform this type of work? Could you refer me to someone else for more information about opportunities in this field?

Be prepared with questions   Moving from a general categorical framework to more specific detail, here is a list of typical questions you might ask in your information interviews.

1. What do you like most about your job and why?

2. What do you like least about your job and why?

3. How did you decide to get into this field, and what steps did you take to enter the field? What alternative ways can one enter this field?

4. What training would you recommend for someone who wanted to enter this field now? What skills and background are needed to get into this field now?

5. What is the salary range for a person in this field? Entry-level to top salary?

6. What personal qualities do you feel are most important in your work and why?

7. What are the tasks you do in a typical workday? Would you describe them?

8. What types of stress do you experience on the job?

9. What types of people survive and do well in this field?

10. Are resumes important in getting a job here?

11. What are the opportunities for promotion?

12. Is this field expanding? Taking any new directions?

13. What related occupations might I investigate?

14. Can you give me the names of three other people who share your enthusiasm for this kind of work? How can I contact them?

15. Is there anything else about this field that would be helpful for me to know?

When you approach professionals in your field of interest from a research point of view and *not* as if you want a job, they will often be happy to talk with you. Even the busiest executives will often find time for you. If one person doesn't have time, ask to be referred to another professional in the field. It is the secretary's job to protect the boss from distractions. When a secretary asks, "What is this call regarding?" you might respond, "I was referred to Jane by her associate Don Reid." Be certain to sound confident and friendly. It's best to call on a Tuesday, Wednesday, or Thursday between 8 A.M. and 11 A.M. If the person isn't in and you must leave a message, leave just your name and phone number.

Interviewing people who work in a field that interests you will provide you invaluable information, either confirming or revising your views. But even better, you will make contacts who may be able to help you actually find a job in the future. These contacts can suggest groups or associations to join, colleges to attend, and classes to take, as well as the current status of employment activity in their field. If you use this information wisely, you too can become visible in these inner circles. It's never too early to start. If you would like to read some sample interviews on the Web, go to www.careerchase.net and click on "Career information categories."

PRACTICING INFORMATION INTERVIEWS

Some people prefer to practice information interviews until they become confident in approaching people about their career. If you need to practice, you might try one of the following approaches. Either you can interview someone you already know about a hobby that sounds interesting or you can ask people about their hobbies and careers at any informal gathering you attend. These informal activities tend to build your self-confidence in asking questions. Once you get started, you might find you enjoy interviewing for leads through other people.

Information interviewing leads to contacts and careers

Two interesting success stories may help you get started. Thomas Shanks, a college assistant professor of communications, tells how one of his students moved from California to New York. For three months, the student sent his resume everywhere and knocked on the door of every friend, relative, and remote acquaintance that he could find. He even found out which after-hours spots the television crowd preferred, and he frequented those places. He eventually got offers from all three networks. Another student, a freshman, was a business major with an interest in art. In November, the vice president of industrial relations at an engineering firm gave a talk in her leadership class. After class she asked him about summer jobs with his firm (notice how early she did so). By January, he had arranged for her to interview in the graphic arts department of his firm. She got the summer job, one many graduates of art programs would have coveted.

Last, if you are a student or have access to a college campus, teachers are valuable resources. Many faculty members have interesting summer jobs or worked in other positions prior to becoming a teacher. They have valuable contacts. In turn, if you are a teacher interested in a career change, you might find a lead through a student. Many times a teacher can design a lesson plan to find out the occupations of parents and then invite parents to speak in their class about their career. These parents can become future contacts for both students and teachers!

Networking

*N*etworking refers to the process of developing and maintaining contacts. While conducting information interviews, you will meet many people. Besides gathering information, you are making contacts. Contacts, if cultivated and used wisely, can lead to or become potential employers. As the job market becomes more competitive and economic conditions create uncertainty, more people will be seeking fewer available jobs. In this climate, networking becomes the key element for success in getting a job. Contacts often make the difference between your being selected or being passed by. This is true for several reasons. Often jobs need to be filled before there is time to advertise. Additionally, as has been mentioned, the majority of new jobs that are available each year are filled through business leads—they go to candidates who already have some connection, even if indirect, to the employer. Most people hear about jobs by word of mouth. You need to let people know that you are looking.

Networking provides the edge

The best networking appointment is personal and never manipulative. The meeting is not a "hard sell" or a sales transaction. It is all about gaining trust, building visibility, and listening carefully to the contact's wisdom, experience, and insight. The respect and attention you communicate for the

Information Interviewing Outline   **ACTIVITY**

Below is an outline/review of the points we have discussed about information interviewing. Use this form as a guide in preparing for each interview.

1. **Find someone with whom to start the interview process.** Make sure you get the person's name. Call the person directly, by name.

   What is the name of the person you're going to call?

   _____

2. **Make a specific appointment, for a specific length of time.**

   When is your appointment, and for how long?

   _____

3. **Make a list of specific questions, things you want to know about the job.**

   Your questions for this interview. (See list on pages 227–229.)

   _____

   _____

   _____

   _____

4. **Explain why you're calling for the interview.** Some explanations:

   a. You want to know more about this kind of work before you decide that you're interested, or before you decide you should choose it as a career.

   b. You are getting ready for a job interview and would like to get some advice from someone in the field before the interview.

   c. You are interested in the field but haven't found much information on it and would appreciate someone filling you in on it.

   d. You are doing some research for a career class and would like some specific information in this field.

   Which explanation will you give when you call?

   _____

   _____

   (Create your own if you wish.)

5. **Tell the employer who recommended that you call.** (A reference helps.)

   Who is your reference for this interview? _____

6. **After the interview, send a note thanking the person for the time and help.**

   Date sent: _____

valuable time provided to you at the meeting are crucial to any further contact, referral, or consideration. Skilled networkers learn to put the contact person at ease. Always remember, the purpose of the meeting is not to request employment. It is to help you learn more about the field and company and about strategies or job search efforts that would be useful in increasing your chances of becoming successful in that field.

The term *network* is both a noun and verb. As a noun, a *network* is defined as a group of individuals who are connected to and cooperate with each other. As a verb, *to network* is to develop contacts and exchange information with other people for purposes of developing business or expanding one's career opportunities. The verb form often becomes action-oriented and is changed to *networking*.

Your network can develop each day; anyone you know can be a good source. Each has friends and contacts and can make a difference in helping you secure an information interview. Think about it: The more people you get to know, the more information you gather. The more visible and proactive you are, the greater your chances will be of finding the right job. It may be a relative or neighbor who points you to a hidden job opening or provides you with valuable strategies.

You probably have many acquaintances willing to provide names and ideas to help you be successful in finding your preferred career. These friends and acquaintances may come from any of the following groups: clubs, organizations, health and sports team affiliations, teachers and professors (past and present), religious groups, coworkers, and previous employers. Exercise 9.1 will suggest people to contact.

Join professional associations

One form of networking is to meet professionals where they gather. For example, if you are interested in human resources management (HRM), you will find HRM personnel at such association meetings as American Society for Training and Development (ASTD); if you are interested in personal communications services, read the trade journal *Radio Communications Report* to find out about local meetings or national conventions.

Attend conferences

Check the local business section of the newspaper to keep up on what's happening in your community. Review the list of groups using your city's convention center, and plan on attending conventions related to your interests. For example, one trade show related to theme parks had 20,000 registrants and 800 exhibitors occupying 2,600 booths; it lasted four days. Students majoring in communications, radio–TV, theater arts, business, and computer science would all find experts related to their majors at such a conference. Such conventions usually offer reduced fees for attending only one day or entering the exhibit area only.

Use all available sources for contacts

Many professional associations have related student groups or student sections. You should already know whether there are groups active on campus related to the field you want to pursue. If you don't, make this your first networking step. Use the resources listed in Chapter 7 to obtain association names and addresses, or ask your adviser. For example, a very complete source is *The Encyclopedia of Associations,* but the *Occupational Outlook Handbook* also lists names and addresses after each occupation. Consider writing an association to inquire about local meetings and the possibility of becoming a student member.

These are all ways of meeting professionals in your field of interest, a key factor in finding the job you want. A survey of 1,500 successful job applicants by *National Business Employment Weekly* found that 67 percent got their jobs through networking, 11 percent by answering an ad, and only 2 percent by sending out resumes and filling out applications.

While conducting information interviews or discussing people's careers at a conference, take advantage of these opportunities to find out what kinds of questions *they* were asked in interviews; ask what they considered to be the most difficult questions in their interviews. Another good question is to ask them what makes a candidate the best candidate. Their answers to questions like these will be helpful when you begin to practice for job interviews.

MOVING BEYOND THE FEAR OF NETWORKING

Many people are reluctant to develop contacts by networking. They may feel they are imposing on busy individuals whose time is precious. This hesitation can be overcome, however, by realizing that many people truly enjoy talking about themselves and their profession. Many remember their own difficulties in connecting to a new career and are, therefore, very receptive to others' requests.

Remember that as you meet people, you are finding out about the real work these new contacts do and finding out if you feel comfortable with their environment. You should also be finding out if your skills would be helpful in solving problems or meeting needs in each workplace you visit while networking. Let the contact know what you can do for them—you may be just the person they need! One graphic design student visited the company of a graphic designer who had spoken in her art class. When asked if she had used Adobe Photoshop (software for modifying photographs electronically), she was very enthusiastic in her answer about using the program in one of her classes. She was hired for a summer job on the spot!

Some job seekers find it difficult to network because they are introverts by nature. If this is the case for you, consider writing an introductory note to ask for a brief meeting. Then, stick to the agreed-upon time. Knowing general conversational techniques helps. For instance, use mutual professional interest when making the contact.

Finally, be sure that every contact is made with courtesy and tact, and be prepared with specific questions. Thanking your contacts for assistance pays huge dividends in the future. The best networking is not simply a one-time association, but a continuing connection. Networking can positively affect your job search and every aspect of your life.

Job Search While Unemployed

Although experts agree that it is best to look for a job while you are still employed, not everyone can be in that position. If you are unemployed and seeking employment, you will benefit by disciplining yourself to stick to a daily job search schedule. Otherwise, your best intentions may be thwarted by procrastination. Procrastination can then turn into the paralysis described in Chapter 8 related to poor decision-making strategies.

Create a disciplined job search to replace the work schedule missing from your life. You will be more productive if you begin the day as if you were

Meet Susan

As an assistant to a county supervisor, Susan finds many of her assignments relate to land development. While finishing work toward her bachelor's degree in business (attending college after work hours), she increasingly represents her supervisor when land developers appeal to the Board of Supervisors for zoning and code changes. When her supervisor decides not to run for reelection, Susan is hired as a director for the business-industry association to lobby the county for the industrialization of farmland. Within a few years, she becomes a consultant to land developers and interacts with her present boss, who hires her into his prospering real estate development firm as vice president of government relations.

Even while working in an entry-level job, Susan met people working in the field of her interest, real estate. As an assistant to the county supervisor, she met people in government, nonprofit associations, and private industry. She maintained high visibility by speaking at community events, representing her supervisor when necessary, and joining relevant organizations and community clubs. When Susan wanted to make a job change, she had already identified and made contact with the types of places and people with whom she wanted to work.

going to work. Get dressed, have breakfast, and begin the day with a few hours of phone calls. Identify employers who can use your skills. Be aware that successful phone contacts rely on sheer numbers. The greater the number of calls you make, the greater are your chances of getting an interview.

Because many cold calls will result in responses such as "No one can speak to you today" or "Sorry, we have no openings," your daily routine must include predictably positive activities. For instance, plan to spend a portion of your day at the library or online researching job information, a portion looking for leads, and a portion filling out job applications. Another important part of the day should include being with supportive people, for example, attending networking and association meetings (local newspapers have business sections that announce weekly association meetings), joining friends for lunch, and enjoying recreation. Keeping active will reenergize you and keep you visible to those who might be able to refer you to a job. Somewhere in your present circle of friends, coworkers, and acquaintances is someone who can link you with your next job. This process is further discussed under the topic of networking.

Your daily routine should include using the Internet

Reserve the final part of your day for returning phone calls and e-mails, redrafting letters, revising your resume and cover letter, and writing specific thank-you letters to people you have met. Planning and preparation can make the critical difference in turning telephone calls into interviews and interviews into job offers. (See Chapter 11 for interviewing techniques.)

Many unemployed people use the services of their state employment agency. (The unemployment office usually requires you to contact a minimum number of employers each week or month to remain eligible to collect unemployment insurance.) However, the state employment agency also offers workshops on job search strategy, assistance in writing a resume, and a computerized job bank. Some offices also conduct targeted group meetings for workers in designated fields, for example, aerospace, automotive, bank-

Susan had contacts who were insiders and could recommend her for jobs even before they were announced. But even more important, she had discovered the hidden job market. She knew the needs of the business-industry association and could tell its people how her skills and contacts could benefit them. She was able to sell herself. She knew she had skills and contacts with government that could enhance her present employer's expansive plans. She was hired because she was able to describe the job she wanted to do in the firm and because her ideal job meshed with the vision of the president of the company. She actually created her current position.

1. What job strategy did Susan use to great advantage?

2. How did Susan develop visibility while working on the job?

3. How did Susan use her knowledge and contacts to create the job of her dreams?

4. How can you develop your network through your job, internship, volunteer, or service learning experience?

To answer these questions online, go to the *Real Stories* module in Chapter 9 of the Companion Website.

ing, executive, manufacturing, and the like. Support groups may meet on a regular basis to offer both encouragement and leads.

Planning for Action

astly, effective job search strategy requires that you master the skills of goal setting and action planning. This means that you set objectives such as those indicated in the following five suggestions and designate specific times to complete each one:

1. Schedule planning time.
2. Maintain a list of activities to get done; for example, write up a weekly calendar and enter each item per day or hour. A pocket calendar may be sufficient for one person whereas a notebook may work better for another.
3. Start a notebook with one section for contacts' names, addresses, and phone numbers and another section for notes about different companies.
4. Develop an Internet bookmark of often-used addresses. (A bookmark allows quick access to favorite sites.)
5. Review your progress by checking off completed activities.

An effective job search requires clerical and organizational skills. Every week you will need to update specific names, obtain more exact titles, and confirm addresses. This information can be kept in a file box or in your home computer. (Exhibit 9.1 provides a sample contact record.) Being able to retrieve at a moment's notice the information you have been collecting can make the difference between getting your resume to the potential employer today or tomorrow (which may be a day too late). The fastest way to update a resume is to have it stored in your own home computer or on a floppy disk for use in a personal computer at school, at a local copy center, or at a friend's home.

9.1   *Sample contact file format.*

1. Company:	Phone No.:	Contact Person & Title:	Type of Contact & Date: Letter _____
	Referred By:	E-mail:	Phone _____ Resume _____ Application _____
Address:	Job Target:		Interview _____
Follow-up:		Conclusions:	

2. Company:	Phone No.:	Contact Person & Title:	Type of Contact & Date: Letter _____
	Referred By:	E-mail:	Phone _____ Resume _____ Application _____
Address:	Job Target:		Interview _____
Follow-up:		Conclusions:	

3. Company:	Phone No.:	Contact Person & Title:	Type of Contact & Date: Letter _____
	Referred By:	E-mail:	Phone _____ Resume _____ Application _____
Address:	Job Target:		Interview _____
Follow-up:		Conclusions:	

4. Company:	Phone No.:	Contact Person & Title:	Type of Contact & Date: Letter _____
	Referred By:	E-mail:	Phone _____ Resume _____ Application _____
Address:	Job Target:		Interview _____
Follow-up:		Conclusions:	

5. Company:	Phone No.:	Contact Person & Title:	Type of Contact & Date: Letter _____
	Referred By:	E-mail:	Phone _____ Resume _____ Application _____
Address:	Job Target:		Interview _____
Follow-up:		Conclusions:	

Software packages can help you create a tracking system for all of your contacts and activities. One software program, for example, leads you through planning, analysis, targeted markets, and commitment to a schedule of tasks. After working through the program, you will have created a list of potential employers, a resume, and a cover letter, and you will have prepared for the interview.

If you do not already have Internet access, consider investing in a service such as America Online or Earthlink that provides access to computer bulletin boards. More and more companies are advertising job openings through these bulletin boards and even requiring electronic transmission of resumes (more about this later in Chapter 10). Also, company insiders may provide information about job openings via these bulletin boards.

It is advisable to have a designated area in your home for all of your career information. Keeping careful records of all contacts made, applications submitted, resumes sent, interviews held, and correspondence sent and received will make your job search more effective and easier to manage.

Implementing Your Job Search: A Lifelong Venture

The comprehensive approach to job hunting involves putting yourself in the right place at the right time again and again throughout your lifetime. It involves strategies that assist you in finding openings in your target area before the openings are publicly announced. In situations when you do not appear to be the ideal candidate, this approach will assist you in getting noticed and getting an interview.

Many times, this approach works best while you are still employed because potential employers tend to defer unemployed inquirers to the personnel office. Ideally, before starting a job search, you will have a specific field and job objective in mind. Let's say you have selected business administration and want to specialize in real estate finance. Your first decision is whether you want to work for a commercial bank, private developer, the government (such as an appraisal office or bureau of land development), or a related association that employs people to interact with the government. The box entitled "Meet Susan" (pages 234–235) offers an example.

Confirm your career objectives

High visibility helps

Networking opens up the hidden job market

Summary

This chapter has discussed the comprehensive job search. It is important that you confirm your impressions about your ideal job. You won't know the accuracy of your researched information until you volunteer in the field, do part-time work in the field, or find a job that will put you around the people doing the type of job you really desire. Only then will you know how you feel about the real job environment. It also takes practice to remember to ask everyone you meet about his or her job. The more jobs you learn about, the more alternatives you will have.

A large but hidden job market exists out there, and the people you meet through the process of information interviewing can help you uncover it by informing you about potential jobs before they are advertised.

Selected Online Employment Databases

Searching online can be overwhelming. Thousands of websites are available for job searching, but you may feel comfortable with only a few. Find a service suited to you and remember, the more you target your search, the more efficient it will be. Rather than typing "job search," use terms like "entry-level job" or "job in advertising." Here are a few sites to get you started.

The Monster Board (www.monster.com) *The Monster Board* has a database with more than one million job listings and includes a resume bank. There, you can develop your online resume and use it to apply for jobs. It will be matched to employers' needs at no charge. Students may find that their college lists jobs designed with the student in mind at a related site, www.monstertrak.com.

America's Job Bank (www.ajb.dni.us/index. html) *JobBank USA* is one of the largest and most diverse databases, with more than 250,000 jobs. This site provides resume writing, networking, and information services to job candidates, employers, and recruitment firms. This is a free service to job hunters.

FlipDog (www.flipdog.com) *FlipDog* offers job listings, resume tips, salary guides, company information, and practice interview information.

CareerBuilder (www.careerbuilder.com) The *CareerBuilder* site has its own database of job opportunities; it lists more than 500,000 jobs and directs the user to online job fairs, employer profiles, and special resources for students. Instructions and tips about electronic resumes are provided. You may search by job type, by industry, or by company. Again, this is free.

Nation Job Network (www.nationjob.com) In addition to the standard search by job title or company name, this site features Personal Job Scout, which keeps an eye on listing updates and notifies you via e-mail about related jobs. Again, this service is free but also offers "for fee" services.

The Riley Guide (www.rileyguide.com) *Riley's Job Guide* provides a wealth of information with many good links regarding job listings, resume postings, employer profiles, and current articles. It also contains articles from real job searchers who have tried electronic job searches and can tell you how it really works.

The Richard Bolles Parachute Site (www.Job HuntersBible.com) The author of *What Color Is Your Parachute?* has an abundance of career information and resources on his site, including job search information, resume writing tips, and company information. He also provides tips for using the Internet to conduct your search effectively.

Virtual Job Fair (www.vjf.com) This site is sponsored by BrassRing.com. *Virtual Job Fair* is especially useful for those looking for high-tech jobs. There are more than 45,000 jobs and links to career resources, magazines, and expos, as well as a resume-posting service.

Resumail Network (www.resumail.com) The *Resumail Network* has created a standard for electronic delivery of properly formatted resumes by linking its software directly to employers' software. There is a fee for the software, but privacy is guaranteed. This site also has links to more than 150 sites related to associations, career fairs, and other career information. Jobs may be searched by company or category.

Online Services with Good Career Sections

America Online: (800) 827-6364 (www.aol.com)

Microsoft Network: (800) 386-5550
  (www.msn.com)

Earthlink: (www.earthlink.com)

Yahoo! (www.yahoo.com)

Check with your local university or 800 directory for more online services.

Search Engines and Browsers Below is a list of the most-used search engines as well as some unusual ones. Following the name is a description of how it catalogs various sites. Big search engines (such as AltaVista) are best for obscure searches because they cast a wider net, which increases your chances of finding what you want. Novices should start with Google, Yahoo!, or Lycos, all of which target mainstream users and are considered user-friendly. Consult the instructions for each search engine to learn how to search most effectively.

AltaVista (www.altavista.com) is one of the most comprehensive indexes of documents on the Web. Unless you're very specific about your search criteria, it often turns up so many matches that you will have more than enough to meet your needs. This engine will locate the most obscure topics.

Excite (www.excite.com) gives you reviews of all the sites it catalogs. You can also use Excite to search Usenet discussion groups and classified ads.

Google (www.google.com) rates sites by how many pages link to the site.

Infoseek (www.infoseek.com) catalogs individual webpages rather than entire sites and displays an excerpt for each page that matches your search criteria.

Lycos (www.lycos.com) also catalogs webpages rather than entire sites and provides you with an outline and abstract for each page that matches your criteria.

Searcher (www.searcher.com) is an excellent reference site.

Yahoo! (www.yahoo.com) organizes sites by category. When Yahoo! finds a site that matches your request, it displays a summary of the site and link to the site's category.

Similar to Yahoo! (searching by category) are the following: www.looksmart.com and ask.com.

Search Engine Watch (www.searchengine watch.com) provides a tutorial on using search engines and also rates them for a variety of subject areas.

Targeting Your Job Search

The written exercises that follow serve to increase your ability to network effectively. Exercise 9.1 asks you to identify specific people who are part of your network. Exercise 9.2 suggests that you conduct information interviews. Exercise 9.3 helps you expand information about your job target by using practice information gathering, expert information gathering, and interviewing for employment strategies.

To answer these questions online, go to the *Exercise* module in Chapter 9 of the Companion Website.

Support Network Checklist

Fill in the names of people who might help you in the list below. Specifically ask yourself: How can this person help (provide information, introduce me to someone, offer advice, write a reference, etc.)?

Former employers: _____

Former coworkers: _____

Present employer: _____

Friends: _____

Relatives: _____

Civic group members: _____

Professional association members: _____

Alumni group members: _____

Religious group members: _____

Clients: _____

Counselors: _____

Teachers: _____

Clergy: _____

Neighbors: _____

Classmates: _____

Bankers: _____

Accountants: _____

Financial planners: _____

Insurance agents: _____

Real estate agents: _____

Stockbrokers: _____

Salespeople: _____

Retail store owners: _____

Medical professionals: _____

Other: _____

_____

_____

_____

_____

Information Interviews

E X E R C I S E 9.2

Select three individuals who work in fields that are interesting to you, and conduct brief information interviews using the list of sample information interview questions given in this chapter as your guide. Write a brief report of each.

Personal Contact Log

E X E R C I S E 9.3

Prepare a log of personal contacts (at least five) that you make using the approaches described in this chapter under Interviewing for Information and Practicing Information Interviews. Focusing on your own job target, see how much information and how many new contacts you acquire. Use the appropriate format below for each type of contact made.

Name: _____   Job Target: _____

PRACTICE INFORMATION GATHERING

Hobby or interest: _____

Contact: _____

Information gathered as a result of the interview: _____

_____

_____

_____

Other possible contacts: _____

_____

_____

EXPERT INFORMATION GATHERING

Occupational interest: _____

Contact (who, where employed, how you found this person): _____

_____

Information gathered: _____

_____

_____

New contacts: _____

_____

Any contradictions: _____

_____

Conclusions: _____

_____

_____

_____

_____

INTERVIEWING FOR EMPLOYMENT, APPRENTICESHIP, OR VOLUNTEER EXPERIENCE

Choice of possible work site: _____

_____

What do you want (job, apprenticeship, volunteer experience)? _____

_____

Who is in a position to hire you? _____

Your approach (telephone, letter, in person): _____

Outcomes and follow-up: _____

_____

_____

WWWebwise

For additional activities online, go to the WWWebwise module in Chapter 9 of the **Companion Website.**

Exercise Summary

Write a brief paragraph answering these questions.

What did you learn about yourself from these exercises? How does this knowledge relate to your career/life planning? Did you use the Internet? Was it helpful in locating job information? What was most useful?

_____

_____

_____

_____

_____

_____

_____

_____

_____

_____

_____

_____

_____

_____

_____

_____

_____

_____

_____

_____

_____

_____

_____

Preparing a
Winning Resume

CHAPTER 10

Every good fitness program includes a chart that indicates visually where you started, where you are currently, and where you are going. In a career fitness program, this chart is called a *resume*. Eventually, in the course of job hunting, you will be asked to present a resume to a prospective employer. Some career counselors warn that the resume isn't going to get you an interview unless you already have a good contact inside the company; others suggest that a good resume can help you get your foot in the door. These days, a resume can be transmitted electronically via computer to reach thousands of potential employers at once. In any case, your resume will be an essential job search tool. A resume is:

1. A systematic assessment of your skills in terms of a specific job objective.

2. A memory jogger useful in an interview in responding to the following common requests/questions by interviewers:

    a. Tell me about yourself.

    b. Why should I hire you?

    c. What skills do you bring to this job?

3. An aid in filling out application forms.

4. A marketing device used to gain an interview.

This chapter offers guidelines for writing a resume and distributing it electronically. It presents three sample formats: functional, chronological, and a creative combination. Additionally, the importance of cover letters and application forms is addressed. Once you have completed this chapter, you will be prepared to compile your own winning resume.

The Resume

The purpose of the resume is to get an interview. Like an advertisement, the resume should attract attention, create interest, describe accomplishments, and provoke action. Brevity is essential; one page is best, and two are the limit. The resume tells the prospective employer what you can do and have done, who you are, and what you know. It also indicates the kind of job you seek. The resume must provide enough information for the employer to evaluate your qualifications, and it must interest the employer enough so that you will be invited for an interview.

Writing a well-constructed resume requires that you complete your research before compiling the resume. You need to keep in mind the type of employer and position as well as the general job requirements in order to tailor your resume to the specific requirements and personality of the employer. To be most effective, your resume should be designed to emphasize your background as it relates to the job you seek. It should look neat, clean, and organized. This means word-processed with no errors, and then laser-printed or photocopied on high-quality paper.

By now you should have completed all the necessary research. Utilize the information you gathered in Chapter 7, Information Integration, and Chapter 9, Targeting Your Job Search. Integrate your answers with the categories listed in the box titled "Resume/Portfolio Review" on page 249.

PORTFOLIOS

The portfolio is an expanded resume. It is usually a folder containing the basic resume and samples of your work related to the job objective. It is a good idea to begin storing work samples now. For instance, a marketing specialist might send a potential employer a resume along with fliers, brochures, and ads created in past jobs. For a marketing student with limited experience, the folder could include copies of term papers, proposals completed for classes, and homework assignments related to the job objective. Portfolios are useful to have during information interviews, when you are at association meetings and networking, or upon request in an interview.

PREPARATION FOR COMPOSING YOUR RESUME

Although stating an objective is considered optional by some experts (because it can be stated in your cover letter), it is to your advantage to include it on the resume. In actuality, one resume should be designed for each job objective. Remember, there are no jobs titled "anything."

The job objective is a concise and precise statement about the position you are seeking. This may include the type of firm in which you hope to work (e.g., a small, growing company). A clear objective gives focus to your job search and indicates to an employer that you've given serious thought to your career goals. When time does not allow you to develop a resume for each of several different jobs that interest you, the job objective may be emphasized in the cover letter (which will be discussed at the end of this chapter) and omitted from the resume.

A job objective is sometimes referred to as goal, professional objective, position desired, or simply objective. It can be as specific as "community worker," "personnel assistant," or "junior programmer"; it can be as general as "management position using administrative, communications, and research skills" or "to work as an administrative assistant in a creative atmosphere and have the opportunity to use my abilities." The more specific the objective statement, the better, because a clear objective enables you to focus your resume more directly on that objective. The effect is pointed, dramatic, and convincing.

A resume summarizes your particular background as it relates to a specific job. It summarizes your career objectives, education, work experience, special skills, and interests. Visualize a pyramid or triangle with the job objective at the top and everything beneath it supporting that objective.

In writing the rough draft of your resume, prepare 5" × 8" index cards for each job you've held (see Exhibit 10.1). The index card should contain the following information:

FRONT OF CARD

1. Name, address, phone number of employer, and immediate supervisor at work site
2. Dates employed (month/year to month/year)
3. Job title
4. Skills utilized (review the skills discussion in Chapter 5)

BACK OF CARD

Duties divided into functional areas

In choosing information to include in your resume, avoid anything that may not be considered in a positive light or that has no relationship to your ability to do the job (e.g., marital status, number of children, political or religious affiliation, age, photos). When in doubt, leave it out. One clue: In the next chapter, you will be given information about illegal questions in an interview. If information is illegal for an employer to request in an interview, then it's unnecessary in a resume.

Put the most relevant information first

Front and back of resume index card (the format can easily be adapted for use in creating a computer file)

Elaine's House of Coffee
555 Stevens Circle   April 2003–Present
Roanoke, VA 23640
(540) 555-1211

Supervisor: Position:
Joe Smith   Bookkeeper & Shift Supervisor

Skills Utilized:

Related well with continuous flow of people. Attentive to detail; organized; energetic.

Bilingual—Spanish/English

Functions:

Management	—Coordinated service with customer needs, payroll, scheduled employees.
Communications	—Welcomed guests. Directed staff in performing courteous and rapid service. Responded to and resolved complaints.
Bookkeeping	—Maintained records of financial transactions. Balanced books. Compiled statistical reports.

USING ACTION WORDS

Select "power" words

Remember that your writing style communicates the work activity in which you have been involved. Use phrases and document experiences that both involve the reader and make your resume outstanding and active. Following are basic guidelines for selecting your "power" words:

- Choose short, clear phrases.
- If you use complete sentences throughout, keep them concise and direct.
- Use the acceptable jargon of the work for which you are applying. Remember: You want your prospective employer to *read* your resume.

Resume/Portfolio Review

A. **Personal Data**

   1. Name

   2. Address

   3. Phone

B. **Current Job Objective**

C. **Education** (This category may follow category D, Work Experience, on your actual resume, depending on which is more relevant to the position sought.)

   1. High school and college

      a. Favorite subjects

      b. Samples of best work in classes related to job objective

      c. Extracurricular interests

      d. Offices held

      e. Athletic achievements

      f. Other significant facts (e.g., honors, awards)

   2. Other (military service, volunteer work that provided training, correspondence courses, summer activities, languages, technical skills, licenses, and/or credentials)

D. **Work Experience** (This may precede category C, Education, on your actual resume. Refer to your experiography or your skills analysis for this information.)

   Employer

   Length of employment

   Position

   Skills and accomplishments (These may be featured in a bulleted list following Job Objective.)

   Samples of best work if relevant

E. **Publications**

F. **Associations, Volunteer Work, and Community Involvement**

G. **Special Skills** (e.g., language proficiency, computer skills)

- Avoid general comments such as "My duties were . . ." or "I worked for . . ." Begin with action words that concisely describe what your tasks were; for example:

  Implemented new filing system.

  Developed more effective interviewing procedure.

  Evaluated training program for new employees.

- List the results of your activities; for example:

  Reduced office filing by 25 percent.

  Developed interview evaluation summary form.

  Increased efficiency in delivering services.

- Don't dilute your action words with too many extraneous activities. Be *selective* and sell your *best* experiences.

- Target your words to the employer's needs.

USING THE RIGHT KEY PHRASES

In many large companies, human resources personnel now scan resumes into computer files and databases for storage and later retrieval. According to a poll by a management consulting firm, 31 percent of 435 human resource

Meet Eduardo

It is almost one o'clock in the morning and Eduardo Garza is just finishing his shift at Elaine's House of Coffee. On Friday and Saturday nights, a small band plays at Elaine's until midnight. Eduardo has been working these weekend shifts ever since his mother's illness. Mrs. Garza is a single mother of five children, recently underwent surgery, and will not be able to work for approximately six months. Eduardo is the oldest child and he takes much of the responsibility for his family. Until his mother is well again, he must bring in as much of the income as possible.

Eduardo graduated from high school and attended community college for one year but he dropped out because of his family situation and because he was having trouble in some of his classes. He is a very quiet young man and likes to spend his spare time reading and listening to music. In high school, his favorite subject was math. Eduardo has a strong work ethic and his supervisor at Elaine's promotes him to manager. He is not comfortable managing other employees, but he does enjoy his bookkeeping responsibilities.

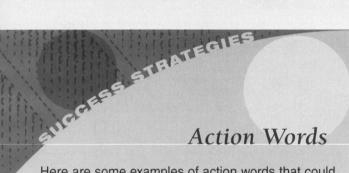

Action Words

Here are some examples of action words that could be used in your resume:

accomplished	evaluated	negotiated
achieved	expanded	organized
analyzed	facilitated	oriented
arranged	guided	planned
built	implemented	processed
controlled	improved	produced
created	increased	proved
demonstrated	initiated	raised profits
designed	inspired	reduced costs
developed	interpreted	researched
directed	invented	sold
effected	led	supervised
encouraged	managed	supported
established	motivated	wrote

For additional action verbs, see the section "Identifying Your Skills" in Chapter 5, including the Assessing Your Skills activity.

professionals indicated their firms use resume banks for recruiting. Many experts say the percentage of large and midsize companies using such programs is far higher, with employers such as Walt Disney World Company leading the way in their use of resume banks. A growing biotechnology firm, Amgen, Inc., receives more than 225 resumes a day, about 60 percent in conventional paper format and 40 percent by e-mail or fax. All end up in an automated tracking system. The manager of employment systems at Amgen says automated tracking allows the company to consider all applicants for all available jobs—which is especially important in a growing company. When an opening occurs, employers search their banks and databases for resumes using certain key phrases relevant to the position. For example, a company looking for "B.S., Information Systems, Cisco Certification" would first retrieve resumes containing these key words.

Depending on the field in which you hope to work and the type of companies you will apply to, this information may be vital to your writing a resume that gets retrieved during a key word search. In such cases, the appearance and style of your resume will be less significant than the manner in which you describe your specific skills: be certain to use concrete nouns to summarize past experience.

Eduardo looks in the want ads daily for better-paying jobs with hours that will let him be home in the evenings, but many of the positions require a resume. Eduardo does not feel that he has enough skills to put on a resume, and he is very concerned about his ability to compete for a better job.

1. Based on the information you have about Eduardo, prepare a resume for him.

2. Where could Eduardo go for help in preparing a resume?

3. What other resources could Eduardo use to look for a job?

4. What might help Eduardo strengthen his self-esteem?

5. What resources might be available to help Eduardo's family?

 To answer these questions online, go to the *Real Stories* module in Chapter 10 of the Companion Website.

REFERENCES

The expression "References available upon request" is usually not necessary on a resume. If references are requested, you will probably need to submit their names and contact information on a separate form. Although you don't have to list specific names on the resume, you should have at least three people in mind who can talk about your work habits, your skills, and your accomplishments. When you are job hunting, ask these people in advance if you may use them as references, informing them of your job objective so that they will be prepared if a prospective employer calls.

Many college placement centers act as a clearinghouse for the collection of resumes and references. You establish a file, and the center sends out your resume and references when you make a request. The placement center often makes this service available for alumni, and it may have reciprocal agreements with other colleges across the country.

The Appearance of Your Resume

The appearance of this document is critical. Your resume must be clearly typed, well spaced, and visually attractive. Remember that many employers skim only the first page of a resume. Thus, it is crucial that your material be strategically placed so that what is most likely to be read is most relevant to the job desired. Employers may receive hundreds of resumes each day, giving them only minutes to review each one. Therefore, even if you must use two pages, the first is more crucial.

Experts advise against using a resume preparation service. An employer can usually spot a canned resume and might assume that the applicant lacks initiative or self-confidence. The time you spend writing your resume will be time well spent. It will give you the opportunity to summarize what you have to offer to an employer.

Resume appearance counts

251

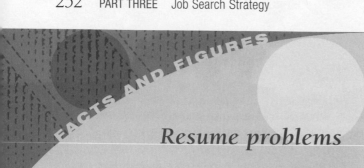

Resume problems

When scanning a resume, the HR manager looks for key "knockout" factors. On the other hand, survey results from human resources managers indicate that the following items help them to decide that the candidate has *not* matched their resume with the needs of the company:

1. Job objective incompatible with current openings
2. Inappropriate or insufficient educational credentials
3. Incompatible salary requirements
4. Geographic restrictions incompatible with current openings
5. Lack of U.S. citizenship or permanent resident status
6. Resume poorly organized, sloppy, or hard to read
7. Too many employers in too short a period of time
8. Too many pages
9. Too many (or any!) errors in spelling

Source: www.FlipDog.com, July 2002.

WHAT DO YOU THINK?

1. Have you ever created or submitted an electronic resume?
2. Do you know anyone who has gotten an interview by sending an electronic resume?
3. What do you think is the advantage of sending your resume by e-mail?
4. See Exhibit 10.4 for suggestions for composing your resume. Which points seem to be most relevant for you?
5. In addition to an electronic resume, what other steps or method of communication would you use to get a position?

 To answer these questions online, go to the *Facts and Figures* module in Chapter 10 of the Companion Website.

Personal computers and resume writing or word processing software can help turn an average-looking resume into a class act. If possible, store your resume and cover letter on a floppy disk or in hard-drive memory for easy retrieval and updating. Many duplicating shops have personal computers available for an hourly fee.

Although offset printing was once the preferred method of producing resumes, quick copies made at professional copy centers are now acceptable if they are reproduced on high-quality equipment and are clean and free of smudges. Use an attractive bond paper for these copies of your resume; usually a neutral color such as ivory or white is best. Copy centers typically have a wide selection of stationery available. It is often useful to have a career counselor, potential employer, family member, or friend review a draft of your resume before you duplicate your final copy. Ask for a careful check of content, format, grammar, spelling, and appearance. Even if you plan to send your resume electronically via computer, make sure it is completely error-free.

Electronic Resumes

Whether you prepare your resume yourself or have it prepared professionally, once you have a document you can be proud to send to potential employers, you will need to make slight modifications to create the scannable version. Electronic resumes are entered into a resume bank, which means they are subject to electronic, as well as human, scanning. You may need to create two or more versions of your resume, emphasizing various skills and key words.

You will find this process easier if your resume is on computer disk. You are then free to copy it and make changes to the copy. This allows you to keep your hard work safe and protected in the original file. If your resume is prepared professionally, you may also want to have the service prepare an electronic version, or you may request a disk containing the file, so you may create the electronic version yourself if you feel competent to do so. The key is to work from a copy—not the original!

Another reason to have your resume on disk is that employers and online resume distribution services often have different requirements for file formats and design specifications. The website for an online resume distribution service or potential employer will provide you with company-specific details; it may also offer assistance in preparing this very important promotional piece about you. The human resources department of a potential employer may also be able to provide you with electronic resume information.

Although it is highly recommended that your traditional resume be no more than one page, your electronic resume may be longer. The computer will easily scan more than one page. It uses all the information on your resume to determine if your skills match available positions. The computer searches for key words. Those key words can often be found in a general job description matching the position title for which you are applying. They also appear in classified ads and job postings. Or you may be able to glean some during information interviews. Be sure to write your resume to reflect the skill needs of the position—another reason why you may want to prepare multiple versions of your resume.

Please refer to the box titled "Guidelines for Preparing and Submitting Electronic Resumes" for detailed how-to information. You may wish to learn more about electronic resumes. Your career center, many books on the subject, and resume Internet sites (see Chapter 9) are excellent sources for additional information.

Types of Resumes

To reiterate, there are three general types of resume: functional, chronological, and combination. Comparing the two sample work experience entries in the box on page 255 (taken from Exhibits 10.5 and 10.11) will give you some idea of the basic difference between functional and chronological resumes. The next part of this chapter will discuss all three types in detail. The combination resume, as the name implies, is a combination of functional and chronological.

SUCCESS STRATEGIES

Guidelines for Preparing and Submitting Electronic Resumes

- Your resume will likely be viewed with 80-character lines and 24 lines to a screen page.

- Use an 8 1/2" x 11" page format. (If you plan to fax it, print it on white paper.)

- Use an easy-to-read typeface (font), such as Times, Helvetica, or Courier, at a point size of 11 or 12.

- Avoid tabs (use the space key), underlines, boxes, columns, italics, and shading. Also avoid boldface, vertical or horizontal lines, columns, graphics, and bullets.

- Use capital letters for section headings. Use commonly recognized headings such as the ones shown in this book.

- Use key skill words from a job description or advertisement. Key words are normally nouns rather than action verbs. Key words indicate qualifications and knowledge. For example, an administrative assistant might use key words such as *data entry, filing, database management, word processing,* and *Microsoft Office Professional.*

- Some resume banks offer fill-in-the-blank templates, complete with instructions.

- Be concise, but you may use more than one page if necessary. The computer can handle multiple-page resumes.

- E-mail a copy of your resume to yourself to see what it looks like. (You can do this from an Internet site that allows you to create your own resume using this format.) When including a resume in the body of an e-mail, use a 65-character line with a hard return at the end of every line.

Resume Template

Name
Address
Phone Number/E-mail Address

Job Objective State and describe your objective as specifically as possible. Refer to O*NET or the *Dictionary of Occupational Titles* for appropriate descriptive vocabulary.

Education Depending on your job objective and the amount of education you have had, you may want to place this category directly after Job Objective. (However, if your job experience is more relevant to the position or if your education is not recent, you will want to list job experience *prior* to education.) The most recent education should be listed first. Include relevant credentials and licenses.

As employers, educational institutions are usually more concerned with appropriate degrees than are other employers. Include special workshops, noncredit courses, and self-taught skills when they are appropriate to your job objective.

Experience Describe *functionally* (by activities performed) your experience relevant to the particular job for which you are applying; start with the most relevant and go to the less relevant. Include without distinction actual job experience, volunteer experience, your work on class projects, and school and class offices held. Alternatively, show your experience *chronologically,* listing your most recent professional experience first.

There is no need to stress dates unless they indicate that you have been continuously advancing toward this job objective.

Use action verbs; do not use full sentences, unless you decide to write your resume as a narrative.

Use the *Dictionary of Occupational Titles* or O*NET to help you describe accurately what you have done, always keeping in mind how your experience relates to your job objective. Remember to use words and skills related to your job objective to describe yourself in the cover letter and during the interview. (See Chapter 5.)

Special Skills Put this optional category directly after Job Objective if you feel that your professional experience does not adequately reflect the talents you have that best support this job objective.

Examples: Facility with numbers, manual dexterity, patience, workshops you have led, writing ability, self-taught skills, language fluency.

References Include references only if you have space and if the names are well known to potential employers.

THE FUNCTIONAL RESUME

A functional resume presents your experience, skills, and job history in terms of the functions you have actually performed rather than as a simple chronological listing of the titles of jobs you have held. Like any resume, it should be tailored to fit the main tasks and competencies required by the job you are seeking. Essentially, you redefine your past experiences according to the functions in the job for which you are applying. You should select and emphasize those activities from previous employment that relate to the specific job sought and deemphasize or omit irrelevant background.

For example, an administrative assistant might perform some administration, communications, and clerical functions. A secretary for an elementary school rewrote his resume to highlight these categories. In order to better define the skills used in his secretarial job, he researched the job description of executive secretary and office manager in his school personnel manual and located the description of administrative assistant in the *Dictionary of Occupational Titles*. (See the section titled "Suggestions for Job Descriptions" that follows.) He then compiled his resume to show how his executive secretarial responsibilities relate to the administrative assistant position desired. (See the functional resume in Exhibit 10.5, at the end of this chapter.) Review the organizational divisions described in Chapter 7 to assess how your past work or life experience can be described in such categories as marketing, human resources, finance, community services, or research and development.

SAMPLE FUNCTIONAL ENTRY UNDER PROFESSIONAL EXPERIENCE

- Budgeting/Financial

  Analyzed and coordinated payroll recordkeeping, budgeted expenditures, requisitioned supplies, prepared attendance accounting reports, and initiated budget system for $10,000 of instructional monies allocated to the school.

SAMPLE CHRONOLOGICAL ENTRY UNDER PROFESSIONAL EXPERIENCE

- Sales Associate

  Builders Emporium, Wadsworth, Texas 76199, 2002–Present

  Operated cash register and made change, worked well with public, motivated fellow employees, encouraged customers to buy products.

Suggestions for Job Descriptions

Descriptions in the *Dictionary of Occupational Titles,* in O*NET, and in some personnel manuals provide helpful phrases and statements to use in describing your own job history and experience. The following two descriptions, for example, would be useful to you in composing a functional resume for a job in business. However, you would use only relevant sentences, adapting them to your personal background.

OFFICE MANAGER

Coordinates activities of clerical personnel in the organization. Analyzes and organizes office operations and procedures such as word processing, bookkeeping, preparation of payrolls, flow of correspondence, filing, requisitioning of supplies, and other clerical services. Evaluates office production, revises procedures, or devises new forms to improve efficiency of work flow. Establishes uniform correspondence procedures and style practices. Formulates procedures for systematic retention, protection, retrieval, transfer, and disposal of records. Plans office layouts and initiates cost reduction programs. Reviews clerical and personnel records to ensure completeness, accuracy, and timeliness. Prepares activity reports for guidance of management. Prepares employee ratings and conducts employee benefits and insurance programs. Coordinates activities of various clerical departments or workers within department.

ADMINISTRATIVE ASSISTANT

Aids executive in staff capacity by coordinating office services such as personnel, budget preparation and control, housekeeping, records control, and special management studies. Studies management methods in order to improve work flow, simplify reporting procedures, and implement cost reductions. Analyzes unit operating practices, such as recordkeeping systems, forms control, office layout, suggestion systems, personnel and budgetary requirements, and performance standards, to create new systems or revise established procedures. Analyzes jobs to delineate position responsibilities for use in wage and salary adjustments, promotions, and evaluation of work flow. Studies methods of improving work measurements or performance standards.

If you are applying for a specific job, ask the human resources department for a copy of the job description; then tailor your resume to the skills listed in that description.

Creative Functional Resume

Beginning or returning workers who have had no paid experience often find it particularly hard to make their activities sound transferable to the world of work. They dismiss their experience as academic work or homemaking, which they mistakenly think differs markedly from work in business. However, they usually have been performing business functions without realizing it. People without paid work experience and people returning to the job market after taking time out to be homemakers can persuade employers to recognize their ability and practical experience if they describe their life in categories such as these:

MANAGEMENT

- Coordinated the multiple activities of five people of different ages and varying interests, keeping within tight schedules and continuous deadlines.
- Established priorities for the allocation of available time, resources, and funds.

OFFICE PROCEDURES

- Maintained lists of daily appointments, reminders, items to be purchased, people to be called, tasks to be accomplished.
- Handled all business and personal correspondence—answered and issued invitations, wrote to stores about defective merchandise, made hotel reservations.

PERSONNEL

- Recruited, hired, trained, and supervised household staff; negotiated wages.
- Motivated children to assume responsibilities and helped them develop self-confidence.
- Resolved problems caused by low morale and lack of cooperation.

FINANCES

- Established annual household budget, and monitored costs to stay within budget.
- Balanced the checkbook and reconciled monthly bank statements.
- Calculated take-home pay of household staff, made quarterly reports to the government on Social Security taxes withheld.

PURCHASING

- Undertook comparison shopping for food, clothing, furniture, and equipment, and purchased at various stores at different times, depending on best value.
- Planned meals according to savings available at different food stores.
- Shopped for insurance and found lower premiums than current coverage, resulting in substantial savings.

Pros and Cons of the Functional Resume

The functional resume is especially useful if you have limited work experience or breaks in your employment record, or if you are changing fields. You need not include dates or distinguish paid activities from nonpaid volunteer activities. By omitting or deemphasizing previous employers' names, you downplay any stereotyped assumptions that a prospective employer may make about previous employers (McDonald's, the PTA, a school district). Similarly, highlighting skills and deemphasizing job titles help direct the future employer to the fact that you are someone with specific abilities that may be useful in the present job opening. This format also can emphasize your growth and development.

To use this format effectively, you must be able to identify and write about your achievements. This sometimes requires the assistance of an expert resume writer. Additionally, some employers may prefer resumes that include exact dates and job titles.

Exhibits 10.5, 10.6, 10.7, and 10.8 (at the end of this chapter) are examples of functional resumes for various positions.

THE CHRONOLOGICAL RESUME

The chronological resume is the traditional and most frequently used resume style. It lists your work history in reverse chronological order, meaning the most recent position or occupation is listed first. The work history should include dates employed, job title, job duties, and employer's name, address, and telephone number.

Pros and Cons of the Chronological Resume

The chronological resume is most useful for people with no breaks in their employment record and for whom each new position indicates continuous advancement or growth. Recent high school and college graduates also find this approach simpler than creating a functional resume.

As dates tend to dominate the presentation, any breaks or undocumented years of work may stand out. If your present position is not related to the job you desire, you may be eliminated from the competition by employers who feel that current experience is the most important consideration in reviewing resumes. However, if you emphasize skills in your present job that will be important to the new position, this will be less of a problem.

Exhibits 10.9, 10.10, 10.11, and 10.12 (at the end of this chapter) are examples of chronological resumes tailored to various positions.

THE COMBINATION RESUME

If you have major skills important for success in your desired job in addition to an impressive record of continuous job experience with reputable employers, you can best highlight this double advantage with a *combination* of the functional and chronological styles of resume. This combination style usually lists functions followed by years employed with a list of employers. The combination style also satisfies the employer who wants to see the dates that you were actually employed. See Exhibits 10.13 and 10.14.

Cover Letter Guidelines

 ant to turn off a prospective employer? Send a resume with no cover letter. Or send a form letter addressed to Personnel Manager. Or address your letter Dear Sir, only to have it received by a female manager.

A cover letter announces your availability and introduces the resume. It is probably one of the most important self-advertisements you will write.

The cover letter should indicate you have researched the organization and are clearly interested in a position there. Let the person to whom you are writing know what sources you used and what you know about the firm in the first paragraph—to get his or her attention and show your interest.

You may have heard people say, "It's not *what* you know, but *who* you know that counts." This is only partly true, but nonetheless important. You can often get to know someone with only a little effort. Call or, better yet, visit the organization and talk to people who already hold the job you want. Be tactful and discreet, of course. You're not trying to take their position from them. See the section titled "Interviewing for Information" in Chapter 9. Ask about training, environment, salary, and other relevant issues. Then in your cover letter, mention that you talked with some of the firm's employees, and that these discussions increased your interest. You thereby show the reader you took the initiative to visit the company and that you know someone, if only casually. This is all part of networking, as discussed in Chapter 9.

Basic principles of letter and resume writing include being self-confident when listing your positive qualities and attributes, writing as one professional to another, and having your materials properly prepared. The next page offers a cover letter template.

First, address your letter to a specific person, with the name spelled correctly and the proper title. These details count. Your opening paragraph should contain the "hook." Arouse some work-related interest. Explain (very briefly) why you are writing. How did you become interested in that company? Summarize what you have to offer. Details of your

Resume Cover Letter Template

Address
City, State, ZIP
Phone/E-mail
Date

Name of Person
Company Name
Street Address or P.O. Box
City, State, ZIP

Salutation   (Dear M _____: or Greetings:)

The first paragraph should indicate the job you are interested in and how you heard about it. Use the names of contact persons here, if you have any.

Sample Entry   Your employment advertisement in Tuesday's *News Chronicle* indicating an opening for an administrative assistant is of special interest to me. Mary Smith, who is employed with your firm, suggested I write to you. I have heard that Rohn Electronics is a growing company and needs dynamic employees who want to learn and contribute to the firm.

The second paragraph should relate your experience, skills, and background to the particular position. Refer to your enclosed resume for details, and highlight the specific skills and competencies that could be useful to the company.

Sample Entry   During the last five years, I worked as office manager. In this position, I improved office efficiency by investigating and selecting word processing equipment. I understand that your opening includes responsibilities for supervising and coordinating word processing procedures with your home office. I was able to reduce my firm's operating costs over 30 percent by selecting the best equipment for our purposes.

The third paragraph should indicate your plans for follow-up contact and that your resume is enclosed.

Sample Entry   I would appreciate the opportunity to apply my skills on behalf of your company. For your examination, I have enclosed a resume indicating my education and work experience. I will call your office early next week to determine a convenient time for an appointment to further discuss possible employment opportunities.

Sincerely,

NOTE: Don't forget
to sign the letter.

Your first and last name
Enclosure (or Attachment)

259

background can show why you should be considered as a job candidate. The self-appraisal that went into preparation of your resume tells what you *can* and *like* to do and where your strengths and interests lie. Your research on the prospective employer should have uncovered the qualifications needed. If your letter promises a good match—meaning your abilities match the company's needs—you've attracted attention.

Keep your letter short and to the point. Refer to your resume, highlighting relevant experiences and accomplishments that match the firm's stated needs. Ask for an interview. Indicate when you will be calling to confirm a convenient time for the interview. Let your letter express your individuality but within the context of the employment situation.

The cover letter should be individually typed for each job. Always review both the cover letter and resume for good margins, clarity, correct spelling, and accurate typing. Appearance does count! Review the sample cover letters in Exhibits 10.16 through 10.20, following the exercises.

Application Forms

A final type of form, accepted sometimes as a substitute for a resume, is an *application form*. The employment application is a form used by most companies to gain necessary information and to register applicants for work (see Exhibit 10.2). This information becomes a guide to determine a person's suitability for both the company and the job that needs filling. You should observe carefully the following guidelines when completing an application form.

You will probably be asked to fill out an employment application form before the interview takes place. Therefore, it is good practice to arrive at the employment office a little ahead of the time of your interview. Bring along a pen and your resume or a personal data sheet. You will be asked to provide your name, address, training or education, experience, special abilities, and possibly even your hobbies and interests. Practically all application forms request that you state the job you are seeking and the salary you have received in the past. Most firms require an applicant to complete an application form.

Many times the employer wants to make certain rapid comparisons and needs only to review the completed company employment application forms on file. For example, Ms. Ford needed a stenographer who could type fast. She examined many application forms of people who had word processing skills. By referring to the same section each time, she quickly thumbed through dozens of applications, eliminating all candidates who had only average speed. Thus, there was no need for her to examine resumes or read dozens of letters to find out exactly how fast each candidate could type.

Filling Out Application Forms

(See the next page for a sample form.)

1. Fill out the application form in ink—or use a type-writer.

2. Answer every question that applies to you. If a question does not apply or is illegal (see Chapter 11), you may write *N/A*, meaning *not applicable*, or draw a line through the space to show that you did not overlook the question.

3. Give your complete address, including ZIP code.

4. Spell correctly. If you aren't sure how to spell a word, use the dictionary or try to use another word with the same meaning.

5. A question on job preference or "job for which you are applying" should be answered with a specific job title or type of work. Do not write "anything." Employers expect you to state clearly what kind of work you can do.

6. Have a prepared list of schools attended and previous employers. Include addresses and dates of employment.

7. Be prepared to provide several good references. It is advisable to ask permission of those you plan to list. Good references include:

   - A recognized community leader
   - A former employer or teacher who knows you well
   - Friends who are established in business

8. When you write or sign your name on the application, use your formal name—not a nickname. Your first name, middle initial, and last name are usually preferred.

9. Be as neat as possible. Employers expect that your application will be an example of your best work.

NEATNESS COUNTS

The way in which an application form has been filled out indicates the applicant's level of neatness, thoroughness, and accuracy. If two applicants seem to have equal qualifications but one's form is carelessly filled out, the application itself might tilt the balance in favor of the other applicant. Unless your handwriting is especially clear, print or type all answers. Look for "please print" instructions on the form.

Sometimes you may apply for a job by mail, and a form will be sent to you. Fill out the application form carefully, completely, and accurately. When you have completed the application, go over it again. Have you given the information asked? When an item asked for is not applicable, have you written in *N/A?* Return the completed application to the company. You may attach a copy of your resume, if you wish.

Summary

This chapter has provided diverse examples of resumes, cover letters, letters of introduction, and application form reminders. Putting the resume together is now your job. Use the exhibits and ideas in the following written exercises as well as the tips throughout the chapter to assist you in getting your resume into shape.

10.2   *Sample employment application.*

Date _____

PERSONAL INFORMATION:

Name _____
         Last   First   Middle

Address _____
              Street   City   State   Zip

Telephone Number (____) _____   Are you over 17 years of age? ☐ Yes ☐ No

POSITION WANTED:

Job Title _____ Date Available _____ Salary Desired _____

Check any that apply: ☐ Full Time   ☐ Part Time   ☐ Day Shift   ☐ Night Shift

EDUCATION:

Begin with high school; include any military school you may have attended:

NAME OF SCHOOL   LOCATION OF SCHOOL   DEGREE OR COURSE OF STUDY
_____
_____

List any academic honors or professional associations:
_____
_____

WORK EXPERIENCE:

List last three employers. Start with the current or most recent.

Name and Address of Employer _____
Dates Worked _____ Pay _____ Reason for Leaving _____
Job Title _____ Job Description _____

Name and Address of Employer _____
Dates Worked _____ Pay _____ Reason for Leaving _____
Job Title _____ Job Description _____

Name and Address of Employer _____
Dates Worked _____ Pay _____ Reason for Leaving _____
Job Title _____ Job Description _____

Computer Skills (describe)   Typing Speed _____ *wpm*
   (if applicable)   (if applicable)

Do you have any physical condition or handicap that may limit your ability to perform the job applied for? ☐ Yes ☐ No
If yes, what can be done to accommodate your limitation?

Have you ever been convicted of a felony? ☐ Yes ☐ No   If yes, give kind and date.
A conviction will not necessarily disqualify you from employment.

Are you legally entitled to work in the U.S.? ☐ Yes ☐ No   Can you provide proof of citizenship after employment? ☐ Yes ☐ No

Are you a veteran? ☐ Yes ☐ No   If yes, give dates:

List the names of three references whom we may contact who have knowledge of your skills, talents, or technical knowledge:
(1)   *(2)*   *(3)*
Name and Relationship
(Supervisor, Teacher, etc.) _____
Address _____
Telephone & Area No. _____

I certify, by my signature below, that any false or omitted important facts in my answers on this application may be cause for dismissal.

_____   _____
Applicant's Signature   *Date*

Preparing a Winning Resume

The written exercises that follow will enable you to prepare a resume as well as critique it. Exercises 10.1 and 10.2 help you to organize pertinent information about yourself. Exercise 10.3 asks you to draft a resume. Exercise 10.4 reminds you to save copies of work for a portfolio. Exercises 10.5 and 10.6 provide guide- lines for critiquing your own resume and obtaining valuable feedback from others. Exercise 10.7 reminds you to write a cover letter and get feedback before sending it.

To answer these questions online, go to the *Exercise* module in Chapter 10 of the Companion Website.

Resume Review Sheet

Fill in the review sheet on the following page. The answers will help you prepare a com- plete resume.

Create a Card File

Create a card file (or a computer file) describing your work experiences, using Exhibit 10.1 as a guide. This gives you a chance to write your job tasks in func- tional terms.

Write Your Resume

Choose the format desired and write your own resume, referring to Exercise 10.1 for data. Refer to the suggestions in the chapter and the samples that follow this chapter.

Save Sample Work for a Portfolio

Start now to keep a folder of the best work you have done in work-related classes and past jobs, internships, and volunteer positions.

Resume/Portfolio Review

A. PERSONAL DATA

  1. Name _____

  2. Address _____

  3. Phone _____

B. CURRENT JOB OBJECTIVE _____

C. EDUCATION

  1. High school and college _____

      a. Favorite subjects _____

      b. Work samples _____

      c. Extracurricular interests _____

      d. Offices held _____

      e. Athletic achievements _____

      f. Other significant facts (e.g., honors, awards) _____

  2. Other (military, volunteer, correspondence, summer work, languages, technical skills, licenses, and/or credentials) _____

D. WORK EXPERIENCE

  Refer to your experiography or your skills analysis.

  1. Employer _____

     Length of employment _____

     Position _____

     Skills/accomplishments/work samples _____

  2. Employer _____

     Length of employment _____

     Position _____

     Skills/accomplishments/work samples _____

  3. Employer _____

     Length of employment _____

     Position _____

     Skills/accomplishments/work samples _____

E. PUBLICATIONS _____

F. ASSOCIATIONS, SPECIAL SKILLS, AND COMMUNITY INVOLVEMENT

  _____

G. REFERENCES (Do not include specific names on resume, but do homework regarding possible references *now*.)

  _____

  _____

Critique Your Resume

Use the resume checklist and critique form (Exhibit 10.3) to evaluate your resume.

Resume checklist and critique form.

	Strong	Average	Weak	Plans for Improvement
1. Resume format. Does it say "READ ME"?				
2. Appearance. Is it brief? Did you use a clear, engaging layout? Type clearly? Use a correct format?				
3. Length. Are the key points concise?				
4. Significance. Did you select your most relevant experiences?				
5. Communication. Do your words give the "visual" impression you want? Is the job objective clearly stated?				
6. Conciseness. Does your information focus on the experiences that qualify you for the position?				
7. Completeness. Did you include all important information? Have you made a connection between the job desired and your experience?				
8. Accuracy. Does the resume represent you well enough to get you an interview?				
9. Skills. Does your resume reflect the skills necessary for the job?				

Ask Others to Critique Your Resume

EXERCISE 10.6

Ask other people (e.g., career counselors, those who have been receptive to you during informational interviews, teachers, friends) to give you feedback about your resume. Use the checklist of Dos and Don'ts in Exhibit 10.4 to help others give you feedback.

EXHIBIT 10.4   Resume DOs and DON'Ts.

DO

- Focus your job objective to illustrate specific skills and responsibilities.

- Interest your reader with significant employment, education, accomplishments, and skills.

- Present yourself positively, honestly, and assertively.

- Keep the resume to no more than two pages.

- Use an attractive and readable layout, including top-quality paper, for a professional appearance.

- Have your resume carefully proofread prior to its final printing.

DON'T

- Be too wordy or use buzzwords and unnecessary verbiage.

- Provide personal data on your age, race, marital status, religion, or other private matters.

- Suggest abilities or objectives beyond your reach or qualifications.

- Make reference to a desired salary or income.

- State a reason for leaving a previous job.

- Provide names of references in the resume.

Write a Cover Letter

EXERCISE 10.7

Referring to Exhibits 10.16–10.20, write a cover letter to accompany your resume. Ask others to critique it, as you did in Exercise 10.6 with your resume.

WWWebwise

 For additional activities online, go to the WWWebwise module in Chapter 10 of the Companion Website.

Exercise Summary

Write a brief paragraph answering these questions.

What did you learn about yourself from these exercises? How does this knowledge relate to your career/life planning? How do you feel?

_____

_____

_____

_____

_____

_____

_____

_____

_____

_____

_____

_____

_____

_____

_____

_____

_____

_____

_____

_____

_____

_____

_____

_____

_____

_____

_____

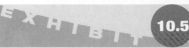

SAMUEL GILDAR
P.O. Box 1111
Cincinnati, OH 14528

Day Phone: (513) 555-1212
E-mail: sgildar@aol.com

GOALS

To work as an administrative assistant in a creative
atmosphere and have the opportunity to use my abilities.

SUMMARY OF EXPERIENCE

Ten years of increasing responsibility in the area of office management involving organization, problem-solving, finances, and public relations.

MANAGEMENT

Initiated and organized procedures used in the office, coordinated activities of clerical personnel, and formulated procedures for systematic retention, protection, transfer, and disposal of records. Coordinated preparation of operating reports, such as time and attendance records, of performance data. Reviewed, composed, and answered correspondence. Directed services, such as maintenance, repair, supplies, mail, and files. Aided executive by coordinating office services, such as personnel, budget preparation and control, housekeeping, records control, and special management studies.

PUBLIC RELATIONS

Coordinated communications with state, county, and district officials as well as district and local employees, student body, staff members, and parents in our community. Planned and coordinated social functions for school, staff, and two social clubs. Promoted sales of jewelry, gourmet foods, and liquors in sales-related jobs.

PROBLEM SOLVING

Made decisions according to district policy in the absence of the principal. Worked under constant pressure and interruption while attending to student problems regarding their health and welfare. Liaison between school and community, resolving as many problems as possible before referring them to superior.

BUDGETING/FINANCIAL

Analyzed and coordinated payroll recordkeeping, budgeted expenditures, requisitioned supplies, prepared attendance accounting reports, and initiated budget system for $10,000 of instructional monies allocated to the school.

CREATIVE

Created news copy and layouts using PageMaker and QuarkXPress. Designed fliers, posters, calendars, and bulletins sent home from school to parents. Personal hobbies include ceramics, oil painting, sculpting, and interior design.

EMPLOYERS

Cincinnati Unified School District
1115 Old School Road
Cincinnati, OH 14528
(513) 555-2345

Cincinnati Blue Cross
5900 Erwin Road
Cincinnati, OH 14526
(513) 555-3698

OLIVIA MARTINEZ
2406 Adams Avenue
Los Angeles, CA 90025
213-555-0862
e-mail: om@msn.com

PROFESSIONAL OBJECTIVE:

Management position utilizing administrative, communications, and research skills.

SUMMARY OF SKILLS:

Administrative

Designed and implemented evaluation program for compensatory education project.

Coauthored grant proposal.

Served as liaison between volunteers and university administration.

Directed registration program and coordinated staff at registration desk, Western Psychological Association Annual Convention, 2001.

As student senator, initiated Earth Day activities and helped establish faculty evaluation program.

Communications

Planned discussion sections, provided guidance to students, cowrote and graded examinations for undergraduate courses in developmental psychology and statistics.

Prepared tutorials in science and study methods and offered educational guidance to economically disadvantaged high school students.

Participated in human growth seminar led by clinical psychologist, trained in therapy methods, and helped devise therapy program for young people.

Research

Designed and conducted study investigating memory in four-year-olds.

Studied mathematical structure underlying Piagetian developmental theory.

Implemented computer simulation model of certain cognitive behaviors of children. Analyzed and categorized data for cognitive anthropologist and psychologist.

EDUCATION:

M.A., August 2002 Developmental Psychology, University of California, Los Angeles, California. California State Graduate Fellow, National Science Foundation Honorable Mention.

B.A., 2000 Psychology, University of California, Irvine. *Summa Cum Laude*, Outstanding Scholar, Honor Scholar.

EXPERIENCE:

Teaching Assistant and Reader. Psychology Department, University of California, Los Angeles, August 1999–June 2002.

Administrative Assistant. Psychology Department, California State University, Fullerton, February–June 1998.

Business Manager, Education Motivation. Community Projects Office, University of California, Irvine, August 1996–January 1997.

Research Assistant. Departments of German and Russian, University of California, Irvine, October 1995–June 1996.

10.7   *Functional resume for a teacher changing careers.*

STACY L. MOLLARD

1001 Gainsborough Street   stacymollard@cox.net   312-555-3581 (home)
Chicago, IL 60664   312-555-4343 (work)

POSITION OBJECTIVE:

Employee Training Specialist

QUALIFICATIONS IN BRIEF:

B.A. in English, Mundelein College, Chicago.

Six years' elementary teaching with experience in communications, human relations, instruction, and supervision.

Bilingual (English, Spanish).

EXPERIENCE SUMMARY:

COMMUNICATIONS:

Conducted staff development workshops; presented new curriculum plans to parent groups, sent periodic progress reports to parents, and developed class newsletter; presented workshops in parent effectiveness training at state and local conferences.

HUMAN RELATIONS:

Directed effective problem solving/conflict resolution between individual students and student groups; initiated program of student self-governance; acted as liaison between families of diverse cultural, ethnic, and economic backgrounds and school personnel/services; conducted individual and group conferences to establish rapport with parents and discuss student progress.

INSTRUCTION:

Developed instructional modules to solve specific learning problems; developed instructional audiovisual materials; used audiovisual equipment such as overhead, opaque, and movie projectors and audio- and videocassettes; did extensive research in various curricula; served as a member of curriculum development committee; introduced new motivational techniques for students.

CURRENTLY EMPLOYED:

Austin Elementary School, Chicago, Illinois

COMMUNITY INVOLVEMENT:

Board member, Chicago Community Services Center

Allocations Committee, Chicago United Way

RICHARD ROTH
66 Cheyenne Dr.
Billings, MT 46060
(712) 555-1212
rroth@earthlink.net

Professional Objective

Administrative assistant position utilizing administrative, bookkeeping, and communications skills.

Summary of Skills

Administrative

Answered phones, scheduled appointments, sorted mail, filed
Implemented new filing and retrieval system
Software programs used include Windows XP and Office Professional XP
Maintained appearance of office

Bookkeeping

Handled cash register
Closed cash register at the end of the evening
Recorded cash transactions

Communications

Served as peer counselor for 2 years
Assisted in dental office
Demonstrated proper dental hygiene to children
Fed, clothed, and entertained children

Education

Billings Community College, Transfer Program, 2002 to present, Dean's List
Billings High School, graduated 2001

Experience

Lombard Medical Group, Billings, MT, October 2002–present
Sandy Murphree, Billings, MT, February 2000–present
Oakbrook Dental, Billings, MT, June 1999–October 1999
Fantastic Sam's, Billings, MT, June 1998–August 1998
Blue Wave, Billings, MT, December 1997–June 1998

EXHIBIT 10.9 *Chronological resume for a high school graduate with limited experience.*

JOHN JONES

(480) 555-1221

1050 Baez Street
Mesa, AZ 85201
jj123@aol.com

OBJECTIVE:	An entry-level position as a *(list one or two related job titles)* that affords opportunities to learn and progress.
SUMMARY:	Three years of part-time and summer employment related to sales, public contact, and accounting while attending high school.
EDUCATION:	*(List your most recent education first.)* 2003 Red Mountain High School, Mesa, Arizona Graduated with emphasis in mathematics and business. Courses included:

Word processing   Trigonometry
Excel   Geometry
English   Business math
Journalism   Accounting principles
Algebra

EXPERIENCE:	*(List most recent experience first.)* 2001–03 Mesa General Store, Mesa, Arizona <u>Salesperson</u>. Sold apparel in men's and children's departments. 2000–01 Tower Records & Video, Mesa, Arizona <u>Counterperson</u>. Assisted customer selections. Handled monetary transactions. 1999–2000 Miscellaneous employment: babysat for four families with one to four children. Stayed with children weekends and while parents were on vacation, and assumed full responsibility for normal household routines.
HONORS:	*(If you had a high grade point average, include it. List offices held in a student or community organization. List publications. If none of these apply, omit this section from your resume.)*
ACTIVITIES:	Future Business Managers Association, Journalism Club, Student Tutoring Association, Young Republicans Club

THUY NGUYEN

532 Castilian Court   (206) 799-1212 (Home)
Seattle, WA 98102   (206) 555-1212 (Work)
                                                           thuynguyen@netstar.net

---

OCCUPATIONAL OBJECTIVE:

A position as office manager leading to increased responsibilities for business operations.

SUMMARY OF QUALIFICATIONS:

Three years of increasingly responsible experience in different positions.

BOOKKEEPER   *Hungry Hunter and El Torito Restaurants*
                                                      Seattle, WA 2002 to present

Kept records of financial transactions, entering them in computer. Balanced books and compiled reports to show statistics, such as cash receipts and expenditures, accounts payable and receivable, and other items pertinent to operation of business. Calculated employee wages from time cards and updated computerized records.

RESTAURANT GREETER   *Hungry Hunter Restaurant*
                                                      Thousand Oaks, CA 1999–2002

Welcomed guests, seated them in dining area, maintained quality of facilities. Directed others in performing courteous and rapid service; also assisted in settling complaints. Related well with the continuous flow of people, coordinating the service with customers' needs.

SPECIAL ACCOMPLISHMENTS:

National Forensic League, vice president (third place, statewide oratory competition); Athletic Association (gymnastic team); Honor Roll and Dean's List; Alpha Gamma Sigma; *Who's Who Among American High School Students,* 1998–1999.

EDUCATION:

Seattle Pacific University, Seattle, WA

Majoring in Business Administration

GPA: 3.5 on a 4.0 scale

10.11   *Chronological resume for a bank teller position.*

ELEANOR RUTLEDGE
3388 North Dallas
Wadsworth, TX 77065
909-555-0026
eprutledge@theriver.net

JOB OBJECTIVE: A position as a bank teller that offers opportunities to learn and progress.

EDUCATION: 2001 to present—Glencoe College, Dallas, Texas
Courses included:

Accounting	Sociology 1
Business Computers	English 1A
Excel	

2000—Wadsworth High School, Wadsworth, Texas
Graduated with Honors; Treasurer for Honor Society
Courses included:

Windows 2000	Algebra
English	Geometry
Public Speaking	

SPECIAL SKILLS: Facility with numbers, manual dexterity, patience, excellence in telephone communications, organized fund-raisers for church group.

EXPERIENCE: 2001–2003—Cashier, Builders Emporium, Wadsworth, Texas. Operated cash register and made change, worked well with public, motivated fellow employees, encouraged customers to buy products.

2001–2000—Miscellaneous employment: babysat for local families; assumed full responsibility while parents were away; helped children with their homework.

SARITA SANDHA
980 Victory Blvd.
Brooklyn, NY 11321
(405) 555-4150
ssandha@aol.com

JOB OBJECTIVE:	**Public Representative or Community Service Worker**
SUMMARY OF QUALIFICATIONS:	Six years' experience in public relations, media work, and writing press releases and newsletters. Organized concerts, rallies, walk-a-thons, and volunteer-a-thons. Basic qualifications in office procedures: phone networking, word processing, mailing, leafletting, outreach, and public speaking.
EDUCATION:	**Brooklyn College, currently attending, 2001–present** Sociology major. Additional specialized institute training at Loyola Marymount University in social organizing. Two years as teacher's aide in New York City school system. Interrelated with a variety of cultural groups. **Alemany High School, graduated**
EXPERIENCE:	**2000–2003 Community service organizations in New York** Organized, educated, persuaded, created social change, raised over $25,000 and performed security work. **1998–2000 Self-employed** Managed and maintained family residence. **1996–1998 Receptionist and secretary** Interviewed applicants for positions in sales, maintained records, answered phones, and performed light clerical work.
SPECIAL SKILLS:	Interact easily with diverse people while under pressure. Knowledge of fund-raising practices. Self-motivated. Experienced in analyzing and working with issues and strategies underlying a particular campaign. Computer literate.

10.13 *Combination resume for a sales executive position.*

JOHN BENNETT
304 Amen Street
Columbia, SC 29260

(803) 555-3692 (w)
(803) 555-1126 (h)
E-mail: jben@msn.com

OBJECTIVE

MARKETING DIRECTOR

SALES PROMOTION

Designed and supervised sales promotion projects for large business firms and manufacturers, mostly in the electronics field. Originated newspaper, radio, and television advertising. Coordinated sales promotion with public relations and sales management. Analyzed market potentials, and developed new techniques to increase sales effectiveness and reduce sales costs. Created sales training manuals.

As sales executive and promotion consultant, handled a great variety of accounts. Sales potentials in these firms varied from $100,000 to $5 million per annum. Raised the volume of sales in many of these firms 25 percent within the first year.

SALES MANAGEMENT

Hired and supervised sales staff on local, area, and national bases. Established branch offices throughout the United States. Developed uniform systems of processing orders and maintaining sales records. Promoted new products, as well as improved sales of old ones. Developed sales training program. Devised a catalog system involving inventory control to facilitate movement of scarce stock between branches.

MARKET RESEARCH

Originated and supervised market research projects to determine sales potential, as well as need for advertising. Wrote detailed reports and recommendations describing each step in distribution, areas for development, and plans for sales improvement.

SALES

Retail and wholesale. Direct sales to consumer, jobber, and manufacturer. Hard goods, small metals, and electrical appliances.

EMPLOYERS

2001–Present	B. B. Bowen Sales Development Co., Columbia, South Carolina	Sales Executive
1998–2001	James Bresher Commercial and Industrial Sales Research Corp., Oakland, California	Senior Sales Promotion Manager
1995–1998	Dunnock Brothers Electronics Co., San Francisco, California	Order Clerk, Salesworker, Sales Manager

EDUCATION

University of California, Berkeley, B.S.; Major: Business Administration

ALBERT CHAN
111 East Maple
Minneapolis, MN
(508) 866-1592 • albertchan34@aol.com

JOB OBJECTIVE	Programmer trainee or Junior Programmer
QUALIFICATIONS BY EXPERIENCE	Flowcharted, coded, tested, and debugged interactive programs for the HP3000. Created a system of five programs from a system problem statement and flowchart. Built a KSAM file for use by the system. Designed system flowcharts and wrote other documentation for improved payroll system for previous employer, as Systems Analysis course project.
	Tutored students in Visual BASIC, C+ and C++, working with Hispanics, Vietnamese, and reentering adults, as well as other students.
	Currently creating a bibliographic database as a volunteer at Minneapolis Public Library and designed library's Web page.
EDUCATION	2003 Associate in Science Degree in Computer Science, Minneapolis Central College. Courses included UNIX and C++.
	3.6 GPA in computer science classes.
	2002 B.A. in English, Florida Southern College.
	Graduate work in research methods.
	Supported self through college by security work at various firms. Gained secret clearance while at IBM Federal System Division.
SPECIAL SKILLS	Attentive to detail, organized, work well with little supervision, enterprising, enjoy problem-solving and interacting with others to plan projects, work well under pressure, able to see relationships between abstract ideas, good at communication, concise.
COMMUNITY SERVICE EXPERIENCE	Organized CROP Walks (fund-raisers for Church World Service), which resulted in raising $6,000 in 2000 and $10,000 in 2001.
	Chaired the planning committee, recruited members, mapped walk route.
	Obtained parade permits and business tax exemptions.
	Wrote press releases and walkers' instruction sheets.

10.15   *A poorly constructed resume (see corrected version on the following page).*

Omit entirely

Place name, address, phone on top of page in correct format; include e-mail address

List as job objective, with specific summary

Edit and highlight key responsibilities

Same as #4

Omit years (if over 10) and reduce excess words

Too wordy and unrelated to job objective. Edit to highlight language ability.

Separate and edit

---

1 PROFESSIONAL EXPERIENCE AND TRAINING OF SARA CRANE: SOCIAL CASE WORKER

2 4234 S. Platt Avenue, Salt Lake City, Utah 84100 (801) 765-4321

3 Social case worker with RN degree wants a responsible position with a large medical firm that could benefit from my experience in both nursing and social work.

EXPERIENCE

4 2000–present . . . Family caseworker. Working through Parker General Hospital Services in Salt Lake. Worked directly with families at their homesites. Met with family and formulated a plan after consultation and comprehensive investigation of needs. Developed assistance and support as appropriate with follow-up services.

5 1991–2000 . . . RN and convalescent services. Grandjunction, Utah. Treated patients with disabilities. Reviewed financial aspects and fee payments, all inpatient and outpatient services, and full family participation in health program to ensure cooperation and support.

EDUCATION

1988–90 . . . Bachelor of Science. Social Work. Brigham Young School of Social Work. Training in all areas of social work including internships in pediatrics, psychiatric, rehabilitation, and gerontology sections.

6 1985–88 . . . Registered Nurse. Baker College, Salt Lake City, Utah. General nursing curriculum including family health concerns. Took additional courses in specialized nursing for retired patients and also advanced psychiatric techniques. I realized that my experience and interests were becoming directed into social work.

PROFESSIONAL AFFILIATIONS

The National Association of Case and Social Workers

INTERESTS

7 Travel and reading. Conversational abilities in Spanish and French, including reading knowledge. Good cook and enjoy theater productions. Any references regarding my education or work experience **8** may be requested at any time.

SARA CRANE

4234 S. Platt Avenue
Salt Lake City, UT 84100
(801) 765-4321
scrane@earthlink.net

JOB OBJECTIVE

Social Worker utilizing skills developed as a Registered Nurse and Financial Planner

EXPERIENCE

Family Caseworker. Parker General Hospital, Salt Lake City, Utah, 2000

Report to Social Services Director of largest family assistance program in Salt Lake City, attached to hospital intake services. Duties include:

- Interviewing family members at the hospital and in their homes to determine needs.
- Investigating claims and proposing plans for assistance.
- Counseling and guiding families in special circumstances, including personal and health issues.
- Providing follow-up treatment and reports.

Convalescent Service as an RN. Grandjunction Hospital, Grandjunction, Utah, 1991–2000.

Reported to Health Services Center with following responsibilities:

- Interviewed patients' families to determine financial capabilities.
- Arranged fee structures.
- Planned outpatient plan and referral services.
- Counseled families for inpatient and/or convalescent needs.

EDUCATION

Bachelor of Science, Social Work, Brigham Young University, School of Social Work, Provo, Utah.

Internships in pediatric, psychiatric, rehabilitation, and gerontology sections.
Additional courses in Financial Planning.

Registered Nurse, Baker College, Salt Lake City, Utah.

Full training in general nursing with specialization in psychiatric nursing. Workshops in family health led to social work career path.

SPECIAL SKILLS/AFFILIATIONS

Fluency in Spanish and French. Membership in the National Association of Case and Social Workers.

March 4, 2004

Mr. Harvey J. Finder
Executive Director
Lung Association of Alma County
1717 Opportunity Way
Santa Ana, CA 92706

Dear Mr. Finder:

I am interested in the position of community health education program coordinator with the Lung Association of Alma County. I feel that my education, skills, and desire to work in this area make me a strong candidate for this position.

My education has helped me develop sound analytical abilities and has exposed me to the health-care field. My involvement with health-care and community organizations has provided me with a working knowledge of various public and private health institutions, which has increased my ability to communicate effectively with health-care professionals, patients, and the community at large. This combination of education and exposure has stimulated my interest in seeking a career in the health-care field.

Please review the enclosed resume and contact me at your convenience regarding a personal interview. If I do not hear from you in the next week, I will contact you. I look forward to talking with you.

Sincerely yours,

Denise M. Hunter
18411 Anticipation Drive
Northridge, CA 91330
(213) 555-0217
DMH@hotmail.com

Enclosures

532 Glendora Avenue
Anytown, IN 45420
April 1, 2004

Ms. Joan Addeman
Director of Personnel
ABC Corporation
Anytown, MO 90000

Dear Ms. Addeman:

I am applying for the administrative assistant position currently available at your firm. I have been impressed for some time with the outstanding reputation that ABC Corporation holds in our community.

As you read my resume, please note that my twelve years of business experience directly relate to the needs of your company. One of my greatest assets is seven years in motivational psychology related to personnel management and public school teaching. I am aware that strength in business and management is considered important in your firm, and I would like the opportunity to discuss with you, at your earliest convenience, how we might work together for our mutual benefit.

Enclosed is my resume for your review. I will telephone your secretary next week to see when we might set up an appointment to further discuss the administrative assistant position and any other ways that I could serve your corporation.

Sincerely,

Gerald Burnes

Enclosure: Resume

EXHIBIT **10.18**   *Cover letter for an electronics technician position.*

412 Melbrook Avenue
Omaha, NE 77050
June 17, 2003

Mr. Lloyd Johnson
Sonat Technical Supervisor
Lear Electronic Company
1229 Van Owen
Knoxville, TN 37917

Dear Mr. Johnson:

I am interested in working for your company as an electronics technician in the field of systems installation and calibration.

During my tour of duty in the service, I became acquainted with many of your electronic systems aboard ship and was extremely impressed with their design and documentation. I have since pursued a course of studies at Hastings College to increase my competence in the field of electronics. For these reasons, I feel I would be an asset to your company.

I have enclosed a copy of my resume for your consideration. I will contact you by telephone next week to set up a meeting to discuss employment opportunities with your company.

Sincerely yours,

Emilio Reyna

Enclosure

1234 Evanston Avenue
Cambridge, IL 61238
May 16, 2004

Mr. Harrison MacBuren
Director of Personnel
North Hills Mall
Cambridge, IL 61238

Dear Mr. MacBuren:

I am very interested in the position currently available in your public relations department for an assistant to the director of public relations.

As you can see by my resume, my previous administrative experience would be a definite asset to your company. I feel that a vital part of any public relations job is the ability to deal with people. This is a skill I have acquired through many years of volunteer work.

I would like to meet with you to discuss how we might work together for our mutual benefit. I will be contacting you within the week to arrange a convenient meeting time.

Sincerely,

George Herounian

Enclosure

EXHIBIT **10.20** *Cover letter for a marketing manager position.*

1736 D Street NW
Washington, DC 20006
(202) 555-8192
May 3, 2004

Ms. Emma Major, President
Vendo Corporation
1742 Surf Drive
Fort Lauderdale, FL 33301

Dear Ms. Major:

I was intrigued by the write-up about your new portable vending centers in *Sales Management* magazine. I think it is an extremely good idea.

As you will note from the enclosed resume, my marketing, planning, and sales management experience could be of great assistance to you at this early stage in your project. Enclosed are some specific marketing ideas you might like to review. I would like to make arrangements to meet with you in Florida during the week of May 17 to discuss some of these ideas.

Because of my familiarity with the types of locations and clients you are seeking, I am sure that if we were able to work together in this new venture, the results would reflect my contribution.

I am looking forward to meeting with you and will call next week to arrange for an appointment.

Very truly yours,

Janet Perrill

Enclosure

Letter of introduction.

EXHIBIT 10.21

TO WHOM IT MAY CONCERN:

This will introduce Mary Smith, a trusted and valued member of my staff for the past two and a half years.

During this time she has held a key position, performing a variety of secretarial tasks, as well as having full charge of the ordering procedures, maintenance work, and updating in our career resources library. She is keen at spotting deficiencies and was instrumental in developing a more efficient system of updating our materials.

She has been recognized by other members of the staff, including the counselors and our program director, the dean of student personnel, as being outstanding in poise, appearance, and reliability. Additionally, and probably most important, she has been exceptionally effective in working with the students, faculty, and professionals who use the resources of our center.

Mary is a good organizer, capable of dealing with concepts and goals and devising systems approaches to problem solving. She is loyal and discreet in dealing with unusual situations and those calling for confidentiality.

If there is anything more you feel you would like to discuss regarding Mary's qualifications, please feel free to contact me.

Very truly yours,

W. T. Jones
Philo Corp.

Interviewing Successfully

CHAPTER 11

Once you begin to feel comfortable with the notion of networking and practice interviewing, you are ready to begin preparing for the "Olympic Finals"—the interview.

Before the Interview

Here are the three most important tips to consider as you approach your first interview or refine your current interviewing style: *prepare, prepare, prepare*.

Some of the best preparation for the interview occurs when you research the prospective employer. Your goal is to show the employer why you will be the best person for the job, relating your personal strengths and past accomplishments to this particular enterprise. Specifically, you want to tell the employer how you can help with current problems or function as a valuable member of the organization. To find out more about a prospective employer and the job you're interviewing for, call or write the organization to request a current publication that describes the organization, such as an annual report, along with the job description. You may find recent newspaper or magazine articles about the company in your library's computerized retrieval system or through such computer networks as America Online or msn.com. Also refer to Internet sources listed in Chapter 9 for company information locations on the Web. If the firm does business with the government, you may also find relevant information in the library's government section.

Before the interview, or at least early into it, try to find out what the essential responsibilities of the job are. Make a mental note of them, and throughout the interview, feed back the kind of information from your background that shows you can handle these responsibilities.

Don't let a formal job description disqualify you for a job. Remember that job descriptions are only guidelines; once in a job, you are allowed to imprint your own style. Additionally, it is expected that over 50 percent of the work in any job is learned on the job.

287

*The trouble is,
if you do not risk anything,
you risk even more.*

SUCCESS STRATEGIES

Job Search Tips

- Your ability to express what your skills are, how you can contribute to the company, and your willingness to learn new skills is as important as being able to do each task listed in the job description. In fact, if you can already do each task described, you might be labeled as overqualified and not get the job!

- Your resume and cover letter become the written and mental outline upon which you elaborate to translate your skills into potential benefits to the employer. Use your resume as a point of reference; write on index cards the key points you want to remember and convey during the interview. It's fine to bring these cards with you to your interview.

- In applying for jobs, a male increases his chances by trying to enter a field that has previously been primarily a female domain (e.g., nursing). Similarly, a female increases her chances if she applies for a position that has previously been primarily a male domain (e.g., electronics).

- Don't be afraid to reapply and reinterview at the same company. Your interview skills will probably have improved in the meantime, and different areas of the company may be interested in you for different positions.

- Be creative if you are applying for a creative job (advertising, design, sales, art), but be conservative if you are applying for a conservative job (banking, insurance, accounting).

- Before the interview, verify the particulars. Write down the interviewer's name, the location, and the time and date of your appointment. Last-minute nervousness can block such details from your memory. Plan on arriving 15 minutes early.

- Apprehension, tension, and anxiety are a normal part of the preinterview jitters. Relaxation techniques, deep breathing, and chatting with the receptionist may help.

- The successful job candidate demonstrates how he or she is the best person for the job.

If you are turned down for the position, consider calling to get information to improve subsequent interviews: "I realize that this is a bit unusual and I am aware that you've chosen someone else for the job, but could you spend a few moments giving me some ideas as I continue my job search?" You could end up with some valuable leads; it's worth a try!

Interviewing becomes easier as you gain practice. Don't be overly discouraged if you don't get the first job for which you interview. Interviews and even rejections are actually invaluable opportunities to reassess and reaffirm your qualifications, strengths, weaknesses, and needs.

In the competitive job market of today, you can maximize your chance of successful interviewing by doing practice interviews and being prepared to answer an employer's typical questions. Always be prepared to support your general answers with specific examples from your experience. Your interviewers will remember your examples! Consider using a video camera to sharpen your interviewing skills. Ask a friend or classmate to be the interviewer. Using the questions below and those found beginning on page 293, practice your responses. Then play the tape, and use the "Interview Critique Form" in Exhibit 11.2 on page 300 to evaluate your performance and improve your answers for the next interview.

The sample questions below are representative of the types of questions commonly asked in an employment interview. Review these, and be prepared beforehand to answer such questions.

Ask for feedback

1. Tell me about yourself.

Refer mentally to your resume; do not assume that the interviewer has even read it! Briefly recap your skills and experiences as they relate to this particular job. Include a clear demonstration of the ways your education, training, skills, and experiences match the needs of the company.

2. Why do you want this job? Why did you apply here?

Refer to information about *this job* and *this company* or institution that makes it particularly appealing to you. Do not give the impression that you're here just because the firm has a job opening. Refer to the company's history, products, and services. Let your interviewer know that you have researched the organization.

3. Why should I hire you?

"Because, with my skills, experience, positive attitude, and enthusiasm, I am obviously the best person for the job. I agree with your philosophy and feel that I will fit in. I will be an asset to your enterprise." (Reemphasize your strengths.) Also emphasize how you can contribute to the company.

4. What are your career plans? Where do you see yourself five years from now?

Employers generally like to think you will be with them forever; you can't make any promises, but you can indicate you would like to be with a company that allows you to grow, asks you to assume more responsibility, and challenges you continuously.

5. What salary do you expect?

If you have done your homework, you should have an idea of the general range for the position. Find out whether this company has a fixed salary schedule. You may want to defer the matter until you know more about what the job entails. If the interviewer does not mention salary, it is best not to bring up the subject at a first interview.

6. Why did you leave your last job?

If asked why you left your last position, avoid mentioning a personality conflict. Rather say, "I felt I had gone as far in that company as possible, and I was ready for more responsibility, challenge, hours (etc.)." If your work history reflects many job changes, explain how you have transferred existing skills and learned new skills that can now benefit this employer.

7. Are there any questions?

You might ask just what kind of person the interviewer is really looking for, then show how you fit the bill. Or you might clarify expected follow-

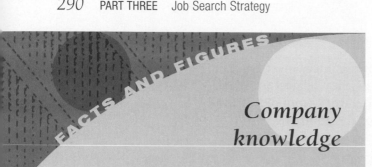

Company knowledge

A recent survey reveals that a lack of company knowledge is—by far—the most frequent interview mistake. The chances are great in any given interview that you will be asked some variation of the question, "What do you know about our company?" The questions could be "What attracted you to our company?" or "Why do you want to work for our company?" or one of a number of other variations. Employers want to see that you've done your homework; in fact, 44 percent of executives recently surveyed by Accountemps said the most common interview pitfall for today's candidates is insufficient company research.

WHAT DO YOU THINK?

1. What are you doing now to make sure that you know about the company for which you are interviewing?

2. Name the sources that you will use when you have to find out information about a company or industry.

To answer these questions online, go to the *Facts and Figures* module in Chapter 11 of the Companion Website.

---

up, or add some information. "When can I expect to hear about the position?" "Oh, yes, I forgot to mention earlier that . . ." "I would like to reiterate that . . ." (See the box titled "Sample Questions to Ask at the Interview" on page 302).

Leave the interviewer convinced that you are ready and able to do the job. Never answer a question "No" without qualifying it positively. "Are you familiar with Excel?" "No, but I have mastered other software, and I'm certain I won't have any problems learning." "Can you 10-key?" "No, I didn't realize it was part of the job description. If it's necessary, I can learn. Just how much numerical data entry will be involved?"

Interview Guidelines

The interview—and ultimately, a job—is the goal of your job search strategy. Generally, people who are interviewed are assumed qualified to do the job; the question becomes one of an appropriate meshing of personalities. Both the interviewer and interviewee are relying on their communications skills, judgment, intuition, and insight. It is a two-way process. While you are being evaluated, you should be evaluating the position and the people offering it. Remember that a good interview is a dialogue, an exchange of information.

DRESSING FOR SUCCESS

An interview is a two-way process

The moment we see someone, we form powerful first impressions that are hard to change. Much of a first impression comes from the visual impact of an individual, and much of the visual impact comes from what we choose to wear. Our clothes and accessories speak and sometimes shout volumes about us. What we want to communicate to prospective employers is that we fit in and that we can be trusted to interact appropriately with other employees and customers.

Many workplaces have become increasingly more casual in dress norms, and in many instances, "casual Friday" has now been extended to every workday. You may be looking forward to this more casual, comfortable norm, but it is generally a good rule to dress a bit more formally for the interview. More people are passed over for jobs because they were too casually dressed than because they were too formally dressed. In this instance, when in doubt, you should err on the side of formality. This also communicates a sense of respect for the potential interviewers who are evaluating you and comparing you with other candidates. You are communicating that this is not just another casual encounter but a meeting that has importance to you.

It's always best to check out the scene firsthand before the day of your interview to get a general sense for the "look" of fellow employees. Of course, having done your informational interviewing, you will know how employees in your field of interest generally dress. For the interview, it is generally accepted that you should dress one or two levels up from the job you are applying for, while remaining consistent with the occupational norms of your field.

With these general guidelines in mind, it is best to have an interview outfit or two selected and ready to wear. Except for certain fields such as fashion, the arts, entertainment, and advertising, it is always best to err on the conservative and understated side for an interview so that your outfit or accessories don't compete with you for the interviewer's attention. It is also wise to get feedback on your outfit from trusted friends and advisers before the day of the interview.

Take a good look at yourself. If you are serious about getting a job, then you had better look and dress the part. No interviewer will tell you what you are supposed to wear, but the person will measure your maturity and judgment partially by your appearance. Remember that the first impression is often a lasting one. It's often not the best qualified person who gets the job, but the one who makes the best impression. *You never get a second chance to make a good first impression!*

PRACTICAL PREPARATION

If possible, drive by the interview site a day or two before so you'll know where it is, where to park, and how long it takes to get there. Plan to arrive for your interview at least 15 minutes early. Establish a friendly relationship with the secretary or receptionist. Develop a firm handshake (practice), and use it when being introduced. Practice good eye contact. Above all, try to relax. Remember, you will be talking about someone you know very well—you!

You may have to handle some trick or stress questions; be prepared beforehand with responses that feel comfortable to you (see the sample questions beginning on page 293). If a question seems inappropriate, you may ask, "How does this information relate to or affect my employment here?" This may prompt an employer to express the real concerns, such as your record of stability on the job, age, child-care needs, or commitment to the job and company. You may even consider bringing up these relevant issues. Often seemingly unimportant conversation is an attempt to put you and the interviewer at ease or to assess your ability to socialize.

Remember that many interviewers are just as nervous about the process as you. Feel free to make the first attempts to break the ice; when you try to relieve another's anxiety, yours becomes secondary. Note the office decor, the cordial welcome, whatever makes sense. If you are nervous, you will find that focusing on the question "What would it be like to work here?" rather than "How am I being perceived by them?" will relax you. Relax in the chair; a rigid posture reinforces your tenseness. Actually, a slightly forward position with head erect indicates interest and intimacy. Maintain eye contact. In answering questions, use your knowledge of yourself to transmit the idea that you are the best person for the job; allow strengths such as goodwill, flexibility, enthusiasm, and a professional approach to surface. Bring samples of your work if they are related. On an index card, note your strengths or key selling points in addition to the questions you may have and some cue words like "smile, speak up, relax"; review them from time to time, especially just before you go into the interview. Forthright statements about what you do well, with examples of accomplishments, are of key importance. Talk with pride, honesty, and confidence about your accomplishments and your potential, your interest and commitment, and your readiness to learn on the job.

Express yourself *positively*. You are selling yourself; allow your personal *energy* and *enthusiasm* to surface.

Segments of an Interview

 lthough every interview is different, most follow a general pattern. A typical half-hour session can be roughly divided into four segments:

1. The first five or 10 minutes are usually devoted to establishing rapport and opening the lines of communication. Instead of wondering why the interviewer is taking valuable time chatting about the weather, your parking problems, etc., relax and enjoy the conversation. He or she will get to deeper subjects soon enough. The interview begins the moment you introduce yourselves and shake hands. Don't discount the initial period. Your ability to converse, expressing yourself intelligently, is being measured.

2. The adept interviewer will move subtly from a casual exchange to a more specific level of conversation. The second part of the interview gives you a chance to answer some "where, when, and why" questions about your background—to supply information that does not appear on your resume.

Now is the time to describe some extracurricular activities or work experience that may explain your less-than-perfect GPA. Or to talk of changes you effected as president of a campus organization or community group. This is your chance to elaborate on your strong points and emphasize whatever you have to offer. Don't monopolize the conversation; let the interviewer lead. But don't confine your statements to yes-or-no answers. Ask some questions to let the interviewer know you have researched the firm thoroughly and have a keen interest in the position.

The interviewer will be interested not only in what you say but also how you say it. Equally as important as the information you communicate will be the evidence of logical organization and presentation of thoughts. The interviewer will be mentally grading your intelligence, leadership potential, and motivation.

3. Part three begins when the interviewer feels your skills and interests have been identified and can see how they might fit the organization. If a

good match seems possible, the interviewer will discuss the company and the openings available.

4. At the end of an interview, try to find out where you stand. "How do you feel I relate to this job?" "Do you need any additional information?" "When can I expect to hear from you?"

Ask questions

After you leave, take 10 or 15 minutes to analyze how you did. What questions did you find difficult? What did you forget to say? How can you might even keep a diary or log with written notes on each of these concerns as well as a list of the specific interview questions asked and a note about how you responded. Also list any specific things that you can do in following up with an employer to increase your chances of getting the offer you want. If you feel you forgot to mention something or there was a misunderstanding, correct or elaborate on these points in a letter or telephone call. Send a thank-you letter to the interviewer, recalling a significant fact or idea of the interview that will set you apart from the other applicants. Write the letter while the interview is still fresh in your mind. One paragraph is usually sufficient. See the sample thank-you letters on the following page.

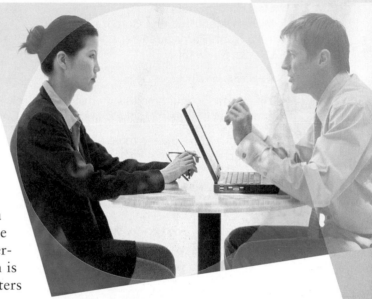

Practice Questions

T he following are questions that may be asked during interviews, intended to create a *stress* response. Often they are asked out of pattern, intended to throw you. The interviewer sometimes is more interested in *how* you respond than in what you say, to observe how you react and how you think on your feet. Decide which of the following questions are likely to be asked of you in your situation. PRACTICE!

1. What kind of job do you expect to hold five years from now? Ten years? Twenty years?
2. Why do you want to work for this company?
3. Why did you choose this company over our competitors?
4. Why did you choose your particular field of work?
5. What do you know about this company?
6. Describe your perfect job.
7. What qualifications do you have that make you feel you will be successful in your field?
8. What are your salary expectations?

Sample Thank-You Letters

Use these sample thank-you letters as a guide and write your own to an imaginary or real interviewer.

19574 Delaware
Detroit, MI 48223
February 8, 2004

Ms. Dorothy Smith
Michels' Manufacturing Corporation
1928 North Berry Street
Livonia, MI 48150

Dear Ms. Smith:

Thank you for your time this morning. I was certainly impressed with the efficiency, friendliness, and overall climate of Michels' Manufacturing Corporation.

Now that you've told me more about Michels' recent contract with the U.S. Tank Command, I feel my degree in industrial engineering and two years of part-time work in task force analysis should be of value to you.

I hope you will consider me favorably for the position of junior project engineer.

Sincerely,

Steven B. Boyd

1010 Yourstreet Avenue
Elizabeth, NJ 07208
July 12, 2003

Mr. John Jones
Widget Manufacturing Company
345 Widget Avenue
Newark, NJ 07210

Dear Mr. Jones,

Thank you for an interesting and informative interview on July 12, 2003. The position of manufacturing representative is of considerable interest to me, as I am most impressed with Widget's excellent growth record.

One point was not brought out in our interview that may be of interest to you. In my previous position with Ferrals Manufacturing, I took ten weeks of intensive training in billing and credit, skills that would directly relate to the position as you described it.*

Again, thank you for the time you spent interviewing me.

Yours truly,

Rosario Ortega

---

*NOTE: This is your chance to mention anything helpful to your campaign that you forgot to tell the employer in the interview. However, the point should be brief and precise.

9. What determines a person's progress in a good company?
10. Do you prefer working with others or by yourself?
11. Describe how you handle stress.
12. How do you react to criticism?
13. What interests you about our product/service?
14. What is your major weakness? (What are three of your strong points? Three of your weak points?)
15. Are you willing to go where the company sends you? Travel? Relocate?
16. What kind of supervision gets the best results from you?
17. What are your own special abilities?
18. Do you object to working overtime?
19. What is your philosophy of life?
20. Do you have any objections to a psychological test or interview?
21. What are the main elements needed to develop a team spirit?
22. What are your career goals?
23. What are the things that motivate you?
24. In what ways will this company benefit from your services?
25. If you were me, why would you hire you?
26. How would you describe yourself as an employee?

How to Handle Illegal Questions

ertain hiring practices, employment application form questions, and specific interviewing procedures are illegal under the Fair Employment Practices Act, the Americans with Disabilities Act, and other governmental regulations. Review Exhibit 11.1 to familiarize yourself with the subject matter and specifics of the illegal issues.

If the question is on an application, you always have the option to put N/A in the blank. If you are asked illegal questions in an interview, try to anticipate the concerns a potential employer might have about hiring you and bring them up in a manner that is comfortable for you.

Example:

Interviewer: "Do you have any children?"

Interviewee: "I guess you are wondering about the care of my school-aged children. I'd like you to know I have an excellent attendance record. You are welcome to check with my past employer, and, besides, I have a live-in sitter. Additionally, I have researched the needs of this position and can assure you that I have no family responsibilities that will interfere with my ability to do this job."

Not only will employers appreciate your sensitivity to their concerns, but your statement provides you with an additional opportunity to sell yourself and to evaluate whether this position is one that you want to consider. It is often advisable for you, the interviewee, to bring up any issue that may be on the employer's mind but that, because of legal concerns, will not be

Anticipate concerns and address them

11.1   *Preemployment inquiries: lawful and unlawful.*

SUBJECT	ACCEPTABLE PREEMPLOYMENT INQUIRIES	UNACCEPTABLE PREEMPLOYMENT INQUIRIES
Photograph	Statement that a photograph may be required after employment.	Requirement that applicant affix a photograph to application form. Request that applicant submit photograph at applicant's option. Requirement of photograph after interview but before hiring.
Race or Color		Complexion, color of skin, or other questions directly or indirectly indicating race or color, such as color of applicant's eyes and hair.
Citizenship	Request that applicant state whether residency status is: (a) U.S. citizen. (b) Legal right to remain permanently in the United States. Statement that, if hired, applicant may be required to submit proof of citizenship.	What is your country of citizenship? Inquiry whether an applicant or applicant's parents or spouse are naturalized or native-born U.S. citizens; date when applicant or parents or spouse acquired citizenship. Requirement that applicant produce naturalization papers or first papers.
National Origin	Inquiry into applicant's proficiency in foreign language must be job-related.	Applicant's nationality, lineage, national origin, descent, or parentage. Date of arrival in United States or port of entry; how long a resident of the United States. Nationality of applicant's parents or spouse; maiden name of applicant's wife or mother. Language commonly used by applicant; "What is your mother tongue?" How applicant acquired ability to read, write, or speak a foreign language.
Education	Inquiry into academic, vocational, or professional education of an applicant and schools attended.	Any inquiry asking specifically the nationality, race, or religious affiliation of a school.
Name	Inquiry about having worked for the company under a different name. Maiden name of married female applicant, assumed name, or change of name, if necessary to check education or employment records.	Former name of applicant whose name has been changed by court order or otherwise.
Address or Duration of Residence	Inquiry into place and length of residence at current and previous addresses.	Specific inquiry into foreign addresses that would indicate national origin.

(continued)

EXHIBIT 11.1

Preemployment inquiries: lawful and unlawful, continued.

SUBJECT	ACCEPTABLE PREEMPLOYMENT INQUIRIES	UNACCEPTABLE PREEMPLOYMENT INQUIRIES
Gender		If not based on a bona fide occupational qualification,it is extremely unlikely that gender would be considered a lawful subject for preemployment inquiry.
Birthplace	Requirement that applicant submit, after employment, a birth certificate or other proof of legal residence.	Birthplace of applicant, applicant's parents, spouse, or other relatives.
Age	Requirement that applicant submit, after employment, a birth certificate or other document as proof of age.	Requirement that applicant produce proof of age in the form of a birth certificate, baptismal record, employment certificate, or certificate of age issued by school authorities.
Religion		Inquiry into applicant's religious denomination, affiliation, church, parish, or pastor, or which religious holidays observed. Applicant may not be told, "This is a Catholic/Protestant/Jewish/atheist, etc., organization."
Workday and Shifts	Request that applicant state days, hours, or shift(s) available to work.	It is unlawful to request applicants to state days, hours, or shift(s) that they can work if it is used to discriminate on the basis of religion.

addressed unless you mention it. Such issues as age, children, spouse's feelings about this position, gender, disabilities, and qualifications can all be addressed by you in such a way as to enhance your chances of getting the job. Basically, you want to show how your age, qualifications, gender, or disability will be an advantage to your employer. This requires some thinking on your part before the interview. The payoff—getting the job you want—is well worth the effort.

The Behavioral/Situational Interview

Employers use this type of interview to gain information from an interviewee about possible job performance and to ascertain your ability to problem-solve in stressful job situations. It includes a series of questions that challenge the candidate about how job stress was managed in the past to determine the probability of success in the future. Some of the behavioral characteristics that interviewers have deemed to be most important include:

- **Listening skills:** Active and caring responses showing empathy and concern for others.

Meet Jose

"I can't believe how poorly I did on my interview," Jose said to his friend Debra. "My hands were so sweaty and I know the committee members tried not to notice when I shook their hands, but I could see it in their eyes."

Jose had just finished his first interview after graduating with his bachelor's degree in applied science. He had asked a friend to help him rehearse his answers to a list of general questions he found in a career planning pamphlet, and he felt confident going into the interview. But everything went downhill from the moment he sat down. He lost his concentration a

couple of times and had to ask for the question to be repeated, and he completely forgot the questions he had prepared to ask the committee. He did feel that he connected with the committee on a couple of questions, and they seemed pleased that he did. After the interview, he was given a tour of the facilities and he was still so upset that he missed several opportunities to redeem his previous behavior.

At home that night, Jose thought about his preparation for the interview and how he could have prepared differently. He was so upset and sure that he would not be called for a second interview that he didn't bother to

- **Writing skills:** Clear and concise communication to resolve issues utilizing shared action plans with suitable outcomes.
- **Organizational/teamwork skills:** Assuming responsibility for self and others; developing mutual agreements, monitoring progress and evaluating results.

For each of these behaviors, the interviewer challenges the candidate to provide examples of real situations where concerns were addressed and resolved. A sample question related to working effectively with others might be: *"Can you give me an example that would show you have been able to develop and maintain productive relations with others, even though they may have differing points of view?"*

Since these types of questions cannot always be clearly anticipated, you can best prepare by analyzing the requirements of the job before the interview and thinking of situations that occurred in previous job settings. By preparing in advance, you will be better able to provide clear and concise examples that will impress the interviewer.

Body Language

Your body language speaks just as loudly as your words. Eye contact is crucial. Remember that at a distance of five or six feet from another person, you can be looking at the person's nose or forehead or mouth and still maintain the sense of eye contact. Try it with friends.

Present yourself
assertively

Voice tone, volume, and inflection are important. A soft, wispy voice will seldom convince another that you mean business; a loud or harsh voice tends to be blocked out. Listen to yourself on a tape recorder or, preferably, write thank-you notes. Two days later, Jose received a call inviting him back for a second interview.

1. Describe how Jose was feeling after his interview.

2. What led Jose to believe he didn't perform well in the interview?

3. What suggestions would you give Jose regarding interview preparation?

4. Why do you think Jose was given a second interview?

5. Would it be appropriate for Jose to bring thank-you notes to his second interview? Would it be

too late to mail them, knowing they will arrive after the second interview is over?

6. Do you think Jose was too confident before his interview?

7. What advice would you give Jose to reduce his stress level for the next interviewing opportunity?

To answer these questions online, go to the *Real Stories* module in Chapter 11 of the Companion Website.

---

watch yourself on videotape. How do you sound to yourself? Remember, however, that our own recorded voice always sounds odd to us, so ask others for their comments. Lessons in voice and diction are available in most schools. Try varying your voice pitch and volume while reading something into a tape recorder. You may find a range that sounds better.

Don't chew gum!

Try accenting your words with appropriate hand gestures to gain emphasis. Before the interview, analyze your practice interviews. Consider the option of being videotaped during a practice interview. The instant feedback is very helpful, particularly if you use the form set out in Exhibit 11.2 to critique your performance. If you are in a class, practice with one or more classmates, evaluating your own and your classmates' interview techniques according to the critique form.

Video Interviewing

Some companies are beginning to use video as a prescreening and screening tool. Video interviewing occurs most often in the fields of education, government, and private manufacturing. According to *EEO BiMonthly (Equal Employment Opportunity Magazine)*, six factors are important to consider:

1. Are you articulate? How do you come across on videotape?

2. Be prepared; practice what you will say before you are taped.

3. If you are a person who usually plays off another's body language in an interview, you will need to practice to make your answers and conversation flow as if you were actually talking to someone.

EXHIBIT **11.2**   *Interview critique form.*

	Very good	Satisfactory	Fair—could be better	Needs improvement	Comments
Name _____ (individual being interviewed)					
1. Initial, or opening, presentation (impression).					
2. Eye contact.					
3. Sitting position.					
4. General appearance: grooming (hair, makeup, shave, beard, mustache, etc.), clothing.					
5. Ability to describe past work experiences, education, and training.					
6. Ability to explain equipment, tools, and other mechanical aids used.					
7. Ability to explain skills, techniques, processes, and procedures. Ability to emphasize how skills are related to job.					
8. Ability to explain personal goals, interests, and desires.					
9. Ability to explain questionable factors in personal life (functional limitations, frequent job changes, many years since last job).					
10. Ability to answer questions or make statements about company or job being applied for.					
11. Ability to listen attentively to interviewer's questions and to notice and respond to interviewer's body language.					
12. Manner of speech or conversation (voice, tone, pitch, volume, speed).					
13. Physical mannerisms (facial expressions, gestures).					
14. Enthusiasm, interest in this job.					
15. Attitude (positive?), confidence.					
16. Overall impression. Would you hire this applicant?					

4. Dress professionally and conservatively; pay attention to the colors and patterns you wear. Solid colors work best on video.

5. Communicate with enthusiasm and confidence through facial expressions and voice tone.

6. Do not exaggerate your movements. Overdone gestures can be distracting and may even cause "waves" in the air.

Learning from the Interview

As much as they are interviewing you, you are in turn interviewing the representatives of a company. Ideally, you will do only about 40 percent of the talking. In the remaining time, you can listen and assess whether or not you want to work for that company. Although an interview tends to be rather formal, you can still gain a feeling about the climate of the organization. Entering its offices, you can observe the receptionist, support staff, people talking or not talking in the hallways. The colors and decor of the furnishings should generate a positive or negative impression.

Take note of whether the interview begins punctually, the arrangement of the seating in the interview room, and the dress of the interviewers. The entrance and handshake are important first impressions. Some companies deliberately set up awkward or uncomfortable situations to observe your response. They may ask tough questions just to see how well you think on your feet. If you can maintain your composure and enthusiasm in the interview, they will probably conclude that you are able to work equally as well under stress.

In selecting your own questions, you might ask who the last person in the position was and what happened to him or her; if the person resigned, you may ask why. Another related question would be, "Given the current economy, how have careers at my level been affected?" You may also ask about the background of your potential supervisor and professional mobility within the company. Although you want to emphasize your interest and commitment to the position for which you are interviewing, these questions can illustrate your interest in a future with the company.

A final bit of information that you should gather or confirm about the company relates to its *corporate culture*. Corporate culture refers to the personality of the potential employer. Primarily you want to seek employment with a firm that is likely to meet your personality needs. Do you need a competitive environment in order to thrive? Most likely a job in a high school or a government position won't satisfy those needs. Do you need security? The aerospace field may be a bit too unsteady for you. The prime question that is related to corporate culture and that you may ask during an interview is, "Can you explain the management style or philosophy of your company?" If you want to have the opportunity for input into management, you might also ask about the use of quality circles or the potential for the use of total quality management in the organization. If you are hoping to enter the field of business but have little relevant background, it might help to take a college class or read a book on the world of business so that you can ask intelligent questions about business practices.

Sample Questions to Ask at the Interview

Going one step further than just *answering* the interviewer's questions involves being prepared to take the initiative in *asking* several questions.

- Where does this position fit into the organization?
- Please describe your ideal candidate for this job.
- Is this position new?
- What experience is ideally suited for this job?
- Was the last person promoted?
- To whom would I be reporting? Can you tell me a little about these people?
- What have been some of the best results you have received from these people?
- Who are the primary people I would be working with?
- What seem to be the strengths and weaknesses of the people with whom I would work?

- What are your expectations for me?
- May I talk with present and previous employees about this job?
- What are some of the problems I might expect to encounter on this job (e.g., efficiency, quality control, declining profits, evaluation)?
- What has been done recently regarding . . . ?
- How is this program going? Is it growing?
- What kind of on-the-job training is allocated for this position?
- What is the normal pay range for this job?
- When will I hear from you about the outcome of this interview?
- If you don't mind, can I let you know by (*date*)?

Factors Influencing Hiring

We have seen that many things must be considered in preparing for an interview. Some of these factors we can control; other considerations are beyond our control. Look over the box on the following page to distinguish between the two.

A national survey of employers (NACE, 2002) found 10 top qualities that employers seek in new employees. To make an outstanding and lasting impression, emphasize the traits listed below during any contact with a company (e.g., informational or formal interview). As you review the list, check each item you feel comfortable discussing in an interview:

____ 1. Communication skills (verbal and written)

____ 2. Honesty/integrity

____ 3. Teamwork skills

____ 4. Interpersonal skills

____ 5. Strong work ethic

____ 6. Motivation/initiative

____ 7. Flexibility/adaptability

____ 8. Analytical skills

____ 9. Computer skills

____ 10. Organizational skills

Realize that interpersonal skills may consist of many of the "emotional IQ skills" discussed in Chapter 2. It is interesting to note that some traits listed 10 years ago as important are not as important today, such as competitive spirit and self-

Factors That Influence Your Success

OUT OF YOUR CONTROL

- Too many applicants.
- Cannot pay you what you are making.
- Indecisiveness on part of business owner.
- Only trying to fill a temporary position.
- A current employee changed plans and decided not to leave.
- Introduction of new personnel policies.
- Death of a company management employee.
- Looking for a certain type of person.
- Lack of experience on part of interviewer.
- Accepting applications only for future need.
- Looking for more experience.
- Looking for less experience.
- Your skills are more than are needed for the position.
- Company management decided that morning on a temporary freeze on hiring—for many business reasons.
- Illness of interviewer.
- Change in management.
- Further consideration of all applicants.
- A more important post must be filled first.
- Company stock went down 65 percent since you applied.
- Company went bankrupt.

FACTORS YOU CAN CONTROL OR GUARD AGAINST

- A poor personal appearance.
- An overbearing, overaggressive, conceited attitude; a superiority complex; being a know-it-all.
- An inability to express yourself clearly; poor voice, diction, or grammar.
- A lack of career planning; no purpose or goals.
- A lack of interest and enthusiasm; appearing passive, indifferent.
- A lack of confidence and poise; nervousness, being ill at ease.
- An overemphasis on money; interest only in best dollar offer.
- A poor scholastic record; just squeaking by.
- An unwillingness to start at the bottom; expecting too much too soon.
- Making excuses; evasiveness, hedging on unfavorable factors in record.
- Lack of courtesy; being ill-mannered.
- Talking negatively about past employers or coworkers.
- Failure to look interviewer in the eye.
- A limp, fishlike handshake.
- A sloppy application form.
- Insincerity; merely "shopping around."
- Wanting job only for short time.
- Lack of interest in company or in industry.
- Emphasizing whom you know over what you can do.
- An unwillingness to be transferred.
- Intolerance; strong prejudices.
- Having narrow interests.
- Arriving late for interview without good reason.
- Never having heard of company.
- Failure to express appreciation for interviewer's time.
- Failure to ask questions about the job.
- Directing a high-pressure style at interviewer.
- Providing vague responses to questions.

knowledge. Employers now want to know that you are a team player who has the ability to learn and make decisions (motivational skills and analytical skills).

Each of the traits you checked can strengthen your chances for a successful interview. Those you did not check are areas for additional homework prior to preparing the final version of your resume and going to the interview.

A greater range of jobs now require a college degree. Often a degree will be required primarily because so many applicants have degrees. Even your liberal arts degree can compete with a specialist degree in business if the following factors apply:

1. You have an excellent grade point average.
2. You have a record of extracurricular activities (club or community involvement). It's especially good to have had leadership positions.
3. You worked your way through college (it helps even more if the work was at the company with which you seek full-time employment or at least in the same field).
4. You've made some contacts within the firm who can serve as positive references.
5. You either minored in business or, at least, selected business courses as electives (e.g., accounting, economics, marketing, information systems).
6. You have defined goals, exude enthusiasm and confidence, and can verbalize these characteristics in an interview.

For example, Walt Disney World Company employs thousands of new college graduates each year; more than one-third are liberal arts graduates.

Generally attributed to all college graduates, but especially to liberal arts graduates, are intellectual ability (verbal and quantitative) and skills in planning, organizing, decision making, interpersonal relations, leadership, and oral communication. The less your major is related to the job desired, the more effectively you must be able to discuss your transferable skills.

If You Are Offered the Job

 ongratulations! Your career fitness efforts have paid off. Before deciding to accept a job offer, it's important to determine how well the position meets your needs. Consider the following questions before making a decision:

- How does this job fit into your long-range career goals?
- If it doesn't fit well, are there factors that may influence your decision to accept the position anyway?
- Have you considered the scope of the job, the reputation of the company, the possibility for growth and advancement, the geographic location, the salary and benefits package?

NEGOTIATING FOR SALARY AND BENEFITS

Although you may be excited and eager to accept a job offer, it's important to realize that your prospective employer is trying to hire the most talented individual at the lowest possible salary. If you are offered a position, your aim should

Summary: Reviewing the Interview Process

PREPARATION

- ✓ Have resume, contacts, and letters of reference.
- ✓ Make interview log for contacts; write initial contact letters.
- ✓ Mail letters out; make appointments with contacts.
- ✓ Make 3" x 5" cards on each interview.
- ✓ Maintain attitude "I can do it." Visualize that you have the job.
- ✓ Dress the part.
- ✓ Know your resume. Bring extra copies to the interview.
- ✓ Know something about the company (use *Dun and Bradstreet, Moody's, Standard & Poor's, Fortune 500,* annual report, magazine articles).
- ✓ Have five or six good questions. Know when to ask them.
- ✓ Keep a computer log or journal.
- ✓ Keep control.
- ✓ Be on time!

THE INTRODUCTION

- ✓ Maintain good posture, shake hands, breathe.
- ✓ Use good eye contact and posture.
- ✓ The first four minutes are key—establish rapport and generate the proper chemistry.
- ✓ Tell what you can do for the company, your major strengths, your background.
- ✓ Be positive—convert negatives to pluses.

THE INTERVIEW

- ✓ Smile.
- ✓ Supply information, referring to your resume.
- ✓ Seek the next interview (or the job).
- ✓ Overcome any objections—try to anticipate objections.
- ✓ Keep answers brief.
- ✓ Ask questions about the field.
- ✓ Know the rules, including when a decision will be made.
- ✓ Ask for the job if it exists.
- ✓ Be positive.
- ✓ Ask "When will you make a decision?"

AFTER THE INTERVIEW

- ✓ Debrief yourself—make notes (name, address, phone, impressions; if a panel of interviewers, write down names and positions of all panel members). Add to computer journal.
- ✓ Formally thank the employer or panel chairperson by letter.
- ✓ Plan a follow-up strategy—if you don't hear from them, call and ask if a decision has been made.
- ✓ Don't be defeated—keep interviewing!

ALTERNATIVES

- ✓ Continue learning and searching.
- ✓ Consider volunteer work to gain more experience.
- ✓ Join or create a job support group.
- ✓ Keep current and updated.

be to start at the highest possible salary. In order to achieve your goal, it is important for you to determine what the salary range is for comparable positions. There are numerous sites on the Internet that will assist you in this research. Check out the Web exercises at the end of each chapter for specific sites.

It is always wisest to wait for your employer to bring up the topic of compensation, which includes salary and benefits. In some instances, the salary is fixed, as with government jobs, but in most cases there is a range. You will usually be offered a salary at the bottom of the range, and it is up to you to move it up. The most effective way to do that is to hold off accepting the first offer by saying, "I'll think about it," or "Is that the very best you can offer me?" Don't worry about offending your employer. This is an expected negotiation and will only confirm in your employer's mind that you know your value in the job market. Even if the initial salary cannot be raised, you can ask for an earlier performance review date, which normally has a raise attached for good performers. In addition to or instead of a higher salary, you may be able to negotiate a fringe benefit package that is uniquely tailored to your needs and preferences. Such fringe benefits as flexible working hours or reimbursement for continued education may be equal to or far more valuable than a pay increase! Remember that the best time to negotiate is before you accept the job offer. Summon up your courage and assertiveness, and ask for what you want and deserve.

If You Do Not Get the Job

Should you find that, despite your solid efforts, you do not get the desired job, remember that all your dedicated preparation will pay off in time. The next interview will be easier; you will benefit from your experience. The key is to keep a positive attitude and not to give up. Keep your goals in mind, and remember that persistent people achieve their objectives by focusing on the target and believing in the future.

Unfortunately, continuing unemployment can undermine a person's confidence. You will be better prepared to handle temporary setbacks and rejection if you remember that your situation is far from unique; everyone with a job was once a job searcher. As you persist in your job search, remind yourself that you *will* find a job and build a career.

How well you cope with stress and rejection will depend on your attitude and actions. Put any anger or frustration you feel to positive use. Concentrate on your strengths; review them each day. A healthy diet, physical exercise, and adequate rest are time-tested prescriptions for overcoming worry and anxiety.

One of the best antidotes for feeling depressed is doing something to help someone else. You have time, talents, and skills that will mean a great deal to others. And remember, each time you volunteer, you gain valuable experience and contacts.

Finally, try to accomplish something every day. Accomplishments are activities that make you feel good about yourself. Even minor tasks such as cleaning out a closet or refining your resume can invigorate you and give you new direction.

When you take care of yourself and strive to maintain a positive attitude, your self-image is enhanced, and you improve your chances of success.

Interviewing Successfully

The written exercises that follow serve to prepare you for a job interview. Exercise 11.1 asks you to review and be ready to answer sample questions. Exercise 11.2 asks you to practice and critique an interview.

> To answer these questions online, go to the *Exercise* module in Chapter 11 of the Companion Website.
>
>

Question Review

EXERCISE 11.1

Review the interview questions listed under Practice Questions, beginning on page 293, and be prepared to answer all of them.

Practice Interview

EXERCISE 11.2

Arrange a practice interview with a friend, colleague, career counselor, or potential employer (someone you've met during your information interviewing). If possible, have the practice interview videotaped so you can review your performance. Use the Interview Critique Form (see Exhibit 11.2) to evaluate your practice session.

WWWebwise

EXERCISE 11.3

For additional activities online, go to the WWWebwise module in Chapter 11 of the Companion Website.

Exercise Summary

EXERCISE 11.4

Write a brief paragraph answering these questions:

What did you learn about yourself from these exercises? How does this knowledge relate to your career/life planning? How do you feel?

_____

_____

_____

_____

_____

_____

Future Focus

LEARNING OBJECTIVES

**At the end
of the chapter
you will be able to . . .**

- **Understand the concept
  of lifelong career
  management and career
  fitness**

- **Recognize the role of the
  future in your current
  career-planning efforts**

- **Explain the philosophy of
  personal empowerment
  and career flexibility**

By the time you reach this chapter in your career fitness workout, you may find that your career is in shape and you are exercising your options in a career of your choice. Alternatively, if you are not yet in the career of your choice, you now have the skills to find and enter your most desired field. This book has provided tools to help you identify who you are; define what you want to do; research, identify, and develop your skills; and create a context in which you are able to find meaningful work. Following the book's guidelines puts you in full control, for you are creating your own possibilities instead of spending time preparing for the "predicted future" only to find that it does not exist. The only predictable future is the one that you create for yourself. During positive economic times there are plenty of opportunities for you to find your ideal position; during down economic times, you are guaranteed nothing but your own persevering attitude. With the right attitude, you can stay focused on the need for constant self-renewal, continuous lifelong learning, and deliberate lifelong networking.

*Obstacles are
what a person sees
when he takes his eye off his goal.*

Although congratulations are in order for completing this book, you haven't completed your career fitness program—you've just started it! The job of managing your career has just begun.

Managing Your Career

Every job or work activity, whether it's your dream job or not, is a step in your career. You have the choice on a daily basis merely to get by or to put your all (your values, interests, skills, and unique personality) into your work. Employers are eager to acknowledge and reward individuals who have a strong work ethic. These individuals routinely arrive on time, display an optimistic, can-do attitude, and are not only willing to do their job but are eager to take on additional assignments. They are savvy enough to know that they are responsible for their own career development. They recognize that in these uncertain times, a promotion may not be around the corner, but there are always opportunities to grow on the job. This willingness to take on new challenges not only results in job enrichment for the employee, but it also sets that individual apart from those individuals who may not be as willing to jump in when needed. This attitude is what often determines whom an employer chooses for a promotion, above and beyond the required skill sets.

It is, in fact, the personality factors as reviewed in Chapter 2 that make the difference when a promotion or a raise is available. Not only are these qualities essential to getting the right job, they are also critical in successfully managing your career. It is in your best interest to cultivate a developmental outlook on your current job. Every opportunity you take to learn, grow, stretch, and further develop your skills is an opportunity that no one can take away from you. The experience becomes part of your portfolio. You are enriched and your marketability is enhanced. Yes, there are cynics who might think that you are being taken advantage of; after all, it's not really your job. You may even be putting in some of your own time to learn and demonstrate your newly acquired skill sets. But the successful career decision maker knows that as you build mental muscle and develop your skill sets, you have a better chance of sustaining a lead in the competitive job market. Even more important, you become more deeply connected to your profession and you demonstrate the courage to be the person (in your work) who you really want and need to be. We are using the work *courage* because it is derived from the old French *cuer*, which means heart. To be courageous means to be heartfelt. It is only when your heart connects with your work that you become the best person that you can be—and others will respond.

Developing Your Relationship Savvy

t's often been said that it's not what you know but who you know. In today's world, it's both. As you move up and around the career ladder, individuals often move away from technical tasks to jobs where people skills and communication skills are essential to success. Take every opportunity to participate in meetings and special projects that will put you in contact with people outside your everyday work team. According to the manager of accountancy at Sony, quoted in Chapter 5, 80 percent of her job was dealing with people. Her subordinates also have to deal with these people. Consider taking a leadership position when appropriate. Develop and nurture your relationships at work. Refer back to the information on personality types in Chapter 4 to remind you of the natural differences among individuals that must be acknowledged and appreciated. If an individual is puzzling or perplexing, take the extra effort to try to understand this person and to cultivate a relationship. This exercise will develop your relationship skills and provide you with a rich network of associates and colleagues. You will cultivate mutual respect and appreciation for each other's uniqueness, and you will develop a strong support network in the process.

Although on one hand employers want you to think and act as if you owned the company so that you will feel empowered to make wise decisions on behalf of the company, even more so, you will also be expected to be part of a team. As a team player you will be expected to act as a part of something bigger than yourself. There is a unique energy that a team experiences when they are working well together. It's called synergy, and it means that something bigger and better can come from combining the forces of several people working together. Can you think of a time when being part of a group or team was a definite advantage in accomplishing a goal? There are endless examples from the sports world and the performing arts. Think about your favorite singer. Could he or she be a success without the many people that make up the team? Being a team player means being willing to listen to and learn from others, even when their ideas or approaches to solving a problem seem very different. It also means being willing to contribute your ideas and thoughts genuinely even when you know they will probably be modified or perhaps discounted as part of the process.

Developing Career Stamina

ven if you are following your passion, doing what you love, there will be some times in the course of your work when you may feel stuck, frustrated, unmotivated, burned out, stressed out, or bored. It's similar to what happens when we are on our physical fitness path. There are times when we've peaked and may be in a slump or a plateau. According to George Leonard in his book *Mastery,* the cycle of learning, growth, and mastery has its ups and downs. Since plateaus are part of the process of regrouping, reflecting, and getting ready for another leap, accept them as part of the cycle, and use them to reflect and recoup your physical and mental resources. Again, think about some of your favorite sports and entertainment figures. They have all experienced painfully public moments of stall before going to ever greater heights.

Embracing Career Fitness as a Way of Life

You are responsible for your own development. Learning to learn will be the most essential survival skill of this new millennium. If you are constantly on the lookout for new ways to use your current skills and new skills, you will remain in demand in the job market. Even if you feel content and secure in your current position, you must constantly be aware of emerging trends, opportunities, and danger signals that may affect your situation. In essence, make the world your classroom; learn something new from everything you do!

Your future is determined by the choices you make in the present. For that reason, this book has emphasized the development of your decision-making skills. This takes the focus away from *predicting* your future and puts the emphasis on *creating* your future. As we experience the 21st century, the world is in flux and you are continually changing, so why shouldn't your career evolve as well? No longer are people staying in one job until retirement. Unfortunately, however, it is human nature to resist change. Thus, many people do not turn to career counselors or books about career change until they are terminated from what they had assumed was a secure job. If you are wise enough to prepare for change before it is forced on you, you have a head start. The time to seek the career of your choice is while you are still employed or still in school!

Life transitions and unemployment can lead to feelings of desperation and a closed or confused mind. The anxiety and confusion generated by a life crisis make career planning difficult, if not impossible. If you are unemployed or underemployed, you are likely to feel depressed, lethargic, and hopeless about the future. It is precisely during this time that you need to immerse yourself in the career-planning process. During times of personal transition and uncertainty, this process will give you a structure to cope with anxiety and depression and to reconnect with your dreams and passions. Each time you begin a job search, review the accomplishments and skills you recorded in this book. This may help relieve your apprehension about another job search. You will be reminded of the skills you have and the many alternatives that can be equally satisfying

Risking

To laugh is to risk appearing the fool.

To weep is to risk appearing sentimental.

To reach out for another is to risk involvement.

To expose feelings is to risk exposing your true self.

To place your ideas, your dreams before the crowd is to risk their loss.

To love is to risk not being loved in return.

To live is to risk dying.

To hope is to risk despair.

To try is to risk failure.

But risks must be taken because the greatest hazard in life is to risk nothing.

The person who risks nothing does nothing, has nothing, is nothing.

One may avoid suffering and sorrow, but one simply cannot learn, feel, change, grow, live, or love.

Chained by certitude and safety, one becomes enslaved.

Only the person who risks is free.

—Unknown

---

career goals. Your emotional intelligence will enable you to recognize that the uncertainty of transition provides you with fertile ground on which to learn and grow. In fact, a change of direction *now* may become the best opportunity of your lifetime.

In the course of reevaluating your personal strengths and skills, your self-confidence will blossom. You will regain a sense of purpose and direction by setting meaningful and achievable goals. Through networking, information interviewing, and volunteering, your interaction with people will enable you to choose, confirm, or change current goals and be energized and inspired by people who are doing the kind of work you find challenging and rewarding.

Exercising your options may take more effort than crystal-ball gazing, but the results are worth it. Finding a career is a full-time effort. We hope you have pulled, stretched, and grown in the process.

References

"20 Facts on Women Workers." 1999 & 2001. *Statistical Abstracts of the United States.* Washington, DC: U.S. Bureau of Labor Statistics, U.S. Department of Labor, Women's Bureau.

Adams, Bob. 2001. *The Job Interview Book.* New York: Adams Media Corp.

America's Top 300 Jobs: A Complete Career Handbook. 2002. 8th edition. Indianapolis, IN: JIST Works.

Appalachia Educational Lab. 1997. *Worker Trait Group Keysort Deck.* Bloomington, IL: McKnight.

Basta, Nicholas. 1991. *Major Options.* New York: HarperCollins.

Beatty, Richard H. 2000. *The Resume Kit,* 4th Edition. New York: John Wiley & Sons.

Bolles, Richard Nelson. 1996. *Quick Job Hunting Map.* Berkeley, CA: Ten Speed Press.

Bolles, Richard N. 1999. *Job Hunting on the Internet.* Berkeley, CA: Ten Speed Press.

Bolles, Richard N. 2003. *What Color Is Your Parachute? A Practical Manual for Job Hunters and Career Changers.* Revised edition. Berkeley, CA: Ten Speed Press.

Bridges, William. 1995. *Jobshift: How to Prosper in a Workplace Without Jobs.* Menlo Park, CA: Addison Wesley.

Bridges, William. 1998. *Creating You & Co.: Learn to Think Like the CEO of Your Own Career.* New York: HarperCollins.

Bridges, William. 2001. *The Way of Transition.* Cambridge, MA: Perseus Publishing.

Brooks, Jake, ed. 1999. *Nice Job: Guide to Cool, Odd, Risky & Gruesome Ways to Make a Living.* Berkeley, CA: Ten Speed Press.

Burnell, Ivan. 1999. *The Power of Positive Doing—12 Strategies for Taking Control of Your Life.* Center Ossipee, NH: IPO Publishing.

Business 2. 2003. *Employment Outlook 2003.* www.business2.

BusinessWeek Online. 2002. *Hiring Outlook 2003, Parts 1 and 2.*

Career America. Washington, DC: U.S. Office of Personnel Management.

Career Opportunities News. Garrett Park, MD: Garrett Park Press. (Six issues annually.)

Career Planning and Adult Development Newsletter. San Jose, CA: CPAD Network. (Twelve newsletters and four journals annually.)

Career Planning Program Handbook. 1981. American College Testing Program.

Cetron, Marvin, and O. Davies. 1990. *American Renaissance: Our Life at the 21st Century.* New York: St. Martin's Press.

Cousins, Norman. 1995. *Anatomy of an Illness as Perceived by the Patient: Reflections on Healing and Regeneration.* New York: W. W. Norton.

Coxford, Lola. 1998. *Resume Writing Made Easy.* 6th edition. Upper Saddle River, NJ: Prentice Hall.

Crispin, Gerry, and Mark Mehler. 2002. *Career X Roads.* New York: MMC Group.

Cubbage, Sue A., and Marcia P. Williams. *National Job Hotline Directory: The Job Finder's Hot List 1999–2001.* Planning Communications.

DiCamillo, Mark. 1999. *California Work and Health Survey.* UCSF, The Field Institute.

Dickerson, Marla. 1999. "Women-Owned Businesses Gain Strength." *L.A. Times,* May 11, Section C, p. 2.

Dictionary of Occupational Titles. 1991. Washington, DC: U.S. Department of Labor, Employment and Training.

Douglas, Merril, and Donna Douglas. 1993. *Manage Your Time, Your Work, Yourself.* New York: AMACOM.

Dyer, Wayne. 1992. *Real Magic.* New York: HarperCollins.

Edwards, Paul, and Sara Edwards. 2001. *Changing Directions Without Losing Your Way.* Los Angeles: J. P. Tarcher.

Edwards, Paul, and Sara Edwards. 1999. *The Best Home Businesses for the 90s: The Inside Information You Need to Know to Select a Home-Based Business That Is Right for You.* 2nd edition. Los Angeles: J. P. Tarcher.

Eikleberry, Carol. 2002. *The Career Guide for Creative and Unconventional People.* 2nd Edition. Berkeley, CA: Ten Speed Press.

Ellig, Janice, and William Moran. 2001. *What Every Successful Woman Knows.* New York: McGraw-Hill.

Elliott, Myrna. 1982. *Transferable Skills for Teachers.* Moorpark, CA: Statewide Career Counselor Training Project.

Enelow, Wendy, and Louise Kursmark. 2001. *Expert Resumes.* Indianapolis, IN: JIST Works.

Eyler, David R. 1999. *Job Interviews That Mean Business.* 3rd edition. New York: Random House.

Eyler, David R. 1999. *Resumes That Mean Business.* New York: Random House.

Farr, Michael. 2003. *Best Jobs for the 21st Century.* Indianapolis, IN: JIST Works.

Fein, Richard. 1997. *Cover Letters! Cover Letters! Cover Letters!* Franklin Lakes, NJ: Career Press.

Fortune Magazine. 2003. "100 Best Companies to Work For." Jan. 20.

Fournier, Myra, and Jeffrey Spin. 2000. *Encyclopedia of Job Winning Resumes*. 2nd Edition. Ridgefield, CT: Round Lake Publishing.

Garber, Janet. 2001. *I Need a Job, Now What?* New York: Silver Lining Books.

Gardner, Howard. 1993. *Frames of Mind: The Theory of Multiple Intelligences*. New York: Basic Books.

Gardner, Howard. 2000. *Intelligence Reframed: Multiple Intelligences for the Twenty-First Century*. New York: Basic Books.

Gawain, Shakti. 2000. *Creative Visualization*. Novato, CA: New World Library.

Gelatt, H. B. 1991. *Creative Decision Making: Using Positive Uncertainty*. Menlo Park, CA: Crisp.

Germer, Fawn. 2001. *Hard Won Wisdom: More than 50 Extraordinary Women Mentor You to Find Self-Awareness, Perspective, and Balance*. New York: Perigee.

Gilbert, Sara D. 1997. *Internships 97: The Hotlist for Job Hunters*. 2nd edition. New York: Arco.

Golden, Bonnie, and Kay Lesh. 1997. *Building Self-Esteem: Strategies for Success in School and Beyond*. 2nd edition. Upper Saddle River, NJ: Prentice Hall.

Goleman, Daniel. 1995. *Emotional Intelligence*. New York: Bantam Press.

Goleman, Daniel. 2002. *Working with Emotional Intelligence*. New York: Audio Renaissance.

Graber, Steven (ed.). 2000. *Adams Job Almanac 2000*. Holbrook, MA: Adams Media Corporation.

Gray, John. 1999. *How to Get What You Want and Want What You Get*. New York: HarperCollins.

Guide for Occupational Exploration. Supplement to the *Dictionary of Occupational Titles*, Volume 2. Washington, DC: U.S. Government Printing Office. (1990 Edition published by Circle Pines, MN: American Guidance Service.)

Half, Robert, and Max Messmer. 1999. *Job Hunting for Dummies*. Chicago, IL: IDG Books Worldwide.

Handy, Charles. 1995. *The Age of Paradox*. Boston, MA: Harvard Business School.

Handy, Charles. 2002. *The Future of Work*. Maiden, MA: Blackwell Publishing.

Hayes, Cassandra. 2002. *Black Enterprise: Guide to Building Your Career*. New York: John Wiley & Sons.

Herzberg, Frederick. 1966. *Work and the Nature of Man*. New York: World.

Hirsch, Arlene. 1994. *Interviewing*. New York: John Wiley & Sons.

Holland, John. 1985. *Making Vocational Choices: A Theory of Vocational Personalities and Work Environments*. 2nd edition. Englewood Cliffs, NJ: Prentice Hall.

Interest Checklist. 1979. Washington, DC: U.S. Department of Labor Employment and Training Administration, U.S. Employment Service.

Jackson, Tom. 1996. *The New Perfect Resume*. New York: Doubleday.

Jaffe, Dennis T., and Cynthia D. Scott. 1994. *Rekindling Commitment: How to Revitalize Yourself, Your Work, and Your Organization*. San Francisco: Jossey Bass.

Jaffe, Dennis T., and Cynthia D. Scott. 1995. *Self-Renewal*. Menlo Park, CA: Crisp.

Job Choices. Bethlehem, PA: National Association of Colleges and Employers 2000. (Annual publication.)

Jones, Laurie Beth. 1996. *The Path: Creating Your Mission Statement for Work and for Life*. New York: Hyperion.

Journal of Career Development. New York: Human Sciences Press.

Judy, Richard, and Carol D'Amico. 1997. *Workforce 2020: Work and Workers in the 21st Century*. Indianapolis, IN: Hudson Institute.

Jung, Carl. 1923. *Psychological Types*. New York: Harcourt Brace.

Karl, Shannon, and Arthur Karl. 1997. *How to Get Your Dream Job Using the Web*. Albany, NY: Coriolis Group Books.

Kauffman, Draper L., Jr. 1976. *Teaching the Future: A Guide to Future Oriented Education*. Palm Springs, CA: ETC.

Kaye, Beverly L. 1997. *Up Is Not the Only Way: A Guide to Developing Workforce Talent*. Palo Alto, CA: Davies-Black Publishing.

Kaye, Beverly L., and Sharon Jordan-Evans. 1999. *Love 'Em or Lose 'Em: Getting Good People to Stay*. San Francisco: Berrett Koehler.

Keirsey, David, and Marilyn Bates. 1984. *Please Understand Me: Character and Temperament Types*. Del Mar, CA: Prometheus Nemesis.

Kelly, Robert E. 1998. *How to Be a Star at Work: Nine Breakthrough Strategies You Need to Succeed*. New York: Random House.

Kenig, Graciela. 1998. *Best Careers for Bilingual Latinos*. New York: McGraw-Hill.

Kennedy, Joyce Lain. 1995. *Hook Up, Get Hired! The Internet Job Search Revolution*. New York: John Wiley & Sons.

Kleiman, Carol. 2002. *Winning the Job Game*. New York: John Wiley & Sons.

Krannich, Ronald. 1997. *The Directory of Federal Jobs and Employers*. Manasses, VA: Impact Publications.

Krannich, Ronald. 1999. *Find a Federal Job Fast: How to Cut the Red Tape and Get Hired*. Manasses, VA: Impact Publications.

Krannich, Ronald, and Caryl Krannich. 1998. *The Best Jobs for the 21st Century*. Manasses, VA: Impact Publications.

Kreigel, Robert, and Marilyn Kreigel. 1985. *The C Zone*. Garden City, NY: Fawcett.

Lawrence, Gordon. 1993. *People Types and Tiger Stripes: A Practical Guide to Learning Styles*. 3rd edition. Gainesville, FL: Center for Applications of Psychological Type.

Leonard, George. 1991. *Mastery*. New York: Dutton.

Levinson, D. J. 1978. *The Seasons of a Man's Life*. New York: Knopf.

Lore, Nicholas. 1998. *The Pathfinder*. New York: Fireside, Simon & Schuster.

Martin, Charles. 1995. *Looking at Type and Careers*. Gainesville, FL: Center for Applications of Psychological Type.

Martinez, Michelle. 1996. "Video Interviewing." *EEO Bimonthly*, Vol. 27, No. 6, November/December, p. 8.

Maslow, Abraham. 1987. *Motivation and Personality*. 3rd edition. Upper Saddle River, NJ: Pearson Education.

Medanger, Talane. 2000. *Coach Yourself for Success*. New York: Contemporary Books.

Moreira, Paula, and Robyn Thorpe. 2002. *Ace the IT Resume*. New York: McGraw-Hill.

Myers, Isabel. 1962. *Manual: The Myers–Briggs Type Indicator*. Palo Alto, CA: Consulting Psychologists.

Nadler, Burt. 1998. *Liberal Arts Jobs*. Princeton, NJ: Peterson's Publications.

National Business Employment Weekly. Published quarterly. P.O. Box 300. Princeton, NJ 08543.

Newman, Betsy Kaye. 2000. *Getting Unstuck: Moving Ahead with Your Career*. Boston: Pearson Custom Publishing.

Nickles, Liz. 2001. *The Change Agents: Decoding the New Work Force and the New Workplace*. New York: St. Martin's Press.

Occupational Outlook Quarterly. 2000–2001. Washington, DC: U.S. Department of Labor, Bureau of Labor Statistics.

Otterbourg, Robert K. 2001. *Switching Careers*. Washington, DC: Kiplinger Books.

Pallatto, John. 2002. "Learning Makes the Grade." *Internet World*, Sept., p. 30.

Parker, Yana. 2002. *The Damn Good Resume Guide*. Berkeley, CA: Ten Speed Press.

Pedras, K., and R. Pedras. 1997. *Jobs '97*. Englewood Cliffs, NJ: Prentice Hall.

Peters, Tom. 1999. *Reinventing Work: The Brand New You*. New York: Knopf.

Peterson's Internships 2003. 2003. Princeton, NJ: Peterson's Guide Publisher.

Phelps, Stanlee, and Nancy Austin. 1997. *The Assertive Woman, A New Look*. San Luis Obispo, CA: Impact.

Planning Your Career. 1981. ACT Adult Booklet.

Podestra, Sandra, and Andrea Paxton. 1996. *201 Killer Cover Letters*. New York: McGraw-Hill.

Reich, Robert B. 2002. *The Future of Success: Working and Living in the New Economy*. New York: Vintage Books.

Rifkin, Jeremy. 1995. *End of Work*. New York: Putnam Publishing Group.

Riley, Margaret, Frances Roehm, and Steve Oserman. 1999. *The Guide to Internet Job Searching*. Lincolnwood, IL: VGM Career Horizons.

Rocks, Celia. 2001. *Organizing the Good Life: A Path to Joyful Simplicity—Home to Work and Back*. New York: Demand Press.

Roehm, Frances E., and Margaret Riley Dikel. 2002. *The Guide to Internet Job Searching*. Chicago: Contemporary Books.

SCANS (Secretary's Commission on Achieving Necessary Skills): What Work Requires of Schools: A SCANS Report for America 2000. June 1991. Washington, DC: U.S. Department of Labor.

School to Career Handbook. 1995. Sacramento, CA: California Community Colleges.

Sheehy, Gail. 1996. In Joelle Delbourgo (ed.), *New Passages: Your Life Across Time.* New York: Ballantine.

Siebert, Al, and Bernadine Gilpin. 1997. *Adult Student Guide to Survival and Success.* Portland, OR: Practical Psychology Press.

Siebert, Al. 1996. *Survivor Personality.* Berkeley. CA: Perigee Books.

Siegel, Bernie. 1998. *Prescription for Living.* New York: HarperCollins.

Simon, Sidney B., Leland W. Howe, and Howard Kirschenbaum. 1995. *Values Clarification.* New York: Warner Books.

Snodgrass, Jon. 1996. *Follow Your Career Star: A Career Quest Based on Inner Values.* New York: Kensington.

Stamp, Dan. 1996. "Managing Priorities." *Executive Excellence,* No. 1. January 1996, pp. 6–7.

Super, Donald E. 1957. *The Psychology of Careers.* New York: Harper.

Tieger, Paul, and Barbara Barron-Tieger. 2001. *Do What You Are.* New York: Little, Brown & Company.

Tracy, Brian. 1997. *Thinking Big: The Keys to Personal Power and Maximum Performance.* New York: Simon & Schuster. (Audiocassette.)

Tracy, Diane. 2001. *Take This Job and Love It.* Naperville, IL: Sourcebooks.

Tulgan, Bruce, and Carolyn Martin. 2001. *Managing Generation Y.* Amherst, MA: Human Resource Development Press.

Vicusi, Stephen. 2001. *On the Job: How to Make It in the Real World of Work.* New York: Three Rivers Press.

Wall Street Journal, "Work and Family," June 21, 2000.

Washington, Tom. 1992. *The Hunt: Complete Guide to Effective Job Finding.* Mt. Vernon Press.

Wellington, Sheila. 2001. *Be Your Own Mentor: Strategies from Top Women on the Secrets of Success.* New York: Random House.

Wendleton, Kate. 2002. *Kick Off Your Career.* New York: Career Press.

White, Dave. 2001. *Work as a Pilgrimage of Identity.*

Wilson, K. 1999. *The Millennium Candidate.* Boston: Element Books.

Working Mother. 2002. "Annual Survey of Best Companies," October. www.workingmother.com/list/shtml.

Yaeger, Neil M., and J. Hough. 1999. *Power Interviews.* New York: John Wiley & Sons.

Yate, Martin. 1999. *Career Smarts: Jobs with a Future.* New York: Random House.

Yate, Martin. 2003. *Knock 'Em Dead: The Ultimate Job Seeker's Handbook.* Holbrook, MA: Adams.

Index

About.com, 171

Accomplishments, 95–97 (*see also* Skills)
  analyzing, 96–97
  description exercise, 111
  identifying skills used in, 111
  listing exercise, 110–111

Action:
  initiating, 32–33
  planning for, 235, 237 (*see also* Job search)

Action words, 248–249, 250

ADA, *see* Americans with Disabilities Act

Adaptive skills, 104

Administration, as organizational division, 158

Adolescence, 6

Ads, classified, 166, 218

Adulthood, 6

Affirmations, 40
  change and, 184
  self-esteem and, 28–29

Affirmative action, 122, 123, 125

Age, questions concerning, 297

Ageism, 122, 123

Agencies:
  employment, 219
  temporary, 132–133

Age of Paradox, The, 102

AltaVista, 239

America Online, 170

American College Testing (ACT) Program, 73

American Society for Training and Development (ASTD), 222, 232

Americans with Disabilities Act (ADA), 122, 125, 295

America's Job Bank, 162, 171, 238

Appearance:
  interviews and, 290–291
  of resume, 251–252, 265

Application forms, 260–261, 262

Artistic personality type, 18, 75

Assertiveness, 26

Assessment:
  American College Testing (ACT) program, 73
  experiography and, 110
  Guide for Occupational Exploration, 73
  Holland Interest Environments, 73
  instruments, 66–71, 73
  interest, 73–91 (*see also* Interests)
  of interview technique, 300
  personal, 3–5
  personality, 66–71
  of resume, 265
  of skills, 100–101, 110–105, 92–115
  using classifieds in, 90
  using college catalog for, 91

Assets, accentuating, 123

Associations, professional, 232

Assumptions, testing, 200

Attitude, 14
  assertiveness, 26
  positive outlook and, 24–26

Baby boomers, 133

Balance, finding, 52–54

workaholics and, 52

Barriers, 122

Behavioral interviews, 297–298

Belief system, self-esteem and, 25

Benefits, job, 228, 304, 306

Bias, gender, 122

Birthplace, questions concerning, 297

Body language, 292, 298–299

Bolles, Richard, 96, 238

Brainstorming:
  decision making and, 184
  jobs, 156–157

Bridges, William, 8

Briggs, Katherine, 66

Browsers, 239

Businesses:
  home, 223
  organizational divisions, 157–159
  small, 131–132
  starting your own, 223–224
  Web organization in, 158
  woman-owned, 132, 223

California Work and Heath Survey, the, 126

Career (*see also* Careers; Career planning):
  age and, 123
  changing, 12–14, 123
  choosing, 12–14 (*see also* Career planning)
  clusters, 86–88
  defined, 216
  equality in the workforce and, 121–125
  experiography and, 110

family and, 121
fantasy, 41–42
fitness, embracing, 312–313
gender roles and, 121–22
identifying ideal, 112
identifying personality and
    interests, 64–91
importance of lifelong learn-
    ing, 127
importance of values in choos-
    ing, 49–50
interests and, 85, 90
managing your, 310–313
objective, 12, 216, 237
paths, 157–159
self-employment, 102 (see also
    Entrepreneurship)
societal influences on, 120–125
stamina, 311–312
tasks identified in SCANS,
    106–107
technology and, 127–130
transferable skills and,
    102–103
values related to, 61
vs. job, 8–11
women in, 124
CareerBuilder, 171, 238
Career clusters, 86
    American College Testing Pro-
        gram (ACT) system, 86, 87
    map of, 88
    U.S. Office of Career Educa-
        tion system, 86
Career Information System (CIS),
    109, 167–168
Career planning (see also Job
    search):
    application forms and,
        260–261, 262
    as continuous loop, 11
    entrepreneurship and,
        223–224
    franchising, 224
    identify personality and inter-
        ests, 64–91
    information interviews and,
        225–230
    job search, 215–243
    management of career and,
        310–313
    networking and, 230,
        232–233

resumes and, 244–285 (see
    also Resumes)
using, 224–225
Careers:
    artistic/multimedia, 139
    basic science, 139
    brainstorming options,
        156–157
    business services, 139
    computer science/information
        systems, 139
    creative, 137
    decision making and,
        178–202
    educational services and
        products, 139
    engineering, 139
    environmental sciences, 139
    fastest-growing, 144, 147
    financial services, 139
    food service, 139
    for artistic types, 78
    for conventional types, 79
    for creators, 78
    for doers, 78
    for enterprising types, 79
    for helpers, 79
    for investigative types, 78
    for organizers, 79
    for persuaders, 79
    for realistic types, 78
    for social types, 79
    for thinkers, 78
    goal setting and, 179, 187–188
    government, 161–162 (see
        also Government jobs)
    growth in next decade, 139
    health services, 139
    Holland Interest Environments
        and, 77
    hotel management and recre-
        ation, 139
    human resources and person-
        nel, 139
    in media-related fields, 137
    in-demand, 133
    information technology, 129
    Internet, 138
    liberal arts major and,
        133–135
    lifelong learning and, 135–137
    limiting factors, 140
    maintenance and repair, 139

nontraditional for women,
    140–141
options, 160–161
overseas, 172
paths, 157–159
professional organizations/
    trade associations, 160–161
projected openings, 145
research, 160–172
researching requirements,
    158, 160–161
salaries, 141, 142–143
sample paths, 159
SCANS skills and, 135
setting goals for, 203–212
stress management for,
    189–190
time management strategies,
    188, 189
training, 191
trends in growth, 137–138
with largest increase, 146
with largest job growth, 148
Career satisfaction, 9–11
    quality of life and, 9
    self-knowledge and, 66
Career sites, Internet, 170–172
Career success, self-knowledge
    and, 66
CD-ROM, products for job
    search, 168, 169
Center for Women's Business
    Research, 223
Change:
    affirmations and, 184
    conditions for, 184
    deciding on, 191–192
Checklist:
    emotional intelligence, 40
    values grid, 56
    Worker Trait Groups, 80–83
Chronological resumes,
    257–258, 272–275
CIS (Career Information System),
    109, 167–168
Citizenship, questions concern-
    ing, 296
Classified ads, 90, 218
Clothing, interviews and,
    290–291
College (see also Education):
    catalog, in interest assessment,
        91

starting salaries for graduates, 143
Combination resumes, 276–277
Companies:
customization in, 131
e-commerce and, 130–131
efficient, 130
flat management structure of, 130
flexibility and, 130
internal job postings, 167
knowledge of, 290
management-directed vs. team-directed, 130
mega-corporations and, 131
newsletters, 167
organizational divisions, 157–159
outsourcing and, 130
temps and, 130
traits for success in global economy, 130–131
virtual corporations and, 130
Web organization, 158
Compensation, 228, 289, 304, 306 (see also Salaries)
Competencies, in SCANS report, 105
Computerized information sources, 167–172
Conferenccs, attending, 232
Contacts, 232
cultivating, 225 (see also Information interviews; Networking)
file format, 236
personal log for, 241–242
Continuing education, see Life-long learning
Conventional personality type, 18, 76
Cooperative education, 222
Cooperative Education Association, 222
Corporate:
culture, 301
relations, as organizational division, 158
universities, 136
Cover letters, 258–260
exercise, 266
samples, 280–284
template for, 259

Creativity:
brainstorming, 156
careers and, 137
visualization and, 156
leisure and, 54
Creators, 75, 78 (see also Holland Interest Environments)
Cross-functional skills, 158
Culture:
corporate, 301
influence on career, 120–125
perception of needs and, 51
Customer needs, small businesses and, 132
Customization, 131

Databases, 238–239
Decision making, 178–202
assumptions about, 181–182
avoiding ultimatums, 182
change and, 184, 191–192
examining behavior, 182–184
exercises for, 193–202
feelings about, 182
generating outcomes, 184
goal-setting review, 193–194
intuitive, 185, 187
luck and, 187
major and, 190–191
model for, 185, 186
overcoming barriers to, 180
personality and, 185, 187
ranking yourself, 193
rational/linear, 185
risks and, 183
strategies, 180–184
stress and, 189–190
styles, 185
training and, 191
visualization and, 183
Decisions, making, 178–202 (see also Decision making)
Department of Labor, interest inventory, 73
Desire, and job market, 138
Dictionary of Occupational Titles (DOT), 98–99, 162, 168, 255
Digital Economy 2002 report, 129
Directories:
employer, 164
list of useful, 165

Disabilities, and workplace accommodations, 125
Discipline, self, 33–34, 136
DISCOVER, 168
Discovering Careers, 168
Discrimination, 122
age, 123
sexism, 122
Disengagement, in Super's self-concept theory, 5
Distance learning, 136
Diversity, 125
Doers, 74–75, 78 (see also Holland Interest Environments)
DOT, 98–99, 162, 168, 255
as source of job descriptions, 98–99
O*NET and, 99
researching skills with, 98–99

E-commerce, 130–131
Economy:
global, 129–131
knowledge-based, 127
NAFTA and, 129–130
new vs. old, 128
service-based, 126
Education:
cooperative, 222
distance learning, 136
Internet and, 136
on resumes, 254
questions concerning, 296
starting salaries for college graduates, 143
trends, 133–137
worth of degree, 142
Electronic resumes, 252–253
E-mail, promoting yourself via, 218–219
Emotional intelligence:
checklist, 40
Goleman's theory of, 35
self-esteem and, 34
Employee, portfolio, 102
Employer directories, 164
Employment (see also Career planning; Careers; Job search; Work)
ads, 218
agencies, 219
Encyclopedia of Associations, 232

Engineering, as organizational division, 158
Enterprising personality type, 18, 76
Enthusiasm, 44
  for job search, 216
  self-esteem and, 27–28
  showing in interview, 292
  values and, 49
Entrance requirements, 228
Entrepreneurship, 223–224
EQ (emotional intelligence quotient), 34–35, 40
Equal Employment Opportunity BiMonthly, 299
Equality, in workforce, 121–125
Equity, definitions of, 122
Establishment, in Super's self-concept theory, 4
Ethics, values related to, 61–62
EUREKA, 109, 167–168
Excite, 239
Experience:
  listed on resumes, 254
  rated by employers, 222
Experiography, 110
Exploration, in Super's self-concept theory, 4
External motivators, 52
Extraverted, personality type, 67, 68

Fair Employment Practices Act, 295
Family, influence on career, 121
Fantasy:
  careers, 41–42
  making it real, 43
Federal Careers Opportunities, 162
Federal Jobs Digest, 162
Fed World, 171
Feeling, personality type, 67, 70
Feminist, 122
Fieldwork, 221
Finance, as organizational division, 158
First impressions, 15
Flat management structure, 130
Flexibility:
  of companies, 130
  self-esteem and, 37
FlipDog, 170, 238

Focus, on job search, 216
Formatting electronic resumes, 253
Fortune.com, 170
Franchising, 224
Freelance career, 102
Functional resumes, 255–257, 268–271
Future:
  creating your, 312
  focus on, 308–313
  predicting, 312
  views of, 25

Gallop Poll, 10
Gardner, Howard, 30–31
Gender:
  and career, 121–122
  bias, 122
  questions concerning, 297
  roles, 121–122
  roles questionnaire, 150
  stereotyping, 122
Generalist, 158
Generation X, 133
  life balance vs. salary, 52
GIS (Guidance Information System), 168
Global economy, 129–131
Goals (*see also* Goal Setting):
  as completed accomplishments, 95, 96
  objectives and, 188
  realistic, 179
  rewards for reaching, 188–189
  self-esteem and, 36
  setting, 187–189, 193–194, 203–212
  short- and long-term, 13, 187–188, 200–201
  specific, 179
  statement of, 194
  timelines for, 188
Goal setting, 187–189
  career, 203–212
  information integration and, 210–211
  review exercise, 193–194
  short- and long-term, 13, 187–188, 200–201
GOE (Guide for Occupational Exploration), 73, 84, 163

Golden years, 7
Goleman, Daniel, 35
Google, 239
Government jobs, 161–161
  America's Job Bank, 162
  DOT and, 162
  Federal Careers Opportunities, 162
  Federal Jobs Digest, 162
  Occupational Outlook Quarterly and, 163
  on O*NET, 162
  One Stop Career Centers, 161
  OOH and, 162, 163
  researching on Internet, 161
  samples of, 162
GPA, 292
Graduate school, 133
Growth, in Super's self-concept theory, 4
Guide for Occupational Exploration (GOE), 73, 84, 163

Habits, in decision making, 183
Handy, Charles, 102
Helpers, 76, 79 (*see also* Holland Interest Environments)
Help-wanted ads, 218
Herzberg, Frederick, 52
Herzberg's theory of motivation, 52, 53
Hierarchy of needs, Maslow's, 50–51
High-order need, 51
Hiring, factors influencing, 302–304
Holland Interest Environments, 89, 73, 74–76
  abilities related to, 77
  artistic type, 75
  careers related to, 77
  conventional type, 76
  creators, 75, 78
  doers, 74–75, 78
  enterprising type, 76
  helpers, 76, 79
  hobbies related to, 77
  investigative type, 75
  majors related to, 77
  organizers, 76, 79
  persuaders, 76, 79
  realistic type, 74–75
  social type, 76

thinkers, 75, 78

Holland types, *see* Holland Interest Environments

Home businesses, 223

Hotlines, job, 225

Human resources management, 232

Humor, self-esteem and, 26–27

Inborn tendencies, identifying, 67–71

Information integration, 154–177, 210–211

Information interviews, 225–230
activity, 231, 241
outline, 227–229, 231
practicing, 230, 231
questions, 228–229

Information technology, wages in, 129

Infoseek, 239

Initiative, self-esteem and, 32–33

Inquiries, preemployment, 295–297

Intelligence:
emotional, 34–35, 40
Gardner's theory of, 30–32
quotient, 34
multiple, 30–32

Interest:
checklist, 80–83
clusters, 73
inventories, *see* Assessment

Interests, 310
Holland Interest Environments and, 73
identifying occupational, 18, 73–91
inventory, 73 (*see also* Assessment)
personality and, 64–91

Internal motivators, 52

International Franchise Association, 224

Internet, 170–172
America's Job Bank, 162
career sites, 170
corporate training and, 136
distance learning and, 136
education and, 136
employment databases on, 238–239
Federal Jobs Digest, 162

government job search, 161
industry searches on, 171
job market research sites, 171
job research and, 161
job search and, 234
library resource centers, 170
O*NET, 162
related growth areas, 138
resumes and, 252–253
trade journals, 171
Yellow Pages, 164

Internships, 220–222

Internships 2003, 220

Interpersonal intelligence, 31

Interviews:
behavioral/situational, 297–298
body language and, 292, 298–299
critique form, 300
factors influencing hiring, 302–304
guidelines for, 290–292
illegal questions and, 295–297
information, 225–230 (*see also* Information interviews)
learning from, 301
sample questions, 289–290, 293, 295
sample questions to ask at, 302
segments of, 292–293
summary of process, 305
thank you letters and, 293, 294
video, 298–299, 301

Intrapersonal intelligence, 31

Introduction, letter of, 285

Introverted type, 67, 68

Intuition:
decision making and, 185, 187
following, 8

Intuitive, personality type, 67, 69

Inventories, interest, *see* Assessment

Investigative, personality type, 18, 75

IQ, 34–35

Job:
bank, 234, 238–239

classifications, 228
clusters, 90
descriptions, 58–59, 167, 228, 255–256
hotlines, 225
identifying ideal, 112, 217
market, Internet sites, 171
objective, 247, 254
offer, 304, 306
performance, leisure and, 54
seeking entry-level, 217
training, 191
transferable skills and, 102–103
trends, 133–148
vs. career, 8–11

Job growth:
in next decade, 139
projected openings, 145
trends in, 137–138

Job satisfaction, 9–11
internal vs. external motivators and, 52

Job search, 215–243
America Online and, 170
America's Job Bank, 171
application forms and, 260–261, 262
as lifelong venture, 237
brainstorming options, 156–157
Careerbuilder.com and, 171
CD-ROM products for, 168, 169
CIS and, 167–168
classified ads and, 166, 218
designing a comprehensive, 216, 217–218
DISCOVER and, 168
Discovering Careers and, 168
e-mail and, 218–219
enthusiasm for, 216
experience and, 222
experiography and, 110
Fed World, 171
Fortune.com, 170
getting started, 218–222
GIS and, 168
government, 161–162 (*see also* Government jobs)
Internet career sites, 138, 170–172

interviewing and, 287–307
(*see also* Interviews)
knowledge sector growth and,
127
library resource centers, 170
lifelong learning and, 135–137
networking and, 230,
232–233
newspapers and, 167
nontraditional for women,
140–141
online employment databases,
238–239
overseas, 172
professional organizations/
trade associations and,
160–161
projected openings, 145
research, 160–172
researching requirements, 158,
160–161
resume writing and, 244–285
(*see also* Resumes)
sample descriptions from
DOT, 98
SIGI Plus and, 109, 168, 169
starting your own business
and, 223–224
stress and, 189
technology and, 127–130
tips, 288
trade journals and, 167
using career planning services,
224–225
volunteering and, 219–220
while unemployed, 233–235
Jobshift, 8
Judging type, 67, 71
Jung, Carl, 66
Jung, personal preferences
according to, 67–71

Key phrases, 249–250
Kinesthetic intelligence, 31
Knowledge workers, 126–127

Learning:
distance, 136
lifelong, 127, 135–137
Leasing companies, 132–133
Leisure:
job performance and, 54
role in life balance, 53–54

stress and, 54
value to workers, 54
Letters:
cover, *see* Cover letters
of introduction, 285
thank-you, 293, 294
Library resource centers, 170
Life:
balance, 52–54
stages, 6–8
transitions, 312
Lifeline, preparing your, 16–17
Lifelong learning, 127, 135–137
distance learning and, 136
Limitations, habits as, 193
Linguistic intelligence, 31
Listening skills, 297
Logical/mathematical intelli-
gence, 31
Low-order need, 51
Luck, 33
decision making and, 187
Lycos, 239

Magazines:
for research, 160
job search and, 166–167
Magellan, 222
Mail, promotion through,
218–219
Maintenance, in Super's self-
concept theory, 5
Majors:
deciding on, 190–191
exploring, 73
liberal arts, 133–135
personality type and, 73
related to Holland Interest
Environments, 77
sampling, 191
Maslow, Abraham, 50–51
Maslow's Hierarchy of Needs,
50–51, 53
Mathematical intelligence, 31
MBTI (Myers-Briggs Type Indi-
cator®), 66, 71
Media careers, 137
Mega-corporation, 131
Men, and gender roles, 124
Mental imagery, 29–30
Mental rehearsal, 29–30
Minorities, affirmative action
and, 123, 125

Model, decision-making, 185,
186
Monster Board, 238
Motivation:
Herzberg's theory of, 52, 53
needs and, 50–52
Motivators:
compared to needs, 53
internal and external, 52
Multimedia, 137
Multiple intelligences, 30–32
Musical/rhythmic intelligence,
31
Myers-Briggs Type Indicator®,
66, 71
Myers, Isabel Briggs, 66

NAFTA, 129–130
Nation Job Network, 238
National Association of Colleges
and Employers (NACE),
129
*National Business Employment
Weekly,* 233
National Multimedia Association
of America (NMAA), 222
National origin, questions concerning, 296
Natural abilities, 103–104
Neatness, applications and, 261
Needs, 50–52
as motivators, 50–52
compared to motivators, 53
cultural perspective of, 51
hierarchy of, 50–51
high- and low-order, 51
physiological, 51
primary, 51
survival, 50
unmet, 50
vs. values, 51
Negotiating benefits, 304, 306
Networking, 216, 230,
232–233
checklist for, 240–241
contact file format, 236
during job, 311
New economy, 128–129
Newspapers, for research, 160
Nontraditional job, 122
North American Free Trade
Agreement (NAFTA),
129–130

Objectives:
    goals and, 188
    job, *see* Job objective
    specific vs. nonspecific, 188, 199–200
Occupational interests, 90
Occupational Outlook Handbook (OOH), 162, 163, 168, 232
Occupational Outlook Quarterly, 163
Occupational status, 19
Occupations, *see* Career; Job
Old economy, 128–129
One Stop Career Centers, 161
O*NET (Occupational Information Network), 99, 162, 168, 254, 255
    researching occupations and skills with, 99
OOH, see Occupational Outlook Handbook
Opportunities, limited, 140
Organizational divisions, 157–159
Organizational skills, 298
Organizers, 76, 79 (*see also* Holland Interest Environments)
Origin, national, questions concerning, 296
Outlook, positive, 24–26
Outsourcing, 130

Peace Corps, 220
People skills, 103
Perceiving, personality type, 67, 71
Persistence, self-esteem and, 33
Personal assessment, 3–5
Personal growth, leisure and, 54
Personal philosophy, self-esteem and, 25
Personal preferences:
    exercise for identifying, 67–71
    extraversion vs. introversion, 67
    four-letter indicator, 71
    four-part framework for, 67
    judging vs. perceiving, 67
    sensing vs. intuition, 67
    thinking vs. feeling, 67
Personality, 310
    career and, 8

decision making and, 185, 187
environments, 73
exploring, 66–73
interests and, 64–91
traits, as assets, 103–104, 109 (*see also* Personality types)
Personality types, 18, 73, 89
    artistic, 75
    conventional, 76
    enterprising, 76
    extraverted, 67, 68
    feeling, 67, 70
    introverted, 67, 68
    intuitive, 67, 69
    investigative, 75
    judging, 67, 71
    perceiving, 67, 71
    realistic, 74–75
    sensing, 67, 69
    social, 76
    thinking, 67, 70
Personnel offices, job search and, 167
Persuaders, 76, 79 (*see also* Holland Interest Environments)
Photograph, request for prior to employment, 296
Point-of-view, self-esteem and, 25
Portfolio employee, 102
Portfolios, 246–247, 249
    review, 264
Position:
    classifications, 228
    descriptions, 228 (*see also* Job descriptions)
Positive outlook, self-esteem and, 24–26
Preemployment inquiries, 295–297
Preferences, 67–71
Princeton Review Online, 221
Procrastination, 233
Productivity, role of leisure in, 54
Professional organizations, for job search, 160–161, 232

Quality of life, 9
QUEST, 168
Questionnaire, gender roles, 150
Questions:
    illegal interview, 295–297

information interviewing, 228–229
    practice interview, 293, 295
    preemployment, 295–297
    sample interview, 289–290
    to ask at interview, 302
Quick Job Hunting Map, 96

Race or color, questions concerning, 296
Rapport, establishing in interview, 292
Realistic, personality type, 18, 75–75 (*see also* RIASEC)
Recareering, 12–13
References, 251
Relationships, developing, 311
Religion, questions concerning, 297
Renewal, 7
Research:
    About.com, 171
    America Online and, 170
    America's Job Bank, 171
    CareerBuilder, 171
    CD-ROM products, 168, 169
    computerized information sources, 167–172
    current events affecting career path, 160
    DISCOVER and, 168
    Discovering Careers and, 168
    DOT and, 162
    employer directories, 164
    exercises, 174–175
    Fed World, 171
    Flipdog.com, 170
    Fortune.com, 170
    GIS, 168
    GOE and, 163
    industry searches online, 160, 172
    in-house bulletins, 167
    Internet, 164, 170–172
    job market, 171
    key employers, 161
    library resource centers, 170
    magazines/newspapers for, 160, 166–167
    newspapers, 166
    O*NET, 162
    Occupational Outlook Quarterly and, 163

occupations, 160
  of career options, 160–161
  OOH and, 162, 163
  professional and trade associations, 160–161
  QUEST, 168
  SIGI Plus, 109, 168, 169
  software for, 167–170
  trade journals, 166, 172
  useful websites for job search, 161
Restabilization, 6
Resumail Network, 238–239
Resume/portfolio review, 249
Resumes, 244–285
  action words on, 248–249, 250
  appearance of, 251–252
  banks of, 250
  chronological, 257–258, 272–275
  combination, 258, 276–277
  common problems with, 252
  cover letters for, 258–260
  critiquing, 265
  do's and don'ts. 266
  electronic, 252–253
  functional, 255–257, 268–271
  index cards for tracking info, 247–248
  Internet resources, 170
  job objective and, 247
  key phrases on, 249–250
  portfolios and, 246–247
  posting online, 170
  references on, 251
  review, 264
  sample, 268–279
  template for, 254
  types of, 253, 255–258
Retirement, 7, 123
Rewards for reaching goals, 188–189
Rhythmic intelligence, 31
RIASEC, 18–19, 74–76 (*see also* Holland Interest Environments)
  artistic type, 75
  conventional type, 76
  enterprising type, 76
  in world-of-work map, 88
  investigative type, 75
  realistic type, 74–75

social type, 76
Richard Bolles Parachute Site, 238
Riley Guide, 238
Risks, 313
  in decision making, 183
Role models, self-esteem and, 32
Rooting, life stage, 6

Salaries, 228, 289, 304, 306
  in government jobs, 163
  in *OOH*, 163
  starting, for college graduates, 143
  trends in, 141, 142–143
Sales, as organizational division, 158
SCANS, 102, 103, 105–108
  competencies, 105, 108
  foundation, 105, 108
  worksheet for identifying skills, 113
SCORE, 223–224
Search engines, 239
Searcher, 239
Secretary's Commission on Achieving Necessary Skills, *see* SCANS
Self-concept, 3
  Super's theory of, 4–5
Self-confidence, self-esteem and, 27
Self-control, *see* Self-discipline
Self-Directed Search®, 74
Self-discipline, 136
  self-esteem and, 33–34
Self-esteem, 24
  affirmations and, 28–29
  assertiveness and, 26
  discipline and, 33–34
  emotional intelligence and, 34
  enthusiasm and, 27–28
  flexibility and, 37
  goals and, 36
  humor and, 26–27
  initiative and, 32–33
  persistence and, 33
  point-of-view and, 25
  positive outlook and, 24–26
  role models and, 32
  self-confidence and, 27
  self-discipline and, 33–34
  self-reliance and, 36

visualization and, 29–30
Self-expression, leisure and, 54
Self-image, positive, 30 (*see also* Self-esteem)
Self-knowledge, 14
Self-motivation, values and, 48
Self-reliance, self-esteem and, 36
Self-talk, 40
Sensing, personality type, 67, 69
Service Corps of Retired Executives (SCORE), 223–224
Sexism, 122
Sheehy, Gail, 7
SIGI Plus (System of Interactive Guidance and Information), 109, 169
Single-parent households, 7
Situational interviews, 297–298
Skills:
  accomplishments and, 111
  adaptive, 104
  analysis software, 109
  analyzing accomplishments and, 96–97
  as source of satisfaction, 109
  assessment of, 92–115
  communication, 103, 311
  critical thinking, 103
  cross-functional, 158
  defined, 94
  describing, 109
  false assumptions about, 94
  homemakers and, 95
  human relations, 103
  identifying transferable, 102–103
  identifying, 94–102
  lifelong learning and, 127
  listed on resume, 254
  listening, 297
  natural abilities as, 103–104
  of liberal arts majors, 133–135
  organizational, 103, 298
  people, 103, 311
  portfolio of, 102
  problem solving, 103
  ranking favorite, 111
  research
  review, 114
  SCANS and, 102, 103, 105–108
  self-discipline, 136

talking about, 95
teamwork, 298
that influence hiring, 302
time management, 136
transferable, 102–103,
    133–135
used in writing term paper,
    97
using past accomplishments to
    reveal, 109
worksheet for identifying, 113
writing stories to identify,
    96–97
writing, 298
Small Business Development
    Centers, 224
Small businesses, 131–132
Social personality type, 18, 76
Social Readjustment Rating
    Scale, 189
Society, influence on career,
    120–125
Software:
    for skills analysis, 109
    job search, 167–170
SOHO, 128
Spatial intelligence, 31
Specialist, 158
Stamina, career, 311–312
Stereotypes, exploring, 150
Stereotyping, 122
Strategies:
    decision-making, 180–184
    stress-management, 189
    time-management, 188, 189
Stress:
    leisure and, 54
    managing, 189–190
    positive vs. negative, 189
    priorities and, 190
    Social Readjustment Rating
        Scale, 189
Strong Interest Inventory®, 74
Success:
    clearly defined goals and, 36
    discipline and, 33
    factors that influence, 36,
        302–304
    flexibility and, 37
    profile, 43
    visualizing, 29–30
Super, Donald, 3
Survival needs, 50

Teamwork, 311
    skills, 298
Technology:
    in workplace, 127–129
    SOHOs and, 128
    telecommuting and, 128
Telecommuting, 128
Temporary agencies, 132–133
Temporary work, as means to
    obtain permanent employ-
    ment, 132
Temporary workers, 130
Thank-you letters, 293, 294
Thinkers, 75, 78 (see also Hol-
    land Interest Environments)
Thinking, personality type, 67,
    70
Timelines, setting, 188
Time management, 136
    strategies for, 188, 189
Trade associations, for job
    search, 160–161
Trade journals:
    job search in, 166
    online, 172
Training, 191 (see also Educa-
    tion; Lifelong learning)
Transferable skills, 102–103, 158
    (see also SCANS)
    of liberal arts majors,
        133–135
    of teacher, 104
Transitions, life, 312
Trends:
    corporate universities, 136
    distance learning, 136
    education, 133–137
    job growth, 133–148
    lifelong learning, 135–137
    marketable skills and,
        133–135
    salary, 141, 142–143
Turning-point years, 6

Underemployment, 312
Unemployment, 312
    job search during, 233–235
UN Volunteers, 220
U.S. Department of Labor publi-
    cations, 162–164

Values, 310
    acted upon, 49

alternatives and, 49
as part of a pattern, 49
choice and, 49
clarification, 46–63
consequence and, 49
criteria for clarifying, 49–50
defined, 48
enthusiasm and, 49
exercises for clarifying, 55–63,
    59–60
exploring, 57
finding balance and, 52–54
grid checklist, 56
job descriptions exercise,
    58–59
public affirmation and, 49
related to ethics, 61–62
relating to careers, 61
strategies for identifying, 54
vs. needs, 51
Verbal/linguistic intelligence, 31
Videotape, interviewing and,
    298–299, 301
Virtual corporation, 130
Virtual Job Fair, 238
Visibility, maintaining, 237 (see
    also Networking)
VISTA, 220
Visualization, 29–30
    and career choice, 156
    in decision making, 183
Visual/spatial intelligence, 31
Volunteering, 219–220

Wages, leisure vs., 54
Want ads, 166, 218
Websites, job research and, 161
    (see also Internet; Job
    search)
Woman-owned businesses, 132
Women:
    and gender roles, 124
    in the workplace, 124
    nontraditional occupations
        for, 140–141
    businesses owned by, 223
Words, action, 248–249, 250
Work (see also Careers):
    environment, 228
    experiography and, 110
    identifying ideal, 112
    relevant experience, 222
    technology and, 127–130

temporary, 131, 132–133
Workaholics, finding balance
 and, 52
Workers:
 traits for global economy, 131
 knowledge, 126–127
 knowledge of global issues,
  130
 new economy and, 129
 temporary, 130, 131
Worker Trait Group Guide, 84
Worker Trait Groups, 73
 categories 84

checklist, 80–83
Workforce, equality in, 121–125
Workplace:
 changing, 126–148
 diversity in, 125
 importance of lifelong learning, 127
 know-how identified in
  SCANS report, 105,
  106–107
 new technology and, 127–129
 non-traditional schedules and,
  126

women in, 124
 workers with disabilities and,
  125
World Wide Web, job research
 and, 161 (*see also* Internet)
World-of-work map, 88
Worldwide Franchise Directory,
 224
Writing skills, 298

Yahoo!, 222, 239
Yellow Pages, research and, 164